Armed Conflicts in South Asia 2008

Armed Conflicts in South Asia 2008

Growing Violence

Editors
D. Suba Chandran
P. R. Chari

LONDON AND NEW YORK

First published 2008 by Routledge

2 Park Square, Milton Park, Abingdon, Oxfordshire OX14 4RN
711 Third Avenue, New York, NY 10017

Routledge is an imprint of the Taylor & Francis Group, an informa business

First issued in paperback 2018

Transferred to Digital Printing 2008

Copyright © 2008 Institute of Peace and Conflict Studies

Typeset by
Star Compugraphics Private Limited
5–CSC, First Floor, Near City Apartments
Vasundhara Enclave
Delhi 110 096

All rights reserved. No part of this book may be reprinted or reproduced
or utilised in any form or by any electronic, mechanical, or other means,
now known or hereafter invented, including photocopying and recording,
or in any information storage or retrieval system, without permission in
writing from the publishers.

Notice:
Product or corporate names may be trademarks or registered trademarks,
and are used only for identification and explanation without intent to
infringe.

British Library Cataloguing-in-Publication Data
A catalogue record of this book is available from the British Library

ISBN 13: 978-0-415-47622-5 (hbk)
ISBN 13: 978-1-138-38029-5 (pbk)

Contents

Preface   *vii*

1. Armed Conflicts in South Asia—An Overview   1
   P. R. Chari

2. Afghanistan: Continuing Violence   20
   Shanthie Mariet D'Souza

3. Pakistan: The Sectarian Conflict   47
   Kanchan Lakshman

4. Pakistan: The War of Tribes   71
   D. Suba Chandran

5. J&K: From Militancy to Jihad?   92
   Kavita Suri & D. Suba Chandran

6. Left Extremism: The Naxal Conflict in India   118
   Mallika Joseph & Devyani Srivasatava

7. Northeast: Island of Peace and Ocean of Conflict   153
   Bibhu Prasad Routray

8. Bangladesh: Islamic Militancy and the Rise of Religious Right   189
   Smruti S. Pattanaik

9. Nepal: State in Dilemma   211
   P. G. Rajamohan

10. Sri Lanka: Thumbs Up to Violence; Thumbs Down to Peace   238
    N. Manoharan

Notes on Contributors   269
Index   273

Preface

The essays in this volume are concerned with armed conflicts in South Asia and the conflict management efforts made over 2006 and 2007 to mitigate these armed conflicts. The present volume is the second in what is intended to be a series. The first volume was published earlier this year (2007) and discusses the armed conflicts that excoriated South Asia in 2005. It was made possible by a generous grant from the Konrad Adenauer Foundation. We are confident that these annual volumes will be as valuable as are the Strategic Surveys published by the International Institute of Strategic Studies (IISS) in London, and the Yearbooks on Armament, Disarmament and International Security brought out by the Stockholm International Peace Research Institute (SIPRI) in Stockholm.

By way of a methodological note, it should be mentioned that the contributors to this volume, as in the earlier one, were requested to follow a standard format in writing their essays. Through this approach they address five issues or themes: they start with a brief history of the armed conflict; identify the principal actors in the conflict; describe the course of the armed conflict over 2006–07 and its major trends; evaluate conflict management measures, if any, undertaken in this period; and, finally, present appropriate conclusions. Two additional chapters on naxalites and sectarian strife in Pakistan were added as they had become relevant over 2006 and 2007. These essays are prefaced by an Overview chapter. The structure governing this volume has advisedly sought to approximate the pattern followed by the SIPRI Yearbooks.

A conscious effort has been made to associate younger scholars with this work in the hope that they would provide continuity to this exercise. The initiative taken by Dr Suba Chandran in this regard merits appreciation; without his tireless efforts this volume would not have achieved fruition within the rigid timeframe set by the publishers. An initial meeting was held with the proposed authors in May 2007, followed by a two-day conference in September to review the first drafts of the chapters.

I am grateful to the scholars who have contributed to this volume, and for adhering to deadlines. Without their willing cooperation this effort would not have fructified. I am also grateful to Mr. Bhambal and Ms Omita Goyal at Routledge for having agreed to undertake this series.

P. R. Chari

1

Armed Conflicts in South Asia—An Overview

P. R. Chari

BY WAY OF A PROLOGUE

In a recent interview, Eric Hobsbawm predicted a bleak future for this century:

> If 21st-century states prefer to fight their wars with professional armies, or contractors, it is not just for technical reasons, but because citizens can no longer be relied upon to be conscripted in their millions to die in battle for their fatherlands. Men and women may be prepared to die (or more likely to kill) for money... [but] in the original homelands of the nation, no longer for the nation-state....War in the 21st century is not likely to be as murderous as it was in the 20th century, but armed violence creating disproportionate suffering will remain omnipresent and endemic—occasionally epidemic—in a large part of the world.[1]

It is no longer disputed that the stability and certainties of the Cold War era have been replaced by the anarchism that is inherent within the international system. Non-state and transnational actors, owing no allegiance to the discipline of the alliance systems of the 20th century, would be contending for space in the international system. Consequently, the problems of terrorism, the proliferation of weapons of mass destruction, the dangers arising from failing states, the malefic aspects of globalization, and the democratic movement would exacerbate socio-economic and ethnic conflict within states, making for a more conflict-prone future. These developments would be more evident in the developing parts of the world.

All these problematical issues and newer threats are excoriating South Asia and have informed the present exercise to study armed

---

[1] http://living.scotsman.com/books.cfm?id=1057902007 (accessed on 6 July 2007).

conflicts in this region. Paradoxically, and contrary to general expectations, and despite being the land that gave birth to and remained the *karma bhumi* (work sphere) of the apostle of peace, Mahatma Gandhi, South Asia is identifiable as one of the most violent regions in the world. It exhibits great ethno-political and religious-communal violence that spills over borders to aggravate regional tensions and instabilities. Next only to Iraq, South Asia has seen the largest number of deaths caused by terrorism over the last seve ral years.[2]

Proceeding further, an immediate definitional problem arises in parsing the operative phrases in this paper's title, i.e., 'armed conflicts' and 'South Asia'. Reversing their order, South Asia is easily recognizable as constituting a unique security complex. Should it be only the eight states comprising SAARC (including Afghanistan)? Should China be included within a more diffused entity of southern Asia, appreciating the logic that it impinges on South Asian security? Extending this logic further, should Myanmar be included, which impinges on regional security and was highlighted during the student-monk agitation in that country? Should one prefer the natural geographical expression 'subcontinent'? Exploring these possibilities would detract from our main purposes; hence South Asia is identified here as coterminous with SAARC, which now includes Afghanistan.

What about the phrase 'armed conflicts', which is also problematical. The Uppsala Conflict Data Program (UCDP) provides a definition for 'major armed conflict', which is seen as 'a contested incompatibility concerning government and/or territory over which the use of armed force between the military forces of two parties, of which at least one is the government of the state, has resulted in at least 1,000 battle-related deaths in a single calendar year'.[3] This definition is unduly restrictive, but ensures that only high-intensity conflicts would be recognized. Earlier, the UCDP definition required that these 1,000 battle-related deaths should have occurred over the entire course of the conflict to qualify as a 'major armed conflict'.[4]

---

[2] See *www.tkb.org* (accessed on 8 July 2007), especially the Chart, '22 Countries with the Most [Terrorist] Attacks, 1998–2004', which places India in the second position. This website is devoted to compiling statistics relating to terrorism worldwide.

[3] *SIPRI Yearbook 2007: Armaments, Disarmament and International Security*, Oxford: Oxford University Press, 2007, p. 91.

[4] *Ibid.*

The scale of violence is obviously central to defining the term 'armed conflict' and making it relevant for security analyses. Viewed from a state perspective, this data is sufficient to initiate peace processes for containing and ending 'armed conflict'. However, there are obvious inadequacies in these UCDP definitions when applied to 'major armed conflicts' in South Asia. They exclude, for instance, the use of armed force between two or more non-state actors, which occurs in sectarian conflict or between militant groups as occurs during Hindu–Muslim communal riots in India, or within communities like the Shia–Sunni violence in Pakistan, or the Sinhala–Tamil ethnic conflict in Sri Lanka or Pashtun–Uzbek clashes in the FATA region. Further, the 'use of armed force' connotes the utilization of troops and militarily trained personnel by the state against guerrillas, insurgents and similar non-state actors. What about deaths caused by hunger and deprivation in the battle zone, or due to the forced migration of the population either fleeing the war zone or being forcibly evicted by the state or by non-state actors? Consequently, the UCDP definitions do not address these broader aspects of collective violence.

These quibbles can be multiplied, but the greatest difficulty arises by raising the bar to 'at least 1,000 battle-related deaths in a single calendar year'. Restricting such deaths to 'battle-related' causes would exclude deaths caused by landmines, improvised explosive devices and so on that cause the most deaths in armed conflicts in South Asia. The death toll qualification, however, does not include civilians caught in the crossfire between the state and insurgent and terrorist forces. In effect, therefore, this numerical limitation would ignore long-enduring conflicts like Sri Lanka's ethnic conflict, the Kashmir imbroglio, and the ethno-political conflicts afflicting northeast India for decades; the total casualties in these conflicts greatly exceed the numerical limits placed by the UCDP definitions if the entire duration of these armed conflicts is reviewed.

It is apparent now that the UCDP definitions were derived from Cold War beliefs that persist; hence, more thought needs to be given to refining the concept of 'major armed conflicts' to have greater relevance for South Asia.[5] Since its situation is unique, this exercise

---

[5] The inadequacy of the present definition of 'armed conflict' is appreciated, while recognizing the need for 'additional research and resources'. See *SIPRI Yearbook 2007: Armaments, Disarmament and International Security*, note 3 above, p. 95. The attendant problems are set forth in Appendix 2 C, ' Collective violence beyond the standard definition of armed conflict', ibid. pp. 94–106.

should be undertaken within the region to cater for these different elements relevant to armed conflicts, especially the death of civilians and the economic damage to the affected territory, apart from battle-related deaths.

PARTICULARITIES OF SOUTH ASIAN ARMED CONFLICTS AND PEACE PROCESSES

National security beliefs are primarily a function of the threat perceptions generated by their ruling elite; they comprehend both external and internal dimensions, but also the linkages between them. Do armed conflicts in South Asia share any common features? Overall, the region's security is characterized by two unique features. First, the tensions and instabilities embedded in the India–Pakistan standoff have acquired a nuclear dimension. Several wars have interspersed their traditional hostile relations, which began soon after they achieved independence in 1947; the inter-war interregnums were really an armed truce, but were marked by various forms of subterranean warfare, which is ongoing in Kashmir today. Their reciprocal nuclear tests in May 1998 made overt the state of recessed nuclear deterrence between them. It could have been hoped that this would strengthen stability and erode tensions; not unexpectedly, this did not happen, and there was no mitigation in the proxy war that had been launched by Pakistan against India, manifested by its support to militancy in Kashmir and terrorist activities all over India. The Kargil conflict (1999) is unique in that it provides an example of a conventional conflict between two nuclear armed countries, the only other example in the nuclear era being the Ussuri clashes that occurred between China and the erstwhile Soviet Union in early 1969. Currently a peace process is underway between India and Pakistan, but at a glacial pace, and opinion is evenly divided on the durability of this modality.

Second, the binding force linking the security perceptions of India's smaller neighbours is their abiding angst regarding its perceived hegemonistic ambitions, which guides and underpins their foreign and security policy. They are convinced that 'South Asia's security problems derive basically from India's expansionist and hegemonic spectre looming over the region, since the main component of Pakistani,

Bangladeshi, Nepali and Sri Lankan threat perceptions focus upon India.'[6] The geo-political structure of South Asia emphasizes its Indo-centricity; an often-cited fact is that no two South Asian neighbours of India have common borders with each other, but India has land or maritime borders with all of them. This geo-strategic reality has profound psychological implications for Nepal and Bhutan, both land-locked countries, while emphasizing the geo-political isolation of the island nations—Sri Lanka and the Maldives—from the region. The national security perspectives of these countries is shaped by these geo-strategic realities, which has strengthened India's belief that it must expand its bilateral and multilateral relations beyond South Asia to its extended neighborhood in Southeast, Central and West Asia, while continuing modest efforts to pursue bilateral ties and regional cooperation in the region through SAARC.

Some distinguishing features of armed conflicts in South Asia can now be discussed. They inform us that:

- First, in line with global trends that have accentuated in recent years, the external aspects of national security in South Asia have yielded precedence to its internal aspects. Following the Indo-Pak war of 1971 and the creation of Bangladesh, there have been several crises between India and Pakistan that could have escalated into a major conflict but did not. These major crises were associated with the Brasstacks Exercise (1987), the Kashmir-related Spring crisis (1990), the Kargil conflict (1999), and the Border Confrontation crisis over 2001–02.[7] There could be several reasons why these major crises did not precipitate an all-out war, which might be attributed to a combination of good sense dawning—belatedly perhaps—on the India–Pakistan leadership, intervention by the United States, a fuller appreciation of the implications of nuclear deterrence among the decision-making elites of the two countries, and plain good fortune. Their current security problems are almost entirely internal

---

[6] P.R.Chari, 'Security Aspects of Indian Foreign Policy', in Stephen Philip Cohen, ed., *Security Aspects of Indian Foreign Policy: American and Asian Perspectives,* Urbana and Chicago: University of Illinois Press, 1987, p. 50. Nothing basically has changed over the intervening two decades.

[7] See P.R.Chari, Pervaiz Iqbal Cheema and Stephen P. Cohen, *Four Crises and a Peace Process,* The Brookings Institution Press, forthcoming.

in nature, comprising threats from jihadi terrorism, Left extremism and so on, which can be aggravated by external actors, but basically illustrates that internal threats far outweigh external threats in South Asia.

Indeed, it has been perceptively noted that 'Lagging economies, ethnic affiliations, intense religious convictions, and youth bulges will align to create a "perfect storm", causing conditions likely to spawn internal conflict. The governing capacity of states, however, will determine whether and to what extent conflicts actually occur. Those states unable both to satisfy the expectations of their peoples and resolve or quell conflicting demands among them are likely to encounter the most severe and most frequent outbreaks of violence.'[8] All South Asian countries are at risk since the lack of governance or, more accurately, misgovernance in South Asia is too marked to require highlighting. The security situation in Nepal, Bangladesh and Sri Lanka exemplifies this assessment.

- Second, the region also exhibits symptoms of the 'contested incompatibility' noticed in the UCDP definitions, deriving from states acting in concert with armed groups under their control to promote dissidence and insurrection in their neighbours. Indeed, several armed conflicts in South Asia exhibit this phenomenon of external–internal factors propelling conflict and exacerbating their virulence. In consequence, large numbers of deaths occur due to terrorist and insurgent violence in the region, including those of innocent civilians caught in the crossfire, which is euphemistically underplayed by describing them as 'collateral damage'. The proxy war instrumentality informs the interventionary foreign and security policies of South Asian countries, as the recent history of India–Pakistan, Indo-Bangladesh and Indo–Sri Lankan relations informs us. Terrorist attacks on specific communities, targeted killings by focusing on individuals within designated political groups or communities are also occurring regularly. For instance, jihadi groups have been encouraged by Pakistan to selectively kill

---

[8] Report of the National Intelligence Council's 2020 Project, 'Mapping the Global Future,' http://www.cia.gov/nic/NIC_global trend2020. html. Cf. 'Pervasive Insecurity', p. 5.

moderate Kashmiri leaders, and the LTTE assassinating leaders in their own Tamil community. Another example is the wanton destruction of property in Sri Lanka by the security forces and the Tamil militants. These examples illustrate the different ramifications of armed conflicts in South Asia, as distinct from its law and order problems which rank lower in the spectrum of violence in the region.

- Third, sectarian and ethno-political violence, apart from insurgency and terrorism, underlies several armed conflicts in the region, which is discernible in a broad span of territory from the turbulent Afghanistan–Pakistan border region to Baluchistan to northeast India to the tribal belt in East and Central India, and further into Sri Lanka. Battle-lines are constantly being redrawn in these conflicts, leading to a loosening of government control over the affected territories, and the armed conflicts in these theatres becoming more intense. The most recent addition to this list of lawless territories is the sensitive Waziristan and Federally Administered Tribal Area (FATA) in Pakistan. There has been an alarming growth of al Qaeda and Taliban influence in this sub-region due to the crusading zeal of these Islamist organizations and the covert support extended by Pakistan's intelligence agencies. There are some 40 million Pashtuns living on both sides of the Durand line in Afghanistan and Pakistan, and it is believed that the birth of a new Pashtunistan state is possible[9] as this region rapidly slips out of the control of both Islamabad and Kabul.

- Fourth, most studies on armed conflicts in South Asia pay little heed to their psychological and economic costs, which are considerable but are difficult to quantify, especially when these conflicts are prolonged over years. The armed conflicts in Kashmir, northeast India and Sri Lanka, for instance, have proceeded for decades. Apart from causing economic hardships to individuals and communities, stultifying regional development and draining the national and state exchequers, these prolonged conflicts are known to have profound psychological, even

---

[9] Selig Harrison, 'The Pashtun time bomb', *The International Herald Tribune*, 1 August 2007. According to the author, traditional wisdom informs that either Islamist or Pashtun identity would triumph in this conflict. But the more plausible alternative is the emergence of an 'Islamic Pashtunistan'.

neurological, effects on the local population.[10] This is particularly true of groups that are generally forgotten in these conflicts, namely women and children, whose sufferings need greater illumining in studies of armed conflicts. The absence of adequate importance to socio-economic costs, however, does not mitigate from their relevance, or the need to configure the affected population, particularly women and children, into reconciliation and rehabilitation programmes devised to manage the post-conflict consequences of the peace processes.

- Fifth, armed conflicts in South Asia exhibit the full panoply of violence. They include cross-border conflicts which have occurred regularly between India and Pakistan, India and Bangladesh, and now between Afghanistan and Pakistan; and, intra-state conflicts within the South Asian countries with varying degrees of virulence. These intra-state conflicts can be further categorized into armed conflicts possessing a communal-religious character, clearly evident in Pakistan and Bangladesh; or having socio-economic roots as apparent in the naxalite movement in India and the Maoist struggle in Nepal; or having ethno-political dimensions as evident in northeast India and Sri Lanka. Intra-state conflicts have arisen when such discontents have morphed and turned societal groups against provincial and central authority and sometimes against each other. All these factors have made South Asia, alongside sub-Saharan Africa and the Middle East, one of the most conflict-prone regions in the world. It could be said that better connectivity between estranged communities and with the state would mitigate such discontents by increasing communications. But better connectivity is a double-edged sword, and improved communications through television or internet can also fuel resentments within communities having common links—religious, ethnic, linguistic and cultural—against insensitive governments or against each other, leading to the growth of local resentments, frustrations against legal authority, and inspiring armed conflicts within the state.

- Sixth, South Asia's extremist groups have inspired these armed conflicts. They fall into five distinct categories: (*i*) Islamic

[10] Kavita Suri, 'Women in the [Kashmir] Valley: From Victims to Agents of Change', in W.P.S.Sidhu, Bushra Asif and Cyrus Samii, eds., *Kashmir: New Voices, New Approaches,* Boulder, Co: Lynne Rienner Publishers, 2006, p. 84.

extremists who seek to impose, extend or defend Muslim rule against non-Muslims; (*ii*) armed Sunni and Shi'a extremists fighting for sectarian control over the Islamic state; (*iii*) Hindu extremist organizations, like the Vishwa Hindu Parishad and Rashtriya Swayam Sevak Sangh, who wish to establish or mould the state on the foundation of Hinduism as opposed to a secular polity; (*iv*) ethno-linguistic groups that use political violence, including guerrilla war and terrorism, to gain their secessionist objectives, like the LTTE in Sri Lanka; and (*v*) Leftist extremists, like the Maoists in Nepal and the Naxalites in India, who are seeking to acquire state power and transform its structure to conform with their ideological goals. Currently, all these violent groups are using conventional weapons like small arms, hand grenades, landmines and improvised explosive devices. However, an anxiety obtains that they will, in time, acquire weapons of mass destruction (WMDs), especially biological and radiological weapons that are comparatively easier to acquire and deliver by unconventional means like using unmanned aerial vehicles (UAVs). Persisting reports, for instance, that the al Qaeda has shown interest in acquiring weapons of mass destruction cannot be dismissed as fanciful. This was recognized in the latest National Strategy for Homeland Security report issued by the United States, which unequivocally states that 'the most serious and dangerous manifestation of this [terrorist] threat remains al-Qaida, which is driven by an undiminished strategic intent to attack our Homeland.'[11] For that matter, the likelihood of states giving WMDs in deliverable form to non-state actors cannot be dismissed.

- Seventh, peace processes in South Asia are common, but proceed fitfully, as between the regional countries and within them. Clearly, the dynamics of peace processes between the South Asian countries are necessarily different from those between the state and non-state actors within their territory. The inter-state peace processes include the ongoing dialogues between Afghanistan and Pakistan, Pakistan and India, India and Bangladesh; the intra-state peace processes include those between the central authority in regional countries with their militant groups, as occurs with the Taliban in Afghanistan,

[11] *National Strategy for Homeland Security,* http://www.whitehouse.gov/infocus/homeland/nshs/NSHS.pdf (accessed on 12 October 2007).

Kashmiri dissidents in India, jihadis in Pakistan, Maoists in Nepal, Tamils in Sri Lanka, and may occur in the fullness of time in the Maldives. These dialogues generally proceed at a leisurely pace; some are halted, while others could be revived.

Going further, the problem remains of sustaining the peace dividend when achieved. The empirical evidence suggests that peace processes in South Asia are easier to initiate than to sustain, as is apparent in Sri Lanka and in Nepal. Ironically, however, agreements reached are scrupulously adhered to, especially if their benefits are clearly demonstrable. A good example is the Indus Waters Treaty (1960), which has withstood the strains of three India-Pakistan conflicts, the continuing dispute over Kashmir, and several major and minor crises that have periodically heightened tensions and instabilities between the two countries over the last half century. Currently the India–Pakistan 'composite dialogue' proceeds at a snail's pace, although some minor agreements have been reached between them on hotlines, giving prior notification on missile flights (cruise missiles are not yet included) and nuclear accidents. More substantive agreements on territorial issues like resolving the Siachen and Sir Creek disputes still await resolution, but remain the subject of interminable negotiations. Significantly, however, both countries have reached an agreement on 'making borders irrelevant' in Kashmir, on the assumption that neither country can extend them further or make them permanent in the foreseeable future. Bus services have been opened between the two countries that permit the divided population on both sides of the Line of Control (LOC) to socialize with each other. Agreements on permitting truck traffic and opening these routes to trade and commerce are on the anvil, and may become possible as mutual suspicions erode. Much the same could be concluded about the several other peace processes that are on in the region. No doubt the complexity of the disputes that lead to armed conflicts militate against their early resolution, but the influence of the security establishment, coupled with the lack of political will, apart from the dedication of the conflicting parties to pursuing their perceived national objectives without compromise, are further reasons for the continuance of these armed conflicts. So, is the glass half full or half empty? Much lies in the eyes of the beholder, but a debate on these issues is useful, even if it remains inconclusive.

The past history of American–Soviet negotiations on arms control, the current Israeli–Palestinian negotiations on evolving an elusive peace agreement, and between North and South Korea to usher peace into northeast Asia informs us that conflict resolution and post-conflict reconciliation are difficult exercises, and can linger for years without progress; patience is therefore essential for their pursuit, since quick-fix solutions can easily unravel. There is little reason therefore for South Asian countries to shun external mediation, which has often helped, though there can be no guarantee that they will always succeed. The Indus Waters Treaty, for example, was finalized after six years of negotiation over 1954–60, chiefly due to the mediatory efforts of the World Bank. More recently, American intervention was a crucial factor that hastened the cessation of the Kargil conflict and the termination of the border confrontation crisis. The signal lack of success, however, of the Sri Lanka Monitoring Mission (SLMM) and the Norwegians to bring peace to Sri Lanka shows that it is for the warring parties to resolve their differences and make the necessary compromises to end regional armed conflicts.

DISCERNING THE BROAD TRENDS IN ARMED CONFLICTS OVER 2006–07

It is not proposed to summarize in this Overview the contents or the conclusions of the various chapters in this volume. Each individual essay is basically reportage and needs to be read fully to appreciate its judgements on facts, and the conclusions derived thereafter. Instead, it is proposed to review here the broad trends that have manifested themselves within the armed conflicts in South Asia over 2006 and 2007, and those that seem likely to either persist and/or exacerbate over the coming years. An identification of these trends would permit revisiting them in future volumes in this series to track developments of interest and changes therein.

It is apparent that the new challenges to security, especially intra-state security, are more likely to ignite armed conflicts in South Asia. Peering into the future, what can one discern about armed conflicts that might arise, or those that would continue and could exacerbate over the coming years? Several indications are available to read the writing on the wall.

- First, there is little doubt that the writ of several South Asian states does not run over their entire territory, and sometimes does not extend much beyond their national capitals, as occurred during the last decades of the Mughal empire. The best example is Afghanistan, which lends credence to the *bon mot* that the Karzai government's writ runs only over Kabul, and that too, only during the daytime! But, it is also evident that the writ of the Pakistan government no longer runs over its FATA region, especially over the Waziristan Agency. The resurgence of the Taliban in south and east Afghanistan and the tribal belt straddling Afghanistan–Pakistan, with its bases located in Balochistan and the North West Frontier Province constitutes a cancerous node in South Asia; it could spread like a contagion leading to instability in Central Asia, but also in Pakistan. This phenomenon of expanding lawlessness and armed conflict is largely financed by the smuggling of drugs from the uncontrolled cultivation of poppy in these criminalized areas. Several parts of South Asia are exhibiting manifestations of state failure demonstrated by the presence of 'black spots' where the symptoms of a failed state are evident. 'One such black spot is the area around Peshawar… which has been repeatedly described as the hiding place for fleeing or regrouping al-Qaeda and Taliban operatives; the area is also a smuggling center where almost anything can be bought or sold on the black market.'[12] It is also the distribution centre for illicit opium and its derivatives produced in Afghanistan for supply to markets across the world. Other 'black spots' are recognizable in the Jaffna peninsula, the Chitagong Hill Tracts, northwestern Nepal, parts of Kashmir and the northeastern Indian states, and, most worrisome, the rapidly growing number of districts in central and eastern India (172 out of some 600 plus districts at last count) that are falling under Naxalite control. These 'black spots' identify the areas out of which armed conflicts could emerge and radiate further into South Asia unless they are effectively dealt with. The coexistence of functioning national and provincial authority, alongside virtual lack of control over broad expanses of its territory, has become a distinguishing feature of violence in South Asia.

[12] Bartisz H. Stanislawski and Margaret G. Hermann, *Transnational Organized Crime, Terrorism and WMD,* Centre for International Development and Global Management (CIDCM), University of Maryland, 15 October 2004, pp. 2–3.

- Second, many South Asian countries have demonstrated a touching faith in the efficacy of fencing and/or mining their borders to keep out militants/terrorists, but also desperate people migrating into their territory hoping for a better quality of life, and often to ensure their personal safety from persecution or by escaping from ethnic and communal conflict. The latest effort is Pakistan's attempt to fence off stretches of the Pak–Afghan border, mainly to convince the Americans that it is 'doing something' to prevent the ingress and egress of the Taliban and al Qaeda elements that have found refuge in its territory. India has fenced off the Line of Control in Kashmir to stop militants and terrorists from entering the state by crossing the Indo–Pak border. This modality has its dedicated supporters and opponents in India. Those in favour point to a marked reduction in the number of militants and terrorists crossing the LOC. But those against this proposition argue that the fence can be breached or tunneled under, and needs to be continuously manned anyway. Moreover, the fence goes down whenever heavy snowfall occurs, permitting the LOC to be crossed. The shifting of mines due to landslides, furthermore, causes more casualties on the Indian rather than the Pakistani side, both to the local people and their livestock. The efficacy of the Indo–Bangladesh fence that is being constructed by India also remains in doubt, chiefly due to the availability of easy alternative river and maritime routes for entering India, apart from the Bangladeshi enclaves in Indian territory and vice versa. Besides, there is no reason for determined anti-social elements to cross the border to enter another country, when the longer but safer modality of entry via a third country is available. Witness the ease with which Pakistani militants and terrorists enter India through Nepal or Bangladesh. Therefore, the chief value of these massive, expensive, but essentially useless efforts to fence off countries seems to be providing an option to slow down the human tide of migrants. Wisdom suggests that a more certain method to achieve this objective would be for South Asian countries to develop their border regions jointly through SAARC. Wisdom also suggests that the implications of sub-nationalism, which transcends borders, be recognized, instead of trying to fence it off.

- Third, minority issues are likely to become the new and more prescient reason for armed conflicts in South Asia. The disconcerting regularity of communal riots in an avowedly secular country like India points to the strength of religious prejudices in the majority community against the minority communities in South Asia. The major communal riots in India in the recent past, for example anti-Sikh (1984), anti-Muslim, after the Babri Masjid's demolition (1992), and Gujarat (2002) highlight both the religious aggressiveness of the majority community, and the hand of the state in permitting, if not promoting, such deliberate breakdown of law and order. This is applicable to the Pakistani and Bangladeshi governments as well in their dealing with, if not also promoting, anti-Hindu riots in the past, as also the Sinhala government's conduct in Sri Lanka vis-à-vis the Tamil minority. In India and Sri Lanka the minorities are too large to be either suppressed or expelled, which only leads to more virulent attacks upon them by the majority community. An equal danger arises from the minority community resorting to violence in retaliation, which need not express itself overtly, but through covert modalities like those embedded in 'revenge' terrorism. Several terrorist incidents in India, like the Bombay blasts in 1993, had a clear nexus with the anti-Muslim riots after the Babri Masjid demolition some three months earlier. A serious majority–minority situation in South Asia currently obtains in Afghanistan where the minority Uzbek community currently dominates the Karzai government, while the Pashtun majority, constituting the bulk of the Taliban militants, is challenging its authority. Past efforts of the international community (read the United States and, for that matter, India) to support the Northern Alliance (largely Uzbek) has alienated them from the Pashtuns, reduced the capacity of the Karzai government to cobble a modus vivendi in Afghanistan, and exacerbated the ethnic divide between the Uzbek and Pashtun communities. A reasonable presumption could be made that South Asia will witness greater sectarianism and communalism in future, leading to violence and armed conflict; the two largest communities in the region—Hindus and Muslims—comprise roughly 60 per cent and 40 per cent of the total population. The empirical evidence reveals, moreover, that the majority community can be responsible while the minority

community is irresponsible, and vice versa, which points to the need for objective judgements, instead of automatic and *a priori* conclusions.
- Fourth, the absence of coordination between the several states in South Asia, as also within these states, is a matter of serious concern. The Terrorism Convention, for instance, which was entered into by the SAARC countries in 1987, remains toothless in the absence of extradition treaties for the eviction of persons wanted for prosecution for serious offences. Nor are the countries where they were provided asylum willing to undertake their prosecution on the basis of evidence provided to them. The situation in India as regards coordinating efforts by the northeastern states, for instance, or the states afflicted with Naxalite militancy, is equally disconcerting. Determined efforts to launch joint operations, share intelligence, investigate cross-state–border offences, and proceed, in short, with a clear sense of purpose against militant and terrorist groups are seriously missing. Ironically, these anti-social groups have established close coordination among themselves to procure arms, set up training facilities and address 'policy' issues to make themselves a more effective fighting force.

CONCLUSIONS

The plea has been made in several fora by well-meaning people that the bilateral and multilateral dialogue processes in South Asia must be strengthened to bring peace and stability to one of the poorest regions in the developing world. But, is peace an end in itself? Can the mere absence of hostilities ensure peaceful and stable conditions for the affected population to pursue their lives and avocations without fear? In northeast India, for instance, negotiating peace and ceasefire agreements has become a meaningless exercise since they proceed side by side with militancy; kidnappings and extortion, for instance, continue even after negotiating such agreements, making them quite irrelevant.

What is often not appreciated are the connections between the national security concerns of the South Asian countries, the common nature of their armed conflicts, and their identical mistakes. Three instances from recent South Asian history are instructive in this regard.

- First, it may be recalled that Indira Gandhi was arrested in mid 1978 and tried on criminal charges after the Janata Party came to power in 1977, immediately after the Emergency imposed by her was lifted. The sympathy wave generated by this vindictive act, and the inability of the Janata government to obtain Indira Gandhi's conviction, led to their ouster in the general elections of 1980. Thereafter, her prosecutors were sidelined, and her trusted officials returned to prominence. This same course of events is unfolding in Bangladesh with the military-backed interim government having arrested former Prime Ministers Khaleda Zia and Sheikh Hasina in mid-2007 on charges framed against them by the Anti-Corruption Commission. At the time of writing, no charges have been pressed against them while the Parliamentary elections have been indefinitely postponed. Should these leaders return to power, which is not unlikely, history might repeat itself, with the prosecutors becoming the prosecuted.
- Second, the forcible entry of the Indian army into the Golden Temple in June 1984 and the storming of the Lal Masjid in Islamabad in July 2007 bear a remarkable similarity. The comparisons between the circumstances leading to 'Operation Bluestar' and 'Operation Silence', the killing of Sant Bhindranwale and Maulana Gazi, and the situation that obtained in Punjab in 1984 and is currently seen in Pakistan in 2007 are striking. The lessons that can be drawn from these two episodes to instruct the leaderships in South Asia is that the nurturing of an extreme leadership to counter moderates in the Opposition might be part of a clever divide-and-rule policy, but it is also fraught with the danger of the extremists getting out of control, and the intended solution becoming the future problem. But, has this lesson been learned? Does prejudice deter the countries in South Asia from learning anything from these Indian examples?
- Third, the co-optation of militants into counter-insurgency and counter-terrorism operations is a modality that has a siren lure for many states in South Asia. Banglabhai in Dhaka, Karuna in eastern Sri Lanka, the SULFA (Surrendered ULFA) in Assam, and Ikhwanis (former militants) in Kashmir are some examples of individuals and organizations being co-opted into the law enforcement machinery to identify and often liquidate their former companions in militant and terrorist outfits. Empirical evidence

reveals that these former militants/terrorists slowly but surely become the problem rather than the solution. Extortion rackets, human rights violations and other anti-social actions are frequently associated with them, sometimes in collaboration with the armed and paramilitary forces of the state. In all such situations the local population fears them more than the militants and terrorists. The result is losing the battle for the hearts and minds of the general population, without whose cooperation counter-militancy and counter-terrorism operations are doomed to fail and destined to continue *ad infinitum*. Still, this modality continues to inspire governments, as is evident from the establishment of the controversial Salwa Judum in Chattisgarh, which has instilled fear in the common people and has raised the hackles of NGO groups across the country. The latest example is President Karzai's offer to initiate a dialogue with Mullah Omar and Gulbuddin Hekmatyar, which in itself is unexceptional, but he also went on to say that 'executive positions in his government could be found for Taliban and Hezb-i-Islami notables'.[13] How this will affect the ethnic arithmetic of his present Cabinet and the power structure in Kabul is not difficult to predict. It would only complicate his task even further.

Regrettably, the similarity in the intrinsic nature of their armed conflicts has not informed the South Asian countries to formulate responses taking into account the experience of their neighbours, since they prefer to learn from their own experience! The same grievous errors and mistakes made elsewhere in the region continue to be repeated. Lessons remain unlearnt, allowing a paraphrasing of Marx's famous judgement on history in the South Asian context: 'History repeats itself as a tragedy, and then as a greater tragedy'. Lest this negative picture seem overdrawn, the positive developments within the region over 2006–07 should be noted. The ceasefire along the Line of Control in Kashmir is holding up, and the earlier artillery duels between India and Pakistan in this region have, hopefully, become a part of their unfortunate history. Elections, despite their obvious imperfections, have been held in Pakistan and Nepal, and,

---

[13] William Maley, 'Talking to the Taliban', *The World Today*, vol. 63, no.11, November 2007, p. 4.

hopefully, will be held before long in Bangladesh. GDP growth, despite violence, has displayed remarkable resilience in India, Pakistan and Bangladesh—the prominent countries of South Asia. There is in all the regional countries a commitment to multi-party democracy, which remains firm despite many slippages in practice. But these few positive developments are a thin silver lining in the dark cloud of growing violence and conflict.

What can we discern about the future of armed conflicts in South Asia? The South Asian countries, except for India and the Maldives, fall in the category of failed and failing states. To make such estimates, an annual 'Failed states Index' has been drawn up by a US think-tank, the Fund for Peace, which is published by the *Foreign Policy* journal in Washington.[14] Nations are ranked on this index according to twelve factors: mounting demographic pressures; massive movement of refugees and internally displaced persons; legacy of vengeance-seeking group grievance; chronic and sustained human flight; uneven economic development along group lines; sharp and/or severe economic decline; criminalization and delegitimization of the state; progressive deterioration of public services; widespread violation of human rights; security apparatus becoming a 'state within a state'; rise of factionalized elites; and intervention of other states or external factors.

How do South Asian countries fare on this Failed States Index? Including Afghanistan, which has recently become a SAARC member, it is disconcerting that, except for India and the Maldives, the other six countries in the region are listed among the first sixty failed states. Their respective positions are Afghanistan (8), Pakistan (12), Bangladesh (16), Nepal (21), Sri Lanka (25) and Bhutan (47). Significantly, Afghanistan, Pakistan and Bangladesh are designated as the most 'critical' countries; Nepal heads the second list of countries 'in danger'; while Bhutan falls in the third list of borderline states. So many failed states being located in South Asia has serious implications for the region's internal security and the propensity for armed conflicts in their territory. The geo-strategic reality must be appreciated that India is ringed by a circumference of tensions and instabilities that react with tensions and instabilities subsisting in India. This factor has profound implications for its external security in the coming

---

[14] Cf. *The Failed States Index 2007*, http://www.foreign policy.com (accessed on 7 September 2007).

years. It can be argued that the Failed States Index exaggerates the situation, since newly de-colonized states could be expected to be economically and politically weak and not cohesive as they are in various stages of state formation. But the existence of one or all of these symptoms of state failure in parts or the whole of different states in South Asia cannot be ignored; they point to their serious vulnerability to social and political chaos, which predisposes them to instability and armed conflicts.

Finally, it could be surmised that terrorism, with its international and regional linkages, is unlikely to show any signs of abatement in South Asia, but will continue to excoriate the region; that the linkages between terrorism and organized crime will further consolidate, but a special danger will arise from the *entree* of these anti-social elements into the inner processes of governance; that the growth of 'identity politics', with primacy being accorded by adherent groups to religion and ethnicity, would lead to greater communal and ethnic violence; that the links between the internal and external sources of armed conflict in South Asia, especially radical Islam, will continue in the foreseeable future; that the growing reach of the electronic media, with its message of consumerism for the endowed, will inspire and strengthen the resentment of the poor against authority, leading to their resorting to violent means for mitigating perceived injustices; that the capacity of regional bodies like SAARC to erode armed disputes will remain marginal; and that bilateralism to proceed with the peace processes would posit itself as a practical necessity.

These issues need to be closely reviewed when considering armed conflicts in South Asia, but they must also be kept in mind to forge the instrumentalities required to meet these challenges to regional security in South Asia. What is important is to nuance these issues to enhance our understanding, but also to recognize their changing trends.

2

Afghanistan: Continuing Violence

Shanthie Mariet D'Souza

A BRIEF HISTORY

The beginnings of the conflict and consequent instability in Afghanistan can be traced to the period 1973–1979, the period preceding the Soviet intervention. This phase was marked by internal coups and external power intervention. In the largest covert operation since the Vietnam War, policy-makers in the United States started supporting the Afghan resistance parties based in Pakistan through the Central Intelligence Agency (CIA). President Carter decided that the US had a 'moral obligation' to help the resistance movement.[1] The US Congress increasingly pushed for more aid and took the initiative in doubling the administration's request for $250 million, plus an extra allocation for anti-aircraft weapons. The entire aid programme was channelled by the CIA through Inter Services Intelligence (ISI), Pakistani's intelligence agency, to maintain deniability.

With the objective of transforming Afghanistan into a 'Soviet-Vietnam' and to bleed the Soviets white in Afghanistan, US policy-makers armed the mujahideen, flirted with Islam and allowed the chaos to intensify. Following Soviet withdrawal from Afghanistan, US policy-makers lost interest in the country. In the 1990s, Afghanistan continued to be wracked by internecine warfare between various mujahideen factions. In the ensuing anarchy, the Taliban began their victory march with active support from Pakistan. There was, however, some apprehension among US policy-makers after the Taliban captured Kabul in 1996. The strict puritanical Taliban regime

---

[1] In July 1979, six months before the Soviet invasion, President Carter signed a Presidential finding on covert action that began as a modest programme of medical aid to the rebels. See John H. Cooley, *Unholy Wars: Afghanistan, America and International Terrorism*, London, 2000, p. 129. For CIA funding see Brigadier Mohammad Yousaf and Major Mark Adkin, *The Bear Trap: Afghanistan's Untold Story*, Lahore, 1992, p. 120.

was led by Mullah Omar along with a ragtag motley group of former Pushtun military commanders, madrassa teachers and a large rank and file from the Islamist religious schools in Pakistan. This largely obscurantist rule was marked by large-scale human rights violations and oppression of women.

The US was at first supportive of the Taliban, hoping that the regime would serve as a stabilizing force to restore peace and order in the country. However, these hopes were belied when the Taliban provided sanctuary to al Qaeda in 1996, following Osama bin Laden's flight from Sudan. The al Qaeda and the Taliban shared a symbiotic relationship, with the former financing and providing a fighting force to the Taliban. When Osama bin Laden was indicted for the 1998 US embassy bombings in Africa, the Taliban refused to extradite him, a stance it maintained till the 11 September 2001 (9/11) attacks on the American homeland. The Taliban, dictated by their tribal code of Pushtunwali, vowed to protect and provide hospitality to their al Qaeda guests.

The present ongoing conflict in Afghanistan can be traced to the US military intervention in that country in response to the 9/11 attacks. The US-led Operation Enduring Freedom (OEF) was primarily targeted at decimating the Taliban–al Qaeda terrorist infrastructure in Afghanistan and depriving the al Qaeda of its territorial base for carrying out future attacks. The military operations that commenced on 7 October 2001 ensured an early victory with the Taliban's ouster from Kabul. The Taliban's withdrawal from Kandahar on 9 December 2001 marked the end of its regime in Afghanistan. On 1 May 2003, US Secretary of Defense, Rumsfeld, declared an end to 'major combat operations'.[2] The announcement of early victory and diverting of resources to Iraq as early as 2002 at a critical state of the war in Afghanistan changed the tide in that country. The shift from CIA specialists and elite Special Forces to conventional troops affected counter-insurgency operations. The reluctance of the Bush Administration to involve itself in nation-building exercises in Afghanistan, and their reliance and support to the warlords to maintain a light security footprint there led to a deteriorating security situation.

The insurgency, which began in 2002–03, continues to wrack the country today. The year 2007 is being viewed as the 'pivotal year'

---

[2] Kenneth Katzman, 'Afghanistan: Post-War Governance, Security, and US Policy', Washington, DC: Congressional Research Service Report, 4 May 2006, p.8.

for NATO and the US forces to arrest, if not reverse, the trend of resurgence of the Taliban. The fractured political processes, inadequate reconstruction, rising instability and alienated populace provides a support base to the Taliban-led insurgency.[3] The top Taliban leaders have found refuge in Pakistan's cities. The Taliban has a wide support base in the Pakistan–Afghanistan border areas, which has ramifications for both Pakistan's and Afghanistan's security. These areas have historically been ungoverned spaces and are predominantly inhabited by the Pushtun tribe, with strong ethno-tribal affiliations to the Taliban. Though the Taliban originated as a social and religious movement, it has a strong ethno-tribal base.[4]

The conflict situation in Afghanistan involves a plethora of internal and external actors with conflicting interests and competing agendas. Some ethnic, tribal, clan and community groups were a part of this environment before the conflict began and were engaged in creative competition. However, the present conflict has accentuated the existing socio-ethnic cleavages due to external support, deepening fissures within Afghan society. In Afghanistan, the ethno-tribal power competition, and the Pushtun domination in the political space, have always been important in maintaining equilibrium in the political system.

THE PRINCIPAL ACTORS

The present, ongoing conflict in Afghanistan has produced a vast array of new actors—an intervening counter-insurgent state (United States) and its coalition partners (OEF & NATO), foreign terrorists with transnational linkages (al Qaeda and its affiliates), international institutions, non-governmental organizations, media and others. In the case of the Afghan insurgency, the Taliban–al Qaeda symbiotic relationship provides al Qaeda with a local partner (Taliban), which has developed linkages with various groups in Pakistan from its sanctuary in the

---

[3] The Taliban-led insurgency includes: a loose alliance of Taliban guerrillas, followers of the Afghan warlord Gulbuddin Hekmatyar's radical group—Hizb-i-Islami, al Qaeda recruits, foreign terrorists, narcotic traffickers, bandits and tribal fighters in the Pakistan–Afghanistan border. This inference was derived from interviews and discussions with the locals in various provinces in Afghanistan—Herat, Kabul, Balkh, Parvan, Baglan, Samangan, Kapisa and Nangarhar—during a field visit to Afghanistan in May–June 2007.

[4] Thomas H. Johnson and M. Chris Mason, 'Understanding the Taliban and Insurgency in Afghanistan', *Orbis*, vol. 5, no.1, Winter 2007, pp.7–8.

Pakistan–Afghanistan border area. This area has emerged as an 'arc of regional conflict formation,'[5] linking the conflict from Chechnya to Kashmir.

The Afghan state led by President Hamid Karzai is viewed as a weak and ineffective state by the international community, insurgents and the local populace. The nascent democratic government in Afghanistan is dependent on external aid for its functioning and for providing security to the population. The writ of the Karzai government is restricted to the capital and he is popularly known as the 'mayor of Kabul'. Large parts of rural Afghanistan, particularly in the south and east, are controlled by the Taliban. The fight against the Taliban is being led by the US, NATO and indigenous Afghan forces.

Afghan National Army (ANA)

The ANA was organized, trained and equipped by the US Special Forces (USSF) in 2002 along the lines of the 'conventional' US light infantry model. However, the ANA, trained as a conventional army, has been primarily employed to augment the Coalition's conventional COIN operations, rather than developing its independent role.

Afghan National Police

The core component of any effective counter-insurgency (COIN) force is a well-trained police force responsible for security and intelligence collection at the community level. The US and Germany are training the Afghan National Police (ANP) force. About 62,000 ANP are on duty, including 3,000 in training, which is approximately the target size of the force. There are seven police training centres across Afghanistan. Like the ANA, the ANP too is saddled with problems of funding, training, recruitment, equipment and desertions. It remains under-trained, under-manned and has minimal control in the Afghan urban centres, a ghost presence and almost no presence in the rural Afghan villages, where they are needed most.

---

[5] Discussions with Barnett R. Rubin, Washington, DC, 4 February 2006. Also see Barnett R. Rubin and Andrea Armstrong, 'Regional Issues in the Reconstruction of Afghanistan', *World Policy Journal*, vol. 20, no. 1, Spring 2003.

Armed Groups

The Taliban-led insurgency includes a loose alliance of Taliban guerrillas, followers of the Afghan warlord Gulbuddin Hekmatyar's radical group Hizb-i-Islami, al Qaeda recruits, foreign terrorists, narcotic traffickers, bandits and tribal fighters in the Pakistan–Afghanistan border region.

Taliban

Vanquished from their political seat in Kabul in December 2001, the Taliban are able to carry out well-orchestrated attacks in Afghanistan from their sanctuaries in the Pakistan–Afghanistan border region. There is no accurate estimate of the number of Taliban fighters, though their strength seems to be increasing with recruits largely from madrassas in Pakistan. Their weapons are vastly improved and more sophisticated, making their attacks more lethal than ever. The influence of the Taliban has been persistent over the southern and eastern provinces of the country and is spreading westwards. Several Taliban leaders are reported to be living in Baluchistan around Quetta,[6] from where they are able to direct anti-Afghan activities.

al Qaeda

The Taliban–al Qaeda symbiotic relationship has further strengthened in post 9/11 Afghanistan. They have found refuge in the sanctuaries in the Pakistan–Afghanistan border areas, particularly Waziristan. The al Qaeda has reportedly forged alliances with Pakistani terrorist groups like Jaish-e-Muhammad (JeM, proscribed in 2002 and presently operating under the banner of Jamaat-ul-Furqan),[7] Harkat-ul-Jihad-al-Islami (HuJI) and Harkat-ul-Mujahideen (HuM) that are responsible for terrorism in Jammu and Kashmir. These terrorist groups, along

---

[6] Declan Walsh, 'Balochistan feeds Taliban's growing power', San Francisco Chronicle, *Chronicle* Foreign Service, 31 May 2006 http://www.sfgate.com/cgibin/article.cgi?file=/c/a/2006/05/31/MNGT1J4ULI1.DTL.

[7] In Pakistan, the JeM operated at least four major military training camps located in Balakot, Muzzaffarabad, Hajeera and Mansehra. For further details see Evan F. Kohlmann, 'The Jihadists of Pakistan', Occasional Report, The NEFA Foundation, August 2006, http://www.nefafoundation.org/miscellaneous/pakistanjihad0806.pdf.

with the al Qaeda, have created a 'lethal concoction' with over-lapping linkages, membership and ideologies.

Warlords and Private Militias

The warlords were regarded as the staunch allies of the Western powers during the initial phase of Operation Enduring Freedom (OEF). Rather than marginalizing the warlords and dismantling their militias, the US, in numerous cases, has relied upon the warlords (particularly from the Northern Alliance) for intelligence gathering and cooperation in efforts to capture the Taliban and al Qaeda remnants.[8] Their limited vision of nation-building and the effort to maintain light security footprint due to their preoccupation with planning for the war in Iraq, security for the Afghan population was to remain the responsibility of regional warlords until a new Afghan national army could be recruited, trained and deployed.[9] This promoted a 'culture of impunity'[10] in addition to increasing the influence of the warlords. This over-reliance on the warlords has created a greater problem for the Afghan government and the international community.

International Forces

United States

In post-9/11 Afghanistan, the United States has been the intervening counter-insurgent state leading a coalition of countries under the OEF. However, compared to its forces deployed in Iraq, the US presence in Afghanistan is clearly not adequate. Even the limited number of

---

[8] Richard Rupp, 'High Hopes and Limited Prospects: Washington's Security and Nation-Building Aims in Afghanistan', *Cambridge Review of International Affairs*, vol. 19, no. 2, June 2006, p. 291.

[9] Discussions with Ambassador James Dobbins, Washington, DC, 7 September 2005. See James Dobbins, 'Preparing for Nation-Building', *Survival*, vol. 48, no. 3, Autumn 2006. Also see James Dobbins, 'Ending Afghanistan's Civil War', testimony presented before the House Armed Services Committee on 30 January 2007, http://armedservices.house.gov/pdfs/FC%20hearing_013007/Dobbins%20Testimony.pdf (accessed 27 April 2007).

[10] 'Countering Afghanistan's Insurgency: No Quick Fixes', *Asia Report*, no. 123, 2 November 2006, http://www.crisisgroup.org/home/index.cfm?l=1&id=4485 (accessed 24 January 2007).

US forces[11] is focused on offensive 'clear and sweep' operations and aerial bombings, resulting in collateral damage and mounting civilian deaths, further antagonizing the population.

OEF–ISAF (International Security Assistance Force)

The complexity of the International COIN response in Afghanistan is compounded by the presence of two major international military coalitions. The first, OEF, is an American-led effort, while the ISAF commenced as a UN-mandated European organization, but then evolved into a NATO-led mission in 2003. This violates the principle of 'unity of command' and creates problems of coordination in the operational sphere. Some countries contribute forces to both the OEF and ISAF, while others contribute only to ISAF. At present, twenty-one nations contribute approximately 3,100 troops to OEF, and 37 NATO and non-NATO nations contribute about 20,000 troops to ISAF.[12]

The NATO countries invoked Article 5 of collective self-defence as a response to post-9/11 attacks on the American homeland. NATO's first out-of-Europe involvement began in Afghanistan under a UN mandate in August 2003. Some non-NATO states like Australia and New Zealand contribute resources to the allied effort. In July 2006, ISAF moved into southern Afghanistan, where US, British, Canadian and Dutch forces (ABCD forces) predominate. In October 2006, during Phase Four, ISAF took control of the entire country.[13] The US-led OEF continues its combat operations in the Pakistan–Afghanistan border areas.

---

[11] According to estimates provided by the US Department of Defense (DoD), there are approximately 19,000 US service members in Afghanistan. The DoD figures show that there were about 139,000 troops in Iraq and 19,000 in Afghanistan as of 1 October 2006. For further details see Amy Belasco, 'The Cost of Iraq, Afghanistan, and Other Global War on Terror Operations Since 9/11', Congressional Research Service (CRS) Report, RL33110, updated 16 July 2007, p.13. In addition to troops involved in combat operations, about 5,000 US troops are involved in training and advising Afghan security forces and another 2,000 are involved in logistical operations and also providing manpower for 12 Provincial Reconstruction Teams (PRTs). Between 23,000 and 24,000 American service members are in Afghanistan, the highest troop level the United States has had in the nation. Jim Garamone, 'NATO, US, Afghan Forces Battling Taliban in Afghanistan', American Forces Press Service, 16 January 2007, http://www.globalsecurity.org/military/library/news/2007/01/mil-070116-afps01.htm (accessed 7 March 2007).

[12] See Andrew Feickert, 'US and Coalition Military Operations in Afghanistan: Issues for Congress', CRS Report RL33503, updated 11 December 2006, p.2.

[13] For details about stages in NATO's expansion in Afghanistan and troop strength, see Paul Gallis, 'NATO in Afghanistan: A Test of the Transatlantic Alliance', CRS Report, RL33627, updated 16 July 2007, p.3.

The NATO-led ISAF has about 39,000 troops. As of September 2007, Canada has 2,500 troops in Afghanistan; Germany has 3,000 troops deployed as part of the ISAF forces on a reconstruction and training mission in the northern part of Afghanistan; the Dutch have about 2,000 troops. Britain, while reducing its contingent in Iraq, has almost doubled its force in Afghanistan from 3,300 to 5,800. Australia has 1,000 troops in Afghanistan, more than any other non-NATO nation. However, the current international troop level remains inadequate.

Provincial Reconstruction Teams (PRTs)

In an innovative COIN approach to resolve the 'security-reconstruction' dilemma in Afghanistan, Provincial Reconstruction Teams (PRTs) were created by the US Department of Defense to provide secure areas for international aid workers beyond Kabul in December 2002. As of 5 September 2007, there are twenty-five PRTs with five regional command centres. PRT activities range from resolving local disputes to coordinating local reconstruction projects, although the US-led PRTs focus mainly on counter-insurgency. They consist of fifty to a hundred US military personnel, representatives of USAID, Defense Department, State Department; and Afghan government (Interior Ministry), and allied personnel.[14] Many United States PRTs in the south and east are 'co-located' with 'forward operating bases' of 300–400 US combat troops.

Regional Powers

Pakistan

Given its geo-strategic position and strong linkages with the Taliban, Pakistan emerged as a 'crucial partner' in the US-led Global War on Terrorism (GWOT). However, after the post- 9/11 reversal of Pakistan's Afghan policy, it continues its quest of regaining 'strategic depth' in Afghanistan. While the leadership of the Taliban combine is ensconced in Quetta, the ISI is actively involved in supporting,

---

[14] Each US PRT operates from a Forward Support Base (FSB) with medical resources, helicopters and reaction forces. See Sean M. Maloney, 'Afghanistan Four Years On: An Assessment', *Parameters*, Fall 2005; 'Afghanistan: The ISAF peacekeeping force and its expanding Afghan role', Agence France-Presse, 6 October 2005, http://www.reliefweb.int/rw/rwb.nsf/db900SID/VBOL-6GWJG4?OpenDocument.

funding and training the Taliban forces in its territory.[15] While Pakistani officials deny the existence of the Taliban and al Qaeda leadership in the country, there appears to be growing frustration among US policy-makers with the lack of progress in arresting 'high value targets' (HVT). In the recently released US National Intelligence Estimate, Pakistan is identified as a 'hub of al Qaeda activity'. The increasing US pressure calling for overt strikes in Pakistan and to cajole the military regime to cooperate in capturing the Taliban– al Qaeda leadership has yielded little result. Prior to the elections in Pakistan, General Musharraf has consolidated his position by making himself indispensable to the GWOT.

Another external actor contributing indirectly to the instability in Afghanistan is Iran. The reported discovery of Iranian arms in the Ghorian district of the western Herat province in September 2007[16] and similar accounts of gunmen in pickup trucks crossing over into Afghanistan's western Farah province from Iran suggest that Tehran could be raising the ante for Washington in Afghanistan. United States' officials have accused Iran of shipping advanced weaponry to militants to destabilize the Karzai government, a charge that has been denied. Further, a statement by Karzai also absolves them. However, while Karzai could be downplaying the issue to maintain good diplomatic relations with Tehran, Afghan officials in the western provinces that border Iran have discussed incursions by Iranians, violations of Afghan airspace by Iranian aircraft, and support to anti-government groups in camps operated by the Iranians. The unfolding of a difficult phase in US–Iran relations could have larger implications for Afghanistan's stability. Iran's involvement in Afghan affairs is being viewed as a 'point of pressure' on multiple fronts for the United States.

CONFLICT IN 2007

Despite early claims of success during Operation Enduring Freedom in decimating the Taliban–al Qaeda combine in Afghanistan, these forces are able to carry out lethal strikes in Afghanistan from their

---

[15] Discussions with Afghan analysts in Washington DC, January–February, 2006. Also see James Risen and David Rohde, 'A hostile land foils the quest for Bin Laden', *New York Times*, 13 December 2004. Also see Christopher Heffelfinger, ed., *Unmasking Terror: A Global Review of Terrorist Activities,* Jamestown Foundation, Washington, DC, 2005.

[16] 'Dumps of Iranian, Russian & Chinese arms found in Herat,' Pakistan Tribune 8 September 2007, http://www.paktribune.com/news/index.shtml?188974

sanctuaries in Pakistan. While south and east Afghanistan continue to be wracked by raging insurgency, the much more stable north is also moving towards instability. The rag-tag Afghan security forces and international forces continue positional warfare and direct combat with the Taliban in Helmand, Kandahar, Uruzgan, Zabul, Ghazni and other provinces in the south, east and west. The geographic scope of Taliban activities has also widened with an increased Taliban presence being observed in the Badghis province.

The Afghan and US governments face insurmountable challenges in curbing the insurgency. The over-reliance by the US on a conventional military approach to COIN with scant attention to 'nation-building and reconstruction' has led to an alienated populace and a discredited Karzai government. The loss of lives, lack of reconstruction and absence of state-building is causing resentment towards foreign forces in the country. History is rife with instances of popular discontent which, if not addressed, reach a 'tipping point' where the populace initially identifies with and then supports the insurgents. In Afghanistan, the perceived lack of security is swaying popular opinion towards the stability and order brought about by the Taliban in the 1990s.

The Taliban Regain Lost Ground

Contrary to the expectations of the international forces that thwarting the spring offensive would turn the tide in 2007, the Taliban are regaining lost ground and occupying areas cleared by the international forces. According to media reports: 'A year after [2006] Canadian and American forces drove hundreds of Taliban fighters from the area, the Panjwai and Zhare districts southwest of Kandahar, the rebels are back and have adopted new tactics. Carrying out guerrilla attacks after NATO troops partly withdrew in July 2007, they overran isolated police posts and are now operating in areas where they can mount attacks on Kandahar, the south's largest city', according to the *New York Times*, 2 September 2007. As troops have to be rotated, the international forces move away after clearing the area, thus leaving it vulnerable to Taliban occupation and control.

According to Afghan officials, 'the Taliban have driven government forces out of roughly half of a strategic area in southern Afghanistan that American and NATO officials declared a success story last fall in their campaign to clear out insurgents and make way for development programs.'[17] The Taliban have also registered their presence in northern Afghanistan in Mazar, Balkh and Kunduz provinces and the western provinces of Herat and Farah The borders along Zabul and Kandahar are used as the main ingress routes by the Taliban–al Qaeda fighters to infiltrate southern Afghanistan, i.e., Kandahar, Uruzgan and Helmand provinces.

Increased Levels of Violence

The levels of violence and insurgent attacks dramatically increased in 2006, as is evident from the numbers on fatalities. The BBC, in November 2006, quoting from a study on the situation in Afghanistan compiled by the Joint Co-ordinating and Monitoring Board (JCMB), pointed out that 'there has been a four-fold rise this year [2006] in the number of people killed in the conflict in Afghanistan.' The report indicated that more than 3,700 people have died since January 2006— about 1,000 of them civilians. The rest included insurgents, members of the Afghan army, the NATO-led international security assistance force, and a separate US contingent of soldiers.[18]

Available data for 2007 portends a similar trend. On 21 September, the UN Secretary-General in a report entitled 'The Situation in Afghanistan and its Implications for International Peace and Security' stated that insurgency and terrorism related violence in Afghanistan had seen an increase of at least 20 percent compared to 2006. 'An average of 548 incidents per month were recorded in 2007, compared to an average of 425 per month in 2006.'[19] The Associated Press news agency said that by September 2007 the tally of war-related deaths had surpassed 5,000, compared to a total of 4,019 deaths in all of 2006.

Asymmetric Warfare: Suicide and Roadside Bombings

In 2006–07, apart from open engagement with Afghan and international forces, the Taliban continues its 'asymmetric warfare' through

---

[17] David Rohde, 'Afghan police suffer setbacks as Taliban adapt', *New York Times*, 2 September 2007, http://www.nytimes.com/2007/09/02/world/asia/02taliban.html?_r=1&th=&emc=th&pagewanted=print&oref=slogin2007 (accessed 3 September 2007).

[18] See 'Afghan conflict deaths quadruple', 13 November 2006, http://news.bbc.co.uk/2/hi/south_asia/6141762.stm (accessed 27 January 2007).

[19] 'The situation in Afghanistan and its implications for international peace and security' (A/62/345–S/2007/555), United Nations General Assembly, September 2007.

roadside and suicide bombings, primarily targeting Afghan police and security forces, government officials and international troops. In his report to the Security Council on 21 September 2007, the UN Secretary-General indicated that, 'there have been over 100 suicide attacks to date in 2007, compared to 123 in all of 2006. While 76 per cent of all suicide missions target international military and Afghan security forces, their victims have been largely civilian bystanders: 143 civilians lost their lives to suicide attacks between 1 January and 31 August 2007.'[20] Afghanistan's civilians—not the national and international security forces—have borne the brunt of these attacks. According to a recent UN study on suicide terrorism in Afghanistan, non-combatants comprise up to 80 per cent of suicide attack victims.[21]

Suicide attacks have been accompanied by attacks against students and schools, assassinations of officials, and the targeting of police in a deliberate effort to impede the establishment of legitimate government institutions and to undermine popular confidence in the authority and capability of the government of Afghanistan. The deadliest Taliban attack in the reporting period was the detonation of a bomb in a bus carrying police instructors in Kabul on 17 June, which killed at least 35 people. In another deadly attack, on 29 September, a suicide bomber blew himself up inside a bus packed with Afghan army officers, killing 30, including six civilians. Suicide attacks were quite alien to Afghanistan until 2002, and have spiralled in the last two years. In September 2007, the UN reported that since January of the same year, 103 suicide attacks have been recorded, compared to 100 in 2006.

Afghanistan's suicide bombers are generally uneducated and unemployed youth, often drawn from madrassas across the border in Pakistan.[22] Suicide assailants in Afghanistan and their supporters seem to have been mobilized by a range of grievances. These include resentment against Western occupation of Afghanistan, anger over civilian casualties, and affronts to their cultural, religious sense of honour perpetrated during search operations.

---

[20] Ibid.

[21] 'Suicide Attacks in Afghanistan', UN Assistance Mission to Afghanistan, September 2007.

[22] 'Suicide attacks in Afghanistan', UN Assistance Mission to Afghanistan, September 2007.

Bargaining Chip: Kidnappings, Killings, Hostage Taking

The Taliban continues to use kidnappings of Afghans and international personnel as a bargaining tool to demand the withdrawal of international troops; the release of Taliban prisoners; for ransom; and to fuel public anger against the military engagement in Afghanistan in the various ISAF countries. On 7 June 2007, the Taliban released four Afghan medical workers kidnapped in Spring in exchange for the body of the recently killed Taliban commander Mullah Dadullah; a fifth hostage had been beheaded by the Taliban shortly before the 'prisoner exchange' deal was struck. On 18 July, two German engineers and their five Afghan colleagues working with the United Nations Assistance Mission in Afghanistan (UNAMA) were kidnapped in the Wardak province; later, the Taliban started raising demands for the release of these Germans. While one of the two Germans was later found dead, the other remains in Taliban captivity. On 19 July, the Taliban also kidnapped 23 Korean aid workers (18 women) in the Ghazni province, demanding the release of Taliban prisoners and the withdrawal of around 200 Korean troops serving with the US-led OEF. Following the release of the hostages, Korea has been contemplating pulling out its troops by the end of the year. While negotiating with the Taliban, the Karzai government is left with limited choices. It was heavily criticized by the US and other countries for the release of Taliban prisoners in exchange for Swiss-Italian journalist Mastrogiacomo in March. With the kidnapping of 23 Koreans, the Taliban have gained unprecedented media coverage and international attention, which reflects their successful use of psychological warfare and which is empowering them far beyond their military strength.

In July 2007, several incidents of kidnapping, attacks and threats against Afghans and foreign nationals working for relief and development organizations were reported. On 31 July 2007, an aid worker with the Danish aid and development organisation (DACAAR) was killed in Badghis province in western Afghanistan. In early August 2007, Afghanistan's Ministry of Interior ordered Afghan security forces not to allow foreign aid workers to travel outside Kabul without an armed escort. In the violence-wracked southern Helmand province, 11 health workers have been killed in the past year, and nearly half of all the health facilities have been closed. According to a statement by the Ministry of Education in June, there has been an increase in the number of students/teachers killed and schools burned down in the past 13 months.[23] Many aid and development workers have witnessed the deteriorating conditions for humanitarian and developmental activities. Due to the role of NGOs in development activities, human rights and democratization programmes, they have been perceived by the insurgents as collaborators with the government of Hamid Karzai and his Western supporters. According to officials of the Agency Coordinating Body for Afghan Relief (ACBAR), Afghanistan is presently experiencing 'diminishing humanitarian space'.[24]

Media: Propaganda and Battle for 'Hearts and Mind'

The major information battle between international forces, the Afghan government and the Taliban, however, is being fought in the media. Reports of high numbers of Taliban insurgents or civilian fatalities at the hands of international troops are used by either side to legitimize their actions and to tarnish the image of the opponent. Reports of an unprecedented number of civilians killed by international forces in June 2007 enraged the Afghan public. It also led to domestic debates in various countries providing troops to ISAF/NATO against the engagement in Afghanistan. Despite several public announcements by NATO officials of using smaller bombs to lower civilian casualties, the international forces have not succeeded in minimizing civilian casualties. This will remain difficult so long as the international forces rely on aerial attacks to compensate for their weak presence on the ground.

Taliban Challenge Karzai Government

The Taliban-led insurgent groups are presently seeking to discredit and undermine the legitimacy of the Afghan government by targeting Afghan and coalition forces, Afghan government officials and President Karzai's support base in the Pushtun Durrani tribal areas. They are also

---

[23] Afghanistan: Trends in conflict and Cooperation Apart, Swiss peace FAST update, no. 3, June–July 2007, www.swisspeace.org.

[24] This inference has been drawn from interviews with NGO and INGO workers in Kabul, Jalalabad, Herat, June 6–9, 2007. The officials of ACBAR made this observation during interviews in Kabul and Jalalabad, June 2007.

attempting to paralyze or fragment the state, and to expel foreigners (infidels). On 10 June 2007, in what seems to be a demonstration of power, the Taliban challenged President Hamid Karzai by firing rockets towards him in the Ghazni province; no one was injured in the attack. At the end of July, in another attempt to undermine the Karzai administration, Taliban insurgents kidnapped and killed four judges from the Paktika province, accusing them of collaborating with the government. This incident occurred a few weeks after an international conference was held in Rome on 2 and 3 July on the rule of law in Afghanistan. International donors pledged US $360 million for the training of judges, the construction of new prisons and other measures to strengthen the frail and corrupt judicial system as part of security sector reforms over the next four years. At the same time, the state judiciary is being challenged by parallel judicial structures established by the Taliban; numerous alleged criminals were publicly tried by the Taliban courts and subsequently hanged.

Collateral Damage and Mounting Civilian Casualties

On 2 August 2007, 200 civilians were killed in aerial bombings in what was seen as a Taliban meeting in the small town of Bughni in the Baghran district of Helmand province during the traditional weekly market. If the reports are confirmed, it would be the highest single casualty figure in an accident in Afghanistan this year. The killings of numerous civilians by international forces, such as in Herat, Helmand, Nangarhar and Kandahar have sparked popular protests in several parts of the country. The high death toll among civilians was also criticized by Karzai, the UN, and even NATO/ISAF when the deaths were caused by the US-led OEF.[25] Civilian deaths not only fuel resentment against international troops but further undermine the credibility of the Karzai government. Thousands of civilians have also been displaced due to fighting between the Taliban and international/ national forces in war-torn areas. According to Associated Press counts, 1,800 people have so far been killed in insurgency-related violence in 2007, including 135 civilians killed by the international forces and the

---

[25] This inference has been drawn from discussions with Afghan government officials and Afghan people in Kabul, June 2007.

Taliban each. According to UN figures, 320–380 civilians have been killed by the Taliban and government/international forces in the first four months of 2007. The Afghanistan Independent Human Rights Commission (AIHRC) has indicated that over 155 Afghan civilians died in ground military operations, aerial strikes and suicide attacks by Taliban insurgents, and by US, NATO and Afghan government forces in September 2007.

Compared to the figures brought out by the Human Rights Watch in 2006, these new figures suggest an increase in civilian casualties of around 40 per cent. In a statement on 29 May 2007, Taliban chief Mullah Omar called for the establishment of an independent body to investigate civilian casualties in Afghanistan.

Taliban Killings

On 13 May 2007, the Taliban's top military commander, Mullah Dadullah, was killed along with his brother Mullah Shah Mansoor and two commanders in clashes with international (reportedly British) and Afghan forces in Helmand province. Although Dadullah's death is unlikely to affect the Taliban command structure, it is a moral blow to the movement. Soon after his death, Dadullah was replaced by his younger brother, Mullah Bakht Mohammed alias Dadullah Mansoor. The death of Mullah Dadullah might strengthen Taliban commanders like Haqqani and Saifullah Mansoor who have their power base in south-eastern, rather than southern, Afghanistan.

Local Support

The US-led military operations, aerial bombings and search operations have caused large-scale discontent among the Afghan people. The local populace is resentful of house-to-house searches and are demanding that foreign military forces seek the Afghan government's approval before private homes are searched. The US troops also serve as a constant reminder to the Afghan people that their government is weak and cannot handle its own internal problems.

A complex web of international networks of armed groups—connected by opium trafficking, ethnic ties, and Islamic fundamentalism—link Afghanistan with Kashmir, Chechnya, Tajikistan, Kyrgyzstan, Uzbekistan, Pakistan, Iran, and Central Asia in an arc of 'regional conflict formation'.[26] Their transnational nature is intertwined and interconnected by the exchange of illegal goods (weapons, drugs, human trafficking), which provides fighters and funds for the Taliban–al Qaeda insurgency in Afghanistan.

Cross-border social and ethnic ties connect these destabilizing networks and undermine the Afghan government's efforts to bring in stability. In addition to the history of Taliban support in this 'ungoverned' area from the ethnic Pashtun, this region is one of the most underdeveloped in the world. In 2005, Afghan authorities continued to apprehend Pakistani nationals fighting alongside the Taliban who claimed to have received recent military training at jihad camps near Mansehra.'[27] The US effort to increase 'military to military cooperation' and counter-terrorism cooperation with the Musharaff regime has not yielded any tangible results.

The Taliban movement itself began among students attending Pakistani madrassas.[28] The Taliban are once again recruiting younger men in the age group 18 to 25 from madrassas straddling the border with Pakistan. Many of these madrassas are financed and operated by Pakistani Islamist political parties such as the Jamaat-e-Ulema Islam (the JUI, which is closely linked to the Taliban), and by foreign sponsors in Saudi Arabia. Despite President Musharaff's public statements to achieve madrassa reform, not much has been done.

Any analysis of the sources of funding for this insurgency boils down to narcotics trafficking. The vast numbers of Taliban-affiliated groups—warlords, narcotics traffickers and organized criminals involved in the drug trade—have formed cross-border networks, enabling an easy flow of drugs from Afghanistan into Central Asia, Iran, Pakistan, China and even India. While around 93 per cent of the world's heroin comes from Afghanistan, UN Office on Drugs and Crime (UNODC) sources indicate that in 2006, the production levels rose by almost 60 per cent to reach a record harvest of 165,000 hectares.

The failure of the reconstruction process post-OEF and the lack of an alternative livelihood programme in Afghanistan have resulted in a

---

[26] See Barnett R. Rubin and Andrea Armstrong, 'Regional Issues in the Reconstruction of Afghanistan', *World Policy Journal*, Spring 2003.

[27] David Rohde and Carlotta Gall, 'In a corner of Pakistan a debate rages: Are terrorist camps still functioning?' *New York Times*, 28 August 2005.

[28] Interviews with Pakistani analysts in Lahore and Islamabad in March 2005. See Mark Sedra and Peter Middlebrook, 'Beyond Bonn: Revisioning the International Compact for Afghanistan', *Foreign Policy in Focus* (Internet edition), November 2005.

growth in Afghan opium production, raising concerns of Afghanistan being a 'narco-state', aiding insurgent groups both in Afghanistan and Pakistan. Defeating the insurgency has been complicated by the growing nexus between smugglers, criminal groups and narcotic traffickers, who have a common interest in preventing the imposition of state authority or corrupting what little state authority exists. In the poppy-cultivating provinces of Badakhshan, Helmand and Kandahar, the state is extremely weak or non-existent through much of the countryside, while corruption is endemic in provincial centres.

The opium trade in Afghanistan is worth about US $3.1 billion and contributes about a third to Afghanistan's total economy. It fills the treasuries of the warlords and insurgents, with less than a quarter going to the farmers. But drug production and trafficking also nurture the insurgency (the Taliban tax poppy trade), fund illegal armed groups, foster corruption and erode the legitimate economy. Profits from the drug trade have enabled the Taliban to purchase more sophisticated weaponry, including Russian and Chinese surface-to-air missiles.

The Karzai government's ambitious plans announced two years ago for fighting the opium trade based on 'eight pillars', including poppy eradication, building the justice system, and funding alternative development programmes, has not taken off.[29] While the Americans are trying to push drastic eradication efforts like aerial spraying, the Europeans are clearly opposed to such forceful eradication for fear of losing the 'hearts and mind' campaign. In Helmand province, for instance, rural communities, in addition to turning anti-government, look towards the insurgents for 'protection' of their poppy crop. Travel across Nangarhar province highlights the absence of any alternative development projects. In other provinces, the alternative crop seeds provided to farmers were either unsuitable due to climatic conditions or have not been profitable. Thus, a string of broken promises have generated alienation and contempt within rural communities, particularly in the south, further weakening their link with the Karzai government.

---

[29] In an interview with this author, former Minister of Counter Narcotics, Habibullah Qaderi (who has since resigned) emphasized the need for a unified and well-coordinated strategy with help from the international community as a way out of this quandary (11 June 2007).

CONFLICT MANAGEMENT

Afghan–Pak Peace Jirga

A joint peace Jirga (tribal assembly) between Afghanistan and Pakistan was convened in Kabul between 9 and 12 August 2007. The idea was first suggested by President Karzai during talks with US President George W. Bush in September 2006. The Jirga was reportedly attended by 700 people including members of the two Parliaments, political parties, religious scholars, tribal elders, provincial councils, civil society and business community members of both countries.[30]

The achievements of the exercise remained limited. Tribal elders from Waziristan refused to attend the Jirga. Taliban supporters said that the Jirga was an attempt to 'deceive the ordinary Afghans'[31] and

---

[30] The principal recommendations made by the Jirga were: 1. The Joint Peace Jirga strongly recognises the fact that terrorism is a common threat to both countries and the war on terror should continue to be an integral part of the national policies and security strategies of both countries. The participants of this jirga unanimously declare an extended, tireless and persistent campaign against terrorism and further pledge that government and people of Afghanistan and Pakistan will not allow sanctuaries/training centres for terrorists in their respective countries. 2. The Joint Peace Jirga resolved to constitute a smaller Jirga consisting of 25 prominent members from each side that is mandated to strive to achieve the following objectives: (a) Expedite the ongoing process of dialogue for peace and reconciliation with the opposition. (b) Holding of regular meetings in order to monitor and oversee the implementation of the decisions/recommendations of the Joint Peace Jirga. (c) Plan and facilitate convening of the next Joint Peace Jirga. (d) Both countries will appoint 25 members each in the committee. 3. The Joint Peace Jirga once again emphasises the vital importance of brotherly relations in pursuance of policies of mutual respect, non-interference and peaceful coexistence and recommends further expansion of economic, social, and cultural relations between the two countries. 4. Members of the Joint Peace Jirga in taking cognisance of the nexus between narcotics and terrorism condemn the cultivation, processing and trafficking of poppy and other illicit substances and call upon the two governments to wage an all-out war against this menace. The Jirga takes note of the responsibilities of the international community in enabling Afghanistan to provide alternative livelihood to the farmers. 5. The governments of the Islamic Republic of Afghanistan and Islamic Republic of Pakistan, with the support of the international community, should implement infrastructure, economic and social sector projects in the affected areas. See 'Text of Pak–Afghan Peace Jirga declaration', *Daily Times*, 13 August 2007.

[31] 'Taleban dismiss Afghan-Pakistan "peace jirga"', *Khaleej Times*, 6 May 2007, http://www.khaleejtimes.com/DisplayArticleNew.asp?col=&section=subcontinent&xfile=data/subcontinent/2007/May/subcontinent_May221.xml

talks that did not include them would be futile. Abdul Ghafoor Haideri, Secretary-General of Pakistan's JUI said, 'This is only a display, which cannot produce the true views of the Afghan people.'[32] In addition, genuine doubts were expressed by analysts as to whether Pakistani Pashtuns are sufficiently unified to implement the goals outlined in the jirga's joint declaration.

Subsequent developments have tempered even what were from the beginning modest expectations from the Jirga. On 15 August 2007, for example, at least four Pakistani elders who attended the Jirga received anonymous letters threatening them with reprisals if they followed through on efforts to curtail Taliban activity in Pakistan.[33]

Taliban Reconciliation

There have been reports of differences between the British and the American approach of reconciliation in Afghanistan.[34] The United States is being seen as approving Karzai's move to include the moderate elements within the Taliban in the future peace proces. On 10 September 2007 President Hamid Karzai offered the Taliban the option of negotiations. On 11 September a Taliban spokesman responded saying, 'For the sake of national interests ... we are fully ready for talks with the government.' He added that the Taliban had a 'limited' number of conditions, but did not explain further.[35] This response is being viewed with scepticism as the Taliban has a history of rebuffing offers for negotiations.

---

[32] 'Unity call as Afghan jirga opens', BBC News, 9 August 2007, http://news.bbc.co.uk/2/hi/south_asia/6938033.stm.

[33] Camelia Entekhabi-Fard and Richard Weitz, 'Afghanistan: Probing for ways to engage the Taliban', 16 August 2007, http://www.eurasianet.org/departments/insight/articles/eav081607.shtml

[34] Disagreement has reportedly surfaced over the US military's desire to air-spray Afghan opium poppy fields with herbicide, and to continue its bombing strikes on Afghan villages, which Britain complains undermines its strategy of 'winning hearts and minds'. Other areas of contention include what Britain regards as Washington's indulgent attitude towards Hamid Karzai, the Afghan President, who is accused of tolerating, even conniving with, widespread corruption inside his government. See 'Britain tells US: We're winning Afghan battles but not the war', 7 September 2007, http://www.timesonline.co.uk/tol/news/politics/article2402986.ece.

[35] Syed Saleem Shahzad, 'Al-Qaeda fights back at Afghan peace bid', *Asia Times*, 13 September 2007, http://www.atimes.com/atimes/South_Asia/II13Df01.html.

However, the latest move to include the Taliban as a stakeholder in the conflict indicates a victory of sorts for the Pakistani viewpoint, which advocated the inclusion of the Taliban in any decision on the future of Afghanistan. For example, during the August 2007 Jirga President Pervez Musharraf said, 'The Taliban are part of Afghan society. Some of them are uneducated and do not know what they do, and to that we must be sympathetic.'[36] For Pakistan, the Taliban can serve as a vehicle for the preservation of its influence in Afghanistan.

The Afghan reconciliation programme, known as *Takhim-E Solh* or 'Strengthening Peace', grants amnesty to middle- and lower-level insurgents who agree to stop fighting and peacefully enter civil society. This programme aims to break the cycle of violence that plagues Afghanistan by assimilating former Taliban combatants into democratic society, thus enabling the country to build a safe and prosperous future. Taliban in the higher tiers and individuals accused of war crimes are deliberately excluded. *Takhim-E Solh* petitioners must pledge loyalty to the government of Afghanistan and renounce violence against Afghan and coalition forces. About 2000 ex-Taliban fighters have already made their peace with the Afghan government.

Combating Narcotics Trafficking

Narcotics trafficking has been identified as the most significant problem confronting Afghanistan's long-term stability and economic growth. Since his 4 November 2004 election victory speech, President Karzai has called on Afghans to join a 'jihad' against the opium trade, later pledging to destroy Afghanistan's poppy fields within two years. Despite these pledges, poppy cultivation has shown a marked increase, primarily due to lack of alternate livelihood programmes and reluctance on the part of the US to deal with this problem by appreciating the interlinkages between counter-narcotics and COIN.

The US military has overcome its initial reluctance to expand its mission in Afghanistan and is playing a greater role in attacking traffickers and their installations. The Bush Administration has also taken new legal steps against suspected Afghan drug traffickers by

---

[36] Camelia Entekhabi-Fard and Richard Weitz, 'Afghanistan: Probing for ways to engage the Taliban', 16 August 2007, http://www.eurasianet.org/departments/insight/articles/eav081607.shtml.

indicting them and putting in place a legal machinery to have them extradited from Afghanistan if caught.[37] However, it is important to focus primarily on funding alternative livelihoods that will dissuade Afghans from growing poppy, rather than focusing only on eradication or interdiction.

There are significant variations, however, in the approach of the allies to the counter-narcotics campaign in Afghanistan. While the US policy has oscillated between avoiding forcible means like aerial spraying, NATO allies are reluctant to do so mainly for fear of losing the 'hearts and minds' battle in Afghanistan. The British also believe that forcible eradication of the poppy crop might result in losing the hearts and minds campaign while broadening the support base of the insurgency. Moreover, while the drug menace looms large in Afghanistan, the counter-narcotics policies of the US and its NATO allies are deepening fissures and reinforcing instability in the southern provinces. For instance, Helmand province today has emerged as a significant centre for heroin processing and trafficking, it is the world's biggest drug supplier and is witnessing increased Taliban activity.

Provincial Reconstruction Teams (PRTs)

Described as the 'leading edge' of the allies' effort to stabilize Afghanistan, the PRTS are integrated civilian–military organizations designed to meet three objectives: improve security, extend the reach of the Afghan government, and facilitate reconstruction in priority provinces.[38] Provincial Reconstruction Teams were established in 2002 with the objective of maintaining light international security 'footprint' and on building the capacity of Afghan institutions to address instability in remote, ungoverned regions.[39]

---

[37] In mid–April 2005, a DEA operation successfully caught the alleged leading Afghan narcotics trafficker, Haji Bashir Noorzai, arresting him after a flight to New York. Another alleged Afghan trafficker, Baz Mohammad, was extradited from Afghanistan in October 2005. For further details see Christopher M. Blanchard, Afghanistan: Narcotics and US Policy, CRS Report, Washington, DC, 10 December 2006.

[38] Briefing on the role of PRT at ISAF HQ, Kabul, 17 June 2007. Also see ISAF PRT Handbook, Edition 3, 3 February 2007.

[39] The PRTs were established in Afghanistan at the end of 2002. For detailed information on PRTs, see Kenneth Katzman, 'Afghanistan: Post-War Governance, Security and US Policy', CRS Report, RL30588.

Likewise, the PRTs are intended to build trust among the population, by participating in the reconstruction of the country, and providing a permanent presence and thereby security. By this principle of classic counter-insurgency—protecting the population from the guerrillas and winning the support of the population in one limited area—the teams can deprive insurgents of that same support.[40] However, there are significant problems limiting the performance of PRTs in Afghanistan. For instance, national caveats in PRTs create a problem of coordination between and among PRTs. Most allies with high-risk aversion are hesitant to actively engage with the Afghan population. With little or no idea of how their funds are managed and projects implemented, PRT projects are stymied by corruption and delays in Afghanistan and are viewed as a 'mixed bag'.[41]

While the performance of the PRTs are plagued, early in their existence, by a lack of funds, expertise, training and poor long-term planning of development projects, major criticisms have been levied against them for their weak inter-agency cooperation and the relations between their military and civilian personnel, in terms of cooperation and leadership.

The PRTs have been criticized by NGO workers for many reasons. They replicate the work of NGOs, while also blurring the lines between military and development work. This places NGOs in danger as insurgents see the NGOs to be partisan. Also, there is concern that the PRTs 'have neither the capacity nor the intent to confront the countrywide security threats now facing the Afghan people and are last to help in times of crisis'.[42] The workings of PRTs, as military-run enclaves that provide safe havens for international aid workers

---

[40] A small number are US civilians, generally a DoS representative, a USAID representative, and a representative from USDA. There is usually an Afghan representative from the Ministry of Interior. Not all PRTs have a full civilian complement. On the military side, there is a PRT commander, two civil affairs teams (with four members each), operational and administrative staff, and force protection elements. For further details see 'Provincial Reconstruction Teams in Afghanistan: An Interagency Assessment', USAID, June 2006, http://pdf.usaid.gov/pdf_docs/PNADG252.pdf (accessed 24 June 2007). Also see Andrew Feickert, 'US and Coalition Military Operations in Afghanistan: Issues for Congress', CRS Report, RL33503, updated 11 December 2006, p.5.

[41] This inference was derived after a visit to PRT-funded projects in Herat, 8 June 2007 and discussions with locals in Mazar-e-Sharif, Kabul and Jalalabad in June 2007.

[42] This was stated by an Afghan NGO security official in Mazar-e-Sharif, 6 June 2007. Discussions with NGO personnel in different parts of Afghanistan in June 2007 also highlighted similar thinking.

Disarmament, Demobilization, and Reintegration (DDR) and Disarmament of Illegal Armed Groups (DIAG) Programme

The DDR is a programme run by the UNAMA to dismantle illegal militias and curb regionalism. This programme, aided by Japan, Britain and Canada, with the participation of the United States, got off to a slow start because the Afghan Defense Ministry did not enact mandated reforms (primarily reduction in the number of Tajiks in senior positions) by the target date of 1 July 2003. In September 2003, President Karzai acted on the issue, replacing 22 senior Tajik Defence Ministry officials with Pashtuns, Uzbeks and Hazaras. The DDR programme had initially been expected to demobilize 100,000 fighters, although that figure was later reduced to just over 60,000 by Afghan officials. According to UNAMA, 63,000 identified militia fighters were disarmed by the time this phase of the programme ended on 8 July 2005, and virtually all of them have exercised reintegration options: training, starting small businesses, etc.

Critics of the demobilization programme call it a 'bad joke' as the promised 'vocational retraining programmes' are virtually non-existent and the militias have actually retained most of their weapons and many are back to their old ways. There has been mounting criticism of the DDR programme for failing to prevent the rearmament of militiamen, for stockpiling of weapons, and for rehiring militiamen in programmes run by the US and its partners.

To address the shortcomings of the DDR, the Disarmament of Illegal Armed Groups (DIAG) was initiated with the objective of disarming, by the end of 2007, perhaps 80,000–100,000 members of 1,800 different 'illegal armed groups' that consist of militiamen and unrecognized local forces who were not on the rolls of the Defence Ministry. As of late March 2006, over 20,250 weapons had been collected from these militia fighters. Kapisa province is considered to be a model for the programme because 38 commanders believed receptive to disarmament attended a ceremony to formally inaugurate the DIAG programme on 1 May 2006. Other provinces that seem receptive are Takhar and Herat; some commanders in Khost also agreed to disarm in late March 2006.

CONCLUSIONS

Afghanistan stands at a critical juncture in its nation-building exercise and the year 2007 is decisive. The reconstruction efforts have been marred by a raging Taliban-led insurgency and in spite of the high casualties inflicted by the international forces, the problem is deepening. We can assume, therefore, that the security situation in Afghanistan remains unstable and will likely further deteriorate since the Taliban have increased their area of operation and stepped up the use of guerilla tactics. The lethality and brutality of Taliban attacks are likely to increase. Mere emphasis on economic reconstruction without adequate security measures and the inadequate capacity of Afghan state institutions will only provide easy and soft targets for the insurgents. Kidnappings and hostage-taking are likely to continue, with the Taliban using them as a bargaining tool. The overall impact of such developments on international participation in the reconstruction process could be negated.

Despite the post-9/11 military action in Afghanistan, the symbiotic relationship between the Taliban and al Qaeda remains intact. In fact, it has further strengthened and the two are entwined in their goals to discredit the Karzai regime and expel international forces from Afghanistan. A complex web of international armed groups, connected by opium trafficking, cross-border ethnic ties and Islamic affiliation, link Afghanistan with Kashmir, Chechnya, Tajikistan, Kyrghyzstan, Uzbekistan, Pakistan, Iran, and Central Asia in an arc of 'regional conflict formation'. They are inter-connected and sustain such networks with the exchange of illegal goods, weapons, drugs, and providing fighters and funds for the Taliban–al Qaeda insurgency in Afghanistan. External state support in terms of providing sanctuaries and safe havens has strengthened the movement. The current COIN efforts will have little disruptive impact on such a network.

In fact, the international COIN effort in Afghanistan seems to be floundering, as is evident from its inability to quell the raging insurgency wracking that country. The failure of US policy-makers in assessing the nature of Afghan insurgency, its shift of attention and forces to Iraq, particularly the Special Forces, and replacing them with conventional forces has turned the tide against the early claims of success in the 'Afghan war'. The predominance of a conventional approach to troops surge, and 'clear and sweep' operations proves to be counter-productive due to collateral damage, hurting cultural sensitivities, and thereby alienating popular support.

This, in turn, is accentuating the problem of the legitimacy of the Afghan government. An effective course of action, thus, would be to strengthen the Afghan face of COIN. An effective COIN strategy reduces the support of insurgents and their perceived legitimacy, while increasing the government's credibility and support. The COIN strategy needs to present a unified effort, actionable intelligence and the appropriate use of force. The current Afghan war will be won or lost within the Afghan villages, especially those on the volatile Afghan–Pakistan frontier and 'ungoverned spaces'. Thus, a 'main effort' indigenous COIN force must have access to the social networks within these villages. This could come from an Afghan constabulary force that is primarily recruited from the local population, lives amidst the local population, operates in the community on a daily basis, and provides security for the local population with easy access to grassroots-level social networks for effective intelligence collection.

An important step forward would be a 'Clear, Hold, and Build'[43] strategy—clear the area of the enemy, hold the territory, build infrastructure and resources, and engage with the local community. The success of this approach will depend on ensuring better coordination and faster delivery by international and local actors, and, ultimately, allowing Kabul to take responsibility and control on its terms.

While the COIN approach has focused narrowly on an instant quick-fix method, the larger goal of institution-building and building the Afghan state's capacity to deal with its internal problems seems to be missing. The international community, particularly the US, has reneged on its commitment made during the 2006 London Conference and the tall claims of the 'Afghan Compact' which identified 'three critical and interdependent areas or pillars of activity' over five years: security, governance, rule of law and human rights, and social and economic development are far from being realized. It is important to have a unified political–diplomatic, socio-economic, psychological–moral, and security–stability effort against those who would violently depose the government. The plethora of international actors in aid and reconstruction efforts has only added to the chaos and dissipation of effort and resources. The need is to unify international efforts under

---

[43] Greg Mills, 'Ten Counterinsurgency Commandments from Afghanistan', Foreign Policy Research Institute, April 2007, http://www.fpri.org/enotes/200704.mills.afghanistancounterinsurgency.html (accessed 16 May 2007).

the aegis of the UN, with a coordinator collaborating and directing the nation-building efforts in Afghanistan.

The raging Taliban-led insurgency will not be able to topple the Karzai government as long as the support of international forces is in place. However, popular discontent with the slow pace of reconstruction and lack of security could tilt peoples' support towards the insurgents. After all, in Afghanistan no one ever laid claims to national power by fighting decisive battles but by winning people's support in times of chaos, anarchy and insecurity. The Taliban took advantage of this scenario in the 1990s and there is every likelihood that they would try exploiting every available opportunity to their benefit even now.

While the insurgency in Afghanistan has an external–internal interface, where shared borders, ethnicity and cultures create transnational networks of criminal groups sustaining the insurgency, a regional approach of coordinated responses would help in breaking these networks. The inability of the participants at the 2001 Bonn Conference to involve and elicit the support of the regional powers to play a useful role exposes their inability to comprehend the complexity of regional power dynamics. Afghanistan's neighbours, in alliance with the provincial leaders, could act to tilt the power balance among the ethnic groups in the event the Karzai government fails to extend its authority, or should the international community wash its hands of Afghanistan. More importantly, the way the international community engages with Afghanistan's problematic neighbours, Iran and Pakistan, would go a long way towards the emergence of a peaceful and stable Afghanistan.

3

Pakistan: The Sectarian Conflict

Kanchan Lakshman

A BRIEF HISTORY

Islamism and, indeed, Islamist militancy, have become deeply and culturally entrenched as a result of their continuous promotion, not only through the vast infrastructure of institutions controlled by the religious parties—the madrassas (seminaries) and the marakiz (religious centres)—but essentially and systematically through the government-controlled educational system as well.[1]

While seeking an explanation for Pakistan's sectarian conflict, it is noteworthy that for decades the country's Shias and Sunnis[2] lived side by side without any major problems. Sectarian killings are a relatively recent phenomenon.[3] Their roots thus lie not in religious differences, but in political and social developments within Pakistan and the region, and they are intimately linked to the country's wider problem of militant extremist Islam.[4]

Pakistan's sectarian landscape, however, is far too complex to be reduced to a simple binary division since there are a multitude of Sunni and Shia sub-sects, local cultural variants and cults, and rival religious traditions. Although the conflict between Deobandi and Shia extremists has been principally responsible for fuelling sectarian terrorism in recent decades, the phenomenon of sectarianism is present in other forms and has the potential to surface in other variations in future.[5] Furthermore, what is commonly called Sunni–Shia violence

---

[1] Ajai Sahni, 'Spoiler of the Field', in Barry Rubin, ed., *Survey of Global Islamism*, forthcoming.

[2] Pakistan has a population of approximately 77 per cent Sunni and 20 per cent Shia.

[3] Iffat Idris, 'The Sectarian Menace', *South Asia Intelligence Review*, vol. 2, no. 5, 18 August 2003; South Asia Terrorism Portal, www.satp.org.

[4] Ibid.

[5] 'The State of Sectarianism in Pakistan', International Crisis Group, Brussels, 18 April 2005.

is more precisely a Deobandi–Shia conflict in which the Deobandis have appropriated the term Sunni for themselves, and are supported in their anti-Shia jihad by the Ahle Hadith.

The origins of sectarian violence in Pakistan can be traced back to the war against the Soviet occupation of Afghanistan. 'American funding and Pakistani assistance promoted the proliferation of a huge number of militant Islamist groups and madrassas (seminaries) inside Pakistan. Washington needed the Islamists to "wage jihad" against the Soviets in Afghanistan, while Islamabad needed them to bring in billions of American dollars. Hence both turned a blind eye to their radical ideology and methods.'[6] After the Soviet Union's exit, 'while radical Islamists in Afghanistan formed the Taliban, their brethren in Pakistan turned their attention towards Indian Kashmir or to sectarian opponents inside Pakistan. Each act of sectarian killing provoked a cycle of revenge killings. Governments failed to curb the menace, either because they wanted the militants to fight Pakistan's corner in Indian Kashmir, or because they lacked the will and the strength to do so. That failure in turn allowed the religious militants to flourish and grow in strength.'[7]

Former Pakistani President, General Zia-ul-Haq, played a significant role in orchestrating sectarian hatred. A Sunni Muslim of the Deobandi sect (a strain of Islam closely allied with the Wahabism of Saudi Arabia), General Zia sought to reinforce his government's legitimacy by championing Sunni Islam.[8] Khaled Ahmed describes the origin of sectarian violence thus:

> After coming to power, General Zia took over the populist slogan of *Nizam-e-Mustafa* and imposed *shariah* on Pakistan. It really meant the imposition of the Sunni *Hanafi fiqh* or jurisprudence followed by the majority population from which the Shias were excluded. Two early laws under *shariah* enforced by him, failed miserably: the first, abolition of *riba* (interest), failed because of the inability of the Islamic scholars to reinterpret Islam for modern conditions; the second, *zakat*, failed because the Shia jurisprudence, called *Fiqh-i-Jaafaria*, had a conflicting interpretation of *zakat*. In 1980, an unprecedented procession of Shias, led by Mufti Jaafar Hussain, laid siege to Islamabad and forced General Zia to exempt the Shia community from the deduction of *zakat*.

[6] Ibid.
[7] Ibid.
[8] B. Raman, 'Sipah-e-Sahaba Pakistan, Lashkar-e-Jhangvi, Bin Laden & Ramzi Yousef', South Asia Analysis Group, 1 July 2002, www.saag.org/papers5/paper484.html.

The concept of Sunni *ushr* is also rejected by Shia jurisprudence. It appears that, when the anti-Shia movement started in Jhang in the 1980s, General Zia not only ignored it but saw it as his balancing act against the rebellious Shia community. This was worsened by Imam Khomeini's criticism of General Zia.[9]

According to Ahmed,

the rise of Maulana Haq Nawaz Jhangvi in the stronghold of big Shia landlords in Punjab changed the sectarian scene in Pakistan. There is evidence that General Zia was warned of Jhangvi's anti-Shia and anti-Iran movement, but he ignored the warning and allowed it to blossom into a full-fledged religious party called Anjuman-i-Sipah-i-Sahaba of Pakistan (ASSP). In small towns, the old Shia–Sunni debate restarted with the fury that had become dampened in the past. The tracts which carried this debate were scurrilous in the extreme and helped the clerics to whip up passions. Meanwhile, in 1986, General Zia allowed a 'purge' of Turi Shias in the divided city of Parachinar (capital of Kurram Agency on the border with Afghanistan) at the hands of the Sunni Afghan mujahideen in conjunction with the local Sunni population.[10]

In 1990, Maulana Jhangvi was murdered at the climax of his anti-Iran and anti-Shia campaign of extreme insult and denigration.[11] The same year, as if in retaliation, an activist of the Sipah-i-Sahaba shot and killed Iranian consul Sadiq Ganji in Lahore and revenge killings thus began, with Maulana Isar-ul-Qasimi, chief of the Sipah, being shot dead in 1991.[12]

There were other external factors that generated sectarianism. According to Idris,

for a period, Shi'a and Sunni sectarian groups were sponsored by Iran and Saudi Arabia respectively. These two rivals fought a proxy war

---

[9] Khaled Ahmed, 'Islamic Extremism in Pakistan', *South Asian Journal*, Islamabad, vol. 2, October–December 2003. See http://www.southasianmedia.net/Magazine/Journal/islamicextremism_pakistan.htm.

[10] Ibid.

[11] A cassette of Jhangvi's speeches distributed by the Sipah-e-Sahaba in Lahore in 1993 is the best example of the kind of orator he was. Jhangvi got his audience to chant Khomeini *kutta* (dog) and sought to prove from orthodox religious tracts that the Shias were not Muslims.

[12] Khaled Ahmed, 'Islamic Extremism in Pakistan', *South Asian Journal*, vol. 2, October–December 2003, see http://www.southasianmedia.net/Magazine/Journal/islamicextremism=Pakistan.htm.

in Pakistan. Their support abated as relations between Tehran and Riyadh improved, but the sectarian groups found other sources of sustenance. They derived ideological inspiration (not to mention a base from where to train and launch their operations) from the ultra-orthodox Taliban that came to power in Afghanistan. The Taliban had strong links with madrassahs in Pakistan, so it was little wonder their hard-line thinking influenced people there.[13]

The result of all these developments was that when President Pervez Musharraf seized power in October 1999, he faced a formidable foe: well-armed, well-trained and well-financed Islamist sectarian organizations, with a huge resource pool of recruits in the country's thousands of religious seminaries.[14]

PRINCIPAL ACTORS

The dramatis personae in the sectarian milieu in Pakistan are the various Sunni and Shia militant groups along with their front organizations, the Pakistani state, including its various security agencies, and foreign countries like Iran, Saudi Arabia and Afghanistan.

The main sectarian groups in Pakistan include:

Lashkar-e-Jhangvi[15]

The Lashkar-e-Jhangvi (LeJ), a Sunni–Deobandi terrorist outfit, was formed in 1996 by a breakaway group of the radical sectarian elements of the Sipah-e-Sahaba Pakistan (SSP), a Sunni extremist outfit, which accused its parent organization of deviating from the ideals of its slain co-founder, Maulana Haq Nawaz Jhangvi. It is from Maulana Jhangvi that the LeJ derives its name. It was formed under the leadership of Akram Lahori and Riaz Basra. The LeJ is one of the two sectarian terrorist outfits proscribed on 14 August 2001 by President Pervez Musharraf. The LeJ is listed in the United Nation's 1267 Committee's consolidated list and as a proscribed terrorist organization by the

---

[13] Iffat Idris, 'The Sectarian Menace', *South Asia Intelligence Review*, vol. 2, no. 5, 18 August 2003; South Asia Terrorism Portal, www.satp.org.

[14] Ibid.

[15] The profile of Lashkar-e-Jhangvi is largely drawn from South Asia Terrorism Portal, www.satp.org.

governments of the United Kingdom, the United States and Canada.[16] The LeJ, part of the broader Deoband movement, aims to transform Pakistan into a Sunni state, primarily through violent means.

Muhammad Ajmal alias Akram Lahori is the present *Saalar-i-Aala* (Commander-in-Chief) of the LeJ. Lahori was originally with the SSP, which he had joined in 1990. Subsequently, in 1996, he along with Malik Ishaque and Riaz Basra founded the LeJ and launched terrorist activities in Punjab. Lahori succeeded Riaz Basra, who was killed in Mailsi, Multan, on 14 May 2002. Lahori is currently in police custody following his arrest in Orangi town, Karachi, on 17 June 2002, based on information provided by Shabbir Ahmed—an LeJ cadre who was arrested by the Karachi police in Gulzar-i-Hijri the same day. On 17 January 2007, the Anti-terrorism Court-5 in Karachi acquitted Lahori and his two associates, Mohammed Azam and Ataullah, in a sectarian murder case due to lack of evidence.[17] The three militants were prosecuted for killing the owner and one of the employees of the Agha Juice Centre on 25 May 2002 in Rizvia Society.

Although Ajmal is officially considered the LeJ chief, Mufti Eid Mohammed is now (as of April 2007) believed to lead the organization and the operational command is understood to have passed to minor figures.[18] A substantial section of the LeJ leadership consists of jihadis who fought against the Soviet forces in Afghanistan. A majority of its cadres are drawn from the numerous Sunni *madrassas* in Pakistan.

Media reports indicate that the LeJ is an amalgam of loosely coordinated sub-units in various parts of Pakistan with autonomous chiefs for each sub-unit. Riaz Basra himself reportedly controls the LeJ's units in Lahore, Gujranwala, Rawalpindi and Sargodha. The success of most of its operations is attributed to its multi-cellular structure, whereby the outfit is divided into small groups which are not in constant touch with each other. The LeJ is organized into small cells of approximately five to eight cadres each, who operate independently of the others. Individual LeJ cadres are reportedly unaware of the number of cells in existence similar to their own, or the structure of their operations.

---

[16] Re-Listing of Jaish-e-Mohammad, Lashkar-e Jhangvi, Asbat Al Ansar, The Islamic Movement of Uzbekistan, The Egyptian Islamic Jihad and The Islamic Army of Aden as Terrorist Organisations, http://www.ema.gov.au/agd/WWW/ministerruddockhome.nsf/Page/RWP9BFF96CA820E4929CA2572B10005BDEF.

[17] 'KARACHI: Lahori acquitted in two sectarian murder cases', *Dawn*, Karachi, 18 January 2007.

[18] Ibid.

After carrying out an attack, LeJ cadres often disperse and then reassemble at the various training camps to plan future operations.

The LeJ's chief area of operation is within Pakistan, where it has admitted responsibility for numerous massacres of Shias and targeted killings of Shia religious and community leaders. While sectarian attacks remain the LeJ's primary objective, elements within the LeJ have broadened its focus to include the targeting of members of the Pakistani state and the Western presence in Pakistan.[19] The LeJ derives a considerable portion of its funding from wealthy benefactors in Karachi, and extortion from Shia banks and businesses is another significant source by which the LeJ raises finances for terrorist operations.[20] Pakistani government security crackdowns since late-2001 have had some success, but the group continues to recruit new members to replace those arrested or killed. Reports in April 2007 indicated that the LeJ has 300 active members.

The current status of LeJ training facilities is not known since its training camps in Afghanistan were destroyed by the United States, and their training facilities in Pakistan have been disrupted by the local police. Being part of a broader Deobandi movement, however, the LeJ can rely on the assistance of other militant Deobandi groups, including its parent SSP, Jaish-e-Mohammed, the Jamiat ul-Ansar (also known as Harkat-ul-Mujahideen), and Harkat-ul-Jihad-al-Islami. The LeJ also has close links with the Taliban and al Qaeda.

The LeJ was involved in many incidents in 2006 and 2007.[21] For instance, on 31 December 2006, intelligence agencies unearthed an LeJ plan to target prominent Shia leaders and scholars and carry out suicide attacks on Shia worship places across the country, including in Lahore, Rawalpindi, Gujranwala, Multan, Khanewal, Layya, Bhakkar, Jhang, Sargodha, Rahimyar Khan, Karachi, Dera Ismail Khan, Bannu, Kohat, Parachinar, Hangu, Hyderabad, Nawabshah, Mirpur Khas and Quetta. Earlier, on 13 October 2006, police arrested eight people allegedly involved in the Ayub Park blast and for planting anti-tank rockets at different locations in Islamabad a week earlier. Preliminary investigations revealed that the arrested people had links with the al Qaeda and LeJ and had visited Afghanistan many times. It was

---

[19] Re-Listing of Jaish-e-Mohammad, Lashkar-e Jhangvi, Asbat Al Ansar, The Islamic Movement of Uzbekistan, the Egyptian Islamic Jihad and the Islamic Army of Aden as Terrorist Organisations, see note 16 above.

[20] Ibid.

[21] South Asia Terrorism Portal, www.satp.org.

reported on 1 October 2006 that the LeJ has started a recruitment drive and is forming new cells at the district and provincial levels. Matiur Rehman, who is believed to have links with the al Qaeda and is one of the prime suspects in the London airline plot, murder of American journalist Daniel Pearl, the multiple assassination plots on President Pervez Musharraf and Prime Minister Shaukat Aziz, and the attack on the US Consulate in Karachi in March 2006 has been tasked with reorganizing Lashkar cells. Abdullah Faryad, the LeJ chief at Ditta Khel in the Punjab province, is helping him.

In 2007 as well, the outfit suffered some setbacks. On 26 August the police killed Fayyaz Dada, a former LeJ cadre, who had joined a local gang allegedly dealing in drugs in Karachi. Earlier on 25 July the police in Quetta, capital of Balochistan, arrested Zahoor alias Choota Waqar, an activist of the LeJ. Zahoor belongs to Dera Murad Jamali and is wanted for the killing of important Shiite personalities of Quetta, and for two bomb blasts in Shia places of worship. On 15 February the police raided a house on Misrial road in Rawalpindi and arrested two LeJ militants, Usman Chotu and Arshad Satti, wanted for sectarian attacks on Shias. The police also seized five hand grenades, two Kalashnikovs and some explosive material from them. Similarly, on 4 February the Lahore police announced that it had arrested five LeJ militants, including one carrying a reward of PKR one million on his head. And, on 22 January the Karachi unit *Amir* (chief) of the Lashkar-e-Jhangvi, Mohammad Ali alias Mama, was arrested during a police raid in the Korangi area of Karachi. He is reported to have become the LeJ Karachi unit chief about a year ago. Ali trained at Kabul's Shah Ismail training centre in 2000.

Sipah-e-Sahaba Pakistan

Earlier called Anjuman Sipah-e-Sahaba, the Sipah-e-Sahaba Pakistan (SSP) is a Sunni sectarian outfit that has allegedly been involved in terrorist violence, primarily targeted against the minority Shia community in Pakistan.[22] It has also operated as a political party and contested elections, and an SSP leader was a minister in the Coalition Government in Punjab in 1993. The SSP is one of the five outfits that were proscribed by President Pervez Musharraf on 12 January 2002. It is

---

[22] The narrative on the SSP is largely based on a profile drawn from South Asia Terrorism Portal, www.satp.org.

reported to have been renamed Millat-e-Islamia Pakistan after the proscription, and has largely remained underground since. Most of its cadres have either joined its armed wing, the LeJ, or are functioning in the name of Millat-e-Islamia.

Maulana Haq Nawaz Jhangvi, Maulana Zia-ur-Rehman Farooqi, Maulana Eesar-ul-Haq Qasmi and Maulana Azam Tariq established the SSP in September 1985 in an environment of increasing sectarian hostility in Pakistan Punjab. The origins of the SSP lie in the feudal set-up of Pakistan Punjab and politico-religious developments in the decade of the 1970s and 1980s.

The SSP wants Pakistan to be declared a Sunni state. While believing in hostility towards the Shias, the SSP also wants to restore the Khilafat system. It also aims to protect the Sunnis and their Shariat (law). The SSP has declared that Shiites are non-Muslims. It came into existence as a reaction to the Iranian Revolution and increasing Shia militancy in Pakistan.

The SSP has been involved in some incidents relating to sectarianism in 2006 and 2007. For instance, on 31 October 2006, two SSP activists, Shahnawaz alias Shani and Shaukat alias Javed alias Chand, were sentenced to death by a Karachi court for killing six employees of the Pakistan Space and Upper Atmosphere Research Commission during an attack on their vehicle in October 2003. Earlier, on 18 October, the police at Mianwali in the Punjab province arrested three SSP militants, Noor Muhammad, Abdul Waheed and Rao Saifullah. Further, on 7 April SSP activists held a rally in Islamabad and reportedly vowed to establish a global caliphate, beginning with Pakistan. In a rally attended by thousands of activists of the banned group to commemorate the birth of Prophet Muhammad, SSP leaders called for an Islamic theocracy in Pakistan. On 4 April, five SSP activists were sentenced to death by an anti-terrorism court in Karachi on charges of killing a police constable and an undertrial prisoner in an ambush on a prison van near the city courts in 2002. The Karachi police detained two top SSP leaders on 21 February in a bid to contain the wave of protests in the city.

On 24 August 2007 unidentified assailants shot dead a 22-year-old SSP activist, Kaleen Ullah, at Dera Ismail Khan in the North West Frontier Province (NWFP). During continuing sectarian violence in the NWFP, the provincial Secretary–General of the SSP, Aslam Farooqui, was shot dead in Peshawar. Alam Zeb, brother of the deceased leader, caught hold of one the attackers and handed him over to the police. A police official said one Shoaib Hussain of Parachinar, who belonged to a paramilitary force, had been arrested.

Sipah-e-Mohammed Pakistan and Tehreek-e-Jaferia Pakistan[23]

Sipah-e-Mohammed Pakistan (SMP, literally 'army of Muhammad'), refers to a Shia group which is involved in sectarian terrorist activity, primarily in Pakistan Punjab. The SMP is one of the two sectarian terrorist outfits proscribed by President Pervez Musharraf on 14 August 2001. It has remained largely dormant since then.

Tehreek-e-Jaferia Pakistan (TJP), or the 'movement of the followers of Fiqah-e-Jaferia', the dominant Shia outfit in Pakistan, was formed in 1992. The origin of TJP can be traced to the Tehreek Nifaz Fiqah-e-Jafria (TNFJ), meaning 'movement for the implementation of Fiqah-e-Jafreia' (a school of Islamic jurisprudence which is traced back to its founder Imam Jafar Sadiq) which was formed in 1979 to protect the interests of the Shiite minority and promote the ideas of Ayatollah Khomeini, who led the Islamic Revolution that overthrew the Shah of Iran in 1979. Since August 2001, the TJP has remained dormant.

Lashkar-i-Islam and Ansaar-ul-Islam

The Khyber Agency in FATA has been severely affected by fighting between the Lashkar-i-Islam and Ansaar-ul-Islam. Writing in the August 2007 issue of *Newsline*, noted journalist Rahimullah Yusufzai stated that,

> these two tribal-based Islamic groups have been using heavy weapons to settle scores and the government has failed to stop the fighting that affected life in Tirah Valley and Bara area throughout 2006 and 2007. Occasionally, the fighting spills over to Orakzai Agency, which suffers from its periodic bouts of sectarian strife between Sunni and Shia tribes. Recently, the neighbouring Kurram Agency, too, witnessed sectarian riots for the first time in 10 years. It also suffers from the fallout of the Taliban-led resistance in the adjoining Paktia province in Afghanistan.[24]

The state is unambiguously on the defensive. This is clearly visible from the fact that on 21 August 2007, Mufti Munir Shakir, head of the Lashkar-i-Islam group in FATA, was released after 13 months

---

[23] South Asia Terrorism Portal, www.satp.org.
[24] Rahimullah Yusufzai, 'Accord and Discord', *Newsline*, Karachi, August 2007, http://www.newsline.com.pk/NewsAug2007/specrepaug2007.htm.

of 'protective custody'. The cleric, in his 40s, heads the Lashkar-i-Islam which confronts the rival Barelvi school of thought group, the Ansaar-ul-Islam.

Sunni Tehreek

A majority of the jihadis in Pakistan swear by the Deobandi school of thought, while the Barelvis, including the Sunni Tehreek (ST), have largely, though not entirely, abstained from militancy. The Barelvis, however, are major players in the 'politics of the mosque'. The ST, for instance, is locked in a battle with the Deobandi groups for control over various mosques in Karachi and over the collection of endowments. While this intra-Sunni confrontation often leads to violence in Karachi, the Muttahida Quami Movement (MQM) regime in the Sindh province is also under challenge from the extremist Muttahida Majlis-e-Amal alliance. And violence between Sunni groups, allegedly at the behest of intelligence agencies in Islamabad, is believed to weaken the MQM and mainstream parties like the Pakistan People's Party.

In one of the lethal incidents of sectarian violence in 2006, at least 57 people, including prominent Islamist clerics, died and more than 200 people sustained injuries in a suicide bomb attack on 11 April at Nishtar park in Karachi, capital of Sindh province.[25] The blast occurred at a stage erected in a park where religious leaders and scores of faithful were offering evening prayers at a meeting to mark the birth anniversary of Prophet Mohammed. Among those killed were the top leaders of the Sunni Tehreek and Jamaat-e-Ahle Sunnat. Indications are that the suicide bomber wanted to decapitate the Sunni Tehreek. Its Chief, Abbas Qadri, Deputy Chief Akram Qadri, and spokesperson Iftikhar Bhatti were killed in the attack. Some leaders of the 'moderate' Jamaat-e-Ahle Sunnat, including Haji Hanif Billo and Hafiz Muhammad Taqi, also died in the blast.

The ST, which is of Barelvi orientation, was formed in 1992 by Maulana Saleem Qadri to counter the dominance of the Deobandi and Ahle Hadith schools of thought. Incidentally, Saleem Qadri was assassinated on 18 May 2001 in Karachi. His attackers were identified as belonging to the now outlawed Sunni group, Sipah-e-Sahaba Pakistan. Under Qadri, the ST grew rapidly due to large sums of money pouring in from the affluent business community in Karachi, who were

[25] Kanchan Lakshman, 'Karachi: Metropolis of Terror', *South Asia Intelligence Review*, vol. 4, no. 40, 17 April 2006; South Asia Terrorism Portal, www.satp.org.

primarily hoping for protection from the other groups like the SSP and its armed wing, the Lashkar-e-Jhangvi. The 11 April 2006 incident was the result of the ongoing conflict between the Barelvi and Deobandi schools. No official determination has still been made regarding those responsible for the incident, but many suspect that the LeJ engineered it.

CONFLICT IN 2007

Although sectarian killings have not been stopped, their number has decreased when compared to the past. However, some believe that sectarianism has increased in Pakistan during the rule of Pervez Musharraf. For example, Khaled Ahmed contends that this is because he is unable to control Pakistan's 'ungovernable spaces' into which non-Pakistani sectarian groups are entering and which may comprise as much as 60 per cent of Pakistani territory.[26]

According to Samina Ahmed,

> More than five years after Musharraf promised to crack down on terrorism and to end the jihadi culture in Pakistan, jihadi and violent sectarian groups, many listed as terrorist by the United Nations and the United States and banned by his government, have been allowed to operate freely under changed names or through front organizations. These include the Lashkar-e-Tayyaba (LeT), renamed the Jamaat-ud-Dawa and the Jaish-e-Mohammad which calls itself the Khadam-ul-Islam. Their leaders operate freely, issuing public calls for jihad, With the jihadi madrasas providing their organizations an endless supply of recruits. The infrastructure of these terror groups and hence their capacity to mount terrorist attacks remain intact.[27]

With jihadi seminaries still indoctrinating Pakistan's youth, justifying the use of indiscriminate force on religious grounds, and providing recruits for home-grown terrorist groups, many with links to al Qaeda, there is good reason for concern.[28] Samina Ahmed aptly notes that 'The Musharraf government's successes against al Qaeda, including its 600

---

[26] Sectarian War: Pakistan's Sunni–Shia Violence and Its Links to the Middle East, http://www.wilsoncenter.org/index.cfm?fuseaction=events.event_summary&event_id=231933.

[27] Testimony of Samina Ahmed on 'Extremist Madrasas, Ghost Schools, and US Aid to Pakistan', before the US House of Representatives Subcommittee on National Security and Foreign Affairs, http://nationalsecurity.oversight.house.gov/documents/20070509164247.pdf.

[28] Ibid.

arrests, appear impressive but should be weighed against its failure to eliminate Pakistan's homegrown terrorist organizations with links to transnational terrorism. In fact, the divide between homegrown terrorists and al Qaeda is artificial at best. Both are motivated by a distorted religious ideology and rely on terror tactics.' The military government has also worked openly with banned jihadi groups including Jamaat-ud-Dawa, the renamed LeT, in the earthquake-hit areas of Northwest Frontier Province (NWFP) and Pakistan-administered Kashmir.

The NWFP is swiftly crystallizing at the core of Islamist militant mobilization in the Pakistan–Afghanistan region even as radical Islamists rapidly expand their presence across Pakistan's other provinces. It is significant that the NWFP is a region where the state's presence has been relatively strong in the past, and the situation has never been even remotely comparable to the traditionally ungoverned Federally Administered Tribal Areas. The deteriorating situation in the NWFP is also an indication of increasing political instability and insecurity in Pakistan, and the weakening of the embattled President Pervez Musharraf's grip on power. Sectarianism in the NWFP is unique in the sense that it can assume tribe-versus-tribe or village-versus-village dimensions and, since the province is awash with arms, partly the legacy of the Afghan conflict and partly the state's failure to prevent proliferation, sectarian violence has often assumed the contours of prolonged conflict in which weapons like rockets and missiles are being used.[29]

According to the Federal Investigation Agency's Special Investigation Group (SIG), the risk of terrorist attacks is highest in the NWFP, followed by Sindh, Punjab and Balochistan.[30] A SIG report states that 56 persons—38 Shias and 18 Sunnis—were killed in sectarian violence in NWFP, while eight cases of sectarian terrorism were also reported in 2006.[31] In 2005, five cases of sectarian violence were reported and four people were killed in the province, while in 2004 no such case was registered and no sectarian killings were reported. The report showed that sectarian violence increased in Dera Ismail Khan during Muharram in 2006, resulting in seven killings. 'Shia–Sunni conflict over Mian Mir Anwar Shah Tomb in Kalaya, Orakzai Agency, had resulted in 52 deaths', the report said, pointing out that the Taliban are trying to enforce their rule in Tank, Kolachi, DI Khan, Bannu and Laki Marwat in NWFP. Specific to the province, the report states that

[29] 'The State of Sectarianism in Pakistan', International Crisis Group, Brussels, 18 April 2005.
[30] 'NWFP most prone to sectarian violence this Muharram', *Daily Times*, 24 January 2007.
[31] Ibid.

Matiur Rehman, Qari Ehsan, Umer Aqdas, Hafiz Mohammad Yasin, Mufti Saghir and Qari Nazakt are still at large and are trying to reorganize the LeJ. Some LeJ militants, like Shabbir Arain and Tanveer Khan alias Tanni, have recently been released from jail and they are now trying to regroup, it added. Sectarian violence has reduced in Quetta after the arrest of LeJ activists Habibullah, Dawood Badini and Usman Kurd in 2006, according to the SIG report. 'There is always a possibility of a terrorist attack in Balochistan because of the influence of outside factors. The Taliban, Balochistan Liberation Army (BLA) and various Afghan elements could exploit the situation and fit bombs with bicycles and vehicles near Shia mourners to create religious disharmony in the province', the report stated. On 16 March 2007, the NWFP Governor Ali Muhammad Jan Orakzai said that continued hostilities between two religious groups in Bara had threatened peace and were hampering development projects in the Khyber Agency.[32]

There is considerable cooperation now between sectarian groups like the LeJ and other militant groups which are currently orchestrating violence across the length and breadth of Pakistan. For instance, on 11 June 2007, Karachi police arrested three terrorists and identified the suicide bomber who was allegedly responsible for the Nishtar park incident in Karachi on 11 April 2006.[33] Two LeJ cadres were arrested during raids in two different areas of Karachi and based on their information, the police conducted an operation in Peshawar in the NWFP where the third terrorist was arrested.[34] All three of them, police claimed, had confessed to their involvement in the suicide attack. The suicide bomber was identified as Siddiq who hailed from Mansehra in the NWFP. Police said the attack was planned at Wana in south Waziristan under the supervision of the LeJ and the local al Qaeda. Karachi police sources said that the Abdullah Mehsud group was involved in the attack and his cousin, Abid Mehsud, resident of Orangi town in Karachi, planned the attack. Earlier in January 2007, the Karachi police announced that the al Qaeda had worked with local sectarian groups to carry out some of the deadliest suicide attacks against sectarian targets in 2006, which left more than 60 dead.[35]

Analysts like Christine Fair point out that militant groups cross-pollinate: those who attack Shias today are the ones who attack

[32] 'Clashes hampering development in Khyber Agency', *Daily Times*, Lahore, 17 March 2007.

[33] 'Nishtar Park bombing: culprit identified', *Daily Times*, 12 June 2007.

[34] Ibid.

[35] David Montero, 'Shiite–Sunni conflict rises in Pakistan', www.csmonitor.com/2007/0202/p01s02-wosc.html.

Western targets tomorrow.[36] 'They have multiple goals. It's an external *jihad*. It's an internal *jihad*', observes Samina Ahmed. For instance, in January 2007 the Karachi police disclosed that the 2 March 2006 suicide bombing in Karachi, which killed a US diplomat, identified as David Fyfe, his Pakistani driver and a Rangers official, was carried out by the LeJ, a sectarian group working with al Qaeda. Further, on 4 June 2007, police said that they had arrested two suspected LeJ militants, identified as Attaur Rehman and Faisal Bhatti, from Kashmor, a town northeast of Karachi, for their alleged role in the 2002 abduction and murder of US journalist Daniel Pearl.

Sectarian Violence in Pakistan, 2007 (till August)

Month	Incidents	Killed	Injured
January	3	5	21
February	0	0	0
March	9	8	1
April	72	121	119
May	2	3	1
June	0	0	0
July	0	0	0
August	2	2	0
Total	88	139	142

Source: Database of the Institute for Conflict Management, New Delhi.

Sectarian Violence in Pakistan, 2006

Month	Incidents	Killed	Injured
January	0	0	0
February	5	52	104
March	1	25	0
April	3	59	204
May	0	0	0
June	1	4	0
July	4	3	3
August	0	0	0
September	1	1	0
October	18	31	13
November	4	22	0
December	1	4	25
Total	38	201	349

Source: Database of the Institute for Conflict Management, New Delhi.

[36] Ibid.

Compared to 2005, when approximately 160 persons were killed and 354 others injured in 62 incidents of sectarian violence, there was an increase in the violence index in 2006 when 201 people died and 349 were wounded in 38 incidents. In 2007, approximately 139 people died and 142 injured in 87 incidents of sectarian violence across Pakistan till end-August.

A deeper scrutiny of the sectarian trajectory in Pakistan indicates patterns of uncertainty and resilience. There are also periods of apparent calm between high-intensity attacks. Further, these sectarian jihadis have demonstrated great resilience over extended periods of time. They have been able to systematically expand their geographical support base and target areas. The Punjab province and Pakistan's commercial capital, Karachi, in the Sindh province, have for long been the primary hubs of sectarian violence. However, continuing violence in places like Quetta, Peshawar, Hangu, Multan, Dera Islmail Khan, Khyber Agency and Kurram Agency suggests an extension in the sphere of sectarian strife. Moreover, the task of security agencies is rendered more complex during religious festivals, since large processions in public spaces are always easy terrorist targets. Attacks on mosques at prayer time and on other religious gatherings, when potential fatalities are high, have been a key tactic of sectarian terrorists.

There have been some major incidents of sectarian violence in 2007.[37] While two people from the Sunni community died in a town in the NWFP where a pre-dawn rocket attack on a Shiite Muslim procession sparked a burst of sectarian violence on 30 January, two people were killed in a shooting incident on an unauthorized Muharram procession in the curfew town of Hangu in NWFP a day later. And on 13 March, gunmen shot dead two persons, a Shia and a Sunni, at Dera Ismail Khan, raising the toll from sectarian violence in the town in the preceding week to seven. Meanwhile, in FATA, authorities imposed a curfew on 6 April in Kurram Agency following sectarian violence in which three people were killed and the army was called out to control the situation. Hospital sources said that three people were killed and 13 injured when Shias were attacked in an Imambargah in the morning. Trouble erupted when Shias staged a demonstration outside their mosque against local Sunnis who allegedly chanted anti-Shia slogans during a religious rally the previous week. The next day, at least 40 persons were killed and an unspecified number wounded in sectarian

[37] South Asia Terrorism Portal, www.satp.org.

clashes at Parachinar and other parts of the Kurram tribal Agency. Further, on 8 April, nine Shias and seven Sunnis were killed in the Kurram Agency as sectarian clashes spread to most parts of the tribal region bordering Afghanistan. Eight more persons were killed on the fifth day of the sectarian clashes in Kurram Agency.

On 10–11 April 2007 at least 45 more people were killed during sectarian clashes in the Kurram Agency as Shia and Sunni combatants continued to attack each other's villages with heavy weapons despite warnings of military action by the government against those refusing to stop fighting. Elsewhere in FATA, six people were killed and 12 others wounded when Lashkar-i-Islam activists and security forces exchanged fire at Bara in the Khyber Agency on 23 April. In the NWFP, unidentified militants shot dead three people in a targeted sectarian attack in the Dera Ismail Khan district on 25 April. The assailants fired from a Kalashnikov rifle on a vehicle in which two brothers from a prominent Shia family, Najaf Ali Shah and Syed Ali Shah, and their Sunni employee were travelling. An unnamed official of the NWFP government blamed the attack on the SSP.

Indicating a spread of sectarianism, unidentified Sunni gunmen shot dead two Shia clerics at Chaubara town near Multan in the Punjab province on 6 May. Further, two activists of the Lashkar-i-Islam were killed and three others wounded in FATA when supporters of the rival Ansaar-ul-Islam attacked a mosque with mortar shells in the Shah Kot area of Bara on 22 May. At least eight people died during clashes between activists of the rival Lashkar-i-Islam and Ansaar-ul-Islam groups at Sandapaal in the Tirah valley of Khyber Agency on 17 August.

Among the major incidents of sectarian violence in 2006, at least 40 people were killed and 50 others wounded in a suspected suicide attack on a Muharram procession of Shia Muslims in the Hangu town of the NWFP on 9 February. Two days later, three people were killed in overnight sectarian clashes in the same town. Earlier, on 28 March, approximately 25 persons were killed and as many injured in gun battles between followers of two religious groups at Bara in FATA. The clashes at Sur Dand area in Khyber Agency commenced on 27 March when supporters of cleric Mufti Munir Shakir laid siege to the house of a staunch follower of rival cleric Pir Saifur Rehman. Mufti Shakir and Pir Rehman reportedly run illegal FM radio channels and the clerics, who used abusive language against each other in sermons on their channels, had left the tribal region some time ago under government pressure.

In continuation of the violent trend, 57 people, including prominent religious personalities, died and more than 50 people were wounded in a suicide bomb attack at Nishtar park in Karachi on 11 April 2006. On 18 April, a prominent Shia cleric, identified as Fazal Hussain Alvi, and his driver were shot dead at Faisalabad in the Punjab province. Further, on 14 July, a suicide bomber killed a high-profile Shia scholar and political leader, Allama Hasan Turabi, along with his nephew near his residence in Abbas town in Sindh province. Two persons were killed while seven others sustained injuries in a sectarian clash between the Ahl-e-Sunnat and Shia sects over a controversial shrine in the Orakzai tribal area of the NWFP on 2 October. At least 20 people were killed in a continued exchange of mortar fire between Shias and Sunnis over the control of the Mian Anwar shrine in the Kalay area of Lower Orakzai Agency on 6 October. On 16 November, at least 22 people died in a sectarian clash between the Lashkar-i-Islam and the Ansaar-ul-Islam in the Bara area of Khyber Agency. On 10 December, four persons were killed and 25 others wounded and four houses demolished in an armed clash between the rival Lashkar-i-Islam and Ansaar-ul-Islam groups in Khyber Agency.

The relative decline in casualties in sectarian violence is primarily traced to the fact that the LeJ, the main Sunni group, has been vigorously targeted by state agencies following its 12 January 2002 proscription. A significant number of its cadres, including the top leadership, were either arrested or killed during various encounters with the police. Till 26 August 2007, at least 56 of them had been arrested. Approximately 44 LeJ cadres, including many top leaders, were arrested during 2006.[38] These include 14 arrests in the Punjab province, 11 in Sindh and four in the Balochistan province. Further, the morale of the outfit's cadre suffered due to various judgements that convicted some of its leaders. For instance, on 3 April 2006, an anti-terrorism court in the Sahiwal district of Punjab province sentenced LeJ activist, Naveed Akhtar, to death for killing advocate Syed Abid Hussain Bukhari and his son Haidar Abbas on 30 July 1997.[39] On 30 May 2006, the Multan Anti-Terrorism Court sentenced Qari Omar Hayat, another LeJ activist, to death on 16 counts of murder. Hayat was arrested for killing 16 Shias while they were listening to a sermon in a mosque in Muzaffargarh on 4 January 1999. Further, on 1 August 2006, the same Court in Multan

---

[38] See profile of LeJ, South Asia Terrorism Portal, www.satp.org.
[39] Ibid.

handed out death sentences to two LeJ militants, Zahid Husain alias Zada, and Shahabuddin, on seven counts for killing six people, including five police personnel. The Court also awarded life imprisonment on seven counts to their accomplice Ghulam Shabbir alias Doctor.

However, the LeJ did activate its cadre and was able to keep alive its subversive agenda. An report dated 2 October 2006 indicated that the LeJ had started a recruitment drive and was forming new cells at the district and provincial levels.[40] Matiur Rehman, who is believed to have links with al Qaeda and is one of the prime suspects in the London airline plot, the murder of American journalist Daniel Pearl, the multiple assassination plots on President Pervez Musharraf and Prime Minister Shaukat Aziz, and the attack on the US Consulate in Karachi in March 2006, had been tasked with reorganizing LeJ cells.[41] Abdullah Faryad, the LeJ chief at Ditta Khel in the Punjab province, was helping him, the report added.

During 2006, a new militant group appeared on the sectarian scene in Pakistan. Pukhtoon militants who fought against the US-led invasion of Afghanistan reportedly formed a new anti-Shia militant group.[42] The new militant group is 'led by Mufti Ilyas and Hazrat Ali of Darra Adam Khel. Its members include men who recently fought against US forces in Afghanistan, and have links with Abdullah Mehsud, the militant leader responsible for the attack on Chinese engineers at the Gomal Zam Dam site, and other militants from Waziristan and Afghanistan. It also includes some women members… the new group has no links with any other militant organization, including the banned sectarian group Lashkar-e-Jhangvi, and is active in Quetta, Karachi and other major cities in Pakistan. It also says the group has established a supply line of weapons and ammunition between Darra Adam Khel and Karachi.'[43]

There was evidence of some cooperation between sectarian groups like the LeJ and other militant groups. According to reports submitted by intelligence agencies to the Interior Ministry, 'Maulvi Inayatur Rehman and Maulana Faqir Mohammad of the Tehreek Nifaz-e-Shariat-e-Mohammadi (TNSM) have pledged before their supporters to target VIPs in Pakistan and US and NATO forces in Afghanistan.'[44]

---

[40] 'LJ forming new militant cells', *Daily Times*, 2 October 2006.
[41] Ibid.
[42] 'New militant group targeting Shia leaders', *Daily Times*, 4 September 2006.
[43] Ibid.
[44] 'Jihadis preparing to avenge Bajaur', *Daily Times*, 18 December 2006.

Leaders of the Harkat-ul-Mujahideen, Lashkar-e-Jhangvi and Khudamul Islam (a faction of the Jaish-e-Mohammed) also pledged to cooperate with the TNSM and called for a joint strategy. Another report stated that some LeJ militants 'with links to Karachi went to Wana [South Waziristan] where they got in touch with the Abdullah Mehsud-led group. They then befriended Abdullah Mehsud's cousin, Abid Mehsud. Through Abid they developed more links with Al Qaeda in Karachi and upon Abid's advice roped in some young men from Orangi Town.'[45] Throughout 2006, LeJ militants, according to intelligence reports, targeted Shia leaders and scholars in various parts of the country, including in Lahore, Rawalpindi, Gujranwala, Multan, Khanewal, Layya, Bhakkar, Jhang, Sargodha, Rahimyar Khan, Karachi, Dera Ismail Khan, Bannu, Kohat, Parachinar, Hangu, Hyderabad, Nawabshah, Mirpur Khas and Quetta.[46]

CONFLICT MANAGEMENT

In sharp contrast to his ambivalence towards Islamist terrorist activities elsewhere, President Musharraf's policy has been unambiguous regarding domestic sectarian terrorism. His internal 'war against terror' has vigorously targeted sectarian terrorist groups, and has had a substantial impact domestically. The relative reduction in casualties in sectarian violence is primarily traced to the fact that LeJ, the main Sunni group, and SMP, the main Shia group, was vigorously targeted by state agencies following its 12 January 2002 proscription. Despite its various reverses, however, the LeJ appears to have retained a substantial capacity to strike, and it has emerged as a key provider of logistical support and personnel to al Qaeda and Taliban in Pakistan.

Among others, the SSP and the TJP lay low temporarily in the aftermath of their proscription. They have not, however, altered their organizational structure and, though their cadres went underground for some time, they continue to function. The SSP even re-commenced publishing its official organ, the monthly *Khilafat-i-Rashida*, which it had discontinued immediately after its proscription.

While President Musharraf has been relatively uncompromising in dealing with domestic terrorism emanating from sectarian groups,

---

[45] 'Qaeda–LJ link in terror attacks', *Daily Times*, 1 January 2007.
[46] 'LJ plans attacks on Shia leaders and worship places', *Daily Times*, 1 January 2007.

the prevailing law and order situation in the country demonstrates that terrorism is not an affliction that can be dealt with in a piecemeal fashion—encouraged and supported in one direction, and suppressed in another. The crackdown targeting sectarian groups has failed to produce the desired impact, and continuing sectarian violence across the country suggests that the underground networks and support structures of sectarian groups, particularly that of the LeJ, remain unimpaired and may, indeed, have achieved greater complexity and resilience through their linkages with other terrorist organizations. Clearly, a more comprehensive strategy is required to destroy the source of their lethality.

In the present milieu, the apparent failure of the Musharraf regime to counter Islamist extremism and sectarianism is all the more inexplicable since the country has handed over more than 600 al Qaeda operatives to US authorities since the war on terror began. The will to contain Islamist extremist groups that are not on America's list of priorities appears to be absent, and a significant number of such groups continue to operate within the country, many of them with apparent immunity. The leadership of several such groups, most visibly the Jaish-e-Mohammed, the Lashkar-e-Toiba, the Harkat-ul-Mujahideen and the Hizb-ul-Mujahideen—despite an official ban on the first three—is regularly reported in the Pakistani media to enjoy full freedom of movement. Complex linkages exist between some of these groups and the Sunni sectarian groups, such as the Sipah-e-Sahaba Pakistan and the Lashkar-e-Jhangvi.

Ambivalence and piecemeal stratagems have marked the state's response to sectarianism in Pakistan. An Anti-Terrorism Act (ATA) against sectarian violence was passed only in 1997, despite the fact that the cycle of sectarian violence dates back to the mid-1970s. Sectarian groups were not outlawed until 2002. Raising serious doubts about the ATA being an effective tool in curbing the sectarian menace, a Pakistani analyst pointed out that 'More emphasis seems to have been put on catching the culprits who actually carried out the attacks rather than on catching the masterminds behind them or squashing the infrastructure that breeds, trains, funds and protects the terrorists.'[47]

The perpetrators of sectarian terror share their ideological platform with Islamist extremist groupings engaged in a wide range of

---

[47] See Kanchan Lakshman, 'Pakistan: The Enemy Within', *South Asia Intelligence Review*, vol. 2, no. 34, 8 March 2004; South Asia Terrorism Portal, www.satp.org.

international terrorist movements, and it is evident that the operational capacities of both these are yet to be significantly eroded. According to Hasan-Askari Rizvi, the missing links in Pakistan's counter-terrorism policies are 'the absence of broad-based support for the government and its failure to engage in popular mobilisation on this issue. There has been no serious attempt to seek policy inputs from the political parties and societal groups that favour strong action against extremism and terrorism.'[48]

Extremist and terrorist actors have, for long, secured physical space to operate within Pakistan, and it is the ideology of Islamist extremism—partially reflected in parties such as the MMA and in political initiatives such as the Hisba Act (in the NWFP), but which also generally pervades the founding ideas and political culture of Pakistan—that makes this possible.[49] The West is only now beginning to recognize the pivotal role of the 'evil ideology' that former British Prime Minister Tony Blair blamed for the 7/7 attacks in London. Blair also recognized the 'battle for hearts and minds' that underlay terrorist acts and responses to them. Regrettably, this recognition is still to produce a significant response strategy in the global war on terror. On the other hand, it has been the core of the Islamist extremist approach, which lays immense emphasis on a future guided essentially by ideological motivators, and has created an enormous institutional and political infrastructure for the propagation and promotion of the ideology of extremist Islam. It is precisely this insidious ideology, 'a belief, one whose fanaticism is such it can't be moderated', and its vast apparatus of support within state and non-state entities in Pakistan, that draws people like 22-year-old Shahzad Tanweer, one of the London bombers, and thousands of others, to the *madrassas*, the *marakiz* and the training camps of Pakistan.

While Pakistan, in the words of John D. Negroponte, Director of US National Intelligence, 'remains a major source of Islamic extremism and the home for some top terrorist leaders',[50] it periodically seeks redemption through a promise—repeated incessantly since 9/11—to

---

[48] Hasan-Askari Rizvi, 'Counter-terrorism: the missing links', *Daily Times*, 4 March 2007.

[49] Kanchan Lakshman, 'The Darkness of "Enlightened Moderation"', *South Asia Intelligence Review*, vol. 4, no. 1, 18 July 2005; South Asia Terrorism Portal, www.satp.org.

[50] John D. Negroponte, Annual Threat Assessment of the Director of National Intelligence, 11 January 2007, http://intelligence.senate.gov/070111/negroponte.pdf.

clean up its seminaries, and to rid them of extremism and hatred. The claim is that this would strike at the root of Islamist terror. This promise has raised great expectations in the West and in South Asia. However, the state of play on the ground tells an altogether different story. During a televised address to the nation on 12 January 2002, President Pervez Musharraf had warned that the greatest danger facing Pakistan came, not from outside, but from Pakistan's own homegrown Islamist radicals—'a danger', he said, 'that is eating us from within'. This danger, more than five years later, has assumed menacing proportions. The rapid escalation of violence orchestrated by Islamist extremists across Pakistan in recent times and cumulative efforts to further radicalize the country have now led General Musharraf's military regime to revisit the idea of *madrassa* reforms. Most of the officially estimated 13,000 seminaries in Pakistan (unofficial estimates range between 15,000 and 25,000, and in some cases go up to 40,000) with an approximate enrolment of 1.5 million students have rejected these tentative reforms initiated by the government in 2003. These reforms essentially require the registration of *madrassas* and the maintenance of accounts, including records of domestic and foreign donors, as well as the teaching of 'secular' subjects as part of the curriculum. They have opposed all changes, alleging that the reforms constituted a conspiracy to 'secularize' (that is, de-Islamize) the education system at the behest of the United States. The networks and support structures of Islamist extremism in Pakistan, painstakingly constructed through the Pakistan–Afghanistan arc, have little evident interest in engaging with the President's 'enlightened moderation'.

A majority of the extremist seminaries that preach and support militant violence are of the Deobandi sect and are associated with the Wafaq-ul-Madaris, the main confederacy of seminaries. According to the International Crisis Group (ICG), 'The two factions of the Deobandi political parties, JUI-Fazlur Rehman [Jamaat-e-Ulema-Islam faction headed by Maulana Fazlur Rehman] and JUI-Samiul Haq [Jamaat-e-Ulema-Islam faction headed by Maulana Samiul Haq], run over 65 per cent of all madrasas in Pakistan.'[51] Rehman and Haq are widely perceived to be the primary backers of the Taliban.

---

[51] 'Pakistan: The Mullahs and the Military', International Crisis Group, Brussels, *Asia Report 49*, 20 March 2003, http://www.crisisgroup.org/library/documents/report_archive/A400925_20032003.pdf.

One of the principal instruments of reform and government regulation of *madrassas* was the proposed registration process.[52] Equally important is the content of the subjects taught to students. Aimed at mainstreaming these religious schools, the government has initiated efforts to introduce subjects like English, General Science and Mathematics. The *ulema* (religious leaders), however, claimed that the registration process was intended to curb the 'independence and sovereignty' of *madrassas* and was, consequently, not acceptable. Five years after its inception, the *Madrassa* Reform Project has been an unmitigated failure. While there is far too much resistance at the ground level, ambivalence and a reluctance to implement the reforms dominates the state's agencies and initiatives. According to the ICG's report of 29 March 2007, 'This is best demonstrated in Sindh Province and its capital, Karachi. After three years of efforts by the Sindh Education Department to help "mainstream" the province's madrassas by including secular education in them, Islamabad asked provincial education authorities in mid-2006 to return more than $100 million in unspent Federal money.' The Project did not have any significant impact since most *madrassas* refused to take the government's help. Incidentally, Pakistan's record in utilizing funds for the socio-economic sectors remains abysmal and, according to one report, 92 per cent of the funds (PKR 51 billion) earmarked for the five-year Education Sector Reforms Programme (2001–2006) has remained unutilized. The collapse of the seminary reform project is a clear indication that Islamabad is either apathetic or clearly does not have the capacity to dismantle the extremist infrastructure across the country.

CONCLUSIONS

Large tracts of Pakistan are now conflict-ridden with a wide array of anti-state actors and terrorists engaging in varying degrees of violence and subversion. A cursory look at the map indicates that FATA, Balochistan and the NWFP are witnessing large-scale violence and subversion. Violence in parts of Sindh, Punjab and Gilgit-Baltistan has also brought these provinces under the security scanner. Islamabad's writ is currently being challenged vigorously—violently or otherwise—in a wide geographical area, and on a multiplicity of issues.

[52] See Kanchan Lakshman, 'Pakistan: More Muscle to the Madrassa', *South Asia Intelligence Review*, vol. 5, no. 41, 23 April 2007; South Asia Terrorism Portal, www.satp.org.

During 2006, 1,471 persons, including 608 civilians and 325 security force personnel, died in terrorism/insurgency-related violence in Pakistan. Crucially, this reflected well over a doubling of fatalities since 2005, when a total of 648 persons (including 430 civilians and 81 SF personnel) were killed in insurgent and terrorist conflicts. In this rapidly deteriorating situation, at least 1,584 people, including 554 civilians, 287 security force personnel and 743 militants, have been killed in 2007 (till 31 August).[53]

The flag of extremist Islam is, thus, fluttering vigorously across Pakistan, even as the state gradually withers away. Moreover, there is now a clear dispersal of the violence linked to radical Islam across hitherto 'peaceful' areas. Violence and mobilization linked to Islamist extremists is now being reported from Swat, Nowshera, Tank, Peshawar, Hangu, Dera Ismail Khan, and other areas in the NWFP, Gujranwala and Multan in the Punjab province, many locations in Sindh province, and the national capital, Islamabad. The writ of the state is clearly on the wane.

At the heart of this rapid march of radical Islam and dissident violence in Pakistan, and the consequent disorders of the past year and more, is the abysmal failure of President Musharraf's much-vaunted vision of 'enlightened moderation'. His call for 'enlightened moderation' in Pakistan is threatened by the very forces that have long been nurtured by successive regimes in the country. Recurrent Islamist violence, it appears, will remain a significant element in the churning process within Pakistan in the proximate future.

The military regime under Pervez Musharraf has had some notable successes against sectarian terrorists, but the demobilization of these groups has become difficult because the end-game of the state remains ambivalent, and that of the extremists does not allow any place for withdrawal or compromise: there is either victory or martyrdom. Solutions to Islamist terrorism, including its sectarian offshoot, will remain elusive as long as the infrastructure of terrorism remains intact in Pakistan, and is supported by the state structure. It needs to be decisively and irrevocably dismantled and destroyed.

---

[53] All data is from South Asia Terrorism Portal, www.satp.org.

4

Pakistan: The War of Tribes

D. Suba Chandran

In 2007, armed conflict continued in Pakistan's Federally Administered Tribal Area (FATA), while the armed conflict in Balochistan considerably declined. Here, we look at the nature and intensity of the armed conflicts in these two tribal regions of Pakistan—FATA and Balochistan.

A BRIEF HISTORY

The Federally Administered Tribal Area is a small region, comprising seven tribal agencies—Bajaur, Mohamand, Khyber, Khurram, Orakzai, North Waziristan and South Waziristan. Except the Orakzai Agency, the other six agencies share borders with Afghanistan in the west and the North West Frontier Province (NWFP) in Pakistan in the east.

As part of their larger strategy vis-à-vis Afghanistan and Russia and what came to be later known as the Great Game, the British created the NWFP in 1901 along with five tribal agencies, which was subsequently increased to seven. After failing repeatedly to establish its writ over these tribal areas, the British formulated an administrative scheme, governing mainly through the Frontier Crimes Regulations (1901), which vested administrative, executive and judicial powers in government officials. Though the Durand Line (1893) divided the numerous Pashtun tribes between Afghanistan and British India, it was never recognized by the local population then or now, which is a major historical reality framing the armed conflicts that one is witnessing today. These agencies had also witnessed armed conflict between the local tribal population and the British Army in the late 19th and early 20th centuries.[1]

---

[1] See the following for military engagements between the tribes of FATA and the British: Captain H.L. Nevill, *Campaigns on the North-West Frontier,* Lahore: Sang-e-Meel, 2003; Evelyn Howell, *Mizh: A Monograph on Government's Relations with the Mahsud Tribe,* New Delhi: Oxford University Press, 1979; Olaf Caroe, *The Pathans,* New Delhi: Oxford University Press, 1984.

Of the seven agencies, today there is a sustained armed conflict in at least four of them—North and South Waziristan, Mohamand and Bajaur. The current round of armed conflict started in 2002 in South Waziristan as a consequence of the US launching Operation Anaconda. As a result, the Taliban/al Qaeda fighters fled Afghanistan looking for safe sanctuaries and entered Waziristan—North and South. When troops deployed, Pakistan in these agencies and started operations against the Taliban/al Qaeda, the militants started fighting back, triggering an armed conflict which continues today. Gradually, the armed conflict spread over to other agencies, mainly Bajaur and Mohamand.

While the Taliban/al Qaeda have been fighting the US-led forces, with a section having their base in these tribal agencies, the armed conflict inside Pakistan—between the security forces and militants—can be divided into distinct phases marked by bloody violence, cease-fires and agreements. While the security forces in Pakistan started military operations against the militants in South Wazirstan from the beginning of 2003, these intensified in October of that year, especially after the suicide attack on General Musharraf in December 2003. It was believed to have been hatched in Waziristan. In April 2004, the government and the militants who primarily belonged to the Wazir tribes reached a temporary understanding in Shakai, in South Waziristan. This agreement, however, unravelled almost immediately, when Nek Mohammad, one of the local militant leaders who was a part of the understanding, resumed fighting. When he was eliminated in a midnight missile attack, the fighting between the security forces and the militants resumed.

In 2005, while the armed conflict continued in South Waziristan, it spread and intensified in North Waziristan. In February 2005, the government reached an understanding with a section of the local militants who belonged to the Mehsud tribe, led by Baitullah Mehsud. However, this agreement was also ineffective as the main local militant leader—Abdullah Mehsud—was not party to it. During this year, the armed conflict in North and South Waziristan also witnessed a parallel conflict between the militants and their local supporters vis-à-vis the local tribal leadership. The attempt to establish their writ, which came to be popularly described as Talibanization of the FATA, also began and intensified during this year. Numerous pro-government elders were murdered and their relatives kidnapped.

In 2006, the armed conflict expanded to include Bajaur Agency, when the US carried out air strikes on a compound in Damadola village, believing that Ayman al-Zawahiri, al Qaeda's second-in-command, and many other senior al Qaeda leaders were present. While Zawahiri and other senior leaders escaped the attack, it was believed that Abu Khabab al-Masri, al Qaeda's chief bomb expert and head of the WMD (Weapons of Mass Destruction) programme, was killed along with more than fifteen locals.

In Balochistan, on the contrary, there has been a decline in the armed conflict during 2007. Though there have been a series of insurgencies since 1947, the current armed conflict became visible in mid-2003 and intensified during 2004–05. For the first time, the existence of the Balochistan Liberation Army (BLA) came into prominence following a cover story published by the *Herald;* according to this expose, the BLA then had 60 camps in the mountains with generators, walkie talkies, satellite phones and tribesmen armed with sophisticated weapons.[2]

In 2005, the armed conflict intensified in Balochistan after a criminal assault on a female doctor in the Pakistan Petroleum Limited (PPL) compound in Sui by army personnel, triggering a series of violent attacks and counter-attacks. The Bugtis, one of the principal tribal groups in the province along with the Marris and Mengals, led the attack by storming PPL installations. In 2006, while the violence continued in terms of bomb explosions, there was no regular armed conflict between the militants and the state. The killing of Akbar Bugti, leader of the Bugti tribes in August 2006, was widely expected to start another round of armed conflict, but this did not happen. However, violence continues to date, with regular bomb explosions within Balochistan.

THE PRINCIPAL ACTORS

The State: Government of Pakistan

The government of Pakistan is a principal actor in both the FATA and Balochistan conflicts. The strategies employed in these two tribal

---

[2] M. Ilyas Khan, 'Back to the hills', *Herald*, September 2004, pp. 51–59. Also see Shahzada Zulfiqar, 'Edging Towards Anarchy', *Newsline*, September 2004, pp. 35–36.

regions are distinctly diverse, since its objectives are also different. The main objective of the federal government in FATA is not to alienate the local tribal Pashtun population, as that would have larger implications for Pakistan–Afghanistan relations and strengthen Pashtun nationalism. All-out military action, the federal government fears, would alienate the local population from Pakistan, leading to the emergence of anti-Pakistani and pro-Pashtun sentiments.

This could be a major reason for Pakistan's dilemma in waging an all-out war against the local militants, al Qaeda and Taliban, in this region. While Pakistan is willing to target the al Qaeda and other foreign militants like the Uzbeks present in FATA, the federal government is extremely reluctant to pursue a confrontationist policy against the Taliban and its local supporters in this region. It is for this reason that the federal government has several times attempted to reach an understanding with the local tribal population in North and South Waziristan, Mohamand and Bajaur agencies. Pakistan has deployed over 80,000 troops in FATA, which includes its regular armed forces and paramilitary forces.

In Balochistan, Pakistan's objectives are to militarily suppress any opposition from the BLA or the various tribal leaders. Since the BLA does not have much external support and lacks credible local support all over the province transcending tribal loyalties, Pakistan believes that this militancy can be suppressed.

The Militants: Taliban/al Qaeda/Local Militants

The militants who are fighting the state in the FATA region are not a monolith. Four separate streams can be identified, though they consider the security forces of Pakistan and the US-led forces in Afghanistan as their main targets. They include: the Taliban, who are primarily Afghan Pashtuns; al Qaeda, whose cadres are from all over the Middle East, including Chechens and Arabs; other foreign militants who are not part of the al Qaeda but are fighting along with the Taliban, like the Uzbeks; and the local militants who owe their allegiance to either the Taliban or the al Qaeda or both.

The main aim of these militant groups is to continue their operations in Afghanistan against the US-led forces to overthrow the Karzai government; to establish Taliban control over Afghanistan; to establish a pro-Taliban administration and/or society in FATA; and to confront the Pakistani state—politically and/or militarily—if obstructs these objectives. Since 2003–04, these forces have been fighting Pakistan's security forces inside FATA and the US-led forces across the Durand Line. Tactically, a section of the militants reached a temporary understanding with Pakistan on many occasions, only to dishonour them later. The politics of these peace understandings are discussed later in this chapter.

The US-led Forces in Afghanistan

The US-led security forces in Afghanistan, though not allowed formally to operate inside FATA by Pakistan, are the third principal actor in the armed conflict in this region. The main objectives of the US-led forces in the FATA region include: to ensure that FATA is not used as a sanctuary or base for military operations by the militants; to pressurize the Pakistani government not to support the militants, politically or militarily; and to force the Pakistani security forces to launch military operations against the militants in FATA.

The US-led forces have indulged in hot pursuit, cross-border firing, and even used drones armed with missiles to strike targets inside FATA towards achieving these objectives. According to a new report, quoting the *New York Times*, the Pentagon has advocated direct American strikes against the al Qaeda training camps inside North Waziristan.[3]

It is also believed that the US has built an excellent network of human and signal intelligence in this region, which it is using either to directly attack targets or is sharing this information with Pakistani security forces and pressurizing them to act. The killing of Nek Mohammad and the attack on Damadola in Bajaur reveals the efficacy of this intelligence network. On both occasions, drones and missiles were used, and the targeting was precise.

Despite the rhetoric in public, there appears to be a serious lack of trust between the US security forces and those of Pakistan. The latter do not totally believe the intelligence inputs from the former; there have been many instances where they were proved wrong. On the other hand, the US forces have their apprehensions about the 'leaks' by Pakistan which warn of an impending attack or a search; hence the need for their unilateral attacks.

---

[3] 'Pentagon for attack on camps in N. Waziristan: NYT', *Dawn*, 20 February 2007.

CONFLICT IN 2007

The armed conflict in Pakistan in 2007, as mentioned earlier, is primarily centred on the various tribal agencies of FATA, while it has declined considerably in Balochistan. Based on the number of attacks, casualties and intensity, one could conclude that, in 2007, the armed conflict in the FATA region progressed to a different level, while in Balochistan it has been reduced to armed violence.

An Overview

Since the peace agreement was signed between the administration in North Waziristan and the local Taliban militants in September 2006, there has been no major confrontation between the security forces and the militants until the second and third weeks of January 2007. On 16 January, the security forces used attack helicopters to target hideouts, resulting in the killing of eight militants in South Waziristan.[4] This was followed by the first suicide attack of the year in Mir Ali in North Waziristan on 22 January, when the bomber attacked a military convoy with a explosives filled car, killing four security personnel.[5]

In March 2007, as explained elsewhere in this chapter, there was an armed conflict within the militant groups led by a section of the local militants in South Waziristan against the Uzbek militants in the region. This fighting continued in April 2007. The local militants, especially a section of Wazirs loyal to Maulana Nazir, had raised a huge tribal militia to fight the Uzbeks, while a section of the Wazirs loyal to Nek Mohammad, who was killed in 2005, supported the Uzbek militants. The state exploited this divide by aiding the Maulana Nazir-led tribal militia. The local tribesmen demanded that the state support them since it provided them with limited air power, arms and ammunition against the Uzbek militants. This internal jihad came to an end during the second week of April, with around 300 casualties, mostly Uzbeks. Maulana Nazir's tribal militia emerged successful, with the Uzbek militants led by Tahir Yuldashev leaving South Waziristan.[6]

---

[4] '8 killed in strike on militant camps in Waziristan', *Daily Times*, 17 January 2007.

[5] '4 soldiers killed in suicide attack', *Daily Times*, 23 January 2007.

[6] See 'Jihad declared against Uzbeks', *Dawn*, 3 April 2007; 'Tribesmen raise 900-man army to fight foreign militants', *Daily Times*, 4 April 2007; 'Jirga seeks govts help to fight Uzbeks', *The Nation*, 6 April 2007.

In April, a sectarian conflict broke out in the Kurram Agency. According to news reports, Sunnis allegedly raised anti-Shia slogans during one of their processions in Parachinar, the headquarters of the Kurram Agency. The Shias came out of their mosque and staged a demonstration after their prayers the following Friday. Violence broke out immediately and continued over almost the entire month, resulting in the killing of more than 50 persons, including both Shias and Sunnis.[7] The reasons and implications of this sectarian conflict are discussed later.

In May, violence continued mainly in North and South Waziristan, with local militants attacking army checkposts and military convoys, and beheading pro-government leaders and locals accused of being spies of the US. During this month, the militants also abducted nine government officials in North Waziristan, though they were subsequently released. Towards the end of the month, local militants attacked the home of the Khyber Agency's political agent with rockets, hand grenades and assault rifles, killing nearly 15 people.[8]

In June, a missile attack in North Waziristan killed more than 20 people, though the reason for the attack remains a mystery. The administration claimed that the attack was carried out by the local militants against foreign militants (most of those killed were of Uzbek origin), but the local population claimed the missile had targeted a madrassa. Later, the Inter-Services Public Relations (ISPR) Director-General, Maj. Gen. Arshad Waheed, denied the involvement of the Pakistan army or the US-led coalition forces in Afghanistan and said that the attack 'was an accidental blast in the area'.[9]

July witnessed the beginning of a series of suicide attacks in the NWFP, following the stroming of the Lal Masjid in Islamabad. On 5 July 2007, Musharraf initiated military action against the madrassas, which had been challenging the writ of the state since January 2007. In January, a small group of girl students wearing burqas occupied a government children's library, protesting against the decision to

---

[7] 'Riot toll in Kurram Agency rises to 50', *Dawn*, 11 April 2007; Editorial, 'Violence in Parachinar', *Dawn*, 10 April 2007; '15 more killed in Kurrum Agency sectarian violence', *Daily Times*, 12 April 2007.

[8] See '13 killed at political agent's Tank home', *Daily Times*, 1 June 2007; Editorial, 'Descent into nihilism and anarchy', *Daily Times*, 2 June 2007.

[9] See '22 die in Waziristan "blast"', *Dawn*, 20 June 2007; 'Missiles hit NWA madrassa: 32 killed', *The Nation*, 20 June 2007; Editorial, 'It's Waziristan again', *Dawn*, 21 June 2007.

bulldoze mosques built illegally. In March, the students, including the girls in the Lal Masjid and Jamia Hafsa, started a moral drive; music and video shops were targeted and the owners threatened to close down their businesses. During the same month, girl students raided a house and illegally detained some women, accusing them of running a prostitution racket. In April 2007, a Sharia court was formed and ten judges were appointed by the administration to issue decrees on religious issues. In May 2007, the students of the Lal Masjid again detained policemen and in June the students kidnapped six Chinese women from a massage centre, accusing them of running a brothel. This led to the military action against the Lal Masjid residents, allegedly under Chinese pressure.

In retaliation, the militants started a series of suicide bombings all over Pakistan. On 14 July 2007, a suicide bomber in North Waziristan rammed an explosives-packed car into a military convoy, killing 23 paramilitary troops. The same day there were simultaneous attacks on the security forces in the districts of Bannu and Dir as well. The following day there were three suicide attacks in the DI Khan and Swat districts. The first two attacks were suicide car bombs targeting the security forces in Swat, killing 11 security force personnel and six civilians. The third attack was carried out by a single suicide bomber in DI Khan, killing 25 people.[10] On 17 July, there was another suicide attack on a security post which killed four persons including three soldiers in North Waziristan.[11] On 19 July, a suicide bomber killed seven people in Hangu Police Training College. The same day, another suicide bomber attacked an army mosque in Kohat, killing 15, mostly army officers, besides a prayer leader and two children.[12]

During the same month there were also conventional attacks on the security forces by the militants. On 18 July, a military convoy was attacked near North Waziristan killing 17 soldiers.[13] Towards the end of July, there was another attack in Miran Shah on the security forces, killing six soldiers.[14]

---

[10] See '45 dead and 108 injured in suicide bombings in Swat and DI Khan', *Daily Times,* 16 October 2007.

[11] '4 die in Waziristan suicide attack', *Daily Times,* 18 July 2007.

[12] 'Bombers target Chinese, police, military, 51 killed', *Daily Times,* 20 July 2007.

[13] '17 soldiers killed in Waziristan attack', *Daily Times,* 19 July 2007.

[14] 'Six soldiers die as militants renew attacks', *Dawn,* 31 July 2007.

Both conventional and suicide attacks continued in August. On 4 August, nine people were killed by a suicide car bomber in Parachinar, Kurram Agency.

Three distinct trends can be identified in the armed conflict in FATA. First, the armed conflict, which until 2005–06 was primarily centred around North and South Waziristan, spread into the other agencies of FATA in 2007. Besides, the conflict has also spread into the settled districts of the NWFP, including Tank, Swat and Dera Ismail Khan (DI Khan). Second, 2007 also witnessed an armed conflict within FATA at two levels. At the first level, there was intense fighting among the militant groups, as between the Uzbek fighters and local militants in South Waziristan. At the second level, there has been a slow but steady process of militants targeting the locals for being pro-government and also for being anti-Islamic. Third, a major trend in the armed conflict in FATA has been the increasing number of suicide attacks, especially after the Lal Masjid operations.

Spreading Anarchy

The armed conflict in North and South Waziristan had its domino effect on the other agencies of FATA like Kurram Agency, but also in some of the settled districts like Tank.

Inside FATA, the Talibanization process in North and South Waziristan had its fallout in the Kurram Agency in terms of triggering a sectarian conflict. Kurram Agency is the only agency to be surrounded by Afghanistan on the north and west (in select areas, even in the south), Khyber and Orakzai Agencies, followed by the Hangu district in the east and Waziristan in the south. Safed Koh, the not so lofty but snowclad mountain range forms a natural barrier in the north with Afghanistan, from where numerous streams and rivulets flow into the Kurram Valley. This geographical encirclement and close proximity to Afghanistan plays an important role in the peace and stability of this region.

Many believe that the recent sectarian conflict has resulted from the entry of pro-Taliban fighters into Kurram Agency and their attempts to impose their version of Islam over a predominantly Shia population. Unlike other agencies in FATA which share the borders with Afghanistan, the main tribes of the Kurram Agency, for example the Turis, do not have a good rapport with the Pashtun tribes of

Afghanistan for religious and historical reasons. The Turis are Shias and never got along with the predominantly Sunni Pashtuns who ruled from Kabul. Ever since the 17th century, when the Turis decided to settle in the Kurram Valley, their relations with their western neighbours were troubled. In fact, during the Second Afghan War they joined the British against the Afghan rulers based in Kabul. The British troops, in fact, invaded Afganisthan through Parachinar, the present headquarters of the Agency, towards Kabul, which is hardly 60 miles away. And the Turis were perhaps one of the few Pashtun tribes to invite the British to take over the local administration due to these internal differences.

What is important in this sectarian clash in Parachinar is the nature and extent of the violence. Within a day, the clashes between the two communities witnessed extensive use of rocket launchers, Kalashnikovs, mortar shells and missiles. What started as a minor clash in Parachinar spread rapidly all over the Kurram Valley to include other towns like Sadda and numerous villages. This is perhaps the only sectarian conflict in South Asia that witnessed the use of rocket launchers. The government had to use helicopters to bomb the positions taken by the rival groups and frequently impose curfew, with the death toll crossing 50 in the first five days.

Events in neighbouring Afghanistan have always triggered a sectarian bloodbath in Kurram. The sectarian clash in Kurram Valley in 1997 coincided with the emergence and rapid growth of the Taliban in Afghanistan. The narrow interpretations of Islam and their intolerance towards other sects, even within Islam, had their repercussions in the Kurram Valley. Clearly, the sectarian violence in Kurram in April 2007 is linked, as mentioned earlier, to the growing influence of the Taliban in the FATA region.

Besides Kurram, the Khyber Agency also witnessed violent clashes in 2007. The conflict here cannot be directly linked to the armed conflict in North and South Waziristan, but it ran parallel to it, with the fighting taking place from 2005. Khyber is perhaps the most important Agency for Pakistan and Afghanistan for strategic reasons. The main road link between Pakistan and Afghanistan (the other road is from Quetta to Kandahar via Chaman) goes via Bara and Landikotal in the Khyber Agency, connecting Peshawar with Kabul. From the Greeks to the British, numerous armies including the Persian, Mughal, Afghan and Sikh crossed what later came to be known as the Durand Line, mainly through the Khyber Pass.

The current round of crisis and violence in the Khyber Agency can be traced to the sectarian clashes between the two sects starting from 2005. Two groups, both adhering to the Sunni faith and led by Mufti Munir Shakir and Pir Saifullah started the violence in 2005. In a single incident in March 2006, more than 20 persones were killed in clashes between these two groups. Through numerous jirgas organized by the local population, the two main leaders of these groups were expelled from the region in 2006. It is surprising that neither Munir nor Saifullah belonged to this Agency. Munir was local, from the Khurram Agency, while Saifullah was an Afghan.

The present violence is an offshoot of this conflict. Two armed groups—Lashkar-e-Islam and Ansar-ul Islam—have been engaged in violent activities. The former is led by Mangal Bagh Afridi who was a part of Mufti Munir's group. Mangal Bagh, after tasting power under Munir in terms of issuing fatwas and imposing fines, does not want to lose his control. The Lashkar-e-Islam has been attempting to impose its own code of Islam. There have been reports linking Lashkar-e-Islam to the stoning and killing of people committing adultery, and issuing fatwas on women who go to markets and public places without blood relatives and who do not offer regular prayers. Those who defied Lashkar-e-Islam's edicts were imprisoned and kept in illegal confinement. Journalists who have been writing on the activities of Lashkar-e-Islam were threatened, illegally detained, and their papers banned. Lashkar-e-Islam has also been running illegal FM radio stations, through which Mangal Bagh is issuing his edicts and fatwas.

Besides, Lashkar-e-Islam is also engaged in a violent conflict with Ansar-ul-Islam, another non-state actor which has gained an element of support among the local population. Both the groups have been attacking the supporters and the properties of the other. Capturing illegal weapons and FM stations, and demolishing houses and shopping complexes belonging to each other have become a regular phenomenon in the Khyber Agency. However, this generally goes unnoticed as the reports from other agencies are more sensational. Lashkar-e-Islam has also been attacking the checkposts of the paramilitary forces, capturing and killing them.

At another level, what is happening in North and South Waziristan had also spilled over to the neighbouring settled districts like Tank and

Dera Ismail Khan. Tank, a town in the North West Frontier Province, exploded during the last week of March 2007 with attacks launched by the Taliban and its supporters in South Waziristan. There was a pitched battle for six to eight hours between the security forces and the Taliban as the latter attempted to take over the town. The local civil administration and police failed to tackle the situation, calling in the army to help. Curfew was imposed and the town was totally sealed with soldiers patrolling the streets and markets, while helicopters were circling to prevent any further attacks by the Taliban and its local supporters. Government figures placed the casualties at 26, mostly belonging to the militants, while the locals believe it could be more.

Tank is situated adjoining the South Waziristan Agency and is a major exit point for the Taliban fighters and the tribes of South Waziristan. The Mahsuds and the Bhittanis are the main inhabitants of this district and Tank is a major town for the Mahsuds living in South Waziristan. Many Mahsuds living in Waziristan now own a house in Tank. Traditionally, they have dominated this town and the region, which has witnessed numerous battles and agreements between them and the British. Events in South Waziristan, especially in the Mahsud dominated areas, are likely to have an influence in Tank and its surrounding areas. The Pakistan government has not understood or has overlooked this historical link between the tribal regions and the settled districts of the NWFP.

The government failed to pay attention to the creeping Talibanization of this district. Perhaps the government believed that once the Taliban controlled the administration in Waziristan, the latter would be satisfied. In fact, one could see a direct link between the agreement that the government signed with Taliban supporters in Waziristan and the growing Taliban influence in the settled districts adjoining Waziristan. The agreement with the local Taliban has only strengthened it; since it has been attempting to influence the administration outside Waziristan, including the areas of Bannu, Darra Adam Khel and Kohat. Attacks on music shops and threats to barbers not to shave customers in the settled areas, at times even in Peshawar, are minor, but are strong indications of the Taliban's efforts to enlarge their influence.

In October 2006, the local community in Tank came out into the streets to protest against this gradual Talibanization and increasing problems of law and order. Ransom demands and taking hostages became a norm, as happened during the British era. Locals belonging to the business community and NGOs were kidnapped; their ransom money ran into millions. Unfortunately, the administration has not been able to cultivate this local support to weaken the Taliban, which has made the latter even bolder in this region.

Clearly, there is a pattern in the Taliban's actions outside the tribal regions. With North and South Waziristan, besides Bajaur, fully under their control, they are expanding their influence into the settled districts of the NWFP, especially Bannu, Tank and DI Khan. The agreements signed between the government and the local Taliban have only helped them to consolidate their position inside the tribal regions. Now they are looking east.

The Conflict Within

While the armed conflict between the state and the militants has been taking place at one level, there is another conflict that goes practically unnoticed or under-noticed at another level. Ever since the armed conflict in FATA got consolidated, especially in North and South Waziristan, the militants have been attempting to impose their writ over the local tribal society; this is referred to as Talibanization of FATA or the establishment of an Islamic Emirate in Waziristan, a process that has witnessed the militants attacking selected locals for being pro-government and US spies.

This process of Talibanization should be seen along with similar issues. *Dawn* commented on this growing crisis within:

> In the town of Khar in Bajaur Agency barber shop offering beard, trims and music shops have been blown up by the 'local' bands of the Taliban; in district Kohats semi-autonomous areas, women school and college teachers have come under increasing threat by similar groups. The Khasadar escorts provided by the government to accompany women teachers to and from their schools and colleges are unable to provide them security, saying that tribal loyalties prevent them from any engagement with the militants in case the teachers are attacked by the latter. Little by little, it seems, more and more territory is coming under the hold of the extremists who are out with a mission to impose a Taliban-style rule in their respective areas.[15]

---

[15] Editorial, 'Spread of Talibanisation', *Dawn*, 6 March 2007.

Besides, 2007 also witnessed an internal power struggle within the militant groups in South Waziristan. This internal conflict broke out during March 2007, when a section of the local Wazir tribesmen turned hostile against the Uzbek fighters under Tahir Yuldashev settled in South Waziristan. Though the government attempted to sell this conflict as being between the local tribes and foreign militants, and ascribe it to the peace agreements signed, the reality was different. This conflict took place between the local tribesmen in South Waziristan against, not all foreigners, but a section of the Uzbeks who fought/fight in Afghanistan along with the al Qaeda and Taliban. Even amongst the tribes, the entire tribal population of South Waziristan did not rise against the Uzbeks. Of the two major tribes in South Waziristan—Wazirs and Mehsuds—a section fought against the Uzbeks and another fought along with them.

Yargul Khel, a sub-clan of the Wazirs, was initially happy with these Uzbek fighters; some of them even settled there along with their families. Their economic condition improved thanks to the cash provided by the Uzbeks, sometimes in dollars. The local population earned a lot through rent for accommodation and providing them with daily provisions. According to a report, during Pakistan's military operations in 2004–05, chicken cost 20 to 30 US dollars. This is why a section of the Wazir tribe supports the presence of Uzbeks in the current fighting vis-à-vis other Wazir tribesmen led by Maulvi Nazir.

What could be the reasons for this internal conflict between a section of the local militants and the Uzbeks in South Waziristan? First, the local tribesmen led by Maulvi Nazir are upset with the Uzbek fighters who increasingly engaged in the targeted killing of Wazir tribal elders. Many locals have been targeted for being either pro-government or American spies. Besides, the Uzbek fighters were also involved in kidnapping, ransom and looting local banks. Hence, the primary reason given is that the deteriorating law and order situation, and the Uzbek involvement in local administration, was not acceptable to Maulvi Nazir, who was appointed as the Amir of South Waziristan by a Taliban Shura that included Siraj Haqqani, son of Jalaludin Haqqani, a veteran mujahideen, and an important leader of the Taliban and also Baituallah Mahsud. Maulvi Nazir wants to impose his writ and make it clear that he is the ruler in the area.

One reason for the sudden hostility was the killing of an Arab fighter belonging to the al Qaeda, allegedly by the Uzbeks. Nazir was furious at this and vowed to remove the Uzbeks from the region. This hints at a divide between the al Qaeda and Taliban vis-à-vis

Yuldashev's IMU. There have also been rumours that Yuldashev has been bribed by foreign elements so his troops are no longer fighting in Afghanistan. This divide between Yuldashev and al Qaeda is a larger question that needs to be further investigated as the current fighting may well be a fallout of this new development.

Whatever may have been the reason, at the end of almost a month-long fight, more than 200 militants have been killed, mostly belonging to Yuldashev's IMU.

Suicide Terrorism

Suicide terrorism in the FATA region increased alarmingly in 2007 as compared to previous years. At a broader level, suicide terrorism in FATA should be viewed through the prespective of what is happening at the national level. Ever since 9/11 and the US-led operations in Afghanistan, suicide terrorism in Pakistan has been on the rise.

The following trends can be identified in suicide terrorism in Pakistan, especially the FATA region. First, there is a direct correlation between the US-led action in Afghanistan and suicide terrorism. Until 9/11, there were no suicide attacks inside Pakistan—either in FATA or the NWFP or elsewhere. Available data clearly proves that suicide terrorism in Pakistan is a post-9/11 phenomenon.

Suicide Terrorism in Pakistan

Year	Outside FATA & NWFP	FATA & NWFP
2002	01	–
2003	02	–
2004	06	01
2005	04	–
2006	02	05
2007 (up to Aug)	06	11

Source: Based on news reports.

Second, in FATA and the NWFP, suicide attacks only began in 2004 after the armed conflict became entrenched in Waziristan. While there were no suicide attacks in 2005 in this region, there were five in 2006 and 11 during the first eight months of 2007.

Third, most of the suicide attacks in FATA and the NWFP have been anti-state, with Pakistan's security forces being targeted outside Pakistan. Until 2007, sectarian causes were motivating suicide attacks. In FATA and the settled districts of the NWFP, it has been primarily anti-state.

CONFLICT MANAGEMENT

Pakistan's efforts to manage the conflict in the FATA region has centred around three strategies. First, a military response, in which one witnesses the use of heavy weapons and even air power. Second, Pakistan has attempted to manage the conflict through a series of peace agreements. Third, Pakistan has also made an attempt to fence the Durand Line.

The Military Response

According to news reports, Islamabad has deployed between 80,000 and 90,000 military and paramilitary forces. However, Pakistan's military response to the armed conflict in FATA has not been uniform. The military action could be broadly classified under three categories. First, there have been periods in which the security forces, though deployed all over the FATA region, remained passive, allowing the movement of local militants. This strategy was linked to the ongoing negotiations between the local militants and the government.

Second, the security forces also undertook a series of military actions against the militants. These military actions were mostly against the foreign militants like the Uzbeks and al Qaeda, and did not primarily target the local militants. These select military actions were either a response to militant attacks, or foment to pressurize the militants to negotiate with the state.

Whenever the state engaged the militants, it used severe means in terms of weapons and strategies. While suicide bombing has been the tactical weapon of the militants in the armed conflict against the state, the latter has been using high-tech weapons, especially laser-guided missiles. For example, in January 2007, South Waziristan witnessed laser-guided missiles being fired from fighter aircraft, piercing rooftops and going at least four feet into the ground.[16]

Third, Pakistan's security forces have also been working selectively with the US-led forces in Afghanistan to prevent cross-border infiltration and also to carry out attacks on the millitants. Though the US has been unhappy with Pakistan's response so far, it has failed to pressurize the latter to carry out an all-out military offensive against the militants or effectively seal the Durand Line.

---

[16] 'Army fired laser-guided missiles in Waziristan', *Daily Times*, 20 January 2007.

Peace Agreements

Pakistan has signed three major agreements with the militants in FATA since 2004. The first agreement, with the Wazir militants in South Waziristan led by Nek Mohammad in April 2004, was actually an 'understanding' as there was no formal signing of any terms and conditions. In this understanding, the government pardoned the five most wanted militants, including Nek Mohammad, the local militant leader, who was also a supporter of the Taliban and al Qaeda. In return, Nek Mohammad agreed that the local tribal militants would 'live peacefully and not use Pakistani soil against any other country'. However, this agreement failed almost immediately and resulted in the killing of Nek Mohammad.

The second agreement was signed between the government and the Mahsuds in February 2005. Initially this agreement was a success for Pakistan's security forces, as the militant–military engagements during 2005 drastically reduced. Suicide attacks in this region, which started in 2004, did not occur in 2005.

The third agreement was signed in Miranshah in September 2006, thanks to the efforts of Lt Gen. Orakzai, Governor of the NWFP. A grand jirga comprising 45 members from all major tribes in FATA initiated the process of reconciliation with the militants. These two agreements were in effect until recently; after the government's action against the Lal Masjid in Islambad, the militants in Waziristan repudiated them and have since initiated a series of attacks all over the FATA region and the NWFP .

Fencing and Mining the Durand

Besides the peace agreements, Pakistan has also attempted to fence the Durand Line as part of its strategy for managing the conflict and cross-border movement. Pakistan has been criticized for not doing enough to control cross-border infiltration. In response, Pakistan has repeatedly emphasized that it would fence the Pak–Afghan border.[17]

However, fencing and mining is unlikely to yield the desired results. First, the economic cost of fencing and the technical problems involved will make this project unviable. Second, fencing will actually

---

[17] 'Border mining, fencing to go ahead: Aziz', *Dawn*, 4 January 2007; 'Border fencing decision final, says Pakistan', *The Nation*, 6 January 2007.

increase Pashtun hostility towards Islamabad. The Pashtuns, who have been living across the Durand Line in Afghanistan and Pakistan, have never considered it to be legitimate; hence this border was respected only in its breach. At the political level, Kabul has never recognized the Durand Line. Commenting on this issue, Hamid Karzai said, 'Our people are convinced that mining or fencing of borders will only divide their families living across the borders and will in no way prevent terrorism or end the root cause of terrorism which needs to be addressed through other measures.'[18]

Third, many inside Pakistan's strategic decision-making process will be averse to fencing the border as they still believe in Pakistan's strategic depth. Since the 1980s, a section amongst Pakistan's military and its Inter-Services Intelligence (ISI) has been heavily engaged in subsequent Afghan conflicts. This section, which has played an important role from supporting anti-Soviet mujahideen groups to creating the Taliban, does not support the fencing idea for it would defeat the very concept of strategic depth.

Fencing and mining thus seems to be part of political rhetoric used by Islamabad in response to the 'do more' campaign launched by Kabul and the US-led forces in Afghanistan.[19] Outside the government and amongst the academic and strategic circles in Pakistan, there is little support for fencing and mining the Durand Line.[20]

CONCLUSIONS

The armed conflict in the FATA region is likely to continue for the following reasons. First, the local population supports the militants and is against the state. The main question they ask is: how have they become terrorists today when they were mujahids till yesterday? The fight against the militants is perceived in the tribal areas as a US conspiracy designed against the Pashtuns vis-à-vis the Northern Alliance. Pakistan and General Musharraf, in particular, are seen as having backtracked from the promises of Jinnah and the duties of Islam. This 'us' vs 'them' feeling is likely to continue and the militants will most likely be the main beneficiaries of this situation.

[18] 'Barbs fly at Kabul meet', *Dawn*, 5 January 2007.

[19] See 'Barbs fly at Kabul meet', *Dawn*, 5 January 2007; 'Pak-Afghan border fencing: no decision yet', *Daily Times*, 13 January 2007; 'Pakistan must address Taliban sanctuary: US', *Daily Times*, 19 January 2007.

[20] See Tayyab Siddiqui, 'Time to restructure Afghan policy', *Dawn*, 5 January 2007.

Second, anti-US feelings are likely to increase. It is unfortunate that the 'War against Terrorism' has turned the local Pashtun population against the US. During the 1980s, when the US was supporting the mujahideen against the Soviet Union, there was unanimous support for them in the tribal areas. However, this started changing slowly after the 1990s. The two Gulf Wars, continuous propaganda by the religious parties led by the MMA Muttalida Majlis-e-Amal, and the war on terrorism against the Taliban and Osama bin Laden has lost the US local support. This is likely to continue and play a crucial role in destabilizing Afghanistan, affecting the US-led war against terrorism. The tribal belt, especially Waziristan, will continue to remain a safe haven for the al Qaeda–Taliban forces.

Third, Pakistan is unlikely to wage a full-fledged war against terrorism inside FATA; the armed conflict will therefore continue to simmer. A full-fledged war is likely to erode the state's writ and wipe out any support for Pakistan. Clearly, it would not be in Pakistan's interests. For these reasons, the state would even allow an element of radicalization of the tribal belt. The fact that an anti-Pakistan feeling has always existed and that a full-fledged war against the local population would highlight the Pashtun factor against Pakistan will play an important role in any anti-militancy drive. Pakistan would prefer to contain Pashtun nationalism and have a radical tribal area under its control.

Fourth, for the reasons already mentioned, coupled with the ongoing drive by religious forces led by the Taliban, the tribal areas would get Talibanized. There have been reports that the Shariah has been imposed in many areas of Waziristan, for instance in the Taliban areas of Afghanistan. Tribal customs are being underplayed, and mullahs are attempting to take over the tribal jirgas in FATA. It is all the more important to make changes in the Frontier Crime Regulations (FCR), 1901, FCR as there is already a movement demanding its replacement by the Shariah. When this proposition was put forward, a series of meetings were held in August and September in 2005 various parts of FATA between the members of the FCR Reforms Committee and tribal elders, religious leaders, intellectuals, social workers and NGOs.[21] The local population reportedly felt that if political activities were allowed in the tribal areas, it would lead to

---

[21] 'Tribesmen demand Shariat rather than FCR', *The News*, 27 August 2005.

civil war and anarchy.[22] According to a media report, 'Music and TV have been banned. Women are confined to their homes. Shops must close five times a day for prayers, an edict enforced by armed religious police who patrol the streets.'[23] Clearly, the tribal regions are speedily getting Talibanized.

Fifth, foreign militants are likely to stay on in these tribal areas. They come from various parts of the world, mainly from Uzbekistan, Algeria, Chechenya and Libya. Among the foreign militants there are many Arabs who had come during the 1980s and have married local women. There is a significant Arab–Afghan population now and they are seen as respectable guests by the local population. The state would never succeed in having them registered; there have been discussions about providing them safe passage, which may not be accepted by the militants in Waziristan. There is widespread respect for the foreigners, a section of whom have married into the local population. Besides, the tribal code of honouring and protecting their guests has always played an important role, which is likely to continue.

To conclude, there is an immediate need to undertake FATA reforms, which has been relegated to the back burner. The FATA region is governed by the FCR, which makes the political agent all powerful, enjoying administrative, executive and judicial powers. There were reports of the government working on a strategy to assimilate the FATA areas into the mainstream by converting them into settled areas, but no progress has been made so far.[24] According to Robert Warburton, born to a British Lieutenant, who fought in the First Afghan War and married the niece of Amir Dost Mohammad, the '[malik] robs his tribesmen, gets rich himself, intrigues against the government, and brings on grave difficulties. Giving a malik power means giving him wealth to injure us...the middleman, therefore...has caused the greatest amount of misery on the Punjab Frontier for the past thirty five years.' (*Eighteen Years in the Khyber*: 1879–1898. 1900. London: John Murray.) This statement made in 1900 holds good even today and this alone speaks volumes for the urgent need for reforms.

Second, Pakistan needs better border management, along with Afghanistan, over the Durand Line, especially in FATA. There are an estimated 80,000 military and paramilitary troops deployed along the

---

[22] 'Bajaur elders reject FCR changes, want Sharia instead', *Daily Times*, 21 September 2005.

[23] 'Militants rule the roost in Waziristan: report', *Daily Times*, 13 December 2005.

[24] 'Plan to revoke FATA status', *The Frontier Post*, 5 January 2005.

Durand Line. However, it has always remained unrecognized, making it convenient for the governments in Kabul and in Islamabad to manipulate each other. The last three decades have made the Durand Line irrelevant and erased it from the minds of the local Pashtun population. A comprehensive border management policy that looks for greater political and psychological acceptance is essential, instead of nationalistic statements regarding fencing the border. Also, the border needs to be better manned; as of now there are around 60,000 to 70,000 troops. If necessary, Pakistan should be able to shift troops from its eastern to its western borders. Pakistan's internal situation is grave and demands such measures.

Third, there is an important need to initiate a serious de-weaponization drive. A Pashtun would never part with either his beard or his weapon; but should SAM (surface-to-air-missile) and rockets be permitted to be part of his equipment? The government has never been serious about its de-weaponization drive. This was clear during the two agreements—Shakai and Sararogha.

Fourth, the state should improve its governance record in FATA. Tribal opposition to effective central governance has been used as an excuse to avoid pursuing any reforms. Unless the FATA region is effectively governed and the political parties allowed to function, the entire tribal belt is likely to witness growing armed conflict.

5

J&K: From Militancy to Jihad?

Kavita Suri & D. Suba Chandran

A BRIEF HISTORY[1]

A distinction needs to be made between the 'conflict of' and the 'conflict in' Jammu and Kashmir (J&K). Ever since the 1920s, conflict in Kashmir has occurred at different levels; the nature and actors varying continuously. The perceived oppressive rule of the Maharaja is the primary reason for the 'conflict in' Kashmir. The local population felt alienated and voiceless. At this juncture, the All Jammu and Kashmir Muslim Conference, one of the first political parties in J&K enjoying mass support, was founded by Sheikh Abdullah in 1932. The two decades immediately preceding Partition in 1947 witnessed a movement against the rule of Maharaja Hari Singh. This movement primarily aimed at better governance by the ruler and better representation of the ruled.[2] Led by Sheikh Abdullah, this movement was peaceful and non-violent.

Later, Sheikh Abdullah changed the name of his party to All Jammu and Kashmir National Conference (NC). After him, the NC was headed by Farooq Abdullah, Sheikh Abdullah's son, and now by Omar Abdullah, his grandson. The NC was fighting for a representative government in J&K in the 1930s and early 1940s. After Independence and the accession of J&K to India, the 'conflict in' Kashmir continued

---

[1] This section on the brief history of armed conflict in Jammu and Kashmir is primarily drawn from D. Suba Chandran, 'J&K: Infiltration Declines Violence Persists', in D. Suba Chandran, ed., *Armed Conflicts and Peace Processes in South Asia*, New Delhi: Samskriti, 2007, pp. 30–66.

[2] For the early political history of J&K before 1947, see Prem Nath Bazaz, *The History of Struggle for Freedom in Kashmir*, Srinagar: Gulshan Publishers, 2003; Prem Nath Bazaz, *Inside Kashmir*, Srinagar: Gulshan Publishers, 2002.

at various levels and with differing intensity against the union government, demanding better governance and power-sharing between the union and the state.³

The 'conflict of' Kashmir began in 1947 between India and Pakistan, following the Partition of British India. In the pre-Independence period, Jawaharlal Nehru and the Indian National Congress came closer to Sheikh Abdullah due to his ideology, secularism and political outlook. At this time, Mohammad Ali Jinnah was campaigning for Pakistan and developed close ties with the Muslim Conference in J&K. Kashmir became significant for Jinnah and the Pakistan movement; its 'Muslim' character enabled Pakistan to put forward its claim to Muslim-Majority Kashmir. Pakistan, to date, refuses to accept the accession of Kashmir to India, considering it to be a fraud.

In 1947, J&K was one of the 550 princely states and was ruled by a Hindu King, Maharaja Hari Singh, a descendant of Maharaja Gulab Singh. The contemporary history of J&K can be traced to the Treaty of Amritsar, signed between the British Government and Maharaja Gulab Singh in 1846. According to Article I of the Treaty, 'The British Government transfers and makes over forever in independent possession to Maharaja Gulab Singh and the male heirs of his body, all the hilly or mountainous country, with its dependencies, situated to the eastward of the River Indus and the westward of River Ravi, including Chamba and excluding Lahul, being part of the territories ceded to the British Government by the Lahore State, according to the provisions of Article IV of the treaty of Lahore, dated 9 March 1846.'⁴

At the time of granting Independence, the 'conflict in' Kashmir was subsumed by the 'conflict of' Kashmir. On the eve of Independence, the Prime Minister of Kashmir sent identical telegrams, on 12 August 1947, to the governments of India and Pakistani suggesting a Standstill Agreement. According to him, 'the existing arrangements should continue pending settlement of details'.⁵ Pakistan became proactive and started taking forcible steps to secure Kashmir's accession.

---

³ For the initial problems between the Union government of India and the J&K government during the 1950s and 60s see Prem Nath Bazaz, *Kashmir in Crucible*, Srinagar: Gulshan Publishers, 2005.

⁴ See the Treaty of Amritsar, 1846, signed between the British Government and Maharaja Gulab Singh.

⁵ See 'Standstill Agreement with India and Pakistan', in Verinder Grover, ed., *The Story of Kashmir: Yesterday and Today*, vol. III, New Delhi: Deep and Deep Publications, 1995, p.106.

Pakistan sent both Pashtun tribesmen and its own troops to capture J&K by force. After the joint forces occupied Muzafarabad on 22 October 1947,[6] Maharaja Hari Singh appealed to Lord Mountbatten, Governor General of Independent India, for help. Following the Defence Committee of India's decision that Indian troops could only be sent after Hari Singh acceded to India, the latter sent a letter to Lord Mountbatten,[7] who, while accepting his request, added a caveat that the accession should be ratified by the people of Kashmir.[8] On 25 October 1947, Maharaja Hari Singh signed the Instrument of Accession, which was accepted by Lord Mountbatten on 27 October 1947. Subsequently, Indian paratroopers were dispatched to Srinagar.

In November 1947, full-fledged fighting broke out between the Indian and Pakistani troops, which continued till December, with one-third of the territory remaining under Pakistan's control. On 20 December 1947, the Indian Cabinet decided to refer the case to the UN Security Council and lodged a complaint on 1 January 1948. Following this complaint, the UN Security Council adopted a resolution on 13 August 1948. It had three parts: the first called for a ceasefire between India and Pakistan; second, withdrawal of Pakistani troops from the disputed area; and, third, withdrawal of troops by India, except for a minimum force needed to maintain law and order; while the future of Kashmir would be decided 'in accordance with the will of the people.' Except for the first part of the resolution, there has been no progress on its other provisions, despite a series of successive resolutions passed by the UN. Since then, the 'conflict of' Kashmir has continued between India and Pakistan and has witnessed conflicts in 1965, 1971 and 1999.

The 'conflict in' Kashmir started gaining momentum in the early 1980s. Several issues, including the problems of governance, narrow political interests of the union and state governments—especially the Congress and NC—social, political and communal mobilization of Kashmiri society, converged in the late 1980s. What lit the spark was the 1987 election, widely perceived as the most unfair in Kashmir's history. The popular disaffection in the Kashmir Valley was exploited

---

[6] Lars Blikenberg, *India-Pakistan: The History of Unsolved Conflict*, vol. I, Odense: Odense University Press, 1998, p. 76.

[7] Verinder Grover, ed., *The Story of Kashmir: Yesterday and Today*, vol. III (New Delhi: Deep and Deep Publications, 1995, p. 108.

[8] Ibid.

by Pakistan to initiate an armed conflict. Thus, after the 1987 elections, the 'conflict of' Kashmir merged with the 'conflict in' Kashmir, leading to an armed conflict.

The armed conflict in Kashmir, however, was not monolithic. Initially led by the Jammu and Kashmir Liberation Front (JKLF), there was a rapid change in the principal actors and their objectives. The JKLF, led by Yasin Malik and Javid Mir, fought for an independent, but secular, Kashmir. Hedging of Kashmir with Pakistan was never its objective. As a result, the JKLF fell out of grace with its supporters across the border. The JKLF is divided into two major factions: one led by Yasin Malik in J&K (on Indian soil) and the other led by Amanullah Khan in Pakistan-occupied Kashmir (PoK). Amanullah's JKLF, even today, refuses to take part in the PoK elections and demands Kashmir's independence.

The second phase of the armed conflict in the early 1990s was overtaken by the Hizbul Mujahideen, the JKLF being the main casualty. During this period, realizing Pakistan's objectives in Kashmir, the JKLF began distancing itself. Throughout this period, Pakistan sent many former Afghan mujahideen to fight in J&K. The mid-1990s saw the Hizbul Mujahideen and the Afghan mujahideen waging an intense war against the security forces. This phase also witnessed the militants, mainly Afghans, abusing the local Kashmiris, especially the Kashmiri women. This generated dissatisfaction among the local population with the militancy, the first positive turn since it began in the late 1980s.

In 1996, the situation improved considerably and elections were held for the first time in a decade. The NC formed the government in J&K; however, neither the union nor the state government seemed to have learnt any lesson. Both governments failed to take advantage of the situation on the security and administrative fronts. Two processes, initiated by Pakistan during this period, transformed the nature of armed conflict in J&K. First, Pakistan allowed the Lashkar-e-Toiba (LeT), with its puritanical beliefs, to take over the militancy. Since then, the armed conflict has acquired a fundamentalist and jihadi streak, with the Hizbul Mujahideen playing a secondary role. Second, it initiated the war in Kargil, partly with the objective of reviving militancy in J&K. This provided a new impetus to the armed conflict, which subsequently saw a series of fidayeen attacks.

The military standoff in 2001–02 and the elections for the legislative assembly in 2002 introduced a new realism. While Pakistan was pressurized by both India and the international community to rein in its support for militancy, the Indo-Pak peace process, which began in October 2003, has contributed to the present thaw in the armed conflict. Much would depend on the success of the bilateral peace process and Pakistan's ability to exercise control over jihadi groups like the Lashkar-e-Toiba and Jaish-e-Muhammad (JeM).

THE PRINCIPAL ACTORS[9]

The principal actors in the armed conflict of J&K include both state actors—India and Pakistan—and the armed non-state actors (NSAs).

State Actors

India

The union government is the principal actor in the conflict 'within' Kashmir and 'of' Kashmir. Since 1947, it has pursued multiple political and military policies. At present, it is pursuing a bilateral political process to resolve all its issues with Pakistan, including the conflict of Kashmir. Internally, it has been pursuing political, economic and military approaches to resolve the conflict in Kashmir.

The policies of the union government have been criticized for being ad hoc and incoherent. Ever since the outbreak of violence in the late 1980s, the union government's major emphasis has been on organizing elections to the J&K state legislature and the union Parliament, supporting the state government, and engaging various political organizations and groups in a dialogue. This political approach, however, has not been consistent; being conditioned by the parties that have formed the government in New Delhi and Srinagar, the union government is generally criticized for allocating more funds to J&K without proper scrutiny.

On the security front, the union government has deployed military and paramilitary forces since the outbreak of violence in J&K.

---

[9] This section on the principal actors in the armed conflict in Jammu and Kashmir is primarily drawn from the previous edition. See D. Suba Chandran, 'J&K: Infiltration Declines, Violence Persists', in D. Suba Chandran, ed., *Armed Conflicts and Peace Processes in South Asia,* New Delhi: Samskriti, 2007, pp. 30–66.

Until recently, the counter-militancy operations were mainly led by these organizations, with the local J&K police providing only marginal support. Three groups need particular mention when evaluating the counter-militancy operations—the Rashtriya Rifles (RR), the Border Security Force (BSF) and the Central Reserve Police Force (CRPF). While the RR was created within the Indian army as a special counter-intelligence force and functions under the union Defence Ministry, the BSF and CRPF are paramilitary police forces functioning under the union Home Ministry. An increasing role is being assigned to the local police.

The main objectives of the union government are to prevent cross-border terrorism and militancy in J&K, reach a permanent settlement with Pakistan on the Line of Control (LoC), and ensure the smooth functioning of the state government. Power-sharing between the state and union governments and the quantum of autonomy to be devolved are major issues for decision at the governmental level.

Pakistan

Pakistan is the second principal actor, both in the conflict 'of' and the conflict 'in' Kashmir. At the bilateral level, Pakistan has attempted to keep the conflict alive both politically and militarily. All the India–Pakistan conflicts (1947–48, 1965, 1971 and 1999) were initiated by Pakistan to achieve its objectives militarily. The 1971 war could be considered an exception to this rule, as it started primarily in Bangladesh, then East Pakistan. Politically, it has attempted to internationalize the Kashmir issue by bringing it up at all major international fora, and inviting external actors to intervene. Pakistan has also been party to many failed bilateral dialogues with India. At present, it is again engaged in a political discourse with India.

Cross-border terrorism, as a covert policy in J&K, emerged in the late 1980s, following Pakistan's involvement in the Punjab militancy. Until then, Pakistan had only provided political support to the separatists. Pakistan's successes in Punjab, and in the Afghan jihad against the Soviet forces, played an important role in its adoption of proxy war as its main strategy in J&K. The fact that the Indian government had failed on the political and administrative fronts in J&K caused immense disaffection and alienation among the Kashmiris against New Delhi, which helped Pakistan to sustain its proxy war.

Cross-border terrorism has now become the cornerstone of Pakistan's policy in Kashmir.

Pakistan's main objective in J&K is to use Kashmir as a means to bleed India; to force India to give up its claims, especially to the Kashmir Valley, and also to annex J&K. There have been slow changes in these objectives. Today, Pakistan's primary objective is not to annex J&K, but to annex PoK permanently, and loosen India's control over the Kashmir Valley.

The Jammu & Kashmir Government

The state government is the third principal actor in the conflict. The successive state governments—ruled by the NC, People's Democratic Party (PDP) and now the Congress—have all been accused of misgovernance, corruption and lack of accountability. Two major policies pursued by successive governments in recent years have been the demand for autonomy and the 'healing touch'. Autonomy for J&K has been the main slogan of the NC, led by Farooq Abdullah, and now by his son, Omar Abdullah. In 2000, the government led by the NC passed a resolution in the J&K legislative assembly demanding autonomy. The union government, then led by the Bharatiya Janata Party (BJP), rejected the resolution without even discussing it. 'Healing touch' was the major political and social approach pursued by the PDP government, led by Mufti Mohammad Sayeed, from 2002 to 2005. It sought to provide good and humane governance.

Ever since the outbreak of militancy, the state government has strengthened its police force, which now plays a significant role in countering militancy. The state police has a special counter-militancy unit—the Special Operations Group (SOG).

Non-State Actors (NSAs)

The armed NSAs are not homogeneous and are divided into various groups based on their objectives, orientation, beliefs and support—both internal and external. Broadly, these armed NSAs could be classified into militants, jihadis and surrendered militants. The Hizbul Mujahideen is the principal militant organization, while Lashkar-e-Toiba and Jaish-e-Muhammad are the principal jihadi groups. The surrendered militants are scattered and are not united under any one particular group.

The Militants: Hizbul Mujahideen

Hizbul Mujahideen, the primary militant group, fights for political objectives and its focus is limited to J&K. Widely perceived as an indigenous organization, the Hizbul is mostly comprised of and led by ethnic Kashmiris. The LeT and JeM, on the contrary, are led by Pakistanis, and their top leadership hails from Pakistan.

Differences exist among scholars on the main objective of the Hizbul—some argue that it fights for an independent Kashmir, whereas others believe that it wants to annex J&K to Pakistan. However, the political nature of Hizbul's objectives is proven beyond doubt; hence it is classified as a militant and not as a jihadi group. Moreover, Hizbul's objective is limited to J&K and it does not seek the destruction of 'Hindu India', openly sought by some other jihadi organizations. Until now, Hizbul's operations were limited to J&K and there has been no single militant act outside the state. On the contrary, the Lashkar is known for its attacks outside J&K.

Finally, the Hizbul, at least a section of it, has shown a willingness to pursue a political path to resolve the conflict. In July 2000, the Hizbul announced a unilateral ceasefire and entered into a dialogue with the union government. Abdul Majid Dar, who was later killed in an internal power struggle within the Hizbul, stated that it would cooperate in a peace process with the Indian government;[10] he was also quoted as saying, 'Our [Hizbul's] activities will lessen in proportion to both countries [India and Pakistan] giving up their rigid stand to solve the Kashmir problem in a realistic approach.'[11] Saiful Islam, who replaced Majid Dar, also stated, 'The Hizb had never closed the doors for a dialogue. If the road to peace opened and talks started the outfit would seriously discuss its role.'[12]

The Jihadis: Lashkar-e-Toiba and Jaish-e-Muhammad

The LeT and JeM are two important jihadi groups fighting for pan-Islamic objectives. For them, Kashmir is a means to achieve their broader objective of establishing their version of Islam, both in the subcontinent and outside it. Mohammad Hafiz Saeed, the *amir* of

---

[10] 'Hizb will cooperate in peace initiative', *The Hindu*, 25 May 2001.
[11] 'Hizb to halt hostilities if India, Pak act realistic', *The Asian Age*, 4 June 2001.
[12] 'Hizb rules out role for foreign militants', *The Hindu*, 21 November 2001.

the Lashkar, stated in an interview, 'There is only one jihad and that is jihad for Allah. All other forms of jihad are also for Allah. Jihad is only for Allah...'.[13] They fight against the Indian security forces and also against those Kashmiris who do not agree with their religious views. A poster of the Al Badr, one of the jihadi groups, claimed, 'We have left our country to fight for your freedom. But still you people feel no sense of gratitude. We urge you to stop helping the Kafirs [unbelievers]. After this, no one who does so will be spared. He who helps a Kafir is also a Kafir. If you still do not pay heed, Allah has given his soldiers enough strength to finish you as well as the Kafirs.'[14]

These jihadi groups and their subsidiaries in the Kashmir Valley also seek to impose their version of Islam. For example, the Lashkar-e-Jabbar, believed to be a Lashkar-e-Toiba subsidiary, had threatened to attack women for not wearing the *burqa*[15] and wanted segregation of the sexes in public transportation.[16] These groups are behind the attacks on the minority communities in J&K.

The Ikhwans: Counter/Surrendered Militants

The third group of armed NSAs are the counter-militants; they are former militants who have now surrendered. The surrendered militants also do not form a monolithic group; most of them are working for the state government, both directly and indirectly. Some of them have been absorbed by the state government, as either Special Police Officers (SPOs) or as part of the SOG. Unfortunately, the counter-militants have neither been assimilated into the state machinery nor rehabilitated to lead a normal life. There have been numerous allegations against them relating to extortion and human rights violations.

The counter-militants are one of the principal targets of the militant and jihadi groups in J&K and most of their top leadership, including Kukka Parray and Javed Shah, have been eliminated by the Lashkar and Hizbul.

---

[13] See 'In defence of jehad', *Frontline,* 9 May 2003, p. 43.

[14] Quoted in Praveen Swami, 'Cloaks and daggers', *Frontline,* 17 January 2003, p. 22.

[15] 'Burqas make a comeback at gun point', *The Indian Express,* 18 August 2001; 'Is Jabbar a front for Lashkar?' *Hindustan Times,* 4 September 2001.

[16] '*Burqa* order is followed by one on buses', *The Times of India,* 6 September 2001.

CONFLICT IN 2007

An Overview

The year 2007 started with anti-US protests in Srinagar led by Syed Ali Geelani, the hardline separatist leader, against the killing of Saddam Hussain. Though this protest cannot be considered a part of the armed conflict in J&K, such protests are led by the over-ground workers of various militant and separatist groups. The organized growth of over-ground workers and their selective promotion of issues, vitiates the atmosphere in the Valley, indirectly providing the base for direct and indirect support to militancy. Slogans in this protest later turned anti-Indian and pro-Azadi.[17] During the same month, Mirwaiz Farooq, leader of the moderate section of the Hurriyat, was quoted as saying that militancy has only resulted in producing more graveyards during his visit to Pakistan.[18]

During January–April, the working groups appointed by the union government to address various issues related to J&K held discussions and submitted their reports. The union government also held the third Round Table Conference on J&K. In March 2007, India and Pakistan held their fourth composite dialogue on designated issues, including Jammu and Kashmir. The Foreign Secretaries of both countries also discussed this issue, but failed to reach any significant agreement.

In July 2007, Prime Minister Manmohan Singh visited J&K and made an important statement related to making borders irrelevant, a concept that he has been advocating for some years as a way forward to resolve the conflict. He observed that the LoC should be converted into a Line of Peace and announced that borders cannot be changed, but they can be made irrelevant with a freer flow of ideas, goods, services and people.

Decline in Armed Conflict

In statistical terms, armed conflict in Jammu and Kashmir came down in 2007. According to the Ministry of Home Affairs, there were 2,565

---

[17] 'Massive anti-US demonstrations held after Eid prayers', *Daily Excelsior*, 2 January 2007; 'Anti-US protests rock Valley', *Greater Kashmir*, 4 January 2007.

[18] 'Militancy has not achieved anything in Kashmir: Mirwaiz', *Daily Excelsior*, 20 January 2007.

terrorist-related violent incidents in 2004, which came down to 1,990 in 2005 and 1,667 in 2006. In terms of percentage, during 2006 the number of terrorist-related incidents came down by 16 per cent com-pared to 2005. While the number of civilians killed reduced by 30 per cent, the number of security forces killed in 2006 also reduced by 20 per cent.

Within J&K, armed conflict in some regions has died down, for example in Rajouri and Poonch, while it is declining fast in Doda, Bhaderwah and Kishtwar regions.[19] The main factors generally considered to be responsible for the reduction in militancy in recent years are: ceasefire along the LoC, border fencing, and a better counter-insurgency strategy.[20] Will this decline continue? Much will depend on how long the ceasefire holds along the LoC and what Pakistan's future strategy will be vis-à-vis Kashmir. If the ceasefire breaks down and Pakistan decides to provide assistance to militancy, the armed conflict in J&K may intensify again.

Two other factors should be taken into account while discussing the decline of armed conflict in J&K. It has undoubtedly come down, but has not completely halted. Cross-border infiltration continues, though there have been contradictory reports and statements. According to General Panag, General-Officer Commanding-in Chief (GoC-in-C), Northern Command, Udhampur, 323 militants have so far been eliminated in 2007, while the number for 2006 was 425. Until the end of August 2007, 278 militants had infiltrated.[21]

Second, making optimum use of the ceasefire along the LoC, Pakistan has also constructed bunkers and strengthened its defence positions. In Jammu division alone, in the three sub-sectors of Akhnoor, Ranbir Singh Pura and Samba, Pakistan has raised over 3,000 metres of earthwork defences in Akhnoor, over 1,000 metres in RS Pura and over 700 metres in Samba. Besides, Pakistan has also constructed concrete bunkers and observation post towers (OPTs) all along the LoC during this period.

Declining Popular Support to Armed Conflict

Active local support to armed conflict has also declined. There is a visible change all over J&K; at the ground level, the local population

---

[19] Interactions with military, paramilitary and police officials in these two regions.

[20] Interactions with military, paramilitary and police officials in J&K.

[21] Interview with Lieutenant General H.S. Panang, GoC-in-C, Northern Command, Udhampur.

does not support violence and prefers a political settlement. A definite change in mindsets, though not uniform in its intensity all over J&K, is prevalent. For example, in Rajouri, Poonch and Doda regions, there is no support to the militant movement, either covert or overt; in Kashmir Valley, however, there is an element of support. Declining support for violence has also forced many militants to surrender and return to a normal life. Especially in the above-mentioned regions, declining popular support has played a crucial role in persuading the militants to surrender.[22] This declining support could also be seen in the local reaction to the killings of militants. In the past, when a terrorist was killed people would take to the streets to protest against the security forces. Today, in regions like Doda, they hand out sweets in celebration, and women spit on their bodies.[23]

Declining Local Recruitment

A significant trend in recent years, which reflected during 2007, has been the decline in recruitment of local youth by militant groups. This phenomenon could be noticed all over J&K, irrespective of the different regions. While there are no concrete numbers to prove this contention, personal interactions with security forces, surrendered militants and the local population substantiate this trend. The security forces and the intelligence community informally confirm this trend, which is corroborated by intercepted messages which call for frantic replacements from across the border, and their frustration in not being able to recruit more cadres. The surrendered militants also agree that the failure to recruit more locals has affected their operations, forcing them to either surrender or get killed. The local population, especially women—mothers, sisters, wives, girlfriends and daughters—play an important role in forcing the locals not to join the militant movement.

Militant groups are therefore finding it difficult to get fresh recruits. Youth in almost all the major districts of Jammu and Kashmir are not joining the militant groups voluntarily, as was the case in the initial years of militancy. The militant groups have either to coerce them or threaten their families with dire consequences if they refuse to allow

[22] Interactions with surrendered militants in Poonch and Doda regions.

[23] In a striking example, villagers in Gundoh in Thathri district distributed sweets when Atta Mohammed, a *tehsil* commander of Harkat-ul-Mujahideen, was killed by security forces in Doda. See Kavita Suri, 'Kashmir terrorist deaths come as a relief now', *The Statesman*, 7 June 2007.

their boys to go with them.[24] Since recruitment by militant groups has dropped drastically, exfiltration has also declined. Today, according to the security forces, there is hardly any movement of militants into Pakistan-occupied Kashmir for training. However, as mentioned earlier, infiltration continues. Foreign militants, mainly Pakistanis, still operate in north Kashmir, while the Hizbul Mujahideen remains the dominant force in Kashmir Valley.

Another interesting issue relating to exfiltration in recent months requires to be noted, though it is not clear whether this can be considered a new trend. There have been instances of youth, especially in rural Kashmir, crossing the LoC, spending time there, taking up guns and returning to Kashmir only to surrender. The reasons are purely economic, as surrendered militants are provided a package as part of the government's rehabilitation policy. It includes one lakh rupees and sometimes a job. In 2006–07, there were seven such cases in Kupwara alone, which is situated close to the Line of Control in Kashmir Valley; eight to nine boys here had crossed over to PoK only to come back and surrender.[25]

Fidayeen Attacks Down, Grenades Up

While the fidayeen attacks had gained notoriety after the Kargil War and reached a peak during 2001–05, there was a visible decline in such attacks during 2006–07. Three reasons could be attributed for this decline in fidayeen attacks.

First, most of the fidayeens have come across the border, mainly from Punjab. With a sectarian and jihadi conflict raging all over Pakistan, it is possible that the suicide bombers have diverted their attention towards Pakistan, rather than fighting in Kashmir.

Second, an analysis of the global trend reveals that suicide attacks in any region generally spiral, only to decline later. In short, suicide attacks have always been seasonal, though there have been incidents of their recurrence. In Palestine and in Sri Lanka, for example, one can trace phases of suicide attacks. In J&K, it can be assessed that the first season of suicide attacks has come to an end.

Third, better counter-militant tactics by the security forces have definitely reduced the lethality of suicide attacks. It should be noted

---

[24] Interactions with security forces, surrendered militants and local population.
[25] Interactions with Rashtriya Rifles units in Kupwara.

that fidayeen attacks in J&K have their special features and are not similar to suicide attacks in other parts of the world. They are more daredevil, high-risk attacks, which the security forces have learnt to cope with by increasing their physical security, intelligence and preparations.

On the other hand, there has been a dramatic surge in grenade attacks. Police officials consider 2006 as 'the year of grenades'. In most cases, unemployed youth and students from the rural areas are involved in these grenade attacks. They were given money and grenades to lob on civilians or security forces. The objective of the militant groups seems to be making sure that incidents of violence continue and normalcy does not return. In short, their objective is to create panic amongst the local population and keep the security forces on the defensive. For the actual perpetrators, these attacks are easy as it does not make them formal militants and provides them quick money. For students, it is money, frustration and a sense of adventure.[26]

High-Tech Terror

In terms of using modern communications, the militants in J&K have become quite advanced in recent years. There have been reports of militants using GPS to help them navigate the terrain. Gone are the days when radio communication was the primary mode of passing information. Radio communication being highly susceptible to interception by the security and intelligence agencies, militants have switched over to mobile phones and the internet to communicate with each other. With local support declining and foreign militants in the armed conflict increasing, the GPS, mobile phones and internet have become popular.[27] There have also been instances of militants using palmtops, Laptops and satellite phones.

The security forces have been concerned about the growing use of mobile phones which is the primary reason for the state going slow on introducing mobile connectivity in J&K. With AirTel and BSNL now operating in the Kashmir Valley, Doda, Rajouri and Poonch regions, more than 80 per cent of these areas that are known for the movement

---

[26] Interactions with school and college students in various parts of Kashmir Valley and Doda district.

[27] Interactions with army and police officers operating in Jammu and Kashmir, especially in Baramulla–Kupwara, Doda, Poonch and Rajouri.

of militants have come under mobile connectivity. Unfortunately, mobile intercepts and making information available to field formations based on such intercepts is mired in bureaucratic procedure involving the intelligence agencies and security forces. The intelligence forces are entrusted with mobile interception and the security forces, which actually need information at the ground level, have to route their request for mobile intercepts through the intelligence agencies. Today, the security forces confess that the number of intercepts has gone down considerably, resulting in either no or poor intelligence, thus hampering security operations. At a few selected places expensive French-made mobile interceptors are available. The security forces in J&K want more such interceptors.

Women as Perpetrators and Silent Participants of Violence

Though the role of women in political and public life in Kashmir is almost negligible, during the initial phase of militancy (1989–1994) when there was a mass uprising, women led the protest demonstrations and mass agitations against the union government. Over almost 18 years of conflict in Jammu and Kashmir, the women have never taken up guns like men.[28] However, in the past few years there has been an increase in the number of women helping terrorists.

There have been reports that the LeT and JeM have recruited women cadres and are training them in terrorist training camps in Pakistan-occupied Kashmir. A Pakistani militant, arrested in Jammu in August 2007, confirmed that after completing their arms training, these women were to be infiltrated. As women are less likely to be searched at checkpoints, this trend is likely to become a major issue—both political and religious.[29]

There have also been arrests of women cadres in recent months belonging to the LeT and Hizbul Mujahideen. Haseena Begum was arrested early this year for being part of a Lashkar module planning to assassinate Chief Minister Ghulam Nabi Azad during a public rally in Ramban district. Haseena, along with a fidayeen squad of the Lashkar, had managed to reach close to where the Chief Minister was to make his speech.[30]

---

[28] Sudha Ramachandran, 'Women lift the veil on Kashmir struggle', *Asia Times Online*, 7 March 2002 (available at: http://www.atimes.com/ind-pak/DC07Df01.html.
[29] Pradeep Dutta, 'Women on the militant radar', *Times Now*, 19 August 2007.
[30] See Kavita Suri, 'Now, it's guns and veils for border belles', *The Statesman*, 22 August 2007.

Besides being a part of the militant movement, women are increasingly taking part in over-ground activities, supporting the separatists and indirectly the militant movement. The alarming growth of Dukhtaran-e-Millat led by Asiya Andrabi is a case in point. Her mobilization of women during the sex scandal in Srinagar highlights this growing trend, especially in urban Kashmir. Even the JKLF has floated a women's wing called Khwateen Markaz to recruit them for a political struggle.[31]

The Over-ground Conflict

Another important trend in recent years has been the growing network of over-ground workers (OGWs) who support the separatists and militants. The reasons are political and monetary. In May 2007, the Kashmir police busted a module of 13 supporters working for Abu Tahir, a Lashkar commander from Pakistan. Monetary considerations rather than political beliefs were the main driving force for this module, which included a woman, since they had no criminal background or known militant links.[32]

According to a high-ranking police official, 'in almost 95 per cent of the cases, the OGWs are helping the terrorists for money. And in just five per cent or less cases, the OGWs come to us because either there is some harassment to them on the hands of the terrorists or there is some personal score to settle or the terrorists are eyes on their girls and daughters. Rest its money and nothing else.'[33] An OGW can get between Rs 1 to 2 lakh for a safe hideout in his/her house for the six months of winter.[34]

Though the army and police officers say there is no jihad left in Kashmir and whatever support is being extended to the terrorists is 'nothing but a money game', another section of OGWs can be classified as political. This section makes use of the monetary rewards, but primarily acts out of political convictions. According to a high-ranking army officer, this section is found among the separatists, business community, and even those working in the government.[35]

---

[31] Pradeep Dutta, 'Women on the militant radar', *Times Now*, 19 August 2007.
[32] Ibid.
[33] Interview with a police official.
[34] Interaction with Kupwara RR officers, September 2007.
[35] Interview with an army officer.

Hizbul Out, Lashkar In

The most disturbing new trend that will have far-reaching implications for the armed conflict in the coming days is the decline of the Hizbul Mujahideen as the most powerful militant group in the Kashmir Valley. Their decline has been in terms of cadres, striking ability and high-profile attacks.

Several reasons could be ascribed to this: surrenders, criminalization, fatigue and better counter-militancy efforts. In the past two years, most of those who have surrendered and given up their guns belong to the Hizbul Mujahideen. Every surrender of a high-profile Hizbul militant triggers another set of surrenders. For example, when the District Commander of the Hizbul in Doda region surrendered recently, those working under him also gave up the gun. Second, with developmental funds pouring in and reaching militant hands, many Hizbul commanders have made money in various ways, besides being bribed by the intelligence agencies. For example, the railway project in Kashmir Valley, starting from Qazikund to Baramulla, has been of great monetary benefit to many of the Hizbul militants. Third, due to these two factors, the security forces have much better intelligence, especially about the hideouts and the movement of Hizbul cadres. This has resulted in the Hizbul facing the brunt of counter-militancy operations in the last two years. More Hizbul commanders have been eliminated as compared to the Lashkar or Jaish. The decline in the Hizbul is not a completely positive outcome since it provides the space for the Lashkar to expand its activities.

The most important question now is whether the al Qaeda is present today in Kashmir or is likely to remain there in the future. The army believes that al Qaeda could outsource its missions to other jihadi groups like the Jaish and Lashkar.[36] Lt Gen. Panag commented on this important issue: 'We cannot say al-Qaeda is not here, but we have not come across any hardcore operative of this outfit. Al-Qaeda is an internationally trained militant organisation having networks all over the world and there can be possibility of the presence of some cells in the country as well as in the state here but till date no case of the presence of al-Qaeda operative has been detected.'[37]

---

[36] 'Al-Qaeda outsourcing its missions: Army', *The Kashmir Times*, 14 September 2007.
[37] Ibid.

CONFLICT MANAGEMENT

The union government has taken measures to address both the conflicts at the bilateral level with Pakistan, and at the national level with various segments of Jammu and Kashmir society.

The Working Groups and Round Table Conferences

In May 2006, as a part of the internal peace process, Manmohan Singh announced the settling up of five Working Groups on the following issues: improving union–J&K relations, enhancing relations across the Line of Control, boosting the economic development of J&K, rehabilitating the destitute families of militants and reviewing the cases of detainees, and ensuring good governance.[38] The Working Groups comprised members drawn from various political parties and representing different opinions.

Each group had an agenda and submitted their reports with significant recommendations. The Working Group on strengthening relations across the LoC recommended the following measures: simplify procedures to facilitate travel across the LoC; increase goods traffic; expand people-to-people contacts; and open up new communication routes like Kargil–Skardu.[39]

The Working Group on confidence-building measures across segments of society in the state recommended the following measures: to improve the condition of people affected by militancy; schemes to rehabilitate orphans and widows affected by militancy; relaxation of conditions for persons who have foresworn militancy; an effective rehabilitation policy for Kashmiri Pandit migrants; and an approach to encourage the return of Kashmiri youth from areas controlled by Pakistan.[40]

The Working Group on the economic development of Jammu and Kashmir made recommendations for improving conditions in the power sector; communications, rural roads and telecom; tourism sector;

---

[38] '5 working groups for Jammu & Kashmir', *The Hindu*, 25 May 2006.

[39] See 'Strengthening Relations across the Line of Control', Report of the Working Group, January 2007.

[40] See 'Confidence Building Measures across Segments of Society in the State', Report of the Working Group, January 2007.

agriculture, irrigation and forests; industrial development and commerce; health; education and employment; and regional development.[41]

The Working Group on good governance suggested measures to increase accountability and transparency in the administration; strengthen local self-government; effectively monitor development programmes; institute zero tolerance for human rights violations; strengthen right to information; and provide adequate security to all segments of society, particularly minority communities.[42]

Unfortunately, the Working Group reports failed to elicit any positive response at the ground level, especially in the Kashmir Valley. People considered these Working Groups and their reports to be a useless exercise as they had failed to include different sections.[43] The main criticism of the local population regarding these Working Groups were (i) that they included only the moderate political sections who do not have any major differences with New Delhi; (ii) that they did not include the separatists in the Kashmir Valley; and (iii) they neither included nor consulted groups like industry, tourists and fruit growers.

Apart from these Working Groups, New Delhi organized the third Round Table Conference in 2007. Presided over by the Prime Minister, this Round Table was held in New Delhi in April 2007; the earlier two Round Table Conferences were held in Jammu in February 2006 and later in Srinagar in May 2006. This Round Table endorsed the reports submitted by the Working Groups. Importantly, the Prime Minister announced the setting up of two committees for the implementation of decisions by the state and also said that the government was working on a 'blueprint of a new future' and a *'naya* (new) Jammu, Kashmir and Ladakh'.[44]

Though this Conference, like the Working Groups, was attended by leaders representing different mainstream parties, this effort was also seen as a futile exercise since it failed to include the separatists. Some of the leaders who were a part of this exercise included Home Minister Shivraj Patil, Chief Minister Ghulam Nabi Azad, PDP leaders Mufti Mohammad Sayeed, Mehbooba Mufti and Muzaffar Hussain

---

[41] 'Economic Development of Jammu and Kashmir', Report of the Working Group, March 2007.

[42] See 'Ensuring Good Governance in Jammu and Kashmir', Report of the Working Group, March 2007.

[43] Interviews and interactions during field trips in both Jammu region and Kashmir Valley during March–August 2007.

[44] 'PM's vision of "naya" Jammu, Kashmir & Ladakh', *Daily Excelsior*, 25 April 2007.

Baig, NC leaders Farooq Abdullah and Omar Abdullah, former Minister and Panthers Party leader Harshdev Singh, CPI(M) leader Mohd Yusuf Tarigami, Congress leader Saifuddin Soz, state BJP leaders Ashok Khajuria, Dr Nirmal Singh, Prof Hari Om, and Panun Kashmir chairman Agnishekhar.[45]

Although an invitation was sent to the Hurriyat to participate in the conference, it declined for various reasons. The Ladakh Union Territory Front (LUTF), on the same day as the Conference was taking place in New Delhi, organized a total *bandh* demanding Union Territory status for the Ladakh region.[46] On the other hand, a large number of refugees from Pakistan-occupied Kashmir, West Pakistan and Chhamb protested against the non-inclusion of their representatives and demands in the Conference, and staged a march towards the international border with the objective of crossing over and reaching their original homes across the LoC. This included all major refugee and migrant groups like SOS-International, West Pakistani Refugees, and United Refugees Front. The security forces prevented their march and the protesters were sent back to Jammu.

Debating an Internal Ceasefire

The call for an internal ceasefire in 2007 initially came from the Hurriyat. The moderate section led by Mirwaiz Farooq urged New Delhi to announce an internal ceasefire within J&K. This section also announced that it would help the union government in pressurizing the militant groups to agree to the same.[47] Mirwaiz, in fact, took this debate forward by asking the militant groups to give up their armed struggle, paving the way for a peaceful resolution of the conflict. Unfortunately, these efforts failed to materialize as both the United Jihad Council and the Hizbul Mujahideen rejected them.[48]

Fencing the LoC

India went ahead with the process of fencing the Line of Control, which it had started many years ago. The government of India, and

---

[45] Ibid.
[46] 'Bandh observed in Leh', *Daily Excelsior,* 25 April 2007.
[47] 'Hurriyat urges Centre to announce ceasefire in J&K', *The Hindu,* 15 January 2007.
[48] See 'Pak-based militants reject Mirwaiz's call', *The Tribune,* 22 January 2007; 'Salahuddin rules out ceasefire possibility', *Greater Kashmir,* 5 January 2007.

particularly the Indian army, have always believed that fencing the LoC will prevent cross-border infiltration. As far back as 2003, Lt Gen. T. P. S. Brar, General Officer Commanding (GoC) 16 Corps, clearly stated that fencing the LoC would a be major step towards discouraging the militants from entering the state to engineer trouble.[49] With the ceasefire in place between India and Pakistan, the LoC could be fenced at a faster pace as there have been no cross-border firings since 2003.

The fencing, according to a statement made by the Defence Minister in Parliament, was completed in December 2004 itself.[50] However, the government is improving the fencing further by way of lighting, installing sensors and related high-tech equipment. Unfortunately, this fencing has not completely stopped cross-border infiltration, though it has considerably reduced. Many security officials belonging to the military and paramilitary forces agree that fencing can only reduce infiltration but cannot stop it.[51] Despite the fencing, militants cross the LoC using various means like rubber ladders. Besides, there is an element of corruption amongst those who are actually maintaining the LoC at the ground level.

Bilateral Initiatives: Making the LoC a Line of Peace

The Indian government's efforts to address the 'conflict of' Kashmir vis-à-vis Pakistan during 2007 was reflected in bilateral meetings at the highest levels. The first such meeting was held in March 2007 when India and Pakistan held their fourth round of the composite dialogue. The Foreign Secretaries of both counties also met during this exercise, discussing numerous bilateral issues including that of Jammu and Kashmir. Nothing much was achieved or even discussed, as one can gauge from the statement by Shiv Shankar Menon, India's Foreign Secretary. After these meetings, he stated on J&K: 'We seek the settlement of all outstanding issues including J & K. With Foreign Secretary Riaz Mohammad Khan, I also discussed the implementation of the existing CBMs and new cross LoC CBMs. We raised the Kargil Skardu route for a bus service and Pakistan side agreed to consider it.

---

[49] 'Border fencing along LoC in Rajouri-Poonch hills', *The Times of India*, 13 May 2003.
[50] 'LoC fencing completed: Mukherjee', *The Times of India*,
[51] Interviews with military and paramilitary officials.

We now start looking at the logistics and modalities of operationaling this. We also discussed trade across the LoC.'[52] All that was decided during this meeting that related to J&K was to 'ensure implementation of the already agreed Jammu and Kashmir related CBMs', 'to ensure operationalization of truck service', and to 'ensure operationalization/ rationalization of the five crossing points'.[53]

On General Musharraf's various proposals to resolve the conflict, Pranab Mukherjee, India's External Affairs Minister, stated in the Rajya Sabha while answering a question on this issue that the Government of India has been discussing the issue of J&K with Pakistan within the framework of the composite dialogue.[54]

In July 2007, Manmohan Singh, during his visit to J&K, announced his vision on converting the LoC into a Line of Peace. He pronounced: 'As I have stated earlier, borders cannot be changed, but they can be made irrelevant. There can no be question of divisions or fresh partitions, but the Line of Control can become a Line of Peace with free flow of ideas, goods, services and people.'[55]

This recent enunciation of the LoC as a Line of Peace should be read along with his earlier statement on making borders irrelevant. For Manmohan Singh, both these proposals mean using the land and water resources of the region jointly for the benefit of the people living on both sides of the LoC.[56] Also, in July 2007, Jairam Ramesh, India's Minister of State for Commerce, announced that Pakistan had agreed in principle to allow trade through the Line of Control. Efforts are underway to open the LoC to allow truck services.

CONCLUSIONS

In recent years, one can visibly see positive developments in both the conflict 'in' Kashmir and 'of' Kashmir. If it succeeds, Manmohan Singh's vision to make the border irrelevant and convert the LoC into a Line of Peace will undoubtedly be a path-breaking effort during the

---

[52] 'Comments by Foreign Secretary Mr. Shivshankar Menon at the Joint Press Briefing with Pakistan Foreign Secretary Mr. Riaz Mohammad Khan on March 14, 2007', http://meaindia.nic.in//pressbriefing/2007/03/14pb01.htm.

[53] See 'Decisions taken at the conclusion of the Fourth Round of the Composite Dialogue between the Foreign Secretaries of India and Pakistan', meaindia.nic.in/pressrelease/2007/03/14pr01.htm.

[54] http://meaindia.nic.in//parliament/rs/2007/03/15rs12.htm.

[55] 'LoC could be Line of Peace if terror, violence end permanently', *Daily Excelsior*, 16 July 2007.

[56] Ibid.

60 years of the Kashmir conflict. Cross-border infiltration has declined, while the ceasefire between India and Pakistan, announced in 2003, has been holding up for the last four years. Within J&K, the Round Table Conference and Working Groups are good initiatives which need to be taken to their logical conclusion.

On the other hand, as earlier mentioned, there have been negative developments in the conflict. Despite the decline in infiltration, violence continues within J&K. There is also a steady growth of over-ground workers and radical groups like the LeT are attempting to take over the armed conflict.

To strengthen the positive and arrest the negative developments, the following measures could be taken to strengthen cross-border relations and improve them within J&K.

Looking Beyond Cross-LoC Bus Services

The current level of cross-LoC interactions is limited to two bus services between Uri–Muzaffarabad; and Poonch–Rawlakot. The first service was started in 2005 and the second in 2006. In 2007, two years after agreeing to start the bus service across the LoC, allowing only divided families to meet, efforts are now being made to further expand cross-LoC interactions. The pace of this expansion is painfully slow, given the hostility, vested interests and hardened mindsets which are not conducive to enlarging interactions across the LoC.[57]

There have been increasing demands from the entire community in the Jammu region and Kashmir Valley to allow trade across the LoC. Currently, interactions are primarily focused on the divided families. Movement of other people as well, along with goods, would bring enormous economic, political and human dividends. The fruit industry in Kashmir Valley, on which more than 80 per cent of the workforce is dependent, will immensely benefit from such an initiative. At present, the fruit industry sends their goods by trucks via Jammu to Delhi and beyond. This route is heavily dependent on access to and security of the Srinagar–Jammu national highway, which passes through the Jawahar tunnel and over unstable mountain ridges. If the LoC is opened for goods, the apples from Anantnag and Sopore could reach Rawalpindi via Muzaffarabad faster than they could reach New Delhi.

[57] See D. Suba Chandran, 'J&K as Land of Contact', *Epilogue,* September 2007, pp. 14–23.

Besides, the Jammu–Sialkot road along with the Kargil–Skardu road should also be opened for the movement of people and goods. Sialkot is hardly 40 km away from Jammu and there are numerous divided families in this region. Until 1947, Jammu was linked with the outside world mainly through bus and rail routes via Sialkot.

Such economic movement across the LoC is likely to have an important political fallout. It would weaken the hold of hawks over local society, since it would be this community that would rebel against unrealistic *fatwas* issued by hawks and their supporters across the LoC, especailly the Hizbul Mujahideen.[58]

Making the Working Groups and Round Tables Meaningful

The five Working Groups set by the union government and the three Round Table Conferences organized over the last two years have undeniably been a good effort. Unfortunately, the local population in all three regions perceive this effort as meaningless and an eyewash. These meetings and Working Groups could be made meaningful by expanding their scope and participation. Many groups, who perceive themselves as direct and indirect victims of the conflict, have been left out of this process. For example, the PoK refugees, people of Kargil and Leh, the economic community and women feel that there should be adequate representation to include them and all other shades of opinion. Outside these groups that are willing to participate are the separatists led by the two factions of the All Parties Hurriyat Conference (APHC) which have steadfastly refused to take part in this process. Unfortunately, the groups that are willing to participate, but are not included in the process, feel that the union government is more interested in roping in those sections which have been refusing to participate.

The moderate section of the Hurriyat led by Mirwaiz Farooq has laid down some preconditions before they take part in any process initiated by New Delhi. If they are not willing to join in the main process, there could be a separate process to address their concerns. On the other hand, those groups that are willing to take part should be included since their inputs would be significant.

[58] Ibid.

Let the J&K Police Lead

Currently, security in J&K is being handled by the army, paramilitary forces and J&K police. They work under the union Home and Defence Ministries and the state government. Besides, there are several intelligence organizations, including the IB and RAW. While in theory these forces and intelligence organizations work together, in reality there are significant differences in their attitudes, functioning style, and the extent of local support they receive. Undoubtedly, the J&K police enjoys more support than the others, although its Special Operations Group evokes the same negative feelings as the Rashtriya Rifles.

Second, the J&K police, being 'locals', are better equipped and suited to collecting intelligence. Filtering and analyzing the inputs received can be handled better by the local police than the federal organizations. Often, the intelligence received by the military and paramilitary organizations is false or deliberately planted. Subsequent follow-up actions only worsen the situation instead of addressing it, thus damaging the state. The popular local reaction against high-handed operations is invariably exploited by anti-national and separatist forces. The local police are in a better position to handle this situation, thereby addressing an important issue causing great embarrassment at the national and international level, i.e., human rights violations. Incidentally, most cases of human rights violations involve the military and paramilitary forces, and not the local police.

A Debate on Demilitarization

Finally, there is growing emphasis on demilitarization at the national and bilateral levels. Both General Musharraf and the separatist leaders have been demanding demilitarization, but New Delhi has been reluctant to consider this idea. While these demands by Musharraf and the separatist leaders may have a dubious rationale, the same cannot be said about the mainstream leaders in the Kashmir Valley. The latter have been arguing for demilitarization on larger political considerations and to assuage human rights conditions—real or imagined.

The larger political questions would be: Can India keep the military and paramilitary forces indefinitely in Kashmir? Is it in the interests of the Indian nation and the future of Kashmir? Is it in the interests of the military and paramilitary forces to remain deployed in counter-insurgency operations over extended periods of time? The present time may not be ripe to initiate demilitarization and it should be linked to positive developments in the ground situation. However, it is definitively time to initiate a debate on these questions and to find alternative solutions.

6

Left Extremism: The Naxal Conflict in India

Mallika Joseph & Devyani Srivastava

A BRIEF HISTORY

The term 'naxalite' draws its origin from an organized armed peasant resistance against the landlords that began in March 1967 in a small village called Naxalbari in the state of West Bengal.[1] Three sharecroppers with the help of 150 members of the Communist Party of India (Marxist–Leninist) (CPI [ML]) lifted the entire stock of grain from a landlord's granary without giving him his share. It signalled the birth of a new movement and since then, all forms of armed struggle with socio-economic development of the downtrodden as the cause have come to be termed 'naxalite'. Other terms that are used to describe the movement are 'leftwing extremism' and 'radical Maoism'.

The evolution of the naxalite movement falls broadly into three phases.[2] The first is the period of intellectual fervour which lasted until the early 1970s. This phase was followed by one marked by armed violence, splintered naxalite groups, and decline of the intellectual discourse in the movement. This phase lasted until the end of the millennium. The third phase, which is the current one, is characterized by increased violence, amalgamation of the various naxalite groups under a single banner, and better organizational capability. Arguably, whatever intellectual moorings the movement started with no longer exists. However, the situation that spawned the naxalite movement—'social injustice, economic inequality and the failure of the system in redressing the grievances of large sections of people'[3]—continues.

---

[1] Naxalbari is a small village at the tri-junction of India, Nepal and Bangladesh.

[2] These phases are suggested for conceptual clarity only, and there are periods of overlap between them as the movement evolved.

[3] Prakash Singh, 'The Naxalite Movement in India', New Delhi: Rupa & Co, 1995, p. ii.

Naxalbari was not the first peasant uprising in India. In 1946, there was the *Tebhaga* (three-share) movement in Bengal that demanded the reduction of the landlords' share to one-third; until then they had received half. The peasants, guided by the *kisan sabhas* (peasant unions), forcibly took away two-thirds of the harvest, leading to violent clashes: the landlords fled and the *kisan sabhas* established control till the landlords once again overpowered them with the help of the local administration. In Andhra Pradesh (AP), too, instances of organized armed struggle emerged as early as 1946 during the Nizam's rule under the generic term, Telengana Armed Struggle. It started as a revolt against the oppression of the poor peasantry and tribals by landlords who fraudulently deprived them of their lands and livelihood with the collusion of revenue officials. The communists directed the movement and soon more than 3,000 villages came under their influence. In 1961, a violent movement under the banner of the Srikakulam Armed Struggle started in Andhra Pradesh; it sought to liberate the deprived hill people from the clutches of the plainsmen, who had deprived them of their land and oppressed them economically.

In 1953, the Indian government passed the Estates Acquisition Act that fixed the land ceiling at 25 acres of agricultural land out of a total of 45 acres that could be owned by an individual. This Act was followed by the Land Reforms Act in 1955. These measures had little effect as landlords continued to have large tracts of land in their possession and oppressed the peasants who leased these lands from them in return for large shares of the harvest.

Then, in March 1967, Naxalbari happened. With little help forthcoming from the government, the peasants in different parts of the country, organized into *kisan sabhas* by the CPI, revolted violently against the landlords with Naxalbari being the example. This spontaneous revolt, over a period of time, transformed itself into the naxalite movement. This phase was marked by ideologues like Charu Mazumdar and Kanu Sanyal who literally used the revolutionary zeal in Naxalbari to spread it to other areas. Their appeal was high among the youth, and many, even from the rich and affluent classes, joined the struggle. Many have linked this phase of the movement with its contemporary global context in the 1960s, which saw the surge of radical struggles larded with a rereading of Marxist ideology. The zeal of revolutionary humanism was apparent in nationalist struggles across the political spectrum from Southeast Asia to

South America and this very zeal was evident in the first phase of the naxalite movement. The government's response to the movement was violent, using increased police action. By strategically targeting the leaders, the state brought the naxalite movement under control within a few months.

In their internal assessment, the naxal leaders felt that the decline of the movement, or rather the inability of the movement to resist the government's action, was due to the lack of a strong party organization, ignorance of military affairs, failure to cultivate a mass base and a structured approach to land reforms. By 1973–74, with most of the naxal leaders captured or killed, it appeared that the movement had been crushed by the government. But this was not true, since the movement, after a realization of its failures in the first phase, morphed into one more adept in guerrilla warfare and with stronger mass support.

The second phase of the naxalite movement saw a marked increase in violence as armed struggle erupted in most states in central India, particularly in Andhra Pradesh and Bihar. This can be attributed to two developments. The first was the elimination of the intellectuals in the movement, who were dealt with ruthlessly by the police, and the second was the division between the moderates and the extremists of the movement. While both categories believed in the cause, there were differences between them on the means to be used to obtain their goals. While one believed that parliamentary democracy provided the space and opportunity to achieve their goals, the other continued to seek alternatives to the existing system through armed revolution. The result was a violent second phase dominated by the People's War Group (PWG) in Andhra Pradesh and the Maoist Communist Centre (MCC) in Bihar. There were various other splinter groups that amalgamated or dissipated as the armed struggle moved along, with this phase being marked also by internecine conflict between the naxalite groups as they struggled to carve out their spheres of influence and action.

While the leaders of the second phase of the movement realized the shortcomings of the previous phase and directed their energies to remodelling the movement, the government remained unable to quell it. This would have been possible if, after its initial success against the movement, the government had addressed some of the key socio-economic issues that had given birth to the movement.

However, the counter-naxal strategy was largely focused on restoring law and order rather than addressing issues of governance; because this approach had worked, it was easier and quicker to do this again, especially when compared to gearing the bureaucracy to deliver justice and fair governance. Police action was the option favoured by most state governments fighting the naxalites. States like Andhra Pradesh, however, realized the inadequacy of police action—though they perfected it to a level envied by other states—and introduced softer measures like the policy of surrender to lure the naxalites back into society, opened channels of dialogue with them and attempted to address the critical issues of governance, especially those relating to land distribution and ownership. However, inconsistencies between the policies and strategies adopted by each state, and within particular states themselves, have marked the problem, coupled with changes within the naxalite movement itself, resulting in the main groups setting aside their differences and amalgamating themselves into a single umbrella organization, which essentially transformed the movement into its current phase.

The naxalite movement in the current phase is far removed from where it started. Bereft of ideology, and left with only the 'revolutionary' part of 'revolutionary humanism' which the movement had started out with, the movement is today characterized only by violence. With over 1,500 incidents and nearly 1,000 casualties each year, it is, as Prime Minister Manmohan Singh put it, the 'single biggest internal security challenge' for the nation. According to the Ministry of Home Affairs (MHA) *Annual Report* in 2006, 76 districts in nine states (Andhra Pradesh, Bihar, Chhattisgarh, Jharkhand, Madhya Pradesh, Maharashtra, Orissa, Uttar Pradesh and West Bengal) are badly affected by naxalism; and there is an emerging naxal presence in three other states (Karnataka, Tamil Nadu and Kerala).[4]

THE PRINCIPAL ACTORS

The principal actors in this protracted conflict are the government actors, the armed groups, the civilian armed counter-naxal group called the Salwa Judum, and civil society groups.

[4] Ministry of Home Affairs, *Annual Report 2005–2006,* New Delhi: Ministry of Home Affairs, 2005, p. 24. According to the 2006–2007 *Annual Report,* about 395 police stations out of a total of 12,476 reported naxal violence in their jurisdictions.

Government Actors

Government actors include the state governments in the various states affected by the naxalite movement, the central government, the state police forces, armed police forces and the central paramilitary forces. The naxalite problem, since its inception, has been viewed as a law and order problem and, in India, maintenance of law and order falls under the jurisdiction of respective states rather than under the central government. As a result, the state governments have adopted different strategies in dealing with the naxalite problem, leading to unevenness in their responses and lack of coordination and cooperation between the various states. For example, when one state is negotiating with the naxal leadership, a neighbouring state bans the organization, and a third one adopts aggressive police action. The naxals often operated in the gaps between respective state jurisdictions and have thrived as a result.

In addition, due to the lack of a coordinated all-India approach, even the counter-naxal strategy adopted by the respective states is affected by inconsistencies. For instance, when they come to power, successive governments in Andhra Pradesh have adopted different strategies to deal with the naxals; it is another matter that most of them come to power with naxal support during elections. By changing the strategies with changes in the regime, the gains accrued by pursuing the previous strategy are lost. This again has benefited the naxals in consolidating their presence in the states. Until recently, this was the approach state governments had taken. However, with the amalgamation of various naxalite parties into one, the central government is adopting initiatives to coordinate the efforts of various state governments to derive a unified counter-naxal strategy. This however, is yet to fructify.

The police forces in the various states affected by naxalism exhibit various levels of expertise and specialization. Since the police forces in Andhra Pradesh have been fighting the naxals for long, their counter-naxal operations are way ahead of the police forces in other states. While there have been attempts at sharing best practices, learning and training with other states, the effects are yet to manifest in other police forces. Adding to this problem is the issue of inadequate numbers in the police force. Across almost all the naxalite-affected states, there are differences between the sanctioned strength and available strength of police forces, and particularly in the numbers of the armed police. Andhra Pradesh has a sanctioned strength of 14,372 armed police personnel. However, the actual numbers are 12,874.[5] Similarly, Jharkhand operates with an armed police strength of 2,412 against the sanctioned 3,490; Chhattisgarh with 9,863 against 10,865; and Orissa with 8,427 against 9,634. Bihar is the worst off with 8,833 armed police personnel against a sanctioned 16,394, which is a shortfall of nearly 53 per cent. And these missing numbers are mostly in the category below Assistant Sub-Inspector, meaning the foot soldiers.

Not only do the naxal-affected states have less armed police than the sanctioned numbers, but they also exhibit the worst police–population ratio. The UN-recommended ratio is 222 policemen for 100,000 population. The Indian average stands at just 122 per 100,000. And in Bihar, the sanctioned strength is 57 per 100,000; Jharkhand 85, Orissa 90, Andhra Pradesh 98 and Chhattisgarh 103. Given the considerable differences between the actual and sanctioned strengths, it is not surprising to find the states struggling to undertake their counter-naxal operations, which have to be carried out in addition to regular law and order and other security duties.[6] In Chhattisgarh, the central government has deployed 85 companies of the Central Reserve Police Force (CRPF), totalling 11,220 personnel, to augment the armed police. This provides about 20,000 armed personnel (though most of the deployed CRPF personnel are for passive defence) for an area of 135,194 square kilometres, while the insurgency-affected state of Manipur in India's northeast, with just 22,327 square kilometres, has nearly 350 companies (more than 45,000 personnel) of army and paramilitary forces.[7]

Armed Group—Communist Party of India (Maoist)

One of the biggest weaknesses of the naxalite movement has been the lack of unity among the nearly 50 or so naxal outfits operating in

---

[5] 'Table 17.2: Sanctioned and Actual Strength of Armed Police as on 31.12.2005', *Crime in India 2005*, New Delhi: National Crime Records Bureau, 2007, p. 497.

[6] In his article 'The Maoists: Their Decisions, Our Abiding Omissions', Ajai Sahni takes the argument further and points out that disproportionate police:geography ratio handicaps the states attempting to counter the naxalite movement. He says, 'The Indian average stands at an inadequate 42.4 policemen per 100 square kilometers; Chhattisgarh has just 17.3; Andhra Pradesh, 28.5; Jharkhand, 30.8; and Orissa, 22.4.' <http://www.satp.org/satporgtp/sair/Archives/5_36.htm#assessment1> accessed on 19 December 2007.

[7] Ajai Sahni, 'The Maoists: Their Decisions, Our Abiding Omissions', *South Asia Intelligence Review*, vol. 5, no. 36, 19 March 2007. Available at <http://www.satp.org/satporgtp/sair/Archives/5_36.htm#assessment1> accessed on 19 December 2007.

various parts of the country; in Andhra Pradesh alone, about 19 groups espoused the naxal cause at one time. This lack of unity was marked also by intense rivalry among these groups. In the mid–1990s there were continuous clashes between the People's War Group (PWG), the Party Unity (PU) and the Maoist Communist Centre (MCC); the death toll in clashes between the Party Unity and MCC was over 150. Notwithstanding these clashes, there were repeated efforts towards dialogue and reconciliation. Since its formation in 1980, the PWG has, in fact, been striving to bring the various naxal groups together under its umbrella.[8] After nearly five years of negotiations, the Party Unity and PWG merged in October 1998. In 2003, the MCC and RCCI-M (Revolutionary Communist Centre of India [Maoist] merged to form the Maoist Communist Centre of India [MCC-I]) merged to form th MCC-I. Finally, in September 2004, after three years of continued negotiations, the MCC-I and PWG merged to form the Communist Party of India (Maoist).

The aim of the CPI (Maoist) is to establish a contiguous revolutionary zone stretching from Nepal to Bihar to Andhra Pradesh and beyond. While continuing their goal of people's democracy, the ultimate aim of the CPI (Maoist) is to seize power through protracted armed struggle. According to the press statement issued to announce the merger,

> The immediate aim and programme of the Maoist party is to carry on and complete the already ongoing and advancing New Democratic Revolution in India as a part of the world proletarian revolution by overthrowing the semi-colonial, semi-feudal system under the neo-colonial form of indirect rule, exploitation and control. This revolution will remain directed against imperialism, feudalism and comprador bureaucratic capitalism. This revolution will be carried out and completed through armed agrarian revolutionary war, i.e. protracted people's war with the armed seizure of power remaining as its central and principal task, encircling the cities from the countryside and thereby finally capturing them. Hence the countryside as well as the PPW [Protracted People's War] will remain as the 'center of gravity' of the party's work, while urban work will be complementary to it.[9]

---

[8] Chindu Sreedharan, 'PWG hopes merger with Party Unity will boost cadre morale', *Rediff On The Net*, 5 October 1998, <http://www.rediff.com/news/1998/oct/05nxl.htm> accessed on 2 February 2005.

[9] 'Maoist-Influenced Revolutionary Organizations in India', <http://www.massline.info/India /Indian_Groups.htm> accessed on 3 March 2005.

According to the same press release, the CPI (Maoist) 'will still seek to unite all genuine Maoist groups that remain outside this unified party'.[10]

The General Secretary of the PWG's Central Organizing Committee, Muppala Laxman Rao alias Ganapati, is the General Secretary of the new party. The organizational structure remains the same, with a Central Committee, followed by zonal/regional committees, state committees, district committees, divisions and squads.

Prior to the merger, the PWG and the MCC had about 3,000 to 3,500 cadres each and an equal, if not significantly higher, number of hardcore supporters and sympathizers. According to the Ministry of Home Affairs, the strength of the CPI (Maoist) is 7,200[11] committed cadres and an unknown but significant number of supporters and sympathizers. The US Department of State, in their list of foreign terrorist organizations and other groups of concern (where CPI [Maoist] features), puts the total strength at 31,000, including 'hardcore militants and dedicated sympathizers'.[12] The military wings of the PWG and the MCC were also merged to form the unified People's Liberation Guerrilla Army (PLGA). The merger also resulted in unifying the areas of operation, thereby giving the new organization a much larger and consolidated area of operation stretching from Andhra Pradesh to Nepal.

Traditionally, the naxalites relied much less on firearms, having only sickles and knives for weapons. However, as the movement progressed from phase to phase, the range of weapons has changed. Currently, the naxalites rely heavily on improvised explosive devices, using gelatine sticks as the main explosive and battery switches as triggers. In addition to weapons snatched from the police during their raids, the naxalites now possess automatic weapons like AK-47s. The source of these automatic weapons is not clearly established, though there is speculation that the naxalites could have procured them from the insurgents in India's northeast. In September 2006, the Andhra Pradesh police seized over 875 rockets and launchers from naxalite hideouts.[13] The source was lathe units located in the outskirts

---

[10] Ibid.

[11] Raman Kirpal, 'More securitymen killed by Naxals than by J&K militants: centre, states discuss today', *The Indian Express*, 30 August 2006.

[12] US Department of State, 'Terrorist Organizations', *Country Reports on Terrorism*, 30 April 2007, available at < http://www.state.gov/s/ct/rls/crt/2006/82738.htm> accessed on 21 December 2007.

[13] 'Maoists turn to Net for making rocket launchers', *The Times of India*, 17 November 2007.

of Chennai in Tamil Nadu, and these units were delivering these armaments for at least three years prior to the activity being unearthed. Senior police officials have speculated that these units could have delivered a minimum of 1,000 rockets and launchers in these three years.[14] Though there is documented use of these improvised rocket launchers by the naxalites, they have been few and far between. This begs the question: where are the rockets which have been delivered over these three years, and why have the naxalites invested in the manufacture and purchase of such large quantities of weapons that they do not use extensively?

Civilian Armed Counter-Naxal Group—Salwa Judum

In June 2005, an anti-naxal campaign named the Salwa Judum came up in Dantewada district of Chhattisgarh. In the local Gondi dialect, the term Salwa Judum means a 'purification hunt'. The beginning of the campaign remains unclear with conflicting versions: while the government maintains that the campaign started in Kutru village with local villagers spontaneously agitating against naxal excesses, media reports and human rights groups argue that the campaign was launched by supporters of the local opposition leader Mahendra Karma against the naxalites. Its origin notwithstanding, the campaign has now evolved into a movement backed and sustained by the Chhattisgarh government. It is largely believed to include three categories of people—victims of naxal violence; those whose traditional position of authority has been challenged by the naxalites, like headmen, *sarpanches* and *panches*; and persons lured into the movement by the promise of free rations and money.

The objective of the campaign is to channelize tribal discontent against naxalite activities into a large-scale mobilization against the ideology and methods adopted by the naxalites. The activities of the movement include mobilizing groups of people, conducting public meetings, speaking against the naxalites, attacking villages and persons sympathetic to the naxalites, forcing their sympathizers to denounce the naxalites, and handing them over to the police in case of resistance. Some members of the Salwa Judum are trained by the

---

[14] 'TN: 7 held in arms seizure case', *Rediff News*, 15 September 2006, available at <http://www.rediff.com/news/2006/sep/15tn.htm> accessed on 21 December 2007.

police and recognized as Special Police Officers (SPOs). The SPOs, numbering around 5,000 in the Dantewada district, are the armed wing of the campaign. While the government provides them with weapons and lets them accompany the paramilitary forces during counter-naxal operations, the SPOs, in turn, provide local intelligence and identify naxal sympathizers. The SPOs also man the checkposts on the roads and wield certain police powers.

The government of Chhattisgarh has set up relief camps for members of Salwa Judum and other tribals who could become naxalite targets, and those who get displaced in this campaign. Set up as a temporary measure, these camps do not offer the comfort of a regular settlement, and the displaced population is unable to move out of the camp for fear of getting caught in the crossfire between the naxalites and counter-naxal groups. According to official sources, nearly 65,000 have been displaced and are residing in these relief camps.

Civil Society

Civil society's response to the naxalite problem in India has been inadequate and reactive. The Committee of Concerned Citizens (CCC), People's Union for Civil Liberties (PUCL), Association for the Protection of Democratic Rights, People's Union for Democratic Rights (PUDR), Andhra Pradesh Civil Liberties Committee (APCLC), Forum for Fact-finding Documentation and Advocacy, and United Struggle Committee against Fake Encounters are some of the organizations that have raised their voice regarding police/government action against the naxalites. They have frequently voiced their concern about the number of naxalites killed in 'encounters'. Labelling them as 'false encounters' because of no corresponding police casualties and the absence of bodies, the activists have insisted on judicial probes into these deaths. They succeeded briefly in getting the attention of the National Human Rights Commission which after investigating 285 cases reported, noted that no prior attempt was made by the police to arrest the deceased persons and concluded that the procedures followed by them were contrary to law.

In Andhra Pradesh, the CCC and PUCL have been trying—unsuccessfully—to negotiate a settlement between the government and the naxalites for several years. They probably suffer from a lack of trust of the state machinery as they have only been decrying the government's response to the naxalite menace, while remaining oblivious to the hardships caused to the people and damage to property by the naxalites. The government sees them as the front organizations of the naxalites. Their decade-long parleys with the government have yielded little, though PUCL President, Kannabiran, was successful in negotiating the release of senior officials and members of the legislative assembly kidnapped by the PWG in 1987, 1991 and 1993. In 2004, civil society organizations paved the way for the first direct parleys between the naxalites and the state government in Andhra Pradesh. Despite their significant potential, the talks broke down in early 2005. In August 2006, PUCL attempted to restore the stalled talks between the government and the naxalites by requesting the government to announce a ceasefire.[15]

Civil society organizations have been active in other naxal-affected states also, particularly Jharkhand, Bihar and Chhattisgarh. In May 2007, the PUCL demanded an enquiry by the Central Bureau of Investigation (CBI) into all encounters in Chhattisgarh since 2005. The request was made following an alleged police encounter in Bijapur on 31 March 2007 that left 12 tribals dead. There is a deep mistrust of civil society organizations among the governments. This is not without reason. For instance, while civil society organizations have been vociferous in criticizing police excesses, they have largely been silent on naxal attacks. This was apparent after the 15 March 2007 attack in Bastar which left 54 policemen dead, but there was no condemnation by civil society organizations. While civil society organizations serve as a useful check on the government, their failure to be balanced in their approach has robbed them of credibility. A democracy cannot do without a vibrant civil society, but currently this characteristic is lacking.

External Actors

In 2001, the naxalite groups in India formed a symbolic alliance with the Maoists in Nepal under the common banner of Coordinating Committee of Maoist Parties and Organizations of South Asia (CCOMPOSA). The CPI (Maoist) are ideological partners of the Nepal Maoists, offering their Nepalese counterparts strategic depth and a safe haven, and who in turn offer the naxalites in India additional manpower and resources that are force multipliers. There are suspicions that Nepalese Maoists were part of the naxalite group that raided

---

[15] 'PUCL for ceasefire between naxals, police', *The Hindu*, 24 August 2006.

Jehanabad prison and the Madhuban attack in 2005.[16] And there are established linkages between the Nepali Maoists and their Indian counterparts.[17]

CONFLICT IN 2007

Three years after the formation of the CPI (Maoist)—following the merger of the Maoists Communist Centre of India and the CPI-ML People's War (PW)—the concerted efforts by the CPI (Maoist) to con-solidate red influence in India seem to be bearing fruit. The naxalites have consolidated their party organization, strengthened their armed wing, upgraded their technology and weaponry, and expanded their mass mobilization activities. Therefore, while incidents of naxal violence and deaths recorded a marginal decline in 2006–07, as noted above, it has been recognized as the 'single biggest internal security challenge ever faced by India'. Chhattisgarh and Jharkhand have emerged as the epicentre of the naxal conflict, suffering the maximum number of incidents and casualties.

Table 1: Trends in Overall Naxal Violence

Head	2003	2004	2005	2006	2007 (till 30 June)
Number of incidents	1597	1533	1608	1509	842
Police personnel killed	105	100	153	157	138
Civilians killed	410	466	524	521	220
Naxalites killed	216	87	225	272	93

Source: Status Paper on Internal Security as on 30 June 2007, Ministry of Home Affairs, Government of India, p. 25.

Evolving Nature of the Naxal Movement

The current phase of the naxal movement, which commenced with the announcement of the establishment of a Compact Revolutionary Zone in August 2001, is marked by two important qualitative changes: militarily and politically. The movement that was earlier restricted to

---

[16] Venkitesh Ramakrishnan, 'Extremism: daring and dangerous', *The Frontline*, vol. 22, no. 25, 3–16 December 2005.
[17] 'Interview with His Excellency, Mr Ved Marwah, Ex Governor of the states of Jharkhand and Bihar', available at <http://www.himalayanaffairs.org/interviewdetails.asp?id=54> accessed on 27 December 2007.

local weapons, small groups and isolated attacks is today 'characterized by growing militarization, Superior army-style organization, better trained cadres, attacks on large targets through large-scale frontal assaults, better coordination and possible external links.'[18] In political terms, the movement has altered its path from 'revolutionary democratic' activities to broad-based 'people's democratic' mass agitations.[19] These changes were reaffirmed by over 100 Maoist leaders who met in early 2007 during their 9th Unity Congress.

Adding a new lease of life to the movement, the CPI (Maoist) successfully held their momentous 9th Unity Congress deep in the forests of Dandakaranya in an area bordering Jharkhand and Orissa in January–February 2007.[20] The Congress, held 36 years after the 8th Congress in 1970, is an event of historic significance for three reasons: one, it achieved a higher level of unity throughout the party by resolving disputed political issues, consolidating the ability of the party to lead the struggle; second, the Maoists were able to maintain secrecy regarding the date and location of the Congress, despite the government placing all the guerilla zones under surveillance; and last, the Congress also charted out an Action Plan for the Maoists. The press release of the CPI (Maoist) stated its agenda clearly in the following words:

> The Unity Congress reaffirmed the general line of the new democratic revolution with agrarian revolution as its axis and protracted people's war as the path of the Indian revolution....*It set several new tasks for the party with the main focus on establishment of base areas as the immediate, basic and central task before the entire party. It also resolved to advance the people's war throughout the country, further strengthen the people's army, deepen the mass base of the party* [emphasis added] and wage a broad-based militant mass movement against the neo-liberal policies of globalization, liberalization, privatization pursued by the reactionary ruling classes under the dictates of imperialism.[21]

---

[18] 'Concluding Remarks at the 2nd Meeting of the Standing Committee of Chief Ministers on Naxalism', *Press Information Bureau*, 13 April 2006, http://pib.nic.in/release/rel_print_page.asp?relid=17128, accessed on 12 October 2007.

[19] Venkitesh Ramakrishnan, 'Naxal terror', *Frontline*, vol. 24, no. 18, 8–21 September 2007, p. 5.

[20] Subhashis Mittra, 'Terror tentacles', *Force*, vol. 4, no. 12, August 2007, p. 38.

[21] 'Press Release, CPI (Maoist) on the 9th Unity Congress, January–February 2007, 19 February 2007', *Maoists Documents, South Asia Terrorism Portal*, available at http://www.satp.org/satporgtp/countries/india/maoist/documents/papers/19feb07.htm. accessed on 13 October 2007.

New Strategies and Tactics

Driven by their dual objectives of armed struggle and mass agitation, the naxalites developed and implemented new strategies and tactics during 2006–07. In order to expand their mass agitation activities, the Maoists identified three broad issues around which to mobilize support: first, fight against the economic development policies of the government, particularly the setting up of Special Economic Zones (SEZs) and other large-scale industrial projects leading to displacement of tribal and forest dwellers; second, resist the continuing discrimination against minorities like Dalits and support their struggle; and third, extend support to the struggle of the oppressed nationalities, particularly in Kashmir and the Indian northeast, for their right to self-determination.[22] The naxalites have focused their struggle around these issues over the last two years; while the first two aims have taken operational effect, the last remains at the level of ideological attachment.

The issue of SEZs, in particular, snowballed into a rallying cry for the naxalites. For this, they employed the tactics of coordinated blockade by disruption of rail and road transport, and commercial activity across several states. Both in 2006 and 2007, naxals successfully imposed a two-day economic blockade in different parts of the country—in parts of Orissa, Chhattisgarh, Jharkhand and Bihar on 14 and 15 June 2006, and extended it to parts of West Bengal and Andhra Pradesh on 26 and 27 June 2007. While violence remained limited during the blockades, it inflicted heavy losses on the economy. For instance, in 2007, Jharkhand alone is reported to have suffered a loss of Rs 150 crore, whereas the Bastar region in Chhattisgarh suffered a loss of Rs 2,000 crore.[23] Through the blockade, the naxalites wish to capitalize on the anti-government sentiment among those displaced by such policies. Moving beyond localized strikes and blockades, the naxalites have demonstrated their ability to sabotage economic activity in the country by coordinating the blockade across six states.

---

[22] 'Call of the 9th Unity Congress of the CPI (Maoist)', *Maoists Documents, South Asia Terrorism Portal*, available at http://www.satp.org/satporgtp/countries/india/maoist/documents/papers/callofunity.htm. accessed on 13 October 2007.

[23] P. V. Ramana, 'Maoists designs', *The Tribune*, 2 July 2007, accessed on 20 October 2007.

At the military level, the naxalites have evolved two important tactics to strengthen their armed struggle: the tactic of simultaneous attacks used extensively in 2005 gave way to 'swarming' attacks, and the 'hit-and-run' tactic was replaced with 'mobile' attacks aimed at hitting specific targets with impunity. The former, as described by Ajai Sahni, involves attacking in hordes, and was first used in Koraput in Orissa in February 2004. There has been an increase in such attacks: from one in 2004, to three in 2005, nine in 2006, and 12 by the end of June 2007. A noteworthy feature of these attacks is that the majority have been carried out in the early hours of the morning to catch the 'enemy' off guard. This precaution seems to recognize their limited capabilities vis-à-vis the state. Supplementing this tactic is a change from 'guerilla warfare to mobile warfare' as pointed out by the Jharkhand Maoist group.[24] Mobile attacks can be conducted swiftly by fewer people, using more advanced technology to attack high-profile targets, for instance the assassination of Jharkhand Mukti Morcha (JMM) Member of Parliament, Sunil Kumar Mahato, on 4 March 2007, and the attempt to kill the former Chief Minister of Andhra Pradesh Nedurumalli Janardhana Reddy and his wife, and state minister N. Rajyalakshmi, on 7 September 2007.

Intensification of the Naxal Conflict

Based on their action plan, the naxalites have resurfaced in states which had managed to contain the movement, like West Bengal and Andhra Pradesh; second, strengthen their support base in states like Chhattisgarh, Orissa, Bihar, Jharkhand and Maharashtra; and third, spread to newer areas in Tamil Nadu, Karnataka, Madhya Pradesh and Uttar Pradesh.

Resurgence of Conflict in Areas Previously Cleared

West Bengal

The state of West Bengal, which had successfully controlled naxalite activities over the past three decades, re-emerged as a hotbed for naxalite agitation and mobilization in 2006–07. This is where the naxalite policy of protesting against the 'imperialist' industrialization

---

[24] Venkitesh Ramakrishnan, see note 19 above, p. 4.

policy of the government found a voice in the anti-SEZ protests by the peasants. These protests began with the proposed SEZ in Singur in November 2006 and intensified with the opposition to the proposed SEZ in Nandigram. The trigger for their resurgence in the state was an incident on 14 March 2007 when 16 peasants protesting in Nandigram became the victims of a crackdown by the state police force. Since the approval of the SEZ Act 2005, around 366 SEZ proposals have been formally approved across the country, and 142 have been notified (as on 29 August 2007).[25] However, the SEZs have encountered widespread opposition, mainly over the acquisition of agricultural land for industrial purposes leading to displacement of peasants and tribals. The naxals have attacked the SEZ policy of the government, particularly the Left government in West Bengal, by creating a safe haven for 'imperialist' multinational corporations (MNCs) and big corporate houses. Post-Nandigram, the spokesperson of the Central Committee of the CPI (Maoist) called upon the oppressed masses 'to transform every SEZ into a battle zone, to create Kalinga Nagars and Nandigrams everywhere and to kick out the real outsiders—the rapacious MNCs, big business houses…'.[26] Reports claim that the Maoists played a role in fuelling the protests.[27]

Apart from the anti-SEZ protests, sporadic incidents of naxal violence also grew steadily in West Bengal from six in 2003, to 11 in 2004, 14 in 2005, and 23 in 2006. The range of naxal violence includes landmine blasts targeting security forces (a CRPF camp on 16 January 2006, a police vehicle on 4 March), mass attacks on India Reserve Battalion camps on 1 August and 23 November 2006, attacks on CPI-Marxist leaders (5 March 2006, 2 July 2006, 19 September 2006, 9 January 2007) and encounters with the police (7 February 2006, 15 December 2006). Another violent incident occurred during the two-day economic blockade called by the naxalites on 26 and 27 June, when around 50 Maoists blasted Biramdih railway station

---

[25] Ministry of Commerce, Government of India, *Fact Sheet on Special Economic Zones as on 29 August 2007*, http://sezindia.nic.in/HTMLS/Factsheet-on-SEZs.pdf. accessed on 15 October 2007.

[26] 'Let us turn every SEZ into a Battle Zone like Nandigram', CPI (Maoist), Central Committee, 15 March 2007, http://Naxalresistance.wordpress.com/2007/03/26/let-us-turn-every-sez-into-a-battle-zone-like/. accessed on 2 October 2007.

[27] Venkitesh Ramakrishnan, see note 19 above, p. 2.

in Purulia district. The main naxal-infested districts are Midnapore, Bankura and Purulia, although the security forces suspect a spread of naxalism in the West Bengal–Jharkhand border areas.

Naxalites have employed both mass agitations and violent attacks to strengthen their movement in West Bengal, and are targeting the Left government's pro-investment industrial policy to expand their support base by translating the grievances of the peasants into support for them.

Andhra Pradesh

In Andhra Pradesh, once the centre of the naxalite movement in India, the number of incidents has come down drastically since 2005. In 2006, there were a total of 183 incidents as opposed to 535 in 2005 while, till June 2007, the figure stood at 63. Clearly, the naxalite movement has suffered reverses in the state. While the naxals used the peace process from May 2004–January 2005 to strengthen their base in the state, they were unable to withstand the heavy police crackdown after September 2005, which proved effective due to close inter-district police coordination. Key naxalite leaders eliminated by the police included the Secretary of Nallamala Forest Division Committee, the Karimnagar East Division Maoist Committee Secretary, and the CPI-Maoist 'Andhra State Secretary'.[28] The police also made some significant arrests in 2006. In addition, the surrenders in the state have shot up from none in 2005 to 60 in 2006 to 110 till August 2007.[29] As a result, the naxal presence has significantly reduced in the northwestern districts of the Telangana region, including Prakasam, Mahbubnagar, Nalgonda, Adilabad, Nizambad, Karimnagar and Warangal.

The naxals are now focusing on recouping their strength in the state in several ways. First, facing a crackdown in the heartland, the naxals have shifted their base to the border areas along Andhra–Orissa, namely Srikakulam, Visakhapatnam, Vizianagaram and East Godavari. Owing to the hilly terrain and dense forests in the region and the

---

[28] 'Major Maoists incidents, 2006', *South Asia Terrorism Portal*, http://satp.org/satporgtp/countries/india/maoist/data_sheets/Major_incidents_2006.htm. accessed on 17 August 2007.

[29] 'Maoists Datasheets', *South Asia Terrorism Portal*, http://www.satp.org/satporgtp/countries/india/maoist/data_sheets/arrsurrender.htm. accessed on 12 October 2007.

porous unmanned borders with Orissa and Chhattisgarh, the threat of the Maoists in Andhra Pradesh remains serious. Second, the naxals have targeted the economic infrastructure in the state to mobilize support. For instance, they blew up the Coffee Board Research Centre near Visakhapatnam, an SEZ location during the economic blockade, which was followed soon after by an attack on several government establishments in the Chintapalli agency on 13 July 2007 to protest against bauxite mining. Third, the naxals also carried out some high-profile attacks to demonstrate their ability to strike at will and boost the morale of their cadres. The attack on the former Chief Minister of Andhra Pradesh, Janardhan Reddy, is an example. Further, a large quantity of ammunition was recovered from Warangal district on 24 September 2007. These incidents, therefore, indicate a probable resurgence of naxal activity in the state.

Consolidation of Naxal Conflict

Chhattisgarh

Emerging as the fulcrum of the conflict in 2006–07, naxal violence shot up in Chhattisgarh from 385 incidents in 2005 to 715 in 2006 to 343 by June 2007. The conflict intensified around two main issues in the state. Foremost is the violence incited by Salwa Judum. When the SPOs, especially trained under the campaign to assist the security forces, began to commit atrocities on the villagers and indulge in arson, loot and mayhem, the naxals retaliated by targeting them and their supporters in the Salwa Judum. Thereby, the tribals got caught in the crossfire, with civilian casualties rocketing to 304 during 2006, as compared to 121 in 2005. Apart from the killings, the campaign also resulted in massive displacement of tribals from their villages with as many as 65,000 people living as refugees and over 600 out of 1,354 villages in the Dantewada district being deserted.[30] Another factor adding to the escalation of the conflict is the targeting of the industrialization drive in the state. In a bid to cripple mining activity in the state, the naxals blew up electricity poles in the Bastar district on 2 June, plunging the area into darkness; blasted 100 metres of the conveyor belt belonging to the National Mineral Development Corporation in Dantewada district on 11 June; and finally, disrupted

[30] Purnima S. Tripathi, 'Strategy gone awry', *Frontline*, vol. 24, no. 18, 8–21 September 2007, p. 1.

road and rail traffic during their two-day economic blockade to stop the movement of iron ore from Dantewada's Bailadila mines.

It is very important for the naxals to retain control over this area, particularly the Dandakaranya forest, because of its rich minerals and forest resources, seen as an important source for meeting the economic needs of the naxals. For this reason, the conflict in this region will only escalate further since the naxals are willing to engage in battle here.[31]

Orissa

Orissa too witnessed an escalation of naxal conflict, with mid–2007 already recording more incidents (45) than in the whole of 2006 (44). Sixteen of Orissa's 30 districts remain affected by naxalite activities, with the border district of Malkangiri emerging as the nucleus of their growth in the state, owing to its proximity with the naxal-affected border districts in Chhattisgarh and Andhra Pradesh, dense forests, and vast *ganja* (marijuana) cultivation (providing a source of income for the naxals). While violence was low-key in Orissa, the naxals stepped up their activity by mobilizing the tribals against the economic policies of the state, as evident from their protest against the proposed steel plant in Kalinga Nagar, Jajpur district; the attack on communication services like the BSNL mobile phone tower in Malkangiri village on 14 June 2007; and obstruction of road traffic during the economic blockade to protest against SEZs in the country. Incidents of violence have also recorded an increase with repeated attacks on police forces and CRPF personnel.

Bihar

According to a March 2007 Bihar police document, 30 of Bihar's 38 districts remain affected by naxal violence: nine districts (Kaimur, Rohtas, Aurangabad, Gaya, Nawada, Jamui, Patna, Jehanabad, and Arwal) have been designated as 'hyper-sensitive', a further nine districts including Bhojpur, Muzzafarpur, Sitamarhi, Motihari, Darbhanga, Saharsa, Banka, Bagaha and Sheohar, fall in the 'sensitive' category, while the remaining 12 districts are categorized as 'less sensitive'.[32] While the total number of incidents dipped to 107 in 2006 from 186 in 2005, records till June 2007 indicate a rise once again. Security forces are increasingly being targeted in Bihar, with a massive attack conducted by the naxals on a police station in Sitamarhi district on

[31] Pravin Sawhney, 'Wound in the heart', *Force*, vol. 4, no. 12, August 2007, p. 29.

[32] Bibhu Prasad Routray, 'Bihar: Deceptive Calm', *South Asia Intelligence Review*, vol.6, no.15, 22 October 2007.

31 March 2007, leading to an hour-long exchange of fire between the naxals and the security forces. This incident was preceded by smaller attacks across Bihar in 2006. Despite the arrest of as many as 257 naxals in the state during 2006, the attacks reveal their lurking presence in many districts of Bihar, particularly in the riverine areas of Purnia, Katihar, Sitamarhi and Saharsa. Bihar also suffered heavily during the economic blockade with road traffic coming to a grinding halt in Arwal, Jehanabad, Gaya and Patna, and the disruption of train services between Bihar and Jharkhand. Another growing cause for concern in Bihar is the shutting down of schools in Aurangabad due to the repeated demand of the naxals for money, which led to protests by the students in October 2007.

Jharkhand

Naxalite consolidation is taking place dramatically in Jharkhand with 21 of its 22 districts currently declared to be naxal-affected (12 are highly affected, four moderately and five marginally). Latest estimates by the MHA indicate a rise in violent incidents in Jharkhand—259 in January–July 2007, as against 191 in the corresponding months of the preceding year.[33] Both the naxalite strategies of mass mobilization and prolonged war have taken concrete shape in Jharkhand. It witnessed the first high-profile attack by naxals in 2007 with the killing of JMM Member of Parliament, Sunil Mahato, on 4 March 2007 in a swarming attack. The incident was preceded by at least five major attacks by the naxals in 2006, targeting police personnel mostly in east and west Singhbhum and Hazaribagh districts, and several minor operations in the first two months of 2007. In addition, three major weapon and explosives seizures have taken place in Jharkhand—recovery of dismantled parts for arms on 23 January 2007 from a private transport firm in Ranchi, 400 bags of explosives and 3,000 detonators from an arrested Maoist cadre from Dumka district on 14 April 2007, and 200 kilograms worth of explosives from Hazaribagh district on 18 November 2007[34]—indicating a large presence of naxals in the state. With mass mobilization activities, the naxals were able to inflict large-scale damage in Jharkhand during the economic blockade. Business was affected, leading to disruption of coal and iron ore production.

[33] Ajai Sahni, 'Jharkhand: Paralysis and Drift', *South Asia Intelligence Review*, vol. 6, no. 8, 3 September 2007.

[34] Bibhu Prasad Routray, 'Tentative Crystallization against the Maoists', *South Asia Intelligence Review*, vol. 6, no. 22, 10 December 2007.

Maharashtra

Although naxal violence remains limited in Maharashtra, the number of incidents recorded has shown an increase: from 75 in 2003 to 84 in 2004, 94 in 2005, 98 in 2006 and 58 till the end of June 2007. The naxalite movement spread to four more districts, namely Chandrapur, Bhandara, Yavatmal and Nanded, apart from its traditional strongholds in Gondia and Gadchiroli. Two reasons have been given: first and foremost is the spillover effect from the seriously affected neighbouring districts of Adilabad, Karimnagar and Nizamabad in Andhra Pradesh, as also Rajnandgaon, Bastar, Kanker and Dantewada in Chhattisgarh.[35] The other reason for increased naxal activity in districts like Bhandara is the killing of a Dalit family of four on 29 September 2006 in Khairlanji village by a mob of 150 upper caste men; their crime was their allegedly reporting 12 upper caste men for committing atrocities against a fellow Dalit. Following this incident, a letter was reportedly received on a CPI (Maoist) letterhead, condemning the Khairlanji incident and calling upon everyone to join the naxal agitation against the government and press for Dalit rights. It further threatened to kill those found guilty in the massacre.[36] Many of the 31 people arrested were charged with having links with the naxalites.[37] Despite doubts about the authenticity of the letter and the charges of the state police, the resolve of the naxals in their party congress to fight for Dalit rights and the proximity of the district to the two naxal-affected districts of Gondia and Gadchhiroli, suggests that there are strong reasons to suspect increased naxal activity in the district over the Dalit issue. In fact, following this incident, there was an increase in naxal-related incidents in Gondia and Gadchhiroli also.

Spread to Newer Areas

The naxals have further expanded their geographical spread across the country. In 2006, in terms of police stations affected, as many as

---

[35] Bibhu Prasad Routray, 'Maharashtra: No Scope for Smugness', *South Asia Intelligence Review*, vol. 6, no.12, 1 October 2007.

[36] 'Naxals vow revenge for Dalit family', CNN-IBN, 17 November 2006, http://www.ibnlive.com/news/Naxals-vow-revenge-for-dalit-family/26438-3.html. accessed on 15 October 2007.

[37] 'Activists allege police harassment', *The Hindu*, 20 November 2006, http://www.hinduonnet.com/2006/11/20/stories/2006112003181300.htm. accessed on 22 August 2007.

seven states reported an increase.[38] Apart from the increase in naxal violence, their area of activity has also increased, as is evident from the discovery of naxal presence in the following states:

- Tamil Nadu: Naxalite presence is suspected in the southern districts of Tamil Nadu like Theni and Tirunelveli, following the arrest of three persons allegedly attempting to start an arms training camp in the Periyakulum forests in Theni district in June 2007. The Tamil Nadu police arrested key naxal leader Sundarmurthy in the same district in July 2007 and, more recently, five suspected Maoists were arrested after a 45-minute gun battle on Varusanadu hills in Theni district on 19 December 2007. Given the limited naxal presence in the northern districts of the state bordering Andhra Pradesh through the 1980s and 1990s, the security agencies suspect a resurgence of naxal activity in the state and have been put on high alert.
- Madhya Pradesh: While the districts of Balaghat, Kawardha, Mandla and Dindori have been declared naxal-affected, the arrest of five suspected naxalites from a residential colony in Bhopal on 11–12 January 2007 has alarmed the government. Apart form the arrests, the police also seized parts of weapons and ideological literature.[39]
- Karnataka: Naxalite activity has been noted in the past months from the districts of Dakshina Kannada, Chikmagalur, Shimoga and Udupi. Most recently, an encounter between suspected naxalites and the police near Menasinahadya village in Chikmagalur district on 11 July upped the ante of the naxalite threat in the state. At the same time, the killing of a Karnataka state committee member of the CPI (Maoist) in the encounter might prove to be crucial in containing the spread of the movement. Incidents in Karnataka, however, are largely being seen as retaliation for the arrests and killing of naxal leaders in Andhra Pradesh.[40]

[38] Naxal Management Division, Ministry of Home Affairs, http://mha.gov.in/security/N.M.Division.pdf. accessed on 12 October 2007.

[39] 'Naxals reach Bhopal, MP worried', *The Indian Express*, 13 January 2007, http://www.indianexpress.com/archive/StoryN-20797-Naxals-reach-Bhopal-MP-worried.html. accessed on 13 October 2007.

[40] 'K'taka plans meet to rein in Naxalites', *The Indian Express*, 17 July 2007, http://www.indianexpress.com/story/205222.html. accessed on 13 October 2007.

- Other States: States like Kerala, Uttar Pradesh, Delhi, Haryana and Punjab continue to be listed as areas likely to witness the spread of naxal activity. Of these, Kerala and Uttar Pradesh have police stations affected by naxal violence—two out of 443 stations in Kerala and seven out of 1,432 in Uttar Pradesh in 2006.[41]

Profile of Violence

In 2006, at least 950 persons including 157 security personnel, 521 civilians, and 272 alleged naxals were killed in conflict. Meanwhile, till June 2007, as many as 451 persons including 138 security personnel, 220 civilians and 93 Maoists have been killed.[42]

Increasing Attacks on Security Forces

As the data drawn from the MHA shows, the number of security personnel killed over the past two years has increased substantially whereas civilian casualties have fallen in 2007 (for the corresponding period in 2006, civilian casualties stood at 304). This could be partly due to the naxalite strategy of targeting security personnel to intensify their armed struggle, and partly the increased presence of security forces in naxal-affected states.

Table 2: Security Forces Casualties

	2003	2004	2005	2006	2007 (till 30 June)
Andhra Pradesh	12	6	22	10	1
Bihar	26	5	24	5	18
Jharkhand	16	41	27	43	7
Chhattisgarh	30	8	47	84	109
Maharashtra	8	6	24	3	1
Orissa	12	4	1	4	2
Other States	1	30	8	8	0

Source: Status Paper on Internal Security as on 30 June 2007, Ministry of Home Affairs, Government of India, p. 25.

---

[41] Naxal Management Division, Ministry of Home Affairs, http://mha.gov.in/security/N.M.Division.pdf. accessed on 12 October 2007.

[42] Ministry of Home Affairs, *Annual Report: 2006–2007*, http://mha.gov.in/Annual-Reports/ar0607_Eng.pdf. accessed on 15 October 2007.

Some of the major attacks on security forces include:

- 28 May 2007: nine police personnel killed in landmine blasts in the Bastar district of Chhattisgarh;
- 26 April 2007: four police personnel killed and 16 injured in a landmine blast in Kanker district of Chhattisgarh;
- 15 March 2007: 55 persons, including 16 Chhattisgarh Armed Police Force personnel and 39 SPOs, killed in an offensive at Rani Bodli village, Bijapur police district, Bastar, Chhattisgarh;
- 16 January 2007: seven CRPF personnel killed in Bastar district in Chhattisgarh.

Increasing Use of Improvised Explosives

Naxals extensively used explosives, including landmines and Improvised Explosive Devices (IEDs), to target both security forces and civilians. While landmines were largely used against security forces, including police forces and CRPF personnel, bomb blasts were used on physical infrastructure like government buildings, road and rail transport, residences of officials and communication towers. In 2007, a growing trend was seen of using 'pressure cookers' and tiffin boxes for triggering explosions. In Jharkhand, the Naxalites have reportedly set up two 'Technical Wings' for the north and south Zone, with an expenditure of over Rs 20 lakh.[43] The sophistication of explosive devices, increasing use of information technology and the use of FM radio devices to intercept communications between the security forces are some naxal achievements in the recent past.

Table 3: Types of Explosives Used

	Landmines	Claymore Mines	Dynamite	Bomb Blasts	IEDs	Gelatine Sticks
2005	14	2	1	10	–	–
2006	25	1	1	31	–	–
2007 (12.09.07)	30	1	4	37	3	1

Source: Date Sheets, Bomb Blasts in 2005, 2006, 2007, Institute of Conflict Management.

[43] Ajai Sahni, 'Jharkhand: Paralysis and Drift', *South Asia Intelligence Review*, vol. 6, no. 8, 3 September 2007.

Attacks against Civilians

Chhattisgarh witnessed massive killings of tribals in 2006 as a consequence of the Salwa Judum campaign. Under this campaign, several relief camps were set up to shield the tribals from naxal violence, but these emerged as the prime targets for the Maoists in 2006. Some major incidents of violence against tribals in these camps include the killing of 25 tribals near Eklagoda village on 28 February 2006 and 33 villagers in the Arrabora village on 17 July 2006, all in Dantewada district.

Table 4: Civilian Casualties in Chhattisgarh, 2006

	Jan	Feb	Mar	Apr	May	June	July	Aug	Sept	Oct	Nov	Dec
Civ.	12	36	36	22	1	19	36	0	9	10	1	3

Source: Institute of Conflict Management.

CONFLICT MANAGEMENT

Naxalite groups feed on the perceived lack of development. Cor-recting this requires a lot of effort. It requires motivated government personnel to work in affected areas, improved road and rail connectivity and better delivery of basic services. I will ask the Cabinet Secretary to chair a Task Force to promote coordinated efforts across a range of development and security activities so that we can tackle the naxal problem in a comprehensive manner. I believe that given the unique nature of this problem, it is time to have a dedicated force just to tackle naxalism. Affected states must set up Special Task Forces on the Andhra Pradesh pattern and the Centre will provide assistance for this purpose. I would also urge the Home Ministry to also consider establishing a dedicated trained force at the Centre either as part of an existing force or as a separate one. Such a trained, dedicated force would go a long way in assisting States tackle naxalite groups.[44]

I notice that in many cases, internal security problems arise out of the uneven development and we also need to address this issue if we are to make any long-term headway in combating extremist ideologies and extremist elements.... I have said in the past that Left Wing Extremism is probably [the] single biggest security challenge to the Indian state. It

---

[44] 'PM's closing remarks at the Chief Minister's Conference on Internal Security', 20 December 2007, available at < http://pmindia.nic.in/speeches.htm> accessed on 21 December 2007.

continues to be so and we cannot rest in peace until we have eliminated this virus. We need a coordinated response to this challenge. The answers to the problem are well known. We need to cripple the hold of naxalite forces with all the means at our command. This requires improved intelligence gathering capabilities, improved policing capabilities, better coordination between the Centre and the States and better coordination between States and most important, better leadership and firmer resolve.[45]

There was only one theme that dominated the Chief Ministers' Conference on Internal Security, held on 20 December 2007, presided over by the Prime Minister—that was the problem of naxalites and the measures needed to tackle this problem. As indicated by these quotes from the Prime Minister's speech and his closing remarks at the Conference, the emphasis of the government's counter-naxal strategy is to be on enhanced development and augmentation of police capabilities. This emphasis is recent, given that the government had until now seen the problem as one meriting a law and order approach. And, with naxal groups operating in various states, and law and order being a state subject under the Constitution, the issue received only local attention. Since the amalgamation of these groups into a single entity in 2004, there has been greater emphasis on coordinating counter-naxal operations. But, a uniform national counter-naxal policy is still being evolved.

The counter-measures adopted and suggested by the central government fall under two categories: policy and operation. Some of the policy decisions are articulated in the Ministry of Home Affairs *Annual Report*:[46]

- The Government will deal sternly with the naxalites indulging in violence.
- Keeping in view that naxalism is not merely a law and order problem, the policy of the Government is to address this menace simultaneously on political, security, development and public perception management fronts in a holistic manner.
- Naxalism being an inter-State problem, the States will adopt a collective approach and pursue a coordinated response to counter it.

[45] 'PM's speech at the Chief Minister's Conference on Internal Security', 20 December 2007, available at < http://pmindia.nic.in/speeches.htm> accessed on 21 December 2007.

[46] Ministry of Home Affairs, *Annual Report 2006–2007*, p. 25.

- There will be no peace dialogue by the affected States with the naxal groups unless the latter give up violence and arms.
- The State Governments will need to accord a higher priority to ensuring faster socio-economic development in the naxal-affected or -prone areas. The focus areas should be to distribute land to the landless poor as part of the speedy implementation of land reforms, ensure development of physical infrastructure like roads, communication, power, etc. and provide employment opportunities to youth in these areas.
- The central government will continue to supplement the efforts and resources of the affected States on both security and development fronts and bring greater coordination between the States to successfully tackle the problem.

Of particular importance are the policies relating to the peace dialogue and the emphasis on fast-tracking socio-economic development in naxal-affected areas. Unevenness in approach by the different state governments has been the biggest flaw in countering the naxalites effectively. As mentioned earlier, successive governments in Andhra Pradesh have attempted to counter the naxalites by adopting strategies that negated the gains made by the previous government. Invariably, all governments start by suspending police operations, lifting the ban on the main naxal group (the PWG) and initiating dialogue. They however resume police operations after the talks have failed to take off and re-impose the ban, by which time the next government comes in and starts this process all over again. The ripple of unevenness spreads beyond the state boundaries. While one state is engaged in talks with a naxal group, a neighbouring state may intensify its police operations against the group while another state bans the organization altogether. This was the situation in 2004: while Andhra Pradesh lifted the ban and was negotiating with the PWG, West Bengal intensified its anti-naxal drive and Tamil Nadu banned the PWG yet again (the PWG was already banned in Tamil Nadu under the Prevention of Terrorism Act [POTA] but was banned again later under the Criminal Law Amendment Act as an 'unlawful organization)'.[47] The central government's articulation of a new policy that restrains the state governments from entering a peace dialogue

---

[47] 'To secure itself, Tamil Nadu bans PWG', *The Pioneer*, 11 September 2004.

unless some specified criteria are first met is a welcome step towards harmonizing policies to counter naxalism.

The central government has also proposed various measures to augment the operational capabilities of the states. Some of these measures include streamlining their security and intelligence structures and raising special police units for counter-naxal operations;[48] sanctioning the setting up of India Reserve Battalions in naxal-affected states;[49] long-term deployment of Central Police Forces; deploying the Sashastra Seema Bal (SSB) along the Indo–Nepal Border; supplying mine-protected vehicles; and, developing a Standard Operating Procedure for inter-state cooperation in counter-naxal operations.

Additionally, the central government has instituted some monitoring mechanisms to oversee state policies and synchronize efforts to evolve an effective counter-naxal strategy. Some of them are:

Task Force on Naxalism: Set up in October 2004, its mandate is to 'to deliberate upon the steps needed to deal with naxalism more effectively and in a coordinated manner'.[50] The members include nodal officers from nine naxal-affected states of Andhra Pradesh, Bihar, Chhattisgarh, Jharkhand, Maharashtra, Madhya Pradesh, Orissa, Uttar Pradesh and West Bengal, and representatives from the Intelligence Bureau (IB), Central Reserve Police Force (CRPF) and the SSB. The last meeting of the Task Force was held on 13 April 2007 in Hyderabad.

Coordination Centre: Set up in 1998, its mandate is to review and coordinate the counter-naxal strategies adopted by the states. Members include the Union Home Secretary, and the Chief Secretaries and police heads of the nine naxal-affected states. Twenty-three meetings have taken place till April 2007. The Coordination Centre called for 'Action Plans to deal with naxal problems, strengthening administrative structures to address both security and developmental aspects, improving ground level

---

[48] Training is currently being offered for these special units by the Greyhounds Training School, Centres of Excellence at the Central Paramilitary Forces, as well as the army. In August 2006, the army had already trained 6,400 personnel in Chhattisgarh, Bihar and Jharkhand in counter-naxal duties and bomb detection. A total of 14,000 personnel were to be trained by May 2007. The actual numbers trained thus far is not known.

[49] The purpose of the India Reserve battalions is not only to strengthen the states police apparatus, but also to provide employment opportunities to youth in the naxal-affected areas. The central government has increased the support for raising a battalion from Rs 13 crore to Rs 20.75 (MHA, *Annual Report 2006–2007*).

[50] Ministry of Home Affairs, *Annual Report 2006–2007*, New Delhi: Ministry of Home Affairs, p. 28.

policing by way of time bound fortification of vulnerable police stations, filling up of vacancies in State police, expeditious raising of IR battalions, ... streamlining of inter-state joint operations, and improving operational and grassroots intelligence on naxal related activities.'[51]

Standing Committee of the Chief Ministers of the Naxal-affected States: Set up following the decision taken at the Chief Ministers' Conference on Internal Security and Law and Order held in April 2005, it consists of the Chief Ministers of 13 naxal-affected states. It has met twice since to monitor the Action Plans of the states and oversee the delivery of socio-economic developmental programmes in the states.

Inter-Ministerial Group (IMG): The central government has also set up an Inter-Ministerial Group headed by an Additional Secretary specifically to monitor and review the implementation of the various centrally-sponsored schemes and programmes being undertaken in the naxal-affected areas. The Group is also monitoring progress in the implementation of land reforms; ensuring that the naxal-affected states take the necessary steps to address tribal-related issues; and assisting states to mount a sustained public awareness campaign to counter naxal propaganda.

Empowered Group of Ministers (EGoM): This was set up following a meeting of the Chief Ministers on Internal Security in September 2006. Headed by the Home Minister and including select Union Ministers and Chief Ministers of naxal-affected states, the aim of the EGoM is to 'monitor the spread of naxalism and evolve effective strategies to deal with the problem'.[52]

Naxal Management Division: Set up on 19 October 2006, the goal of this Division is to 'monitor the naxal situation and counter-measures being taken by the affected States with the objective of improving ground-level policing and development response as per the location specific action plans formulated/to be formulated by the affected States, and review with the concerned Ministries/Departments to ensure optimum utilisation of funds released under, and proper implementation of various developmental schemes in the naxal affected areas'.[53] The Naxal Management Division periodically issues status reports relating to the situation regarding the naxalite problem and the measures that are being adopted to counter it.

---

[51] Ministry of Home Affairs, *Annual Report 2006–2007*, New Delhi: Ministry of Home Affairs, p. 28.

[52] Ibid., p. 29.

[53] < http://demotemp8.nic.in/mha/uniquepage.asp?ID_PK=277> accessed on 21 December 2007.

Police modernization has been a key area of discussion and, under the Police Modernization Scheme, the central government sanctioned Rs 385 crore in 2007 for the naxal-affected states. An additional sanction of Rs 100 crore was also expected.[54] The Security Related Expenditure Scheme reimburses the state governments for monies expended towards training the police, weapons acquisition, etc. The naxal-affected states have been included in this scheme and until 31 March 2007, about Rs 175.5 crore has been reimbursed to the states. The central government has also made available to the naxal-affected states a financial package of Rs 2,475 crore under the Backward District Initiative component of the Rashtriya Sam Vikas Yojna. In January 2007, the central government also passed The Scheduled Tribes and other Traditional Forest Dwellers (Recognition of Forest Rights) Act, 2006 which will hopefully address some critical issues relating to tribals in the naxal-affected areas.[55]

Apart from the central government, the state governments too have adopted measures to address the naxal problem. In January 2007, the Maharashtra government approved formation of Village Defence Committees (VDCs) in 28 villages to counter the naxalites at a cost of Rs 2 lakh per VDC per village.[56] The Orissa government has set up its anti-naxal force and 53 personnel of the Orissa Special Armed Police received specialized training at the Anti-Terrorism Centre in Rourkela.[57] The Chhattisgarh government has set up a Special Task Force, consisting of 900 personnel, on the lines of the Greyhounds (an elite anti-naxal unit that was formed by the Andhra Pradesh state police nearly two decades ago to specifically counter the naxalites) in Andhra Pradesh for counter-naxal operations.[58] In August 2007, the governments of Jharkhand, Orissa and West Bengal formed a Joint Coordination Committee (JCC) for launching joint operations and sharing information about the naxalites.[59] In the same month, the police officials of Jharkhand and Bihar held high-level talks for conducting joint counter-naxal operations.[60]

[54] < http://mha.nic.in/press-release/2007/pr_Naxal Task Force220207.pdf>

[55] < http://mha.nic.in/internal%20security/ISS250907.pdf>

[56] 'Village groups to tackle attacks', *The Indian Express*, 8 January 2007.

[57] 'Cops trained to tackle Naxalites', *The Statesman*, 24 April 2007.

[58] 'Army officer to head anti-Naxal ops in Chhattisgarh', *Rediff.com*, 6 September 2007, http://www.rediff.com/news/2007/sep/06naxal.htm. accessed on 21 December 2007.

[59] 'United effort to curb Naxalites', *The Telegraph*, 14 August 2007.

[60] 'Jharkhand, Bihar to conduct joint operation against naxalites', *The Hindu*, 31 August 2007.

In *Contested Lands*, Sumantra Bose refers to the nature of the insurgency and the possibility of its resolution. According to him, a fragmented insurgency—characterized by multiple groups operating in the same sphere—offers little chance of success for a negotiated settlement. A consolidated insurgency, on the other hand, is more amenable to lending itself to a negotiated settlement.[61] If one were to evaluate the current naxal situation within these parameters, then conflict resolution should be less of a challenge after the amalgamation of the 'fragmented' naxal groups into a single entity. However, conflict management would continue to be a challenge precisely for the same reason. This is indeed a complex situation with no easy answers. Additionally, if any negotiation comes about, who will be the main parties? Since the naxalite movement has moved beyond the confines of individual states, would the central government be one of the negotiating parties? If so, would it not catapult the naxalite movement to a national issue? It is one thing to say that it is the single biggest security challenge, but is the government ready to accord this level of prominence to the naxalites? What would the possible implications be?

One way governments prioritize problems is by securitizing them, which allows them to address the problem more effectively, but also allows governments to resort to military ways to quell the problem because national security is at stake. In the last few years, the naxalite movement has come to be seen as a threat to national security. This hints at the actions the government is likely to adopt. And since it now appears that the government is equally committed to the development of areas affected by naxalism, it is likely that the government will win this battle.

CONCLUSIONS

There is every indication that the current phase of the naxalite movement will be the most violent. An analysis of the conflict in 2006 and 2007 clearly suggests a marked increase in the numbers and violence of naxal incidents. While on the one side there is an attempt at greater synchronization of the efforts undertaken by the union and state governments, there is on the other side greater consolidation

---

[61] See Sumantra Bose, *Contested Lands: Israel-Palestine, Kashmir, Bosnia, Cyprus, and Sri Lanka*, London: Harvard University Press, 2007.

of the naxalite forces. Both sides are likely to be engaged in pitched battles until at least 2012, during which time the violence will surpass currently existing levels.[62]

There is greater emphasis on coordinated police action, augmentation of police forces, better training and modernization. At the Chief Ministers' Conference on Internal Security held in December 2007, the Prime Minister said, 'I would also urge States to establish specialized, dedicated forces to fight Left Wing Extremism. These forces should be led by capable, highly motivated officers who can imbue the necessary fighting spirit in their personnel. The Home Ministry will provide all possible assistance to these forces. States also need to consider joint operations and joint mechanisms for effective police operations in appropriate cases.'[63] His concern to control the naxal problem stems from the effect the naxalites could have on economic development. As he pointed out during the Conference, 'They are certainly targeting all aspects of economic activity. They are targeting vital economic infrastructure so as to cripple transport and logistic capabilities and also slow down any development activity.'[64] At the 9th CPI (Maoist) Unity Congress, it has to be remembered, the naxalites had given a call to 'wage a broad-based militant mass movement against the neo-liberal policies of globalization, liberalization, privatization pursued by the reactionary ruling classes under the dictates of imperialism'.[65] This is exactly why the response of the Indian government is likely to be concentrated, coordinated and conclusive. A new rising economic power will not go soft on any internal threat to its economic robustness.

---

[62] During this period, it is also likely that the institutions of the state become more militarized. While there has been much research on the effect of protracted violence on society, hardly any exists on the effect armed violence has on state institutions. If one were to speculate, it can be reasonably concluded that the institutions of the state, particularly its police, will become more militaristic and perhaps insensitive as the naxalites continue to increase the levels of violence. Unfortunately, at the end of the conflict, it is society which will be left to deal with militaristic state institutions.

[63] 'PM's speech at the Chief Minister's Conference on Internal Security', 20 December 2007, available at < http://pmindia.nic.in/speeches.htm> accessed on 21 December 2007.

[64] Ibid.

[65] 'Press Release, CPI (Maoist) on the 9th Unity Congress, January-February 2007, 19 February 2007', *Maoists Documents, South Asia Terrorism Portal*, available at <http://www.satp.org/satporgtp/countries/india/maoist/documents/papers/19feb07.htm>.

This phase perhaps indicates the beginning of the end of the naxalite movement in India. It has already lost its ideological moorings. The bulk of the people killed by the naxalites continue to be from the section of the people they purport to represent. As Sahni points out, when 'revolutionaries find it necessary to kill more people on their own side than the enemy, it must be presumed either that their cause is widely opposed or that, at least, it leaves the population indifferent'.[66] Since the naxalites have a stake in perpetuating the level of underdevelopment in the areas under their operation, they have opposed and attacked all developmental activities attempted by the state. More than 250 schools have been blown up by the naxalites in Chhattisgarh.[67] The conflict between the naxalites and the state government has resulted in over 75,000 students dropping out of schools in 2006–07. The naxalite movement initially started out with revolutionary humanism. However, the humanistic element has long since vanished from the movement. It has debased itself to such an extent that in one incident, the naxals filled the dead body of a person it had killed with explosives and used it as bait to injure the police who came to recover the dead body.[68] Coupled with allegations of its criminalization, particularly drug cultivation and trafficking,[69] romanticization of the movement is also on the decline.

Indian democracy, however flawed or inadequate it seems, continues to offer avenues for the voicing of grievances. As C. P. Bhambri observes, 'the politics of violence in India cannot bring basic changes

---

[66] Brian Crozier, *A Theory of Conflict*, London: Hamish Hamilton, 1974, p. 129, cited in Ajai Sahni, 'Naxalism: The Retreat of Civil Governance', *Faultlines*, vol. 5, no. 7, 2000, p. 88.

[67] 'Another blow by Naxals, this time its kids' education', *The Indian Express*, 30 June 2007.

[68] 'Maoist violence claims six lives in Chhattisgarh', *Hindustan Times*, 10 April 2006.

[69] In September 2006, the Chief Minister of Madhya Pradesh highlighted the nexus between the naxalites and the drug traffickers in the Malwa region ('More stringent laws needed to tackle naxalism: Chauhan', *The Hindu*, 6 September 2006). In March 2007, the Andhra Pradesh police found that the naxalites in Warangal were selling *ganja* grown in the state to buy weapons ('From marijuana to mines: another Naxal story in AP', *The Indian Express*, 6 March 2007). In June 2007, the Ranchi police seized opium worth Rs 4 crore from an inter-state gang with naxal links, responsible for the cultivation and sale of opium in Jharkhand ('Police see Naxal link to Rs 4-crore opium haul', *The Indian Express*, 4 June 2007). In August 2007, senior police officers in Madhya Pradesh were worried that 'farmers in Naxal-affected areas were being compelled to grow *ganja*, the sale proceeds of which enabled them to fund the supply of arms and ammunition' ('Naxals farm ganja for arms', *The Asian Age*, 24 August 2007).

in society because Indians are committed to the politics of the ballot'.[70] The ameliorating effect of democracy on Left extremism or violence, for that matter, is brought out by Sahni. He says, 'arguments favouring revolutionary violence as an instrument of change in authoritarian or absolutist systems of governance are simply, mechanically and uncritically assumed to apply to a democratic polity. The fact is, democracy does offer institutions and instrumentalities of social transformation and, however inefficient these may be in a particular situation, they are ordinarily more effective than the option of directionless and largely randomised violence.'[71] Unfortunately, the naxalites continue to believe in armed struggle. According to Maoist ideologue and revolutionary writer, Varavara Rao, the Nepal Maoists were, by joining electoral politics, drifting away from the ideology of the party as propounded by Mao Zedong. He stressed that armed struggle was the core principle on which the naxalite movement was built in India.[72] But, the principal question remains, armed struggle for what? The objectives of the movement have changed over time. For instance, in October 2007, a naxal leader called for agitations against the Sethusamudram Ship Canal Project.[73] The stated original aim of the naxalite movement is to capture power through the strategy of protracted armed struggle and area-wise seizure of power by initially building bases in rural and remote areas. These bases would eventually be transformed into guerrilla zones and later into liberated areas that would ultimately extend and encircle the urban centres of power. Some recent pronouncements by the naxalites show no correspondence with their stated aims and objectives. As the Nepal Maoists have proven, it is one thing to capture power, but it is truly a different game when it comes to governing. This is probably why the naxalites are focused on challenging the state but show no inclination to join the mainstream.

Bereft of ideology, unsure of their goals, stripped off the 'humanism' of their revolution, there is only one direction that the naxalites can go. Down. However, that does not mean that they pose no short-term threat to India's internal security. Sadly, the levels of development and governance are so abysmal in many pockets in India that the naxalite

[70] C. P. Bhambhri, 'Maoism: A Failed Ideology', *Hindustan Times*, 21 May 1999.
[71] Ajai Sahni, see note 66 above, p. 84.
[72] 'Do not emulate Nepali Maoists: Varavara Rao', *The Hindu*, 2 May 2006.
[73] 'Maoist leader raises voice against Sethu project', *The Indian Express*, 10 October 2007.

movement, sustaining itself only through armed conflict, continues to get support from the public. As *The Economist* has pointed out,

> Other terrorists attack the Indian state at its strong points—its secularism, its inclusiveness, its democracy. Naxalism attacks where it is weakest: in delivering basic government services to those who need them most. The Naxalites do not threaten the government in Delhi, but they do have the power to deter investment and development in some of India's poorest regions, which also happen to be among the richest in some vital resources—notably iron and coal. So their movement itself has the effect of sharpening inequity, which many see as the biggest danger facing India in the next few years, and which is the Naxalites' recruiting sergeant.[74]

---

[74] 'India's Naxalites: a spectre haunting India', *The Economist*, 17 August 2006.

7

Northeast: Island of Peace and Ocean of Conflict

Bibhu Prasad Routray

For decades, India's northeast has been wracked by multiple armed conflicts. The Naga insurgency that raised its banner of revolt in the early 1950s has been the harbinger of several armed conflicts in each of the seven states of the region. Many of these conflicts, with distinct aims and objectives, have persisted despite the intervention of the state and civil society. Barring a few cases, the government's achievements at ending these conflicts, either through military interventions, peace talks or ceasefire agreements, have been minimal. Dialogue with the militant outfits, wherever it has occurred, has invariably led to ceasefire agreements. However, only a few such ceasefire agreements have actually led to the termination of the conflict. Factions have emerged reneging from the peace talks and have carried on with the armed violence. Over the years, each of these conflicts has developed a nexus and linkages with forces inside and outside the region, and these linkages have contributed immensely to their life span. Most of these conflicts have acquired a criminalized character and display no resemblance to their original objectives and ideology. While states like Tripura and Meghalaya have lately shown signs of breaking the shackles of militancy, other states like Manipur, Assam and Nagaland continue to be affected by a high degree of militant violence.

A BRIEF HISTORY

Insurgency in Nagaland has been described as the 'mother of all insurgent movements' in the northeast. The Naga separatist movement, which had begun before Independence, is based on the premise that Nagas have been historically independent, unconquered by anyone and, therefore, India has no right to subjugate them. Naga representative organizations during British rule had petitioned the government to address their concerns of being submerged in an alien culture after the departure of the British. Though the British had made special provisions for the administration of the hill tribes, this was clearly short of endorsing their demand for independence. Subsequently, after India's Independence, the Nagas, under the Naga National Council (NNC), appealed to the Indian National Congress to set them free. Faced with rejection, the NNC under A.Z. Phizo declared the independence of Nagaland under what he claimed was a plebiscite supposedly held in 1951 in which 99 per cent of the population had voted in favour of independence. The NNC went on to start an insurgency movement as the government of India ruled out the possibility of Nagaland's independence and deployed the army in the Naga hills. Following military intervention by the government, Phizo left the country for London, never to set foot on Nagaland's soil again. In 1975, the Shillong Accord was signed between the NNC and the government of India where the NNC cadres accepted 'without condition, the Constitution of India'.[1] However, a section of the NNC rebelled against the accord and formed the National Socialist Council of Nagaland (NSCN) in 1980. Tribal differences led to a split in the NSCN in 1987, leading to the birth of the Isak-Muivah faction (NSCN-IM) and the Khaplang faction (NSCN-K).[2] Both these outfits continued their movement with the avowed objective of establishing a greater Nagaland comprising the Naga-inhabited areas of Nagaland, Assam, Manipur, Arunachal Pradesh and neighbouring Myanmar. In 1997, the NSCN-IM and the union government entered into a ceasefire agreement and have since held several rounds of dialogue to resolve the conflict. A similar ceasefire agreement was signed between the NSCN-K and the government in 2001, though both sides have yet to start a process of dialogue. The ceasefire agreements with both the outfits have been periodically extended.

Insurgency in Assam started with the popular Assam agitation in 1979. The United Liberation Front of Asom (ULFA) was formed that year with the objective of a sovereign socialist Assam, free from the

---

[1] For the text of the Shillong Accord, see 'The Shillong Accord of 11 November 1975 between The Government of India and the underground Nagas', Naga International Support Center, http://www.nagalim.nl/naga/history/shillong_accord.html (accessed 29 August 2007).

[2] For details of the NSCN–IM's aims and objectives, see the outfit's well-maintained and regularly updated website, http://www.nscnonline.org/. The NSCN–K, on the other hand, does not have a website.

'colonial exploitation of India', as well as halting the flow of illegal migrants from Bangladesh.³ Soon, however, ULFA transformed itself into a terrorist outfit, targeting civilians and security forces. Its military capability is believed to have increased as a result of its ties with the NSCN-IM, which helped it to secure arms and provided training to its cadres. With the Asom Gana Parishad (AGP) government coming to power after the Assam agitation, ULFA's activities received a tremendous boost, with the state government defining them as 'our boys'.⁴ The breakdown of governance led to the declaration of President's Rule in the State and two army operations, Operation Rhino and Bajrang,⁵ targeted the outfit and its facilities within Assam, forcing ULFA's leadership to seek refuge in Bangladesh. Subsequently ULFA was patronized by the Inter-Services Intelligence (ISI) of Pakistan and the Directorate General of Forces Intelligence (DGFI) of Bangladesh. It brought about a drastic transformation in the character of the outfit, which started advocating recognition of the contribution of the illegal migrants from Bangladesh to Assam's economy and development. The outfit also maintained camps in Bhutan and Myanmar. It steadfastly refused to enter into negotiations with the government and continued its militant activities in the state. In December 2003, the Royal Bhutan Army (RBA) launched a military operation against the outfit, clearing Bhutan's soil of the militant presence. During these operations, about 650 militants,⁶ including a majority of ULFA cadres, were neutralized. However, ULFA has managed to survive and continues to launch periodic strikes in Assam.

The ULFA is not the lone insurgent outfit in Assam. In the 1980s, the largest plains tribes in the state, the Bodos, initiated an insurgency on issues like dispossession of their tribal lands by Bengali and Assamese

---

³ Details of ULFA's aims and objectives can be found on the group's poorly maintained website http://www.geocities.com/CapitolHill/Congress/7434/ulfa.htm. For further details also see the outfit's fortnightly *Freedom*, which is electronically distributed to select media persons in Assam.

⁴ For an assessment of ULFA's rendezvous with terrorism, see Bibhu Prasad Routray, 'ULFA: The "Revolution" comes Full circle', *Faultlines: Writings on Conflict & Resolution,* New Delhi, vol. 13, November 2002, pp. 117–39.

⁵ Operation Bajrang was conducted between 27 November 1990 and 10 June 1991. The achievements of this particular operation were minimal. Subsequently, Operation Rhino was launched on 15 September 1991, and was concluded on 13 January 1992.

⁶ Annual Report: 2003–04, Ministry of Home Affairs, Government of India, p. 39, http://www.mha.gov.in/Annual-Reports/ar0304-Eng.pdf (accessed 30 August 2007).

settlers, and apathy shown to the Bodo language and culture by the mainstream Assamese. In 1988, the National Democratic Front of Bodoland (NDFB) emerged with the specific objective of establishing an independent Bodo country. On a parallel front, the All Bodo Students' Union (ABSU) launched a movement that continued till February 1993 when the Bodo Accord was signed between the Bodo Volunteer Force (BVF) and the union government. However, instead of bringing peace to the troubled area, a section of the BVF rejected the Accord and formed the Bodo Liberation Tigers (BLT) in 1996. The BLT has engaged in several terrorist acts, especially in the districts of lower Assam and the Bodo heartland. These activities of the BLT ended with the ceasefire agreement of 29 March 2000. Negotiations between the government and the militant outfit culminated in the creation of the Bodoland Territorial Council (BTC) in December 2003. The NDFB, however, continued to remain outside the ambit of the negotiations till October 2004, when it announced a unilateral ceasefire which has subsequently been extended.

Apart from ULFA and the Bodo insurgency, Assam has been affected by insurgent movements initiated by the Karbi and the Dimasa tribes, the Adivasis and also the Islamists. The Karbis and Dimasas have demanded autonomy for their homelands, whereas the Adivasis have demanded greater recognition of their rights. The government has entered into ceasefire agreements with the Karbi insurgent outfit, the United People's Democratic Solidarity (UPDS), and the Dimasa outfit, Dima Halim Daogah (DHD). But splinter groups of both the outfits, the Karbi Longri North Cachar Hills Liberation Front (KLNLF) and the Black Widow group have continued with their activities. The Islamist outfits, mainly the Muslim United Liberation Tigers of Assam (MULTA), with the assistance of the ISI of Pakistan, based in Bangladesh, have indulged in several acts of sabotage. Security force operations have managed to keep the MULTA cadres in check.

The emergence of insurgency in Manipur is formally traced to the constitution of the United National Liberation Front (UNLF) on 24 November 1964. The alleged 'forced' merger of the Kingdom of Manipur with the Indian union was the cause of great resentment among the people of Manipur. This dissent is said to have been further aggravated by the delay in conferring full-fledged statehood on Manipur. Since then several other outfits, like the People's Liberation Army (PLA), founded in September 1978, the People's Revolutionary Party of Kangleipak (PREPAK) in 1977, and the Kangleipak Communist

Party (KCP) in 1980 have emerged in the valley areas of the state, demanding a separate independent Manipur.

The hill areas of the state, comprising five districts, have been affected by different types of militancy. Kuki tribals, inhabiting the hill areas of the state, initiated their own brand of insurgency in the early 1990s against the oppression by Naga outfits like the NSCN-IM. Following ethnic clashes between the Nagas and Kukis in the early 1990s, several Kuki outfits were formed. Similarly, Islamist outfits like the People's United Liberation Front (PULF) have also been founded to protect the interests of the 'Pangals' (Manipuri Muslims). Most of the militant outfits have tended to resist government offers for negotiations. Today, Manipur is one of the worst affected states in the northeast, where at least 20 militant outfits are active. Except for the Kukis, none of these militant outfits in the state has demonstrated any inclination to negotiate with the government.

Unhindered migration from former East Bengal and subsequently Bangladesh has transformed the demography of Tripura, once a tribal majority state. The migrants have not only managed to push the indigenous tribals to the hills and forests by grabbing their lands, but also dominated the politics and administration of the state. Insurgency started as a protest movement against non-tribal domination. 'First organized-armed tribal movement was known as *Senkrak* which manifested itself in mid sixties ... as a reaction to settling down of non-tribal refugees in the Tribal Reserve Forest Areas. This movement was however, controlled in 1968.'[7] Subsequently, the Tripura National Volunteers (TNV) was founded by B.K. Hrangkhawal with similar objectives in collaboration with the Mizo National Front (MNF). This outfit dissolved in December 1980, but was later revived on 10 November 1982. The TNV continued its activities till the signing of a tripartite agreement on 12 August 1988, which paved the way for the surrender of its cadres. Another militant outfit, the All Tripura People's Liberation Organization (ATPLO), remained active between December 1980 and July 1983.

Some disgruntled TNV cadres formed the National Liberation Front of Tripura (NLFT) in March 1989 led by Dhananjoy Reang. The NLFT has undergone several splits since then. However, the outfit, which is presently based in Bangladesh, remains one of the two most

---

[7] 'Militancy', Website of the Tripura Police, http://tripurapolice.nic.in/amilitancy.htm#b1 (accessed 24 February 2006).

active outfits in the state. The other outfit, in addition to the NLFT, which has steadfastly refused to be drawn into any peace deal with the government is the All Tripura Tiger Force (ATTF), formed in July 1990 as the All Tripura Tribal Force. In fact, the ATTF had signed a memorandum of understanding with the Tripura government on 23 August 1993. However, a faction led by Ranjit Debbarma decided to carry on their armed campaign. Over the years, the outfit has found shelter in Bangladesh and indulges in hit-and-run campaigns inside Tripura. Effective police action since late 2002 has managed to bring about a significant reduction in fatalities.

Militancy in Meghalaya is said to have begun as a movement against the domination of the *dkhars* (outsiders). The Hynniewtrep Achik Liberation Council (HALC) represented the interests of the dominant tribes of the state—the Khasis, Jaintias and the Garos. However, tribal differences led to a split in the HALC in 1992. Two outfits emerged, the Hynniewtrep National Liberation Council (HNLC)[8] representing the Khasis and the Jaintias, and the Achik Matgrik Liberation Army (AMLA) representing the Garos. The AMLA subsequently went into oblivion to be replaced by the Achik National Volunteers Council (ANVC).[9] The HNLC, mostly based in the capital city of Shillong and adjoining areas in the Khasi hills, seeks to convert Meghalaya into 'a province exclusively for the Khasi tribe and free it from "domination" by the Garo tribe'. The ANVC's purported objective is to 'carve out a homeland called "Achik Land" in the areas of Garo Hills'. Both groups entered into a strategic alliance with outfits like the ULFA, the NSCN-IM and the NDFB, in return for allowing them safe passage and providing them with safe houses in the hilly terrains of Meghalaya. Sustained counter-insurgency operations have weakened both outfits. The ANVC entered into a ceasefire agreement with the government on 23 July 2004. However, the HNLC's top leadership, based in Bangladesh, continues to resist any deal.

Insurgency in Mizoram, which started with the infamous *Mautam* famine of the 1960s, ended with the Mizo Peace Accord of 1986. Former insurgent leaders were absorbed into the political stream in the state; following that, the state has remained more or less peaceful, except for peripheral conflicts. Prominent among them has been the

---

[8] For a profile of the HNLC, see South Asia Terrorism Portal, http://www.satp.org/satporgtp/countries/india/states/meghalaya/terrorist_outfits/hnlc.htm (accessed 24 February 2006).

[9] For a profile of the ANVC, see South Asia Terrorism Portal, http://www.satp.org/satporgtp/countries/india/states/meghalaya/terrorist_outfits/anvc.htm (accessed 24 February 2006).

case of the Brus or the Reangs, who were forced out of the state to neighbouring Tripura in 1997, following alleged atrocities on them. Nearly 17,000 of them, whose number steadily grew to about 35,000 by early 2000, were housed in six relief camps in the Kanchanpur sub-division of the North district in Tripura. As the Mizoram government dithered over the repatriation of the Reangs, citing reasons like an inflated number of refugees, militant outfits like the Bru National Liberation Front (BNLF) and the Bru Liberation Front of Mizoram (BLFM) emerged out of these camps, indulging in intermittent violence inside Mizoram and also the border areas in Assam. Peace talks began between the Mizoram government and the BNLF on 7 September 2001. Both sides held several rounds of talks to reach a solution. However, in spite of a peace deal between the BNLF and the Mizoram government on 26 April 2005, repatriation of the refugees into Mizoram is yet to begin.

PRINCIPAL ACTORS

Assam

The 27th Battalion of ULFA suffered the brunt of the military operations in Bhutan in December 2003. However, reports in 2006 indicated that the battalion has been successful in re-establishing camps in Bhutan. 'Hira Sarania, a top leader of ULFA's military wing who is believed to be close to commander-in-chief Paresh Barua, is heading the cadres operating from the camps'.[10] Speaking on 1 November 2006, S.K. Sarkar, Additional Director General of Police (Intelligence) in West Bengal, stated that ULFA, along with the Kamtapur Liberation Organization (KLO), were establishing camps in Bhutan and Nepal and were being helped by the Maoists in Nepal. Sarkar's statement was further confirmed by the Assam police chief D.N. Dutt on 2 November 2006, when he indicated that the ULFA was 'using certain stretches of Bhutan for taking shelter'. Further, the Special Branch of the Assam Police, on 19 November 2006, indicated that ULFA's 7th Battalion had established camps at Kawaimari near Deothang.

For several years, the 28th Battalion of the outfit has remained a major tactical division of the ULFA, key to the outfit's activities in the districts of Tinsukia, Dibrugarh and Sibsagar. The Battalion, primarily based in Myanmar, is led by some of the better-trained and motivated

[10] 'ULFA re-establishes camps in Bhutan', *The Hindu*, 14 August 2006.

'commanders', and it is absolutely vital for the outfit to sustain its sporadic attacks. In addition, Battalion 709 of the outfit, which remained dysfunctional for several years, has started operating in districts like Kamrup and Karbi Anglong. The 27th Battalion, following a deal with the KLNLF in 2006, is known to have set up at least two bases in the district of Karbi Anglong and has coordinated its activities with the KLNLF. Police sources have indicated that about 40 ULFA cadres operate in the Karbi Anglong and have taken shelter in the KLNLF hideouts.[11] Other sources, however, indicate that the number of ULFA cadres in Karbi Anglong could be one hundred.[12]

Among the active peripheral outfits, the Black Widow faction of the DHD and the KLNLF have an equal cadre strength and possess comparable arms and explosives. Both these outfits have engaged in periodic strikes in the districts of Karbi Anglong and the NC (North Cachar) Hills. On most occasions they have avoided attacking the security forces to ensure that a full-scale military operation is not launched against them. Over the years, their cadre strength has remained more or less constant. Islamist militancy, on the other hand, has remained marginal. Police sources maintain that the threat from Islamist militancy is not of great concern.

Strength of the Active Outfits

Outfit	Approximate Cadre Strength	Weapons and Explosives	Area of Influence
ULFA	700–1000	AK series rifles, sniper rifles, grenade launchers, LMGs, pistols, Chinese grenades, TNT and RDX	Dibrugarh, Tinsukia, Sibasagar, Karbi Anglong, Dhemaji, Nalbari, Sonitpur, Kamrup
KLNLF	150–200	Locally made rifles, AK series rifles, pistols, Chinese grenades	Karbi Anglong, NC Hills
DHD (Black Widow faction)	150–200	Locally made rifles, AK series rifles, pistols, Chinese grenades	Karbi Anglong, NC Hills
MULTA	50–100	Locally made rifles, AK series rifles, pistols, Chinese grenades, explosives	Dhubri

[11] Samudra Gupta Kashyap, 'Won't tolerate killings: Jaiswal warns Assam', *Indian Express*, 15 August 2007.

[12] 'Gogoi visits Ampahar, assures more forces', *Assam Tribune*, 12 August 2007.

Manipur

As many as 20 insurgent groups operate in Manipur, at least five of which operate in the valley areas of the state.[13] A report of the state Home Department in May 2005 indicated that 'as many as 12,650 cadres of different insurgent outfits with 8,830 weapons are actively operating in the state'. 'According to government sources, the strength of those concentrated in the valley districts is assessed at around 1,500 cadres for the RPF and its army wing, the PLA, 2,500 cadres for the UNLF and its army wing MPA, 500 cadres for the PREPAK and its army wing, Red Army, while KYKL and its *Yawol Lanmi* is assessed as having a strength of 600 cadres. The KCP's strength is assessed at 100 cadres. Many of these parties now have a strong presence in the hill districts as well.'[14] Over the years, despite arrests and odd surrenders, the strength of the outfits has remained more or less intact.

In Manipur, the valley-based Meitei outfits have remained active and the operations of the security forces have made little difference to their capabilities. The UNLF, PLA, KYKL, PREPAK and the KCP have been involved in some of the serious attacks on security forces. The militants have an avowed policy of not targeting state police personnel unless circumstances demand it. Thus, their practice of attacking the army and the paramilitary personnel, seen as Indian forces, secures vital support from the people who are alienated.

Unlike other conflict theatres of the northeast, not many 'surrenders' have been reported from Manipur, indicating the tight control that the outfits have maintained over their cadres. Armed with an extremely efficient intelligence network and superior fire power, the militants have been able to carve out a number of 'liberated zones' across the state. Security forces operations against such movements have so far achieved only limited success.

---

[13] The Valley-based militant outfits are the People's Liberation Army (PLA), the United National Liberation Front (UNLF), the People's Revolutionary Party of Kangleipak (PREPAK), Kangleipak Communist Party (KCP), and the Kanglei Yawol Kanna Lup (KYKL).

[14] 'Counter insurgency to be reinforced with sophisticated weapons', *Imphal Free Press*, 20 June 2007.

Strength of the Active Outfits

Outfit	Approximate Cadre Strength	Weapons and Explosives	Area of Influence
UNLF	2,250–2,500	AK series rifles, M-16 rifles, UMG, mortars, pistols, grenade launchers, IEDs, Chinese grenades	Valley districts and some parts of the hill districts
PLA	1,200–1,500	AK series rifles, M-16 rifles, UMG, mortars, pistols, grenade launchers, IEDs, Chinese grenades	Valley districts
KYKL	500–600	AK series rifles, M-16 rifles, SLRs, grenade launchers, sniper rifles	Imphal East and West, Bishnupur and Thoubal
PREPAK	400–500	AK series rifles, M-16 rifles, SLRs, grenade launchers, sniper rifles	Valley districts
PULF	75–90	AK series rifles, grenades, pistols	Thoubal, Imphal East & West
KCP	100	AK series rifles, grenades, pistols	Imphal East & West, Bishnupur
NSCN-IM	6,000	AK series rifles, M-16 rifles, UMG, mortars, pistols, grenade launchers, IEDs, Chinese grenades	Hill districts
NSCN-K	600–750	AK series rifles, pistols, IEDs, Chinese grenades	Hill districts

Tripura

Militant outfits in Tripura have weakened over the years. The NLFT faction led by Biswamohan Debbarma remains active along with the Ranjit Debbarma-led ATTF in spite of a gradual decline in cadre strength. The top leadership of both these outfits is based in Bangladesh. Both groups adopt similar tactics and mostly indulge in hit-and-run operations in two of Tripura's four districts. The North and South districts of the state have remained more or less peaceful. Differences between these outfits, however, persist and, despite some reports of a possibility of collaboration,[15] both continue to operate independently. Attacks are primarily targeted against security force personnel, political party workers belonging to the Communist Party of India-Marxist (CPI-M), and businessmen. In the past they used to attack the workers employed in the laying of railway tracks. However, such attacks have reduced after the police started providing security to these projects.

Strength of the Active Outfits

Outfit	Approximate Cadre Strength	Weapons and Explosives	Area of Influence
NLFT-Biswamohan	300	Locally made rifles, AK series rifles, Chinese grenades	West and Dhalai districts
ATTF	200	Locally made rifles, AK series rifles, Chinese grenades	West district

Nagaland

The NSCN-IM remains the most powerful outfit in the state. Reports have indicated that the ceasefire regime which started in 1997 has allowed the outfit to augment its cadre strength and arms in their possession. It has also allowed the outfit to continue operating with 'state sanction' and, thereby, activities like extortion, defined by the outfit as 'tax collection', and gross interference in administrative matters continue unabated. Though the rules of the ceasefire restrict the movement of armed cadres outside their designated camps, they continue to frequent the countrysides in search of finance and their rival NSCN-K cadres.

The NSCN-K, in spite of the losses it suffered in its clashes with the NSCN-IM, has managed to hold on to its areas of influence, primarily in districts like Mokokchung and pockets in Dimapur. The outfit's

---

[15] Amidst reports of a truce between the NLFT and the ATTF, Tripura Police Chief K.T.D. Singh, on 12 September 2007, said that it was not yet clear if both the outfits would engage in joint subversive activity though they had decided to stay away from fighting each other. See 'Rebel truce', *Telegraph*, 13 September 2007.

strength derives from its facilities in the Sagaing division in Myanmar, despite periodic onslaughts by the Myanmarese army. The non-initiation of a dialogue process with the government continues to deprive it of vital popular support, but it remains opposed to the initiation of a dialogue process unless the government calls off its talks with the NSCN-IM.

The NNC, on the other hand, remains a poor shadow of the erstwhile outfit that had initiated the Naga insurgency. Though it has its share of supporters among the older generation, who were associated with the movement started by A. Z. Phizo, the NNC is struggling to keep its identity intact, while being targeted by powerful outfits like the NSCN-IM.

Strength of the Active Outfits

Outfit	Approximate Cadre Strength	Weapons and Explosives	Area of Influence
NSCN-IM	2,000–2,500	AK series rifles, LMGs, UMGs, Grenade launchers, explosives	Phek, Kohima, Tuensang
NSCN-K	1,000–1,250	AK series rifles, LMGs, UMGs, grenade launchers, explosives	Dimapur, Mokokchung
NNC	250–500	AK series rifles, locally made weapons	Phek, pockets of Tuensang, Mokokchung and Wokha

Meghalaya

Following the ceasefire agreement between the government and the ANVC and the subsequent confinement of ANVC cadres in designated camps, the Garo hills of Meghalaya have been peaceful. Since 2004, taking advantage of the vacuum left by the ANVC, several small outfits emerged and disappeared in quick succession. In early 2006, the Liberation Achik Elite Force (LAEF) was formed by a former police commando, Peter Marak. The outfit, which is known to have linkages with the NSCN-K,[16] has been involved in a few incidents in the Garo

---

[16] 'One killed, 11 hurt, newly-formed Liberation of Achik Elite Force prime suspect', *Shillong Times*, 23 June 2007.

hills area. Some other reports,[17] however, indicate that the LAEF is trying to establish links with the NSCN-IM.

The HNLC too has received a drubbing from the state police. Many of its cadres have either been arrested or have surrendered. While its top leadership continues to be based in Bangladesh, the outfit has been rendered incapable of launching attacks. As a result, Khasi militancy has been completely neutralized.

Strength of the Active Outfits

Outfit	Approximate Cadre Strength	Weapons and Explosives	Area of Influence
HNLC	50	Locally made weapons, AK series rifles, grenades	Khasi Hills
LAEF	70–100	Locally made weapons, AK series rifles, grenades	Garo Hills

Mizoram

Mizoram continues to be peaceful barring odd incidents of peripheral militancy. It has managed to bring both the BNLF and the BLFM into the peace fold, thus keeping their nuisance value under control. These outfits remain incapable of posing any serious challenge to the security of Mizoram. Other outfits like the Hmar People's Convention-Democracy (HPC-D), however, continue to carry out their activities beyond the borders of Mizoram, mostly in Assam and Manipur.

Strength of the Active Outfits

Outfit	Approximate Cadre Strength	Weapons and Explosives	Area of Influence
BNLF	Surrendered	SLRs, .303 rifles, revolvers, grenades and locally made arms	Mamit district
BLFM	Surrendered	SLRs, .303 rifles, revolvers, grenades and locally made arms	Kanchanpur sub-division of Tripura and western Mizoram
HPC-D	50	Rifles, grenades and locally made arms	Border areas with Assam and anipur

[17] 'LAEF seeks NSCN-IM help to regroup', *Shillong Times*, 6 September 2007.

CONFLICT IN 2007

The state of militancy in the northeast registered an improvement in 2006 over the previous year. Compared to 869 fatalities in 2005, 780 deaths were reported in 2006, a decline of over 10 per cent. Militancy-related incidents, however, increased by over 2 per cent. While a sharp decline was registered in the fatalities among civilians, the deaths of militants decreased marginally. Fatalities among security forces increased marginally. In spite of these decreases in fatalities, there is little to indicate that the northeast is emerging out of its trough of militancy and chaos. In eleven months of 2007, 1,019 fatalities were recorded in 1,401 incidents. In fact, the following analysis of the conflict situation in the separate states during 2006–07 would reveal that the region, barring states which had already shown signs of improvement by the beginning of 2005, continue to be trapped in a vicious cycle of violence.

Security Situation in the Northeastern States[18]

Head	2003	2004	2005	2006	2007*
Incidents	1,332	1,234	1,332	1,366	1,401
SFs killed	90	110	70	76	76
Civilians killed	494	414	393	309	463
Militants killed	523	404	406	395	480

* As on 30 November 2007.

Assam[19]

Security Situation in Assam[20]

Head	2003	2004	2005	2006	2007*
Incidents	358	267	398	413	442
SFs killed	12	17	7	32	25
Civilians killed	182	194	173	164	268
Militants killed	207	104	74	46	112

* As on 30 November 2007.

[18] *Status Paper on Internal Security Situation*, Ministry of Home Affairs, Government of India, 30 November 2007, p. 12.

[19] Data for Assam and for other states are from the *Annual Report: 2005–06*, Ministry of Home Affairs, Government of India.

[20] *Status Paper on Internal Security Situation,* Ministry of Home Affairs, Government of India, 30 November 2007, p. 14.

In Assam, 242 fatalities were recorded in 2006 in 413 militancy-related incidents. While fatalities have registered a marginal decline over the previous year, militancy-related incidents registered an increase. Fatalities among civilians and militants decreased, while they increased sharply among security force personnel. This was an indication of the augmented capability of the militants, who managed to launch serious attacks on the men in uniform. In 2006, Assam remained the second most violent state in the northeast. The situation further worsened in 2007, when it surpassed Manipur to become the most violent state in the northeast. Between January and November 2007, 405 fatalities were recorded in 442 militancy-related incidents.

The military offensive targeting ULFA began on 24 September 2006 in the districts adjoining the state of Arunachal Pradesh after the government of India called off a six-week ceasefire, blaming the outfit for stepping up violence and extortion. The offensive, by official accounts, was successful. Till 15 April 2007, 48 ULFA cadres had been killed (including 20 top militants of ULFA's 28th Battalion), 81 arrested and another 88 had surrendered.[21] Given the fact that the group's fighting cadres are estimated to be no more than 500, the neutralization of 217 was a serious setback for the outfit.

Even before the success of the military action, ULFA's sporadic activities, largely comprising blasts on oil pipelines in deserted areas and the killing of unprotected and unarmed migrant workers, provided clear indications of the group's diminished ability to carry out 'high-quality' attacks. This indicated a significant reversal for an outfit that has been in the business for nearly three decades, but is also known to have been backed by the ISI and the Bangladeshi DGFI for a considerable period.

In spite of these setbacks, ULFA has survived and cooperated with the local militant outfits to carry out a violent campaign in August 2007 against the Hindi-speaking population in the district of Karbi Anglong. It was the second such attack in 2007 on the Hindi-speaking people, who were also the targets of the outfit's violent campaign in January. In all, during 2007 (till end August) 61 Hindi-speaking persons[22] were killed by ULFA in Assam. The outfit appears to have gained from an

---

[21] Bibhu Prasad Routray, 'Assam: No end to ULFA', *South Asia Intelligence Review*, 23 April 2007, vol. 5, no.41, http://satp.org/satporgtp/sair/Archives/5_41.htm#assessment2.

[22] '6 new PSs, 13 outposts in 'Karbi Anglong soon', *Assam Tribune*, 6 September 2007.

ambivalent government policy that oscillates between peace offers and military operations. In fact, the ceasefire in 2006 was declared despite reservations expressed by the army. Chief Minister Tarun Gogoi had to concede at a later stage that the decision to declare a ceasefire with the outfit was a 'blunder'[23], which allowed it to regroup. The outfit has managed to cast its extortion network far and wide, targeting traders, business establishments, tea gardens, officials, public sector undertakings and civilians. The state has been found lacking in devising a response to these developments.

The existing ceasefire with the NDFB has been periodically extended, the last declaration being made on 28 May 2007. However, with the peace talks going nowhere, 'the ceasefire regime has provided the group with an enormous opportunity not only to consolidate its strength, but also to run an efficient extortion network in its areas of dominance.'[24] The insurgent group has carried out several recruitment drives not only in the BTC districts, but also in the hilly Karbi Anglong district which has a sizeable Bodo population. Its extortion drives have targeted the local civilian popu-lation and the vehicles passing through the area. Since districts like Kokrajhar serve as the entry point to Assam, the NDFB's extortion network casts its net wide, targeting virtually every single vehicle that enters the northeast region. On occasion, the NDFB has also targeted the cadres of its rival outfit, the erstwhile BLT. On 31 March 2007, NDFB militants killed a personal security officer of a BTC executive member at Kumarikata Bazaar under the Tamulpur police station limits of Baska district. Again, on 20 May, NDFB militants killed four persons, including a former BLT cadre, in Sonitpur district.

Peripheral militant outfits like the KLNLF and Black Widow have restricted their activities to the southern districts of Karbi Anglong and NC Hills. Counter-insurgency operations in such districts, directed against a few hundred militants, are characterized by a certain measure of indifference, unless aggravated by 'major' incidents. Both these outfits, throughout 2006 and 2007, indulged in several acts of extortion and attacks on security forces. As a result, there has been a

---

[23] In an interview Gogoi said, 'In retrospect, I admit that the judgment may be a little wrong when we offered a ceasefire to the ULFA'. See 'Truce with ULFA was a blunder, says Gogoi', *Sentinel*, 16 January 2007.

[24] Bibhu Prasad Routray, 'Assam: The NDFB's resurrection', *South Asia Intelligence Review*, vol. 5, no. 46, 28 May 2007, http://satp.org/satporgtp/sair/Archives/5_46.htm#assessment2.

significant increase in their political clout and local politicians have found it expedient to maintain an 'understanding' with them. On 4 June 2007, Black Widow militants shot dead Purnendu Langthasa and his colleague Nindu Langthasa, both politicians of the ruling Congress Party in the NC Hills district,[25] subsequent to a quarrel over the extortion amount.

Manipur

In 2006, Manipur was the third most violent conflict theatre in the country, following Jammu and Kashmir and Left-wing, insurgency-ravaged Chhattisgarh. The 311 militancy-related fatalities in 2006 was, however, a clear improvement over 2005 in which 410 deaths were reported. While fatalities among the civilians and security forces have significantly reduced, a marginal decline has also occurred among the militants. The situation worsened in the 11 months of 2007 in which 355 fatalities were recorded in 546 incidents. Manipur continues to rank among the most violent states in terms of militant domination and the inability of the state to respond to this situation.

Security Situation in Manipur[26]

Head	2003	2004	2005	2006	2007*
Incidents	243	478	554	498	546
SFs killed	27	36	50	28	38
Civilians killed	50	88	158	96	117
Militants killed	128	134	202	187	200

* As on 30 November 2007.

Several areas of Manipur have for long remained under the tactical control of the militants. The Indian army, by a series of major operations since October 2004, was able to purge at least six of Manipur's sub-divisions of militant presence. These six sub-divisions—Thanlon, Parbung, Shinghat and Henglep in Churachandpur district, Jiribam in Imphal East and Chakpikarong in Chandel district—had been under effective militant control for the preceding nine years. However, New Somtal, spread over an area of 1,000 square kilometres and located in the southeastern corner of Chandel district along the Myanmar

[25] 'Militants kill Langthasa son—Gorlosa group strikes before polls', *Telegraph*, 5 June 2007.
[26] *Status Paper on Internal Security Situation*, Ministry of Home Affairs, Government of India, 30 November 2007, p. 16.

border, continued under militant control. Operations by the Indian army to take New Somtal commenced in February 2006, but were quickly abandoned. The General Officer Commanding (GOC) of 57 Mountain Division, Major General E.J. Kochekkan, speaking on 19 September 2006, pointed out the inaccessibility of New Somtal as being the main hindrance. The area's proximity to Myanmar provides the militants an easy escape route, and the absence of a framework for a coordinated effort between the Indian army and its Myanmarese counterpart has created obvious difficulties.

In the second week of December 2006, the Indian army's 10 J&K Light Infantry Battalion launched 'Operation Khengjoi', targeting the New Somtal area. The operation was reportedly launched after Chief Minister Okram Ibobi Singh presented a brief to the Prime Minister on the security situation in the state during the latter's tour of Manipur on 2 December. Contradicting the army's claims of success in purging vast areas of militant presence, Chief Minister Singh pointed out that a great deal remained to be done, particularly in terms of clearing large tracts of the state like Tipaimukh, Barak and Loktak. He admitted, further, that 'There is still a 5–10 kilometre stretch along the Mynamar border [in the Somtal area] where the militants are in control'.

The reign of terror has manifested in other forms as well, since the rule of the militants has synchronized with a complete retreat of civil governance. The militants continue to terrorize and extort with impunity, and people have little option but to obey their diktats. The helplessness of the administration has been repeatedly illustrated by Okram Ibobi Singh. Speaking at a public meeting in Thoubal district on 23 April 2006, for instance, he confessed: 'All development projects have been stalled for interference by militant outfits. The construction of a flyover in Imphal is delayed because the militant outfits are demanding a certain percentage of the project fund. The construction of the Assembly complex has also been similarly stalled.' The Chief Minister further stated: 'Militants are extorting money from each and every one, including barbers, small-time traders and low-ranking Government employees. This has become unbearable for the people. Militant groups have sprung up as cooperative societies in Manipur.'[27]

---

[27] Bibhu Prasad Routray, 'Militancy in India's Northeast', *PINR*, 16 May 2006, http://www.pinr.com/report.php?ac=view_report&report_id=489&language_id=1.

The state administration's general paralysis is, however, inexplicable from a purely security perspective. Apart from the heavy deployment of the army and paramilitary forces in the state, Manipur actually boasts of a dramatically higher police–population ratio, at 535 per 100,000 population, far more than the national average of 122. The state has a top-heavy structure— the ratio of police officials from Director General to Assistant Sub-Inspector compared to Head Constables and Constables is 1:9 against the national average of 1:7.[28] The police remain peripheral to the counter-insurgency effort, largely being confined to the role of passive spectators.

Violence by the Naga groups is also spilling over into Manipur, a substantial part of which is claimed by the NSCN-IM for its grandiose Nagalim—the proposed unified territory of areas claimed by the Naga rebels as being theirs. Several clashes between the NSCN-IM and the NSCN-K have been reported from the hill districts of the state. The NSCN-IM's shadow hung heavy in the electioneering process to the Manipur state legislative assembly polls in February 2007. The outfit not only proposed Naga candidates, but also abducted candidates opposing its activities.

The old rivalry between the Kuki tribe and the NSCN-IM continues to claim lives in Manipur. On 3 September 2007, NSCN-IM cadres killed 10 Kuki Liberation Army (KLA) members at Tangkhul Hundung Khunou village in the Ukhrul district following a dispute over the hijacking of a jeep carrying civilians.[29] The NSCN-IM maintained that this action was necessary as the KLA cadres were involved in 'criminal activities'.[30] Earlier, in March, a civil society organization of the Kuki tribe, Kuki Inpi Manipur (KIM), dispatched a memorandum to Prime Minister Manmohan Singh, demanding the trial of the NSCN-IM cadres for various criminal acts of murder, uprooting and displacing Kukis in the region, before negotiating with the outfit. The KIM has for long been alleging that the NSCN-IM had murdered over 900 innocent Kukis, uprooted over 360 Kuki villages, apart from displacing over 100,000 Kukis during the Naga-Kuki clashes.

---

[28] *Crime in India: 2005*, National Crime Records Bureau, Ministry of Home Affairs, Government of India, p. 501.

[29] S. Singlianmang Guite, 'Kuki armed groups condemn killing of KLA men', *Sangai Express*, 6 September 2007.

[30] 'KLA activities invited executions: NSCN(IM)', *Imphal Free Press*, 7 September 2007.

Tripura

Tripura continues to reap the benefits of its highly successful counter-insurgency policy. The police-led response to militancy continues to reverse the trajectory of violence and, crucially, militant mobilization, despite the support to the militant outfits by Bangladesh and the safe haven each of these outfits has been provided in that country. The number of militancy-related incidents continued to fall from 115 in 2005 to 87 in 2006. The total number of deaths fell from 60 to 50 in the corresponding period, although there was a marginal rise in fatalities among the security forces. However, this is a natural corollary of aggressive policing that seeks greater area domination and, in turn, exposes the forces to attacks by the militants.

Security Situation in Tripura[31]

Head	2003	2004	2005	2006	2007*
Incidents	394	212	115	87	86
SFs killed	39	46	11	14	6
Civilians killed	207	67	28	14	13
Militants killed	50	51	21	22	19

* As on 30 November 2007.

In the first eight months of 2007, 72 militancy-related incidents were reported in Tripura, while 31 incidents were reported from the West district and 32 cases from the Dhalai district. Only nine cases were reported from the North district.[32] This indicated a gradual decline in the area affected by militancy and the expansion of 'safe' zones.

The militant violence, in its present weakened state, still displays the patterns of its violent past. Attacks, mostly of the hit-and-run type, continue to target infrastructure-building projects, security forces, politicians and unarmed civilians. On 27 August 2007, NLFT cadres attacked a railway work site in Dhalai district and killed a para-military personnel of the Tripura State Rifles (TSR) before fleeing with his self-loading rifle.[33] In February 2007, State Transport Minister Manik Dey said that the state government has spent Rs 400 million to provide the necessary security to railway construction workers from Manu to Agartala.[34]

[31] *Status Paper on Internal Security Situation*, Ministry of Home Affairs, Government of India, 30 November 2007, p. 20.
[32] 'Insurgents step up activities ahead of Tripura Assembly polls', *Assam Tribune*, 5 September 2007.
[33] 'Tripura rail site attacked', *Telegraph*, 28 August 2007.
[34] 'Tripura spends Rs 40 cr on security of railway workers', *Sentinel*, 16 February 2007.

Militancy in Tripura thrived for years due to its nexus with the political class. While the Left parties were accused of conniving with the ATTF, the NLFT appeared to be benefiting from its links with the Congress. There appears to be a significant improvement on this front. Politicians, however, continue to be targeted by the militants. On 8 January 2007, a leader of the ruling CPI-M, Phalendra Reang, was abducted by NLFT militants from his residence in the Ashapurnaroaja Para area in Dhalai district. He was released after 39 days in captivity on 16 February. On 8 February, Ratansen Tripura, a CPI-M tribal leader, was killed by NLFT militants at his home in the Ratan Nagar village of Dhalai district. On 13 July, CPI-M leader Manyakumar Tripura was killed by NLFT militants at east Gobindabari, a remote village near the Indo–Bangladesh border in the Dhalai district.[35]

The impact of long years of militancy continues to be felt in Tripura. On 7 March 2007, its Public Works Department Minister, Badal Choudhury, informed the state legislative assembly that 5,317 families had been uprooted due to militancy over the last three years and of them, only 2,786 families had been rehabilitated in their homes. However, such incidents are expected to decline over the years. Tripura, once known as the abduction centre of the northeast, reported the abduction of only 28 civilians in the first eight months of 2007.[36] In 2006, 43 persons were abducted, of whom 31 were released and one killed by the militants.[37]

With the top leadership and the majority of the cadres of the two militant outfits based in Bangladesh, it remains vital to any policy for ending militancy in Tripura. The caretaker government in Bangladesh has, on many occasions, assured Indian authorities of effective action against these militant outfits. But its words are yet to translate into effective action. Intelligence sources maintain that 'no effort has yet been made by the Government of Bangladesh to make the stay of Indian militant leaders in that country uncomfortable, despite providing pinpointed [sic] information about the whereabouts of militants.'[38]

---

[35] Haripada Das, 'Yet Another CPI(M) Leader Killed By Extremists', *People's Democracy*, vol. 31, no. 30, 29 July 2007.

[36] 'Insurgents step up activities ahead of Tripura Assembly polls'.

[37] 'Achievements', Tripura Police website, http://tripurapolice.nic.in/aachieve.htm (accessed 6 September 2007).

[38] R. Dutta Choudhury, 'Bangla yet to put words into action', *Assam Tribune*, 3 September 2007.

Nagaland

The decade-long ceasefire with the NSCN-IM and the six-year-old ceasefire with the rival Khaplang faction (NSCN-K) continue to hold in Nagaland, but in an environment of endemic fratricidal clashes, pervasive extortion and rapid consolidation of the insurgent sway over every segment of society and government. For a state under a 'ceasefire' with both the principal insurgent groups, Nagaland still registers higher levels of insurgent violence than many states with an 'active' insurgency, and the situation appears to be progressively worsening over the years. According to the MHA, insurgency-related fatalities have increased from 97 in 2004 to 99 in 2005, and to a further 147 in 2006. Incidents of insurgent violence registered an increase from 186 to 192 between 2004 and 2005, and sharply rose to 309 in 2006. In eleven months of 2007, 149 fatalities have been recorded in 266 incidents and over 70 per cent of the deaths are in the militant ranks.

Security Situation in Nagaland[39]

Head	2003	2004	2005	2006	2007*
Incidents	199	186	192	309	266
SFs killed	3	0	1	2	1
Civilians killed	13	42	28	29	43
Militants killed	70	55	70	116	105

* As on 30 November 2007.

Virtually all the fatalities are linked to the network of intimidation and the turf wars between IM and Khaplang factions, with the security forces being obvious spectators, accounting for very few of the violent engagements or fatalities. This war of attrition continues with scant regard for the ceasefire ground rules which require the insurgents to stay in designated camps, bans their movement in uniform or with arms, and prohibits extortion. Fourteen designated camps have been set up (seven each for the NSCN-IM and the NSCN-K) by the government. However, as a matter of practice, the militants move out to the state's townships and countryside and carry out their activities. Factional clashes have not only been reported in Nagaland, but have often spilled over into the geographically contiguous hill districts of Manipur.

The NSCN-IM's writ runs supreme in most parts of Nagaland, though the NSCN-K remains dominant in the districts of Mokokchung

[39] *Status Paper on Internal Security Situation*, Ministry of Home Affairs, Government of India, 30 November 2007, p.18.

and Dimapur. While the NSCN-IM's well-oiled 'finance department' engages in widespread 'tax-collection' activities, its 'home department' virtually runs the administration in the state. Its 'crime suppression department' ensures control of its areas of dominance, administering 'justice' to various 'offenders'. Intelligence reports indicate that 'the cadre strength of the NSCN-IM has increased from 800 to about 2,500 since the July 1997 ceasefire announcement'.[40]

Unconstrained insurgent activities have resulted in the occasional civilian backlash. On 22 April 2007, subsequent to the abduction and torture of three Sumi tribesmen by NSCN-IM cadres, a large mob of about 5,000 people attacked Wungram colony, home to several NSCN-IM's leaders in Dimapur, destroying 39 houses and 19 vehicles.[41] The houses of NSCN-IM's 'steering committee member' Rh. Raising, *tatars* (parliamentarians) Samson Jajo, Nithungla and Kamlang, and three leaders of the group's armed wing—Hangshi, Ramkating and Markson—were gutted in the incident. Over 300 civilians belonging to the Tangkhul tribe, from which NSCN-IM's top leadership, including its 'General Secretary' Thuingaleng Muivah is sourced, were displaced from the colony and took shelter at the nearby police station at Chumukedima and the group's camp in Hebron, near Dimapur town. Such occasional, desperate, but rarely planned, mass interventions notwithstanding, the insurgent factions in the state continue to hold sway across wide areas of the state, and engage in continuous efforts to extend their areas of dominance.

Meghalaya

In Meghalaya, 26 fatalities were recorded in 38 militancy-related incidents in 2006, indicating a stagnation in the level of violence compared to the previous year. Only 22 militancy-related incidents were reported till 30 November 2007 in the state, in which 13 militants and five civilians were killed. The state remains one of the safest places for security force personnel, as not a single such death was reported in 2005 and 2006. Although civilian fatalities increased to six in 2006 compared to only one in 2005, Meghalaya has been peaceful.

---

[40] Bibhu Prasad Routray, 'Nagaland: "Peace" under Terror', *South Asia Intelligence Review*, vol. 5, no. 42, 30 April 2007, http://satp.org/satporgtp/sair/Archives/5_42.htm#assessment2.

[41] Iboyaima Laithangbam, 'President's rule in Nagaland sought', *The Hindu*, 25 April 2007.

Mainstream militancy appears to have been fully contained, mostly following the 23 July 2004 ceasefire with the ANVC, and with the neutralization of the HNLC. Effective police action has ensured that the top leadership of the latter remains confined to Bangladesh. Peace with the ANVC has brought tranquility to the Garo Hills, whereas the HNLC's marginalization has been the factor behind the restoration of normalcy in the Khasi and Jaintia hills.

Security Situation in Meghalaya[42]

Head	2003	2004	2005	2006	2007*
Incidents	85	47	37	38	24
SFs killed	7	8	0	0	1
Civilians killed	35	17	1	6	8
Militants killed	37	22	23	20	13

* As on 30 November 2007.

The marginalized HNLC suffered a further setback with the 24 July 2007 surrender of the outfit's chairman Julius Dorphang. He left the camp in Bangladesh's Maulvi Bazar district and crossed the Dawki-Tamabil international border to reach Shillong through the Jaintia hills district along with four other militants and surrendered to the authorities.[43] Touted as the brain behind the outfit, Dorphang was subsequently accused by the outfit's existing leadership comprising Commander-in-Chief Bobby Marwein and General Secretary Cheristerfield Thangkiew of having taken away the 'assets of the organization'.[44] On 15 August, Cheristerfield Thangkiew on the '20th raising day' of the outfit said that his group was keen to end bloodshed and willing to sit for talks.

With the marginalization of the dominant outfits, smaller outfits that primarily rose to fill the vacuum have been responsible for most of the militant violence in the state. One such outfit has been the LAEF in the East Garo Hills district. The outfit abducted two timber smugglers and assaulted them for timber theft in the Dainadubi area. This incident was followed by the abduction of the manager of a coal dealer from the Jadigittim area of South Garo Hills district. He was released unharmed after extensive police operations forced the

---

[42] *Status Paper on Internal Security Situation*, Ministry of Home Affairs, Government of India, 30 November 2007, p. 22.

[43] 'Moderate face of HNLC surrenders', *Telegraph*, 25 July 2007.

[44] 'Surrender an act of cowardice', *Shillong Times*, 31 July 2007.

outfit to abandon their catch and flee. On 22 June, suspected LAEF militants lobbed two hand grenades in Tura town and the coal-rich belt of Nangalbibra in South Garo Hills, killing one civilian and injuring 11 others.[45] Police operations against the outfit met with a strategic success with the arrest of the LAEF chief, Peter Marak, and two of his associates from a site between Jorabat and Khanapara near the Assam capital, Dispur, on 21 August 2007.[46] Following this, Peter's brother Drong Marak assumed command of the outfit.

Meghalaya continues to provide transit passage to groups like ULFA in their journeys between Bangladesh and Assam. On 19 January, police personnel arrested two ULFA militants, identified as Rajiv Basumatary and Wansanlang Rympei, from the Bhoirymbong area near Umroi airport in Shillong, and recovered three kilograms of RDX and a 9-mm pistol from them. Basumatary subsequently admitted to have brought the arms cache from Bangladesh for the 27th Battalion of ULFA.[47] Security force operations within Assam also cause ULFA militants to cross over to Meghalaya and seek refuge. For example, on 22 January, at least 10 to 15 armed ULFA cadres infiltrated into the East Garo Hills district in two groups from the Krishnai–Agya stretch of the Assam–Meghalaya border after counter-insurgency operations were launched in the Kamrup and Goalpara districts of Assam.[48] On 21 March 2007, ULFA militant Ratneswar Rabha was shot dead while crossing over from Bangladesh near Jengjal in the West Garo Hills district. Three kilograms of RDX were recovered from him.[49] The strategic forays by ULFA into Meghalaya were confirmed by the Assam Chief Minister on 21 August 2007. Tarun Gogoi said that ULFA has set up camps in Meghalaya along the India–Bangladesh border. He said, 'The ULFA extremists often commit crime in Asom and slip over to Meghalaya or Bangladesh… Meghalaya is used as a safe passage or corridor by the rebels …. What is now needed is a coordinated approach of all the NE state governments to take on the ultras while keeping the door open for the talks.'[50]

---

[45] '1killed, 11 hurt, newly-formed Liberation of Achik Elite Force prime suspect', *Shillong Times*, 23 June 2007.

[46] 'LAEF chief arrested', *Sentinel*, 22 August 2007.

[47] 'CM balm after ULFA quit notice', *Telegraph*, 20 January 2007. Also see 'M'laya Police: Seized arms were of ULFA', *Sentinel*, 23 January 2007.

[48] 'M'laya Police', Ibid.

[49] 'ULFA militant killed in encounter in Garo Hills', *Assam Tribune*, 23 March 2007. Also see 'ULFA killed', *Shillong Times*, 23 March 2007.

[50] 'ULFA set up camps in Meghalaya: Gogoi', *Shillong Times*, 22 August 2007.

Mizoram[51]

In 2006, Mizoram witnessed a few incidents of violence by the BLFM, mostly in Mamit district, along the state's border with Tripura. On 11 January, BLFM militants attacked a Mizoram armed police outpost at New Kawnpui in Mamit district. On February 6, an encounter between the Mizoram police and the BLFM militants resulted in a militant being injured near Sihthiang hamlet in the Mizoram–Tripura border district of Mamit. In neighbouring Kolasib district, suspected BNLF cadres abducted a sub-contractor on 14 February. On 2 March, an unidentified Bru militant, while trying to extort money from civilians, was shot at and wounded by police personnel near Thaiudawr village in Mamit district. A country-made rifle was recovered from him. On 17 March, police personnel killed a hardcore BNLF militant, Jaingba Reang, during an encounter at Dhalaicherra in the Mizoram–Tripura border area. A few incidents of extortion by Bru militants were also reported in 2006. The year 2007 has mostly remained peaceful, with no reports of militancy-related incidents in the state.

The state police have not only kept militancy at a manageable level, but its anti-militancy efforts have also yielded significant results. On 22 April 2006, a joint team of the Mizoram police and Assam Rifles arrested four top leaders of the BLFM, including its President Vanlalliana, Vice-President Vanrama, Army Chief Romawia Meska, and Lieutenant Lallawma, from different places in the state. The arrests subsequently led to en masse surrenders by the outfit.

CONFLICT MANAGEMENT

Assam

Military operations continue to target ULFA cadres in the state. However, it is becoming clear that these operations being reactive in nature have not been able to rein in the ULFA. While political interference in the operations is a factor behind their lack of success, it is also a fact that there is a critical lack of coordination between the multiplicity of forces engaged in the counter-insurgency operations, seriously affecting their performance. Indications of the divide between army and police personnel were provided by Chief Minister Tarun Gogoi

---

[51] Data on security situation in Mizoram is not available in the MHA's *Status Paper on Internal Security Situation*.

who, on 15 January 2007, became the head of the unified command structure, functioning in the state since 1997. Speaking to the media on 3 August 2007, Gogoi said, 'the army often oversteps its limits, has its own rules for operations and does not take policemen along during operations, which we always insist on.'[52]

Nearly three decades after the start of insurgency in Assam, it is still trying to find a way to deal with this problem. The ongoing modernization of the police force has been slow, barely enabling the state police to deal with the militants, thereby perpetuating its need to depend on the army and the central paramilitary forces. While the state enjoys a healthy police-to-population ratio of 181 compared to the national average of 122, vast stretches of the state remain unpoliced providing the militants a virtual free run. Only after the killing of 36 Hindi-speaking people in the district of Karbi Anglong, one of the largest districts in the state, has the government finalized a plan for dividing it into three police districts.[53] Media reports have indicated that the government is planning to establish 'six additional police stations and 13 additional police outposts'[54] in the district.

Following the dissolution of the ULFA-backed People's Consultative Group (PCG), another body, the People's Committee for Peace Initiatives in Assam (PCIPIA), an umbrella group of 27 Assamese human rights and action groups, comprising mostly ULFA sympathizers, was formed in 2006 to pressurize the government to start the peace process with the ULFA. The PCIPIA led demonstrations and organized public meetings, demanding a halt to army operations. It even said that ULFA's demand for talks on the sovereignty of Assam should be conceded by the government.[55] In truth, there is little to differentiate between the PCG and the PCPIA; hence, it is not surprising that the contribution of the PCPIA to peace in Assam, like its predecessor the PCG, remains minimal.

On the other hand, bodies like the Assam Public Works (APW) are largely seen as propped up and supported by the government. They have led agitations against ULFA's violence, demanding that the

[52] 'Gogoi has no hold on army—It often oversteps limit', *Telegraph*, 4 August 2007.

[53] 'Centre advises Assam to divide Karbi Anglong into three parts', *The Hindu*, 17 August 2007.

[54] '6 new PSs, 13 outposts in Karbi Anglong soon', *Assam Tribune*, 6 September 2007.

[55] 'Sovereignty should be core issue in ULFA-Centre talks', Zee News, 24 March 2007, http://www.zeenews.com/znnew/articles.asp?rep=2&aid=361793&sid=REG (accessed 4 September 2007).

government maintains a firm stand against the outfit. However, while it did contribute to raising awareness in public opinion against the outfit, its role in conflict management remains peripheral.

The October 2004 ceasefire with the NDFB has been extended without a single round of talks being held between the militant outfit and the government. While about 200 cadres of the 900 remain confined to three designated camps, the peace process itself remains stalled over New Delhi's insistence on a charter of demands from the NDFB before negotiations begin. The NDFB's leadership, however, including its Bangladesh-based Chairman Ranjan Daimary, has steadfastly refused to abide by periodic deadlines set by the union government to provide their charter. In an interview published on 22 August 2007, Daimary said, 'We are not fighting on the charter of demands. So it is a new thing for us. The Boro people have submitted charters of demands or memorandums one after another to the Government of India but nothing came out.'[56]

Ceasefire agreements with other outfits like the UPDS, the DHD and the Adivasi Cobra Force (ACF) have been extended, but not much has been achieved in terms of finding a solution to their demands.

Manipur

In September 2006, the UNLF threw a spanner in the works by talking about a plebiscite process for the resolution of the conflict in Manipur. A four-point formula, elaborated by the outfit's Chairman Sana Yaima, included:

- A plebiscite under United Nations (UN) supervision to elicit the opinion of the people of the state on the core issue of restoration of Manipur's independence.
- Deployment of a UN peace-keeping force in Manipur to ensure that the process is free and fair.
- Surrender of arms by the UNLF to the UN force, matched by the withdrawal of Indian troops.
- Handing over of political power by the UN in accordance with the results of the plebiscite.[57]

---

[56] 'NDFB blames Centre for talks delay', *Assam Tribune*, 22 August 2007.
[57] 'UNLF throws plebiscite challenge: Is India bold enough to let people of Manipur decide their future, asks Meghen', *Sangai Express*, 22 September 2006.

Expectedly, the proposal, which generated some interest in intellectual circles in the state, was rejected by the state government.

In the face of the stubborn opposition of the militants groups to the idea of negotiating with the Indian government, army and police operations against them have remained the key to the conflict management process in Manipur. Several military operations have been led by the Unified Command Structure which was established in 2004 against the valley-based militant outfits. Their achievements, however, have been limited and temporary.

The state government appears to have given up its opposition to the Defence Ministry's suspension of operations with the Kuki groups, announced in October 2005.[58] On 31 August 2007, the Manipur cabinet accepted the ground rules proposed by the union Home Ministry for signing a truce between the state government and militant groups with minor changes. It agreed to provide security guards for the militant leaders taking part in the proposed talks. The state government also agreed to allow militants to move out of proposed designated camps in plainclothes, without arms, in groups of not more than five members.[59]

Even as most of the states in the troubled northeast have shown different degrees of progress towards normalcy, exploiting a medley of 'political' and 'military' approaches, Manipur's little wars appear to have become more intractable, without any solution in sight. All the four valley districts of Manipur continue to be affected by militancy and government control over the remaining five hills districts is, at best, tenuous, given the unbridged schism between the Meiteis and the Nagas.

Community-based organizations like the *Meira Paibis* and other civil society organizations like the United Committee of Manipur (UCM) continue with their efforts to reduce violence in the state, but these have achieved limited results.

Tripura

Despite setbacks, both the NLFT and the ATTF continue to refuse starting a process of negotiation with the government. On the other hand, the state government appears to be fairly confident of its police force and, hence, does not see any gains from a negotiation process,

---

[58] In the context of the union government's agreement with the Kuki outfits, the Manipur Chief Minister had said that he does not recognize the agreement and that action by the state police against such groups would continue.

[59] 'Manipur toes truce line', *Telegraph*, 2 September 2007.

at least for the time being. Speaking on 20 August 2007, Tripura Chief Minister, Manik Sarkar, stated that militant hideouts in neighbouring Bangladesh have reduced from 55 to 26 over the past few years.[60]

In August 2006, the ATTF, through its mouthpiece *Choba*, demanded the setting up of a high-powered committee by the union government and, acting upon its recommendations, to protect the interests of the indigenous people. The outfit said that it would only negotiate with New Delhi and not with the state government. 'The dialogue cannot be unconditional, there must be definite parameters for discussion to arrive at a durable settlement of the problems facing the tribals.'[61] The state government, however, maintained that such gestures need to be backed by 'concrete' efforts before being taken seriously. It is evident that the state government prefers to continue imposing costs on the militant outfits before opting for a peace process.

Nagaland

Extending the existing ceasefire with the NSCN-IM and the NSCN-K remains central to the government's conflict management policy in Nagaland. Representatives of the NSCN-IM and the government continue to meet periodically to carry the negotiations forward. However, little success has been achieved to break the deadlock over the outfit's demand for integrating the 'Naga-inhabited' areas of Assam, Manipur and Arunachal Pradesh with Nagaland. Given the strong resentment that the proposal is bound to elicit from states like Manipur, no attempt has been made to involve this state government in the peace process. Both the government of Nagaland and the NSCN-IM, however, took a decision on 31 July 2007 to extend the ceasefire indefinitely, following a dialogue in Dimapur.[62] While the arrangement provides a break from

---

[60] 'Militant hideouts reduced: CM', *Tripura Info*, 22 August 2007, http://www.tripurainfo.com/cgi-bin/news/display.cgi?MODE=Show&ID=5725 (accessed 24 August). The Chief Minister, however, appeared to differ with the assessments of the Border Security Force. On 30 November 2006, the Deputy Inspector General (Tripura Frontier) of the BSF, P.J. Sebastian, said that the NLFT–Biswamohan and the ATTF have 57 hideouts in Bangladesh, and some of them are located in the capital, Dhaka. See 'Rebels still holed up in Bangla: BSF', *Telegraph*, 1 December 2006.

[61] 'Tiger Force for talks, with rider', *Telegraph*, 25 August 2006.

[62] The limited achievement of this development was indicated by the interlocutor of the union government, K. Padmanabhaiah. He said, 'It is a good thing that has happened. Now we don't have to meet every time just to extend the ceasefire.' See Samudra Gupta Kashyap, 'Govt–NSCN ceasefire extended indefinitely', *Indian Express*, 1 August 2007.

the routine extension of the ceasefire, it contributes little in terms of narrowing the differences between the two parties.

The state government has had little to contribute to the peace process. Over the years, it has even failed to bring a semblance of order to the state ravaged by internecine clashes between the rival militant outfits. In fact, Chief Minister Neiphiu Rio is on record claiming that such clashes are a part of the 'political problem' 'between India and Nagaland', thus indicating that these would continue as long as the 'conflict over Nagalim [greater Nagaland]' is not resolved. The Chief Minister's refrain closely echoes the NSCN-IM's position that the factional violence is due to the government's failure to restrict the movement of NSCN-K cadres. The government, on the other hand, insists that the clashes between the insurgent outfits are a law and order problem. On 20 June 2006, Prime Minister Manmohan Singh told a seven-member Congress Party team from Nagaland in New Delhi that the conflict between the insurgent Naga factions was a 'law and order problem' the state's Home Department to solve, and that Delhi could not be expected to take the blame.

Civil society organizations in Nagaland, played an important role in bringing the NSCN-IM to the negotiating table; they also tried, although unsuccessfully, to narrow the differences between the rival outfits. However, over the years they have lost their initiative. In a state which is ruled by the diktats of the NSCN-IM, most of the organizations have found it convenient to reiterate the demands of the outfit. The media in the state follows the outfit's diktats, and the voices of the opposition, mostly located in the separate tribes, find very little mention.

From a strategic point of view, Myanmar, with which India shares a 1,640 kilometre-long unfenced border, remains vital for the Naga outfits, especially the NSCN-K. The group's General Headquarters is located in the Sagaing division of Myanmar, bordering three Indian states: Manipur, Nagaland and Arunachal Pradesh. On 27 April 2007, official sources in New Delhi said that Myanmar has promised to step up military action against all Indian insurgent groups operating from its territory. However, the assurance given by the 18-member army delegation led by Brigadier General Tin Maung Ohn was quite routine and insignificant. Sporadic military offensives in the Sagaing division by the Myanmarese army have taken place since the mid-1980s, but have only temporarily displaced the various insurgent groups from Manipur, Assam and Nagaland. Once the Myanmarese army personnel vacate the area, these groups simply go back to reclaim their facilities. Moreover, a fairly cosy relationship exists between lower-rung Myanmarese military personnel and the insurgents, and the latter are often warned in advance of imminent raids, allowing them to minimize damage.

Meghalaya

Following the 24 July 2007 surrender of HNLC chairman Julius Dorphang, the group expressed its desire on 15 August for a dialogue with the government. In a statement, the outfit's General Secretary Cheristerfield Thangkhiew said that the group was keen to end bloodshed and willing to sit for talks.[63] Although there has been no progress beyond this statement, it could bring about a permanent solution to the problem of militancy in the hill state. Irrespective of the eventual commencement of a peace process, it is useful to interpret this development in light of the enormous costs imposed on the outfit by the sustained operations of the state police department. In its prime, this group had rebuffed several efforts by the state government and church leaders to start a peace process.

The stagnant three-year-old peace process with the ANVC, however, continues to be problematic. On 15 August 2007, Chief Minister D.D. Lapang said that his government had already started peace negotiations with the ANVC.[64] However, details of the peace process are still to emerge.

Any possibility of negotiations with the Assam-based UPDS, which is largely responsible for extortion and other such nefarious activities in the Jaintia hills and Ri Bhoi districts, remains remote after Meghalaya Home Minister R.G. Lyngdoh refused to negotiate with them. He said on 16 February 2007 that the issue of 'disputed' Blocks-I and II areas along the Assam–Meghalaya border will be resolved between the two state governments.[65] Earlier, the Khun Hynniewtrep National Awakening Movement (KHNAM) had offered to become a facilitator in the talks between the state government and the UPDS.

---

[63] 'HNLC willing for tripartite talks', *Shillong Times*, 16 August 2007.

[64] 'Peace negotiations has started in Meghalaya: Lapang', *The Hindu*, 16 August 2007.

[65] 'UPDS slams RG Lyngdoh', *Sentinel*, 17 February 2007.

Mizoram

The April 2005 memorandum of understanding with the BNLF was followed by another significant event in 2006 that had far-reaching implications for the state of militancy in Mizoram. On 26 October 2006, 802 BLFM cadres surrendered before the Mizoram government in Tuipuibari in Mamit district. A week before the formal surrender, the militants had deposited 70 firearms, explosives, AK series rifles, 20 live rounds of ammunition, one 9mm carbine, two 9mm pistols, two explosive grenades, one mortar, two .22 revolvers, two .22 Rifles and 37 country-made pipe guns to the Assam Rifles authorities,[66] which were handed over to the Mizoram police. The surrender, however, was not without its share of con-troversies. On 4 November, Tripura Director General of Police, G. M. Srivastava, accused the Mizoram government and the Assam Rifles of stage-managing the surrender. He said that the BLFM never had such a large cadre and never had more than 20 to 24 weapons. He also said that the surrendered militants were actually inhabitants of refugee camps.[67]

At the beginning of 2007, the Mizoram government initiated a series of steps to bring the HPC-D to the negotiating table. On 5 January, Chief Minister Zoramthanga designated Charlton Lien Amo, a legislator from Manipur, to negotiate with the HPC-D. The group responded by asking for the involvement of the union government in peace talks between them and the Mizoram government. A note issued by the group on 11 January said, 'If there is any negotiation to discuss the fulfillment of the provisions of the 1994 accord signed between the Mizoram government and the HPC, the Centre must intervene'.[68] There has been no further progress in the negotiation process.

CONCLUSIONS

The state of armed militancy in the northeast appears to have improved only in certain states like Tripura and Meghalaya, whereas

---

[66] 'Mizoram: 802 Bru militants surrender', Rediff, 26 October 2006, http://www.rediff.com/cms/print.jsp?docpath=//news/2006/oct/26mizo.htm (accessed 4 September 2007).

[67] 'HQ of NE insurgency shifted to Aizawl: Tripura DGP', *Tripura Info*, 6 November 2006, http://www.tripurainfo.com/cgi-bin/news/display.cgi?MODE=Show&ID=4415 (accessed 7 November 2006). Also see 'Surrender of Bru ultras stage-managed', *Assam Tribune*, 6 November 2006.

[68] 'Hmar group wants tripartite talks', *Assam Tribune*, 12 January 2007.

states like Assam, Manipur and Nagaland are reeling under militant violence. Both Tripura and Meghalaya have benefited immensely from a multi-pronged approach, led essentially by the state police, in which the central paramilitary forces have played a supportive role. Chief Minister Manik Sarkar described the prevailing situation in Tripura accurately during a media interview. He said, 'Insurgency in the state is on the wane but the problem still persists. There are reports of stray incidents of violence. It will take time to weed it out completely.'[69] Similarly, Meghalaya's tryst with militancy appears to be over. While the ANVC has been roped into a ceasefire agreement, the HNLC has been militarily paralyzed and has lost its capabilities to orchestrate attacks.

Assam's rendezvous with ULFA militancy appears to be unending, marked by brief and insignificant interludes of peace. It has recovered from the reverses it suffered in 2003 in Bhutan. Although the quality of its cadres and its attacks have declined (or at best, stagnated), it has been able to exploit the blow-hot, blow-cold policy of the government to survive and make its nuisance value felt. Manipur, on the other hand, continues to be marked by militant violence and the state seems to have no answer to this situation. Militant diktats rule supreme, and the state is further handicapped by the divide between the valley, where the dominant Meiteis live, and the hills, inhabited by several tribal populations. The neighbouring state of Nagaland, too, is exporting its problems to Manipur. In spite of the existing ceasefires with the dominant militant groupings, Nagaland has been marked by unceasing factional clashes and a rampant extortion regime; it has also created security problems for Manipur, Assam and Arunachal Pradesh. Consequently, little respite can be expected from the present state of chaos in the foreseeable future in states like Assam, Manipur and Nagaland.

In spite of the largely reactionary steps of the government for augmenting security, ULFA will continue to be a force to reckon with in Assam. While the state seems convinced that the ultimate solution to the problem of militancy will emerge from negotiating with the group, ULFA continues to exploit such ambivalence to the hilt. On the strategic front, its alliances with peripheral outfits will further widen the area of conflict and scatter the existing security force strength.

---

[69] 'Additional battalion for Tripura', *Telegraph*, 9 August 2007.

The continuing retreat of civil governance is likely to exacerbate militancy in Manipur. A large security presence will, however, ensure that the level of militancy does not cross a threshold level. The stagnant Naga peace process will continue to keep the hill areas on the boil.

With both the NSCN-IM and the union government failing to find a way out of the 'Nagalim' logjam, the Naga conflict will continue. Ceasefire regimes will exist along with large-scale extortion, internecine clashes, and domination of the political process and civil society by the militant groupings.

With elections to the legislative assembly in Tripura due in 2008, militancy is likely to show an upward swing. The militants, especially the NLFT, which has been the target of the ruling Left-front government's decision to give a free hand to the police in its counter-insurgency operations, is likely to engineer violence in a bid to harm the prospects of the party. More attacks and abduction attempts targeting party workers are likely to continue, although the militants would be seriously handicapped by increased policing and reduced cadre strength.

What is the course to counter militancy in the northeast?

Interestingly, ULFA does not dominate any area in Assam and primarily depends on sporadic hit-and-run tactics. Its cadres are mostly based outside Assam and are known to flee into Meghalaya and Arunachal Pradesh following the execution of their attacks. To counter this dissipated threat, the state will have to invest substantially in human and technical intelligence. It has to strengthen its intelligence network at the village level and will have to augment the capabilities of its police stations. For a successful fight against militancy, it also needs to invest in improving the quality of its police personnel.

It is possible to overwhelm the militant movements in Manipur through military efforts, led by the army and the paramilitary forces. However, that would require adequate support from the state police and cooperation from Myanmar. A strategy of encirclement can help. A number of tribes in the hill areas of Manipur have been traditional victims of the violence perpetrated by the valley-based militant outfits. These tribes can be protected, supported and nurtured by the government as an effective source of information on Meitei outfits. Under no circumstances, however, should they be armed by the state.

The government will have to find a way to reduce the factional clashes between the militant outfits in order to establish effective peace in Nagaland. Steps also need to be taken to strengthen the voices urging peace in the state. The militant groups have continued to play on the unfounded fears of the government that the ceasefire can collapse, taking the state back to the days of anarchy, if the outfits are hard-pressed. Several indicators, such as a new generation of cadres, peer pressure and comfort of the ceasefire regime, however, rule out such an eventuality. A bold approach, to be adopted incrementally, would be required by the government to enforce the ceasefire ground rules and disrupt the extortion regime.

During the last Home Secretary-level meeting between India and Bangladesh held in the first week of August 2007, 'the Government of Bangladesh softened its attitude regarding the presence of the militants of the North East and other anti-India forces in Bangladesh soil and even assured to allow India to bring in floating border outposts to Assam for better patrolling of the riverine international border.'[70] However, subsequent reports indicate little action being taken by the Bangladeshi authorities. India will have to find a way to make Bangladesh act against the groups based in that country.

Whereas illegal migration from Bangladesh and the militant camps in its territory has led to an emphasis on the management of the Indo–Bangladesh border, the 1,643 kilometre-long Indo–Myanmar border has not been given due importance. This border, especially in stretches that fall in states like Mizoram, Manipur and Nagaland, have been porous, thus allowing unhindered movement of militants, small arms and drugs into the northeastern region. Militant camps of the Naga and Manipuri outfits situated across the border have survived the intermittent onslaughts by the Myanmarese army. There is a need to monitor the Indo–Myanmar border with the same degree of seriousness as the Indo–Bangladesh border.

---

[70] 'Bangla yet to put words into action', *Assam Tribune*, 3 September 2007.

8

Bangladesh: Islamic Militancy and the Rise of Religious Right

Smruti S. Pattanaik

A BRIEF HISTORY

Militant Islam has emerged as a serious challenge to the largely secular social fabric of Bangladesh. A possible threat from radical Islamic groups was underlined when the media first reported the return of Bangladeshi Talibans and al-Qaeda members after the US started its war on terror in Afghanistan. The four-party nationalistic–rightist regime that was in power dismissed these reports as a fantasy created by the media. The subsequent bomb blasts in cinema halls, cultural events and later suicide attacks in a largely moderate Muslim country reflect the dangers of intolerance and manifestations of a form of Islam unknown in this part of the world. The synchronized bomb blasts of 17 August 2005 epitomized the malaise arising from the larger problem of Islamic radicalism and presented religious militancy as a new threat to the internal stability of Bangladesh. The Jamatul Mujaheedin Bangladesh (JMB), the erstwhile surreptitious group whose radical ideas were not known, announced its agenda through the leaflets attached to the bombs that were exploded on 17 August 2005. The exact social base of this group is largely unknown, but their arrests and confessional statements indicate that some of them belonged to the Quami *madrassa*, which functions outside government control, while others are from the lower strata of society. They were reported to have been funded by Middle East-based organizations and were patronized by the four-parties regime led by the Bangladesh National Party (BNP).

These radical groups were disillusioned by the politics being currently pursued by the four-party alliance, especially the Islamic component. They were convinced that the Islamic revolution cannot be brought about by constitutional means. The differences on ideological issues and acceptance of female leadership by the Islamic parties (JI [Jamaat Islami] and IOJ [Islamic Oikyo Jote]) convinced these fringe elements that it is they who would bring about an Islamic revolution to Bangladesh.

The government came to power in 2001, but till 2005 the Islamic political parties made no move to fulfil the basic Islamic aspirations of a few of its cadres. It needs to be reiterated here that both Banglabhai, Chief of the Jagrata Muslim Janata Bangladesh (JMJB), and Sheikh Abdur Rahman, the JMB supreme, were cadres of the Islamic Chatra Shibir (ICS), the student wing of the JI. In an interview given to Bangladesh media Banglabhai said, 'After my education in 1995 I quit Shibir because by then Jamaat (Jamaat Islami, the religious political party) had accepted female leadership although it had all along been saying that it considered female leadership sacrilege'.[1] Even the Islamic Oikya Jote (IoJ) underwent a split in 2005 on the issue of the 'betrayal of the Jote government' to fulfil some of their common agendas to further Islamic agendas.[2] This disillusionment of some of the Jammat cadres with the main party can be compared to an extent with the ICS split in 1983.[3]

The political base for the resurgence of radical Islam was already visible and the existential announcement of the JMB and JMJB was just a matter of time. What is significant in the case of Bangladesh was repeated denial of the existence of militancy by the government and its reluctance to take any action against the extremists which aggravated the situation. At one point during the five years of the BNP regime, some important ministers in the government, like the Home Minister and the Minister for Industries, went to the extent of saying that the reports on extremism were a creation of the media, and the Finance Minister, Saifur Rahman, went a step further and advised the media not to tarnish the image of Bangladesh. As the opposition political parties blamed the government, accusing it of patronizing fundamentalists, some senior ministers accused the Awami League of conspiring with a foreign power to brand Bangladesh as a failed state.

In Bangladesh politics, rhetorical political statements—blaming one party or the other—limit any scope for further investigations.

---

[1] Shamim Ashraf, 'All 7 JMB Shura men had links with Jammat Shibir', *Daily Star*, 28 April 2006.

[2] Interview with the General Secretary of Allama Azizul Haque faction of Khilafat Majlish, 20 July 2007.

[3] A group of students romanticized the Iraninan revolution and wanted to bring in a similar revolution in Bangladesh through the *ulemas*.

The politically motivated bureaucracy—divided along party lines—further erodes the chances of any fair investigation. As one saw during the rule of the former BNP and the four-party alliance government, politically motivated instructions to the police have constrained fair investigation as the government was disinclined to acknowledge the existence of militants, thereby worsening the matter. The government, dependant on its donors,[4] did not want its image as a 'moderate Muslim' country to be tarnished. Another problem was the emergence of a shadow government under the active patronage and support of Tariq Rahman, Begum Zia's son. Hawa Bhaban became the power centre and some of its activities were carried out in the knowledge and under instructions of this power centre. The BNP government considered militancy to be a law and order issue rather than as the ascend-ancy of fundamentalist forces. This approach in effect limited the government's efforts and therefore it did not conduct any investigation into the militants' patrons and sources of their financial sustenance.

PRINCIPAL ACTORS

The conflict in Bangladesh has three principal actors: government actors, i.e. ministers and law-enforcing agencies; militants (mainly Jamatul Mujaheedin Bangladesh [JMB], Jagrata Muslim Janata Bangladesh [JMJB], Harkatul Jihadi Islami [HuJI] and other Islamic groups); and external actors like non-governmental organizations (NGOs) funded by countries of the Middle East.

Government Actors

The government's attitude played an important role in the consolidation of militant groups. One of these groups, the Jagrata Muslim Janata Bangladesh (JMJB), was involved in extra-judicial killings as

---

[4] Between 1972 and 2004, Bangladesh received $42 billion in foreign aid, of which $19.3 billion was in the form of grants, and the remaining $22.7 billion was received in concessional loans; ADB, World Bank, and Japan provided approximately 60 per cent. During the past three decades, ADB has provided almost one-fifth of Bangladesh's total project aid. External assistance has contributed substantially to the implementation of nearly all the major public sector development projects. Over the years, the share of foreign aid to the nation's total resource mobilization has steadily declined. From nearly 6 per cent of GDP in the second half of the 1980s, net foreign financing fell to 2.6 per cent in the second half of the 1990s, and to less than 2 per cent between 2000 and 2004. See http://www.adb.org/Documents/CSPs/BAN/2005/csp0200.asp accessed on 11 September 2007.

a part of the government's measures to control the criminal groups. According to Masud Mia, the investigating officer, 'We [police] hail you [JMJB] as you are helping us eliminate the Sarbaharas from Rajshahi. We must co-operate with you in the coming days so that people can rest without fear'.[5] Ironically the killings of Sarbohara[6] members in an extra-judicial manner were not challenged by human rights groups in Bangladesh, in turn bolstering the police activities as 'public good'. The government helped the Jagrata Muslim Janata Bangladesh (JMJB) to exhibit its organizational strength to the public. Former lawmakers belonging to the Bangladesh National Party (BNP)[7] and the four-party alliance made it mandatory for the people living in that area to send public and private jeeps, cars, microbuses and motorcycles to ferry people to join the procession led by Banglabhai, which was conducting vigilante action in that region. During the operation undertaken by Banglabhai, the police, due to political pressure, provided security by staying within 500–1,000 yards of the operation area to provide back-up. Earlier, some of the police officers had gone public by saying that they were compelled to turn a blind eye to the activities of Banglabhai. For example, the Inspector General of Police (IGP), Nur Muhammad, who was Deputy Inspector General (DIG) of Rajshahi range in 2004 where the JMJB was active, underlined his helplessness when he said 'I talked to the Home Minister twice or thrice on this matter, but he kept on pushing me towards Aminul Haque. When I talked to the District Minister Aminul Haque he said don't talk in this matter. You do not need to pursue this matter. This has come from the highest level. From Prime Minister to Tareque Rahman everyone knows about it'.[8]

Not only did the mystery of bomb blasts under the BNP regime remained unresolved, but there was also no progress in the investigation of various incidents of bomb blasts since the days of the Awami League (AL) government. These attacks were directed against cultural organizations, street plays (*jatras*), cinema halls and

---

[5] 'Eating own words', *Daily Star*, 24 February 2006.
[6] The Sarbohara's are Left-wing extremists. They are active mostly in the northern part of Bangladesh. These groups have got criminalized and are engaged in killing and looting in places where the administrative machinery of the state is not very strong.
[7] Aminul Haque from Rajshahi constituency-1, Ruhul Kuddus Dulu from Natore 2, Rajshahi Mayor Mizanur Rahman Minu, Nadim Mostafa of Rajshahi 4, Alamgir Kabir of Naogaon helped Banglabhai.
[8] 'JMB ruled supreme with their blessings', *Daily Star*, 27 July 2007.

celebrations of the Bengali New Year. An analysis of the targets reveals that most of them were either AL meetings or cultural organizations; both considered enemies by many Islamic parties. For example: the Islamic parties see the Awami League as their main enemy because of its ideological affiliations, and the fact that it had banned religion-based political parties under the 1972 constitution.[9] The following list reveals the targets of Islamic radicals, mostly political parties or cultural organizations, and sufi shrines that are considered secular or 'unIslamic'.

Date and Year	Target/Place	No. of Persons Killed
6 August 1999	Udichi function, Jessore	10
8 October 1999	Ahmediyas, Khulna	8
15 June 2001	AL office, Narayanganj	22
20 January 2001	Communist Party Bangladesh rally, Paltan Maidan, Dhaka	7
14 April 2001	Pohela Boisakh, Ramana Park, Dhaka	10
3 June 2001	Baruyar char, Gopalganj	10
23 September 2001	AL rally, Bagerhat	8
26 September 2001	AL election rally, Sunamganj	4
28 September 2002	Cinema and circus pandals, Satkhira	3
6 December 2002	4 cinema halls, Mymensingh	21
17 January 2003	Faila Pir Shrine, Sakhipur, Tangail	7
21 May 2004	Shahjalal Shrine, Sylhet	5
5 August 2004	2 cinema halls, Sylhet	1
7 August 2004	AL meeting, Taltala in Sylhet	1
21 August 2004	AL rally, Bangabondhu Avenue, Dhaka	21
16 January 2005	Cultural function in Bogra	2
27 January 2005	AL rally, Habiganj	5

Source: 'Most cases of bomb blasts remain unresolved', *Financial Express*, 18 August 2005.

It is interesting to note that some Bangladeshis continue to feel that extremism is fuelled by external powers to malign Bangladesh's image as a 'moderate' Muslim country. A public opinion poll conducted

---

[9] In an interview with Ahmad Abdul Qader of Khilafat Majlis (Izharul faction), 7 September 2007, Dhaka.

by a magazine reveals this perception. A total of 60 per cent of the respondents felt that a neighbouring country in the region has a hand in bomb blasts in Bangladesh, 40 per cent ruled out this possibility. Thirty-two per cent said it was India, 11.48 blamed the United States, and 1.85 cited Pakistan.[10] This also indicates that the government through sustained propaganda has been successful in portraying the issue of militancy as being a foreign conspiracy, thereby shrugging off its responsibility to address the issue.

Armed Groups

The conflict went through a few phases. Though it is generally believed that the JMB came into existence in 1998, it was not till 2001 that it became active. It has a complex network of organizational linkages and there are media reports that claim that the JMB has connections with the Harkatul Jihadi Islami (HuJI), which announced its birth in 1992. In a meeting of its *shura* committee in Dhaka in 2001, it was christened as the JMB.[11] After its creation, its *shura* members visited the northern districts of Bruhatar Rajshahi, Rangpur, Dinajpur, Bogra, Pabna and delivered lectures on jihad in various *madrassas*. Workers were recruited to carry out the tasks of jihad. As part of their training they were required to pull rickshaws; it was believed this would curb personal pride, strengthen loyalty, and prepare them to make a living during times when it was not conducive to carry out radical action.[12] The JMB initially wanted to work with HuJI but it decided to form a different organization due to doctrinal differences. In 1999, in its effort to launch jihad, JMB leader Sheikh Abdur Rahman visited Pakistan and received training in Pakistan- occupied Kashmir (PoK). The JMB was also influenced by the Alh e Hadith movement (This movement urges people to follow the religious way of life as given in the Quran

[10] 'Bomb blast: people's perception', *Probe*, 14–20 October 2005, p. 14. Some feel that the CIA, RAW and Mossad are involved in helping the militants as these countries have specific interests; an interview with Ahmad Abdul Qader, 7 September 2007, Dhaka. Some highly placed people also said that India and the US are helping the militants as it would pave the way for US intervention; and, since India and the US have become 'friends' it will advance US interest. Interaction with various people at Dhaka University and other organizations between 26 May and 7 September 2007, Dhaka and Sylhet.

[11] Mehdi Hasan Polash, *JMBer ulekhyojog operational Karyakram* (JMB's Significant Operational Work), *Inquilab*, 13 January 2007.

[12] Kamal Hasan, 'JMB blasted bombs for its propaganda', *Prathom Alo*, 4 February 2007.

and Hadith. It does not allow any interpretation of the Quran and Hadith and is puritanical in its belief.) Sheikh Abdur Rahman's father was a top leader of the Alhe Hadith Andolan Bangladesh (AHAB). His relations with this organization date back to his association with the Alhe Hadith *madrassa* in Jamalpur from where he graduated. However, after Sheikh Abdur Rahman returned from Afghanistan he wanted to form the JMB as an independent organization with its own concept of the state—as reflected in a pamphlet that was distributed on 17 August 2005. Sheikh had personally got in touch with Dr M.A.Bari and Professor Asadullah al Ghalib, a professor of Arabic language in Rajshahi University, and a leader of the AHAB. However, these two leaders did not agree with the Sheikh's proposal as they felt that the moment for armed revolution (kital) in Bangladesh was yet to come. Ghalib proposed that the Sheikh join his organization and work with them but Sheikh Rahman placed certain conditions.[13] Even though these two organizations functioned separately, some of the JMB's sympathizers came from the AHAB; some analysts believe that the AHAB is a mass platform for the JMB. The JMB contacted the Rohingya Student Organization (RSO), an armed group operating in Chittagong for training in explosives, but that did not take place. The RSO, in its Ukhia camp in Chittagong, have been training radical religious militants for some time. Most of these militants participated in the anti-Soviet jihad in Afghanistan.

Civil Society Actors

Civil society in Bangladesh has been extremely critical of the government's inaction against the militants. It pressurized the government and the media played an important role in publicizing their concerns. Unfortunately, civil society in Bangladesh is divided along party and ideological lines. However, cutting across party affiliations there was general concern regarding growing extremism. Protest marches were organized and seminars conducted on Bangladesh's tolerant Islamic culture to highlight Bangladesh as a moderate Muslim country. Though civil society actors belonging to the Left parties and the Awami League blamed the BNP and its alliance for the

---

[13] 'Sheikh had tried to contact al-Qaeda', *Prothom Alo*, 3 February 2007.

growing militancy, the members of the BNP were critical of militancy in general, but refused to acknowledge that the government could have any role here. In fact, to rebuff Islamic militancy, people turned up in thousands for the Pohela Baisakh celebration on 14 April 2006, which is observed to mark the Bengali New Year. This celebration had been targeted earlier in 2001 by Islamic extremists who considered these celebrations to be unislamic.

External Actors

The conflict was also fuelled by external actors. It is reported that there are 15 NGOs working to promote Islamic values and culture, while 34 foreign-funded NGOs are registered with the NGO bureau of the Government of Bangladesh. There are several hundred local Islamic NGOs registered with the Social Welfare Ministry which was headed by the JI Secretary General. They act as affiliated organizations of the large foreign-funded NGOs. They do not submit reports detailing their activities in Bangladesh to the Ministry. The funds at their disposal are estimated to be to the tune of taka 200 crore. It is also believed that some Islamic scholars, leaders of religious political parties and heads of *madrassas* regularly visit the countries of the Middle East to collect donations which are given as *zakat* (One of the five pillars of Islam. It is obligatory for Muslims to pay 2.5 per cent of their wealth to the poor.) to charitable organizations and orphanages. There is no account maintained for this money, which is generally channelled through *hundis* (informal transfer of money).[14] Some of these organizations, although not directly involved in terrorism, have contributed to the growth of conservative Islamic ideas. For most of them, religion is the prime identifying factor for generous funding and the basis for their social welfare activities. In the name of spreading the puritan Wahabi Islam these organizations strengthen the hand of radicals who believe that the Islam practiced in Bangladesh is less authentic. Money is spent on building mosques and *madrassas* and other charitable organizations to promote Islamic culture by providing iftar (snacks that are eaten to break the fast in the evening during Ramadan) in mosques. It is important to note that

---

[14] 'These NGOs are Islamic Relief Organisations:, Al-Markajul Islami, Ishra Foundation, Ishrahul Musliman, Al Fokran Foundation and Al Maghrib Eye Hospital', *Daily Star*, 31 August 2005.

Bangladeshi expatriates, especially those working in the Middle East, also contribute substantial amounts for religious purposes, which remains largely unaccounted. Their exposure to Islamic countries also changes the way in which they view religion in Bangladesh.

The media has reported that the militants have also received funds to set up *madrassas* and *maktabs* from United Arab Emirates-based welfare organizations like the Al Fauzia and Khairul Ansar al Khairia Foundation; the Kuwait-based Daulatul Kuwait and Revival of Islamic Heritage Society (RIHS); and the Bahrain-based Daulatul Bahrain. As mentioned, these organizations do not play any direct role but there is no scrutiny of these funds, some of which have gone to *madrassas* that have played an active role in contributing to militancy and the spread of radical ideas. In spite of having a separate bureau for NGO affairs that regulates the foreign-funded NGOs, the government did not consider it important to scrutinize the activities of these organizations, especially the RIHS, which is banned in many countries. For example, the RIHS funded and AHAB patronized Tawhid and Hadith foundations expelled Asadullah al Ghalib in 2002 for embezzlement of funds, but he continued to receive funds indirectly. Instead of account-payee cheques, the RIHS issued bearer cheques to the AHAB even after its linkages to militancy were exposed. The government finally asked the RIHS to end its operations in Bangladesh. Some of the foreign employees who earlier worked for the Al Haramain foundation till it was closed, were thereafter employed by the RIHS. It was only in July 2005 that they were asked to leave when the government got specific data on their direct involvement in fuelling Islamic militancy.[15] Earlier, the government agreed to release RIHS funds after its regional director and country director lobbied for it.[16]

The JI-patronized Islamic Bank also conducted some money transfers that were linked to the militant groups. Around taka 4.5 lakh was transferred in this manner. The Bank did not verify the names of those who issued these cheques.[17] Both the Ghazipur and Savar branches of the Islamic Bank sought to clarify the situation by saying it was an oversight. However, it was hard for the investigators to believe that such mistakes could be repeated so many times.[18] Though the

---

[15] Anwar Ali, 'Agencies for banning Kuwait based group', *Daily Star*, 21 August 2005.
[16] *Daily Star*, 'Government okays release of "Terror Fund", 5 December 2005.
[17] Rezaul Karim Byron, 'Islami bank staffs ignored norms', *Daily Star*, 10 March 2006.
[18] Ibid.

militants had some transactions with the Janata Bank and the Rupali Bank, these accounts remained inactive before the terror incidents.

CONFLICT IN 2007

As mentioned earlier, the government's reluctance to conduct a thorough investigation into the causes of Islamic militancy and their patrons and funders was reflected in its defensive strategy. It was aggressive in denying the existence of extremist militant elements; in fact, in February 2005 it banned the JMB only after the offices of NGOs like Grameen and Brac were attacked. The Islamists consider NGOs to be enemies of Islam as they play a lead role in tackling issues of female education and empowerment. However, the 17 August bomb blasts did not leave much scope for the government to conceal the existence of militancy. The government, without going into the matter seriously, resorted to cheap politics by accusing the Awami League and India. On orders from the High Court, the government submitted two identical reports on 13 and 27 December, providing details of arrest, cases under investigation, cases chargesheeted and property attached, but it did not give details of seized arms and ammunition, bomb-making material and explosives, which could have provided some clues on the capability of the militants.

The government considered introducing a new anti-terrorism law, but it could not make much progress as it became involved in the approaching elections. During Christina Rocca's visit in February 2006, the US proposed to set up an institutional framework to establish a counter-terrorism bureau. However, there has been little progress in this regard. The US government is training the Bangladesh police on how to handle cases of money laundering, and how to interrogate militants.

The arrest of JMB and JMJB cadres started in real earnest after the suicide bomb blasts in various courts which killed two judges. The incident of public outcry and donors' pressure forced the government to arrest the kingpins of these two organizations. Similarly, after the arrest of two sus-pects in the Shahjalal grenade attack case, the government was able to unearth HuJi's hand in it. Later, the government also arrested Mufti Hanan, leader of HuJI, who was the main accused in the Shahjalal shrine bomb blasts that seriously injured British envoy to Bangladesh, Anwar Choudhury. Later, Asadullah al Ghalib, chief of AHAB, was arrested in the same case. The militants, accused in the 17 August bomb blasts and subsequent suicide attacks on the judiciary, were tried and sentenced to death. The government, however, could not carry out these death sentences as the convicts applied for Presidential pardon. But the interesting fact is that, given the preponderant power that the Prime Minister of Bangladesh constitutionally enjoys, the delay in the President's decision on pardon was inordinate. Some Bangladeshi analysts feel that the government, in light of approaching elections, was itself indecisive and hesitant to hang the militant kingpins like JMJB chief Banglabhai and JMB chief Sheikh Rehman. It is the current military-backed caretaker government which implemented the court decision and hanged the militants. The court gave its verdict within 131 days after the cases against these militants were filed in the lower courts, sentencing them to death.

The Jamaat Islami which denies any linkages with the JMB and JMJB was quick to disassociate itself from these militants. To quote Kamruzzaman, the Joint General Secretary of the JI, 'the Jamaat Islami cannot take responsibility for these people who have been cadre members of the ICS in their student days',[19] but left the organization later. Some of the top leaders exposed to the Afghanistan jihad were influenced by the Taliban and wanted to replicate their rule in Bangladesh. In the initial stages some of the influential members of the Jamaat had encouraged *madrassa* students to join the Taliban in Afghanistan and had delivered lectures on jihad.[20] The Habiganj Amir of Jamaat, Saidur Rahman, who was involved with the JMB, is on the run since Banglabhai was arrested. According to the probe conducted by the Bangladesh Bank into the financial linkages of the militants, it was found that suspected transactions of money related to militancy took place from an account which was in the name of Sabbir Ahmed. However, after investigation it was found that this account was actually being operated by Saidur Rahman, the Jamaat Amir of Habiganj. Moreover, due to the intercession of a former Jamaat Islami lawmaker, Abdul Khaleque, the police could not arrest JMB operatives in Khulna and Satkhira. It is also reported that he personally helped and trained women JMB cadres at Chhoygharia Mahila Madrassa in Khulna and Satkhira. Not only some of the members the Jamaat actively helped the JMB, the Islamic Oikya Jote, another alliance partner of the BNP-led, four-party alliance, also supported Banglabhai's fight against Sarbohara's, the radical left.

[19] Interview with Kamruzzaman in Dhaka on 28 June 2007.
[20] Interview with erstwhile leader of IOJ who would not liked to be named, 29 August 2007, Dhaka. In 1991 at a meeting in Gopalganj some members of HuJI took vows to establish Taliban rule in Bangladesh by 2000.

The major drawback of the JMB is that they had no financial power to attract youth to form their backbone. They started, initially, by looting Brac and Grameen offices, even though the money they collected from these crimes was insignificant. The militants tried to generate funds thereafter by investing in shrimp farms and cold stores using fake names.[21] However, the 17 August bombing was planned in great detail which shows that the JMB's operational network, its spread, as well as its organizational ability remain strong.[22] It was also in the process of organizing a women's wing to act as intelligence operatives. The funds for the militants came from *zakat* and other donations. One of the leaders, Sunny, said that two British militant leaders, Abdur Rahman and Sajjad, provided them with £10,000 to carry out the bomb attacks.[23] Rahman got money from Rabita–e-Islam, a Kuwait-based Islamic NGO to run his Al Madina Islamic Cadet Madrassa Jamalpur Sadar Upazilla.

The government has arrested a total of 698 JMB activists in connection with the 17 August 2005 bomb blasts and has filed 183 cases; out of them 56 cases are under investigation, and the trial of 17 cases has been completed.[24]

The regrouping of militants to continue with terrorist activities has been an issue of concern in Bangladesh. There are reports that the JMJB is using the remote Ullahpara village in Kaliganj under the leadership of Abu Ahsan, Imam of the local mosque, who is training its cadres. Another place where the militants are active is Kushtia Islamic University, a stronghold of the ICS. It is again reported in the media that around 12,000 trained cadres belonging to five militant outfits— the JMB, HuJi, Hizbut Towhid, JMJB and Muslim Guerilla Sangstha are active.[25] In Meherpur, the Hizbut is active and it is difficult to arrest them as they are operating under the banner of Tabligh Jamaat.

---

[21] 'Foreign policy, local business keep them going', *Daily Star*, 22 August 2005.

[22] For example, the JMB divided the country into four zones and assigned each zone to its *shura* members. Salauddin was given charge of Jamalpur, Mymensingh and Sylhet; Hafiz Mahmud was given Khulna and Barisal; Ataur Rahman, Dhaka and Chittagong; Abdul Awal was given Rajshahi. The overall charge of coordination remained with Sheikh Abdur Rahman, the head of the JMB. Interestingly, Siddiqur Rahman (Bangla bhai) was not given any responsibility as he was already a known face. Ibid.

[23] Julfikar Ali Manik, 'Secret lies with Rahman', *Daily Star*, 2 March 2006.

[24] Julfikar Ali Manik, 'Foreign link, patron still in shadow', *Daily Star*, 17 August 2006.

[25] Amanur Aman, 'Islamist militants in south-western districts regrouping', *Daily Star*, 27 May 2007.

The JMB is active in the remote char areas which are not easily accessible. Their training continues in different places and some of these cadres were arrested while they were taking lessons in combat using bamboo sticks in the forest camp of the JMB in Mymensingh. The government continues to confine its fight against radical Islamists to making arrests and confiscating arms. The Pabna court remanded three top JMB leaders arrested on 23 May this year. These will have limited effect and will not be sufficient to root out radicalism. After the military-backed caretaker government took charge in January, 11 cases were filed against some of the BNP ministers. The government also probed the links between militancy and some former lawmakers of the BNP. Due to the government's initiatives and support, the law-enforcing agencies were able to bring charges against the political heavy weights, which would otherwise have been impossible. The conviction of former BNP lawmaker Barrister Aminul Haque to a prison term of 32 years for his support to Banglabhai is a case in point. However, out of 25 convicts, 17, including former Minister Aminul Haque, are absconding. Although BNP leaders have been chargesheeted, the government has not taken any action against Maulana Abdul Khaleeq, a lawmaker from the JI. Former IGP, A.S.M. Shahjahan, comments, 'there had been a lot of progress in the JMB case, we may have hanged some top JMB leaders, but its origin has not been unveiled. We have to find out the masterminds who have sown the seeds of this poisonous tree. We should not just limit our arrests within the patrons and leaders of JMB—we must find out the masterminds to end this episode for good'.[26] Sheikh Abdur Rahman and Banglabhai wanted to speak to the media and Banglabhai even tried to smuggle out a letter to the media, but it was confiscated by the police, giving credence to speculation that the government is trying to protect those in higher echelons who have patronized the militants.[27]

There are other small groups involved in extremism and militancy. For example, the government arrested some nine members of Allar Dal in Kushtia this year. Founded by Matin Mehedi, who is in police custody, this group has around 56 members in Kushtia town itself. Among the arrested is Tasnim, son of Khustia Jamaat Amir Abdul Wahid. Although he claims that his son is in Chatra Shibir politics, the

---

[26] Julfikar Ali Manik, 'JMB masterminds yet to be identified', *Daily Star*, 17 August 2007.

[27] 'Let them talk to the media', *The Independent*, 28 March 2007.

police believe he is an activist of the Allar Dal which is suspected to be a front organization of HuJi.[28] The JMB has recast its Majlis Shura under the leadership of Moulana Sayeedur Rahman, alias Abu Zafar, who is reportedly associated with the Insaf Dal—a faction of Alhe Hadith (AHAB). It needs to be reiterated that some of the AHAB leaders are currently in jail and there is a close connection between the JMB and the AHAB. The government has banned the Tanjime Tamiruddin after the arrest of Maulana Abdur Rouf for militant activities. However, the group has renamed itself as Hijbe Abu Omar. Such renaming and proliferation of organizations creates a problem for the government to keep an eye on their activities, as simply banning them is not sufficient. There have been a series of arrests after the caretaker government came to power.

Bangladeshi radicals have gone through various phases of ideological consolidation. A reference point is the Taliban model of Islam. Some of the radicals have been trained in Pakistan and are Afghan war veterans. Their social and political consolidation has been slow but remains extremely significant. Their narrow social base can be attributed to their secrecy and operational problems, which is one of the reasons why they could not make the transition to a larger socio-political movement. Their popular support is insignificant. Without working for grassroots support through a mass awareness campaign about their ideology, they have relied on the false notion that the religiosity of the Bangladeshis would automatically translate into support for an Islamic revolution. The 17 August 2005 bomb blasts created panic and the Bangladeshi people, though largely religious, could not support an organization that used such violent methods.

It was only after the current caretaker government took over that the people tortured by Banglabhai gained the courage to file cases against three BNP lawmakers, former Telecom Minister Barrister Aminul Haque, former Deputy Minister of Land Ruhul Kuddus Talukdar Dulu, and former Parliamentarian, Nadim Mostafa, who provided patronage, especially in the Rajshahi area, in the knowledge of the BNP leaders. The BNP government's inaction emanated from the fact that it refused to recognize the existence of militancy. As Ahmad Abdul Qader, Secretary General Khilafat Majlis (Izharul), explained, 'Government was apprehensive that such recognition will have adverse impact on government's relations with the donor countries,

---

[28] 'Trail of 9 Allar Dal Militants Resumes in Khustia Today', *Daily Star*, 2 September 2007.

mainly the western donors'. The government had reluctantly banned HuJi. It is important to mention here that earlier the BNP government had denied the existence of HuJi when the group attacked Shamshur Rahman, a famous Bangladeshi poet in 1995. On 28 July 2007, the government framed charges against the four accused in the Shahjalal grenade attack case after three years.[29] But there has not been any action in this regard as the present caretaker government's priorities are different.

The government planned to hold a national dialogue to stop terrorist bombings but the opposition refused to participate. The dialogue on militancy began on 12 December 2005; however, some ruling party members accused the Jamaat of supporting militancy. The police continued to seize bomb-making material from across the country in areas like Satkhira, Bogra, Chapainawabganj. The agencies investigating the 17 August bomb blasts found that power gel and electronic detonators were smuggled from India, but other materials were available in the local market. Rajshahi, Sylhet, Chapainawabganj and Naogaon borders were used to smuggle in these goods.

After the execution of the six convicted JMB and JMJB leaders on 29 March 2007, the army-backed caretaker government made more arrests in connection with the 17 August 2005 bombing. It had also arrested the leaders of the AHAB and HuJi, who are currently in jail. The law-enforcing agencies rounded up 50 militants, including two members of Majlis Shura. According to the arrested militants, as reported in the media, a suspected military commander Mostafizur Rahman said that there are around 5,000 operatives still active across the country and some of them have taken up jobs in NGOs as a part of their plot to attack these offices at a future date.[30] The Rapid Action Battalion also arrested some JMB activists from Mirpur in Dhaka with 10 kg of bomb-making material and 10 grenades on 3 August 2007. The government had been alert to this threat as they suspected that the militants would strike while observing the second anniversary of the 17 August 2005 bomb blasts. Some books on jihad were also seized. Whereas these regular arrests and disruption of their network is important, doubts remain about the government's willingness to go beyond these arrests and look deeper into the problem of militancy.

---

[29] Four accused in this case are in police custody: Mufti Abdul Hanan, the HuJi chief, his brother Mofizur Rahman alias Muhib, and HuJi operatives Delwar Hossain Ripon and Sharif Shahedul Alam.

[30] See report in *Daily Star*, 'JMB feared to strike again', 3 August 2007.

There is a need to investigate why the police, although aware of the existence of the JMB and JMJB and their activities, did not take action against the militants before the countrywide bomb blasts. In fact, the Chittagong police had arrested 41 suspected Islamic militants with firearms and military uniforms in 1999. During interrogation these cadres said that they had been trained by Sheikh Abdur Rahman. They were later released. In 2000, the JMB used inaccessible areas in north Bengal to regroup. Some of these areas are also the stronghold of the Alhe Hadith. It is reported that Professor Ghalib received funds from the Middle East through Maulana Abul M Salafi, an Indian preacher of the Islamic movement. In 1988, when Salafi was expelled by General Ershad, Ghalib inherited the huge Saudi funds left by Salafi.[31] It is important to unearth whether there was any political motive that prevented the previous government from taking action against militancy before the 17 August bomb blasts. In fact, in 2005, two lawmakers, Mizanur Rahman Minu from the BNP and Maulana Abdul Khaleq of the Jamaat Islami, certified that Ghalib and the AHAB did not have links with militancy.[32]

Major Trends in the Conflict

After the execution of six prominent leaders of the JMB and JMJB, the organization is trying to regroup itself in the *char* areas of Sirajganj, Jamalpur, Sherpur and Pabna and the *haor upazilla* (bowl shaped land between the levees of the river) of Niklee and Bajitpur. This trend to regroup and reconstitute its *shura* will continue. At the same time, renaming of the organization and their activities is likely to continue. The bomb blasts in Dhaka, Sylhet and Chittagong railway stations on 1 May 2007 by Zadid al Qaeda (a new group which claimed responsibility) is a case in point. Other organizations accused of militancy like HuJI and Alh e Hadith are functioning under different names.

The JMB's linkages with HuJI and Alh e Hadith reveal their political motives and religious underpinnings. Though the HuJI became inactive after the arrest of Mufti Hannan it is still alive. In recent years it has been accused of being involved in various bomb blasts in India. In 2006, HuJI made its appearance in front of Baitul Moqarram mosque

---

[31] Anwar Ali, 'Agencies for banning Kuwait based group', *Daily Star*, 21 August 2005.

[32] 'Government finally cracks down on militants; Ghalib arrested', *Daily Star*, 24 February 2005.

in Dhaka in the name of Sachetan Islami Janata. It is reported that HujI is planning to rename itself as Islamic Gano Andolan under the leadership of Moulana Abdus Salam. Earlier, HujI was constituted of 40 Afghan war veterans, but it split into three groups in 1998 after a faction led by Mufi Hanan was expelled. His faction is the largest; another faction was led by Abdur Rauf who was arrested along with 26 of his associates by the RAB on 2 August 2006 in Bhaluka in Mymensing. This has brought the activities of this group to a standstill. The only organization that is active and functioning is headed by Maulana Farid.[33]

Various arrests, mainly in Dhaka, with huge caches of arms and explosives that being recovered, reflect that JMB has sleeping agents who are helping them to regroup. The JMB support base seems to be wider as its cadre members have been arrested from different parts of the country. And, the explosives and ammunition recovered suggest that these groups can inflict serious damage. It is likely that the militants will strike again to prove that they are committed to their ideologies and to keep the morale of its cadres intact.

Ideologically, the JMB believes in fighting the state which, to them, is unislamic in nature. The 17 August blasts were aimed at announcing their existence and arrival, rather than killing people. Later, suicide bombings targeted the judiciary which they considered 'unIslamic'. To date the JMB has not targeted the masses or tried to kill them. Their attacks are similar to the tactics of HujI, targeting cultural celebrations and cinema halls in Bangladesh which are considered as not conforming to Islam as they understand it.

As the military-backed caretaker government is more focused on political issues, fighting these militants is not a priority; as a result, their activities continue unabated. Law-enforcing authorities too are engaged in various other activities like the pursuit of corruption cases. The government executed the earlier death penalties awarded by the judiciary and has arrested militants and recovered arms. Therefore, it is likely that the government will continue to approach this as a law and order concern and the issue of religious radicalism and militancy will remain a major concern of the country. The focus of the current caretaker government is to hold elections and provide a road-map to democracy.

---

[33] Pinkaki Dasgupta, 'Harkatul Jihad in the wings', *Probe*, 29 June to 5 July 2007, p. 15.

At present the JMB's ability to expand its support base is limited. The current military-backed caretaker government has been extremely strict in its action against militancy. The massive anti-corruption drive has sent a strong message to the people that the government will not take a tolerant approach to this social malaise.

CONFLICT MANAGEMENT

As mentioned earlier, the government has tried to manage the conflict by making some significant arrests. The government's approach to the issue of religious militancy is that of managing the problem rather than dealing with it comprehensively, due to its preoccupation with issues related to the elections. Many analysts feel that the trial and execution of the militant kingpins does not address the larger question of Islamization. These militant leaders were instruments in the hands of some of the leaders belonging to both the religious parties and the BNP and have patrons both inside and outside of the country. Unless this issue is investigated and exposed the entire approach to handling this problem would be a non-starter.

There has been no effort to examine why militants become motivated to sacrifice their lives in the first place. This question assumes significance since Bangladesh is a moderate Islamic country with an extremely religious but tolerant population. If the religious militants only wanted to announce their arrival by coordinated bomb blasts on 17 August 2005, what provoked them to proceed with the objective of implementing their Islamic agenda so swiftly? Without looking into these questions, the government's effort to contain militancy will be limited to suppressing the basic issue.

Arresting the militants regularly indicates that the government is vigilant about their activities. It also points to the fact that these groups, in spite of government action, are not deterred. In 2007, 226 militants from the JMB were arrested, 57 were sentenced to prison terms, 30 were chargesheeted, six hanged and one militant was killed in an encounter.[34] The links between some of the Jamaat members with the JMB and JMJB, which was revealed during the interrogation, created a crisis in the BNP. Some senior leaders who had fought the liberation war opposed the BNP's continued linkage with the rightist parties for electoral reasons. In fact, leaders like Col. Oli Ahmed and Abu Hena

---

[34] Data complied from the South Asia Terrorism portal available at www.satp.org

openly accused the BNP of patronizing militancy by continuing its ties with the Jamaat. They felt that this alliance would go against the BNP in the forthcoming elections. However, it is the younger leaders, led by Tarique Rahman, had thought that the BNP would gain from its alliance with the right. This division within the BNP regarding its approach to militancy and rightist elements was one of the reasons that led to some of these leaders leaving the BNP.[35]

The military backed current caretaker government has a different agenda. The main purpose of the government is to hold elections. It is busy with the preparation of the voters list, political and electoral reforms and pursuing its anti-corruption agenda. Its agenda is largely political. It considers Islamic militancy to be an important issue. In fact, the most significant achievement of the current government is the execution of the militant kingpins, while the outgoing BNP regime seemed reluctant to carry out the court verdict. These executions played an important role in convincing the donor agencies about the conviction of the military to fight Islamic militancy. There also remain, however, some doubts as to whether the government would further investigate the reported links between the Jamaat and the militants. Reportedly, in December 2005, a few bureaucrats known for their sympathies towards the Jamaat Islami were kept under surveillance for suspected links to the militants.[36]

Some of the militants come from the Quami *madrassas*. A speedy trial court in Sylhet on 10 July sentenced two JMB activists Mohsin Khan and Abdul Hye, who were teachers of Dakhil *madrassa* in Jaintapur Upazila, to 10 years rigorous imprisonment for the 17 August serial bombing.[37] The government arrested 27 militants while they were being trained at a Quami *madrassa* in Mymensingh. There is also a need to bring the Quami *madrassas* under greater government control. Though the government formed a Quami Madrassa Board in 2005, there has been little effort to closely examine the curriculum. Since these groups raise their own funds there is also a need to scrutinize their source of funding. The government must establish more schools for general education. In recent years, a large number of *madrassas* have been registered compared to schools for general education. The following table also shows the growth pattern of

[35] Interview with Col. Oli Ahmed, former BNP leader on 29 July 2007 in Dhaka.
[36] '9 JMB men Held: Cops keep Close watch on pro-Jamaat Bureaucratic', *Daily Star*, 21 December 2007.
[37] '2 JMB militants get 10-yr RI in Shylet', *Daily Star*, 11 July 2007.

these institutions under the Awami League and the BNP-led, four-party alliance government. It shows that during the BNP regime the *madrassas* grew at a much faster pace as compared to general schools, thus giving priority to *madrassa* education.

	1996–2000 General	1996–2000 Madrassa	2001–2005 General	2001–2005 Madrassa
Institutions	28%	17%	10%	22%
Teachers	16%	13%	12%	17%
Students	33%	8%	9%	10%

Source: Abdullah A Dewan and Ghulam Rahman, 'The Political economy of Fundamentalism', *Daily Star*, 30 August 2005.

CONCLUSIONS

The most successful achievement of the government in 2007 has been the execution of top JMB and JMJB leaders. It continues to arrest militant operatives and seize arms and ammunition. However, the militants are still active and periodically reconstitute their *shura* membership when some of them are arrested. This is to provide continuity in guiding its members to work towards an Islamic revolution. Most of the Islamic parties' objectives are to usher an Islamic revolution and Islamize society. The methods adopted by the militants and the religious parties are different. While the Jamaat wants to establish an Islamic state through electoral politics, fringe groups like the JMB want to bring about the revolution through armed revolution, and want to change society from the top by bringing in institutional changes to strengthen the Islamic movement. The JI has a bottom-up approach. It wants to prepare the people for an Islamic revolution. Some of the ulema parties have accepted constitutional politics, but there are many who do not want to participate in electoral politics for ideological reasons. The ulema groups are also not strong enough to organize any widespread Islamic movement.

The NGOs funded by western countries have played a very important role in the empowerment of Bangladeshi women, and their work in rural areas has greatly contributed to creating political consciousness. For the time being, it will be difficult for the radicals to make any significant inroads to gain popular support. The donor countries have played an important role in pressurizing the government to take action against the militants. However, they have not persuaded the government to go into the details of the rise of the extremist groups. Though the agenda of the Islamists is currently confined to Bangladesh, it can slowly expand to develop a transnational agenda. For example, HuJI has expanded its network into India, and has linkages with al-Qaeda and other radical Islamic groups. It would not be farfetched to say that the policies of the US and western countries towards the Muslim world would contribute greatly to the political consolidation of the Islamic parties. The Hizbut Tahir, for instance, is active here. It propagates Khilafat and is ideologically more committed. It has a widespread network among the educated people and its support base is largely confined to the urbanized middle class. This is one group that needs to be watched more than some of the other radical groups like the JMB, JMJB, HuJI, and Alhe Hadith.

The politics of religion in Bangladesh has helped the fundamentalist groups ideologically. For example, a relatively secular party like the Awami League did not hesitate to sign a memorandum of understanding with a fundamentalist party like the Khilafat Majlis for the cancelled National Assembly elections. This indicates the relevance of the Islamist parties in a predominantly Muslim country like Bangladesh. Moreover, as a pre-election strategy, the BNP government hastily passed a legislation that would recognize the degrees awarded by the Quami *madrassas*, which are largely private institutions and, until recently, were autonomous of government control. It was only in 2005 that a private body under Befaqul Mudarissin of the Bangladesh Quami *madrassa* was formed to coordinate the activities and regulate the madrassas that are outside government control, and help to develop a uniform curriculum. The Quami *madrassa* laid down a pre-condition that the government cannot interfere with the curriculum that is taught in these institutions. These *madrassas* do not depend on the government for their financial sustenance and have their own sources of funding. On 21 August 2006, the government decided to acknowledge Dawra degrees as equivalent to a Master's degree in Islamic studies or Arabic literature awarded by the general educational system. This recognition was given without upgrading the syllabi and curricula of these Quami *madrassas*.

The culture of political antagonism and deep political division has contributed to the consolidation of radical Islamic elements. The outgoing BNP government's approach of 'winner takes all' politics marginalized the opposition and crippled any effort to arrive at a consensus in dealing with a serious issue like militancy. The slanging matches among political parties diverted attention from many pressing issues. The lack of progress in various incidents of political violence and killings, and political interference in the investigation process, emboldened the militants. They were sure that they could continue their activities as long as they had patrons within the ruling party.

The future of radical Islamic groups and militants will depend on future political dispensation and the shape of the polity that Bangladesh will acquire after the scheduled 2008 elections. A tolerant political culture and respect for the views expressed by the opposition and civil society will go a long way in creating an environment conducive to fighting the threats posed by the militants. A lot will depend on current political reforms, strengthening of democratic institutions that were infiltrated by party favourites, and the collective will of the people being honoured. The signs of armed conflict seem to be distant, but the potential for armed violence certainly exists in Bangladesh. The determining factor in this respect will be the government's actions and priorities, not only to deal with the religious radicals firmly, but to expose their patrons and take action against them. The hallmark of Islam in Bangladesh is its tolerant social culture and religious values. The people of Bangladesh realize this and are aware of the dangers that militant Islam will pose to their cultural entity, in which lies the strength of the country and its ability to fight radicalism. The people of Bangladesh are prepared, but are the government and the political parties listening?

9

Nepal: State in Dilemma

P. G. Rajamohan

With the beginning of the April Movement in 2006, Nepal has been undergoing dramatic historical changes. The country has been relieved of a decade-long Maoist insurgency, but the transition period has posed major challenges to its socio-economic-political and security scenario. Amidst all these threatening issues and stumbling blocks, the government has been under severe pressure to carry forward the ongoing peace process in Nepal. On the one hand, the political parties in the government are pursuing their own party interests and internal differences, and on the other hand, the Maoists are using tactical pressure to intimidate the government authorities. Further, demonstrations by ethnic groups and the unrestrained violence by the newly-formed armed groups severely threaten the smooth transition in the country. While the government managed to reach agreements with some of the agitating groups, it could not prevent the Communist Party of Nepal (Maoist) from walking out of the government when two of their key demands, that is, declaration of a republic and proportionate electoral system, were not met. The Maoists present move has mounted enormous pressure on the ongoing peace process and jeopardized the scheduled constituent assembly elections. However, the country has been strenuously advancing with the peace process and striving to settle every issue that has been raised by various sections of society. Three and a half months after their walkout from the government, the Maoists rejoined the interim cabinet on 30 December 2007. Also, the Constituent Assembly elections have been rescheduled for the third time and all parties have decided to hold it on 10 April 2008.

A BRIEF HISTORY

Nepal is the poorest country in South Asia with significant income poverty and markedly low levels of human development, and has experienced violent conflict over the past decade. The 'People's War' launched by Maoist guerrillas against the state has led to widespread loss of lives and livelihoods[1] and had serious negative effects on the country's development prospects. The inability of elected governments after 1991 to take note of the grievances of the people has encouraged the Maoist armed struggle. Prior to the April Movement in 2006, the actors in the tri-polar political conflict—authoritarian monarchy, parliamentary multi-party government, and the Maoists—had brought enormous suffering on the masses, paralyzed the national economy, and strangulated the political democratic process. This has led to many ethnic and regional liberation groups emerging with their own grievances to demand a political restructuring of the Nepali state. Resolution of the conflicts in Nepal has become more complicated, which inevitably requires a systematic approach in the course of political restructuring of the state. In any such undertaking, Nepal can profitably learn from the experience of other countries around the world which have gone through similar processes, but also from its own past history and the political events and insurgency over the past decade.[2]

Maoist Insurgency

The Communist Party of Nepal was formed under the leadership of Pushpa Lal Shrestha in 1949. During the 1960s and early 1970s, the communist movement developed extremist sections, swayed by the Chinese Cultural Revolution on its north and the naxalite groups[3] functioning along its southern border with India. The extremist groups mobilized the local population in the western and mid-western hill region.[4] Internal schisms and power struggle within the movement were exacerbated by the Sino–Soviet split and its

---

[1] It is estimated that over 13,000 people were killed, properties worth NRs 5.127 billion were destroyed and approximately 200,000 people displaced during the conflict period.

[2] Anand Aditya, Bishnu Raj Upreti and PK Adhikary, 'Countries in Conflict and Processing of Peace: Lessons for Nepal', *Friends for Peace Publications*, Series 011, May 2006, p. 41.

[3] Left-wing extremist groups in India, commonly known as 'Naxalite groups', because of the beginnings of this movement in a village called Naxalbari in West Bengal during the 1960s.

[4] The Hill region in the western and mid-western region is found to be suitable for guerilla war in the country. In the eastern region, the agricultural labourers and the downtrodden were organized by the radical Nepali Communist Party (Marxist–Leninist) which carried out killings of the local feudals (landlords) in and around Jhapa district during the early 1970s. This was known as the Jhapali Uprising and became a landmark incident for the revolutionaries in future.

international repercussions.[5] Under Pushpa Kamal Dahal alias Prachanda, the extremist factions agreed to fight under a common name—Communist Party of Nepal-Maoist (CPN-M).[6] The United People's Front of Nepal (UPFN), led by Baburam Bhattarai, which had nine representatives in parliament, gave its support to the CPN-M.[7] The Maoists then criticized the parliamentary democratic system and warned their cadres to get ready for 'radical change' through armed struggle. This armed struggle at the infant stage centred around the mid-western hill districts. It became serious after the police operations launched in late 1995, Operation Romeo in Rolpa and Rukum districts, and Operation Kilo Siera II around the same region.

The Maoists declared an armed struggle, 'People's War', on 13 February 1996 after submitting a 40-point memorandum that included demands concerning nationality, people's democracy, and questions of the livelihood of Nepali citizens. Other demands included abolition of special privileges of the King and royal family, and promulgation of a new republican constitution by a constituent assembly of freshly elected people's representatives.[8] Subsequently, the Maoist movement became violent in the districts of Rukum, Rolpa, Jajarkot, Salyan, Gorkha and Sindhuli. The People's War path was adopted by the Maoists for establishing a communist society through a 'new democratic revolution' with a people's democratic dictatorship based on the unity of workers and peasants against feudalism and imperialism.[9] They believed in the philosophy of Mao Zedong that 'political power grows out of the barrel of a gun'.[10] Maoists also draw inspiration from Peru's Left-wing extremist guerrilla movement, Sendero Luminoso (Shining Path, founded in 1980), because of commonalities between Nepal and Peruvian society, economy, politics and geography.[11]

---

[5] See, R. Andrew Nickson, 'Democratisation and the Growth of Communism in Nepal: A Peruvian Scenario in the Making?' *Journal of Commonwealth and Comparative Politics*, vol. 30, no. 3, November 1992.

[6] See, Arjun Karki and David Seddon, 'The People's War in Historical Context', in *The People's War in Nepal; Left Perspectives* Delhi: Adroit Publishers, 2003 p. 17.

[7] Sangeetha Thapliyal, 'Maoists in Nepal', *The Hindu* (Chennai), 18 December 2001.

[8] The 40-point demands were published in *Janadesh Weekly*, Kathmandu, 6 February 1996. These demands focused mainly on abrogation of agreements with India, including the Treaty of Friendship in 1950, the Mahakali Treaty, etc.

[9] Excerpts from the document adopted by the Third Plenum of the CC of CPN (Maoist) in March 1995.

[10] It is placed on the Maoists official website; www.cpnm.org

[11] R. Andrew Nickson, see note 5 above.

The regicide in Nepal in June 2001[12] marked an important event in the country, after which it witnessed a deteriorating security situation, political instability, and economic stagnation. In July 2001, the Maoists launched violent attacks on security forces, notably in Rolpa, Rukum and Jajarkot.[13] Simultaneously, they formed a 'People's Council' and set up an alternate 'People's Government' in the areas under their control.[14] Insurgency became deep-rooted and gained a strong foothold in the rural areas after King Gyanendra imposed Emergency and assumed direct executive authority on 4 October 2002. Violence then spread unchecked in the country, with major strikes by the Maoists at Bhimad police post in Sindhuli district and in Sandhikharka, headquarters of Arghakanchi district, consecutively on 8 and 9 September 2002.[15]

The security situation deteriorated further and reached its lowest ebb with the growing political chaos in the country. The Maoist insurgency reached dramatic heights, with almost all the 75 districts in Nepal, including the capital city of Kathmandu, experiencing violence of varying intensity. The Maoists reportedly claimed a presence, strong or marginal, in 80 per cent of the Nepalese territory. The prevailing strategic equilibrium frustrated all government measures to manage the insurgency situation. Meanwhile, the King's direct takeover of the executive powers of the government alienated the political parties, which finally led them to forge an alliance with the Maoists. This has given the Maoists some political legitimacy and their constructive negotiations and alliance with the Seven Party Alliance (SPA) finally

---

[12] 'Nepal Royal Family Massacred', BBC (News Service), 2 June 2001. http://news.bbc.co.uk/2/hi/south_asia/1365393.stm . It was largely believed that King Birendra's 29-year-old son, Crown Prince Dipendra, opened fire on his parents and other family members before turning his sub-machine gun on himself. But many conspiracy theories on this royal massacre still prevail in the country.

[13] On 12 July, along with the nation-wide general strike, Maoist guerillas carried out a raid on the Holleri police post in Rolpa district, taking 70 policemen as prisoners.

[14] On 23 November 2001, a 37-member 'People's Council' was declared under the Chairmanship of Dr. Baburam Bhattarai, Politbureau Member (PBM) of CPN-Maoist. The Council was formed by the conference of the representatives of the People's Liberation Army (PLA), different national and regional liberation fronts, different mass organizations and district United People's Committees. The conference elected Krishna Bahadur Mahara as Vice-Chairman and Deb Gurung as Vice-Chairman and Secretary. The other names of the members are available at http://www.insof.org/news/251101_peoples_council.htm

[15] See *The Kathmandu Post*, 10 September, 2002. More than 100 security force personnel and around 300 rebels also died.

put an end to the King's direct rule. Declaring an end to the People's War on 21 November 2006, the Maoists took part in the newly established interim government along with the SPA on 1 April 2007.

Despite the fact that the bloody insurgency was officially concluded and the Maoists returned to the mainstream politics, the government has not been able to establish a permanent peace in the country. The Terai violence turned into its worst phase and many more ethnic communities started their agitations in the beginning of 2007. While the government was engaged in resolving the newly-emerged disturbances and trying to establish control over the deteriorating security situation, the Maoists felt that they were being sidelined and were particularly worried about the assertion of ethnic communities and armed groups. In their fifth plenum meeting, the frustrated middle-level Maoists leaders reacted against the top leadership for continuing to stand by the government and yet not achieving their demands. In view of the growing dissatisfaction within the party and their declining popularity, the Maoists had set 22 'prerequisites' for continuing in the government and participating in the polls. When Prime Minister Koirala rejected outright two of their key demands—the declaration of a republic through interim parliament and a fully proportional electoral system—the Maoists decided to walk out of the government and increased the pressure tactics. Although the Maoists have not severed the Peace Agreement, their actions have thwarted the November 2008 elections and the peaceful settlement of many existing problems.

PRINCIPAL ACTORS

As the Maoists' decade-long People's War has officially concluded and the peace process is progressing in the country, the triangular power struggle has now become irrelevant. Further, the alliance between the SPA and the Maoists has marginalized the Monarchy, which is defunct; its fate will be decided after the constituent assembly elections. King Gyanendra changed three governments within 27 months of the dissolution of the Sher Bahadur Deuba government on 4 October 2002. He diluted the powers of the political parties but also the government's ability to deal with insurgency. His decision to declare complete authority on 1 February 2005 further weakened the prospects of a peaceful resolution to the conflict. His demand for a three-year period to bring normalcy to Nepal and re-establish a multi-party system kept the political parties out of policy-making, and finally made them forge an alliance with the Maoists to throw out the Monarchy. All the powers of the Monarchy have been stripped and the institution itself is threatened. A resolution was passed in parliament to nationalize all the properties of the royal family. Finally, the Royal Nepalese Army (RNA) and the Nepal police effectively came under the control of the civilian government and have refrained from human rights violations.

The political parties, which were feeble during the King's regime, regained their political power alongside the Maoists in 2006. The SPA[16] began negotiations with the Maoists after they declared a ceasefire in September 2005. After several rounds of secret talks (some reportedly held in India), both the SPA and the Maoists announced the formation of a coalition against the King's rule and declared a 12-point agreement on 22 November 2005.[17] The King's regime threatened that it would treat the SPA as terrorists along with the Maoist rebels if their relationship continued in line with the 12-point agreement. Failing to convince the Monarchy to reach a peaceful settlement with the political parties, the international community, particularly India, the US and the UK, agreed to respect the results of the protest movement in April 2006.

The transition period has clearly been difficult in Nepal as the political actors have not been able to reach a broad consensus on finding an amicable solution to the present crisis. The political wrangling among the coalition partners has created serious problems for the future of the alliance and the interim government. The leaders of the communist parties have advocated a new equation between them and the democratic parties. They have also been trying to polarize opinion on pro- and anti-republic lines. The disunity among the coalition partners has encouraged some groups to declare an armed revolt against the government, thus spearheading action that could seriously threaten the stability of the nation.

The other important force in Nepal, that is, the Maoists, have benefited the most in the present context. After abandoning the People's War, the

---

[16] The Seven Party Alliance includes the Nepali Congress (NC), Nepali Congress–Democratic (NC–D), Communist Party of Nepal–United Marxist Leninist (CPN–UML), Nepal Workers and Peasants Party, People's Front of Nepal, Nepal Sadbhavana Party (Anandi) and the United Left Front.

[17] See the full text of the 12-point agreement in *Nepali Times,* issue 274, http://www.nepalitimes.seacem.com/issue/274/Fromthenepalipress/9190

Maoists have secured five ministerial berths in the interim government and a sizeable representation in the interim parliament. Now the CPN-M has been officially recognized as one of the 62 political parties registered with the election commission.[18] It is believed that 'most' of their cadres and arms are stationed in UN-monitored cantonments[19] and the government has been bearing the expenses for these Maoist armies. However, the Maoist activities have not yet stopped. On the one hand, the Maoist ministers in the government have been pressurizing the government to fulfil their demands. At the same time they are using the ethnic front organizations, students and workers unions to mount pressure on the government through strikes, protest marches, and so on. The newly-formed Young Communist League (YCL)[20] has been active in popularizing the Maoist agenda. Even as the constituent assembly poll was deferred, chiefly due to their rigidity over the electoral process, among other reasons, the Maoists have recently intensified extortion on the pretext of 'ensuring constituent assembly election through yet another movement'.

Terai Groups

Apart from the major actors, the groups operating in the Terai region constitute another important force in the ongoing peace process in Nepal. Their presence in economically and politically significant areas of this region has the potential to thwart any attempt at restructuring of the state. Some of the prominent groups operating in this region are listed below.

---

[18] The CPN (Maoist) registered them with the Election Commission (EC) on 10 April 2007 to participate in the upcoming constituent assembly election. Sixty-two different political parties have registered with the Election Commission in terms of the new provisions enshrined in the interim constitution.

[19] Under the peace agreement, the Maoists agreed to keep their fighters in seven cantonments and 21 satellite camps spread across the country.

[20] The YCL was re-established in December 2006 by the CPN–M Central Committee as a newly-affiliated organization of the CPN–M party and has a growing presence throughout the country, in all regions, districts and village development committees (VDCs). Many of the 45 members of the YCL Central Committee appointed in early February are former People's Liberation Army (PLA) commanders and commissars who left the PLA and transferred to the YCL rather than assemble in the PLA cantonment sites subsequently set up as part of the peace agreement. In addition, YCL leaders at regional and district levels also include former PLA commanders or militia members. See, United Nations Office of the High Commissioner for Human Rights, 'Allegations of Human Rights Abuses by the Young Communist League (YCL)', June 2007.

Janatantrik Terai Mukti Morcha (JTMM)

The JTMM is the splinter group of the Maoists. It was formed in 2004 by splitting the CPN-M to establish an autonomous Terai region. The JTMM has split into two further factions—one led by Jai Krishna Goit and another by Jwala Singh alias Nagendra Paswan. Ever since the split, both the factions of the JTMM and the Maoist cadres have been engaged in violence against each other. Both groups are opposed to the ongoing peace process in Nepal. The JTMM factions believe that the Terai region does not belong to any King of the Shah dynasty. Often the leaders of these groups stated that they would not allow the constituent assembly elections in the Terai region, seeing them as a conspiracy hatched by the Pahadis (hill people) of Nepal.

Madhesi People's Rights Forum (MPRF)

The MPRF is another Madhesi group involved in violence since 15 January 2007. Its demands are: declaration of a republic, federal system and proportional representation; citizenship to all Madhesis; and an end to discrimination against them. Although the MPRF is a major force in the Terai region responsible for violence in the initial months of 2007, the talks between the government and the MPRF struck a positive note on 30 August with the latter agreeing to withdraw all its protest programmes following a 22-point agreement. While the MPRF has been displaying immense political maturity, the agreement has created a division within it and it has also failed to gain support from many of the parties.

Terai Cobra

It has vowed to launch an armed separatist struggle for an independent Terai state. It is also opposed to the presence of hill people in the area. The group has a presence in Bara, Parsa, Rautahat and Sarlahi districts. The head of this group identifies himself as Nagaraj, but remains a mystery figure. The group has occasionally conducted strikes in the Terai districts.

Madhesi Mukti Tigers (MMT)

The MMT, which is an armed group led by Sher Singh Rajput, has been expanding its network in all the 20 Terai districts, including the sensitive central and mid-western Nepal region. The Madhesi Mukti

Tigers, a little-known group which began to draw attention in 2007 with a spate of abductions and robberies, threatened to call a three-day 'Madhes bandh' in nearly 22 districts in the plains to demand the release of detained leaders and the withdrawal of criminal charges against them.

Chure Bhawar Ekata Samaj (CBES)

The CBES has been demanding the establishment of a Chure Bhawar federal region in the Terai. It came into existence when the MPRF refused to include different races and religions of the Terai into its fold, according to Somnath Lama, Chairman of the Samaj. However, the Samaj expressed its willingness to have talks with the government regarding the security of the Pahadi people and other demands.

CONFLICT IN 2007

The year 2006 was a memorable one in the political history of Nepal, marking the end of violent conflict and the beginnings of a new Nepal. Following a peace accord between two of the principal actors in conflict—the Maoists and the Seven Party Alliance—the violence of the past years has declined.

The year 2006 began with the Maoists ending their four-month long unilateral ceasefire on 2 January 2006,[21] which was not reciprocated by King Gyanendra. As the prospects of a solution to the decade-long conflict reached its lowest ebb, the country slipped into an orgy of violence with Maoist attacks being launched across the country, including Kathmandu. Following the breakdown of the ceasefire, the biggest Maoist attack was carried out in Palpa on 31 January 2006, where 24 security force personnel were killed and 29 government officials and security personnel were abducted.[22] Also, 17 security persons were killed in Nawalparasi district on 9 February 2006. Despite the 12-point agreement between the rebels and the SPA and large-scale protest movements by the political

---

[21] The ceasefire was first announced on 3 September 2005 for three months and extended by a month on 2 December 2005.

[22] Later the captives were freed by the efforts of the Informal Sector (INSEC) representatives and journalists on 6 February 2006. See, *INSEC Trend Analysis*, February 2006.

parties, King Gyanendra continued his repressive regime,[23] paying only lip-service to the rhetoric of restoring a peaceful, multi-party democratic Nepal within three years. Things came to such a pass that even the international community criticized the royal government for the collapse of the ceasefire and its uncompromising stance against the democratic forces.

By February 2006, the twelve months of palace rule had only made the security situation more precarious, emboldening the division between the conflicting parties in the country. Despite widespread national and international condemnation, the conflict between the security forces and the Maoist insurgents continued to spread across the country. Eventually, the autocratic King's regime became even more unpopular after the stage-managed municipal elections[24] which were boycotted by mainstream political parties, disparaged by civil society, disapproved of by the international community and threatened by the Maoist rebels. The deteriorating security and political situation did not help to reconcile the existing problems, and pushed the country towards extreme instability. The international community's repeated call for reconciliation between the King and the political parties was in vain and India's last attempt of sending it's high-level mission[25] also ended in failure.

The royal government's repressive measures brought the Maoists and political parties closer to strengthen their alliance against the King. In April, Nepal saw the strongest wave of anti-Monarchy sentiments sweeping the country. The royal addresses on 14 and 21 April were in vain. While agitations began as pro-democracy demonstrations, they eventually turned into anti-Monarchy protests. The demonstrators cautioned the SPA leadership against any political compromise with the King. The demonstrations attracted huge popular support, including government officials, professionals and civil society organizations. Finally, after 19 days of continuous demonstrations across the country and the loss of many lives, the King bowed to the uprising and

---

[23] The regime showed no regard for the people's right to freedom of speech and peaceful assembly. The political leaders were kept under house arrest and prevented from accessing phones, human rights organizations and foreign diplomats. Without heeding any criticism of its action, the government arrested human rights activists as well.

[24] The municipal elections held on 8 February 2006 saw an average voter turnout of 20 per cent. According to the Election Commission, out of 1,443,310 voters in the nation, only 284,225 cast their votes.

[25] 'Karan Singh to visit Kathmandu as special Indian envoy', *Nepal News*, 18 April 2006.

reinstated the House of Representatives (HoR) on 24 April, which had been dissolved in May 2002. While the participation of millions of people from all walks of life made the pro-democracy agitations a historic movement and a success, it also placed on the political parties the onus of delivering a clean and accountable government and resolving the decade-old conflict by bringing the Maoists into the democratic mainstream.

The first meeting of the reinstated HoR[26] on 30 April unanimously passed Prime Minister Girija Prasad Koirala's motion to hold constituent assembly elections. Further, in May the cabinet meeting reciprocated positively to the ceasefire declaration[27] and removed the terrorist tag from the rebels. In addition, a historic HoR proclamation of 18 May clipped the King's powers and privileges, brought the army under its control, declared Nepal to be a secular state, and rechristened His Majesty's Government of Nepal as Nepal Government. Finally, the eight-point agreement[28] between the Maoists and the new government has placed the country decisively on the road to establishing a constituent assembly, while inviting the United Nations to monitor the arms and armies of both sides in order to conduct free and fair elections.

With the signing of a Comprehensive Peace Agreement and Arms Management Accord on 21 November 2006,[29] the bloody conflict in Nepal officially came to an end. The peace-building process witnessed several developments towards the end of the year. The most significant development was, without doubt, the cessation of hostilities and ensuing efforts to manage the peace. The interim constitution was promulgated on 15 January 2007, and a 330-member interim parliament, including representatives of the Maoists, replaced the reinstated HoR. Subsequently, the 35-member UN experts' team for arms management, assisted by the Gurkha Interim Task Force

---

[26] According to the 1999 General Elections, the political parties' representation in the 205-member HoR is: Nepali Congress—113, CPN–UML—68, Rastriya Prajatantra Party—12, Sadbhawana Party—5, Majdoor Kisan Party—1, Samyukta Rastriya Janamorcha—5. See, 'King Gyanendra reinstates House of Representatives', *The Kathmandu Post*, 25 April 2006.

[27] Maoists, responding to a demand by the newly appointed Prime Minister Girija Prasad Koirala, announced a unilateral three-month truce on 3 May 2006.

[28] In 'summit level talks' on 16 June 2006, both the SPA and the Maoist leaders agreed to an eight-point agenda, which includes: framing an interim statute, an interim government, declaring the date for an election to a constituent assembly, and dissolving the revived House of Representatives and the Maoist-declared Governments.

[29] 'Comprehensive Peace Accord signed, armed conflict officially over', *Nepal News*, 21 November 2006.

(ITF), started the registration and storage of Maoist arms at two cantonment sites, Chitwan and Nawalparasi districts. Although the UN involvement helped both conflicting parties to diffuse their mistrust and formulate a reliable and trustworthy means of managing arms, the process has encountered many stumbling blocks because of its potential to highlight more serious issues.

The People's War has been officially suspended, but the other activities of the Maoists like extortion, forceful indoctrination, coercive recruitment and torture continue unabated.[30] They obstructed the government's efforts to reinstall the police posts demolished during the conflict[31] and prevented officials of the Village Development Committee (VDC) from performing their duties. With their continued actions, the Maoists were suspected of trying to malign the credibility of the security guarantees provided by the state and attempting to generate public impatience with the government's inability to maintain law and order. It could be one of the rebels' tactics to overwhelm the system without provoking the Nepali army, which is still considered a major force capable of countering the People's Liberation Army (PLA). However, with the genesis of the peace process and relatively peaceful conditions in the country, nobody would like to see a return to chaos. Continuous pressure from civil society, political parties and the international community, and the distancing of the Nepali army from power politics, has persuaded the Maoists to restrain violence and carry forward the peace process.

Despite the precarious security situation, Nepal has seen many positive political developments and has achieved commendable progress during the peace process in 2007. The formation of the interim government, interim parliament, enactment of an interim constitution, inclusion of Maoists in the cabinet, and keeping the arms and armies of the Maoists in UN-monitored cantonments are some of the achievements in 2007. However, major strikes and brutal violence

---

[30] 'Peace deterrent to abductions, intimidation', *The Kathmandu Post*, 12 December 2006. It said 'Maoists on recruitment drive', *The Kathmandu Post*, 15 November 2006. Maoists were undertaking fresh recruitment drives in the districts of Ilam in fa Rupendehi in Nepal, Sankhuwasabha in the north-east and Surkhet and Nepal.

[31] At least 1 Kosh Raj Koirala e posts were defunct during the decade-long insurgency. 71 police posts restored', *The Kathmandu Post*, 15 January 2007.

(ITF), started the registration and storage of Maoist arms at two cantonment sites, Chitwan and Nawalparasi districts. Although the UN involvement helped both conflicting parties to diffuse their mistrust and formulate a reliable and trustworthy means of managing arms, the process has encountered many stumbling blocks because of its potential to highlight more serious issues.

The People's War has been officially suspended, but the other activities of the Maoists like extortion, forceful indoctrination, coercive recruitment and torture continue unabated.[30] They obstructed the government's efforts to reinstall the police posts demolished during the conflict[31] and prevented officials of the Village Development Committee (VDC) from performing their duties. With their continued actions, the Maoists were suspected of trying to malign the credibility of the security guarantees provided by the state and attempting to generate public impatience with the government's inability to maintain law and order. It could be one of the rebels' tactics to overwhelm the system without provoking the Nepali army, which is still considered a major force capable of countering the People's Liberation Army (PLA). However, with the genesis of the peace process and relatively peaceful conditions in the country, nobody would like to see a return to chaos. Continuous pressure from civil society, political parties and the international community, and the distancing of the Nepali army from power politics, has persuaded the Maoists to restrain violence and carry forward the peace process.

Despite the precarious security situation, Nepal has seen many positive political developments and has achieved commendable progress during the peace process in 2007. The formation of the interim government, interim parliament, enactment of an interim constitution, inclusion of Maoists in the cabinet, and keeping the arms and armies of the Maoists in UN-monitored cantonments are some of the achievements in 2007. However, major strikes and brutal violence

---

[30] 'Peace no deterrent to abductions, intimidation', *The Kathmandu Post*, 12 December 2006; 'Maoists on recruitment drive', *The Kathmandu Post*, 15 November 2006. It said that the Maoists were undertaking fresh recruitment drives in the districts of Ilam in far-eastern Nepal, Sankhuwasabha in the north-east and Surkhet and Rupendehi in western Nepal.

[31] At least 1,271 police posts were defunct during the decade-long insurgency. Kosh Raj Koirala, '904 of 1271 police posts restored', *The Kathmandu Post*, 15 January 2007.

reinstated the House of Representatives (HoR) on 24 April, which had been dissolved in May 2002. While the participation of millions of people from all walks of life made the pro-democracy agitations a historic movement and a success, it also placed on the political parties the onus of delivering a clean and accountable government and resolving the decade-old conflict by bringing the Maoists into the democratic mainstream.

The first meeting of the reinstated HoR[26] on 30 April unanimously passed Prime Minister Girija Prasad Koirala's motion to hold constituent assembly elections. Further, in May the cabinet meeting reciprocated positively to the ceasefire declaration[27] and removed the terrorist tag from the rebels. In addition, a historic HoR proclamation of 18 May clipped the King's powers and privileges, brought the army under its control, declared Nepal to be a secular state, and rechristened His Majesty's Government of Nepal as Nepal Government. Finally, the eight-point agreement[28] between the Maoists and the new government has placed the country decisively on the road to establishing a constituent assembly, while inviting the United Nations to monitor the arms and armies of both sides in order to conduct free and fair elections.

With the signing of a Comprehensive Peace Agreement and Arms Management Accord on 21 November 2006,[29] the bloody conflict in Nepal officially came to an end. The peace-building process witnessed several developments towards the end of the year. The most significant development was, without doubt, the cessation of hostilities and ensuing efforts to manage the peace. The interim constitution was promulgated on 15 January 2007, and a 330-member interim parliament, including representatives of the Maoists, replaced the reinstated HoR. Subsequently, the 35-member UN experts' team for arms management, assisted by the Gurkha Interim Task Force

---

[26] According to the 1999 General Elections, the political parties' representation in the 205-member HoR is: Nepali Congress—113, CPN–UML—68, Rastriya Prajatantra Party—12, Sadbhawana Party—5, Majdoor Kisan Party—1, Samyukta Janamorcha—1, Rastriya Janamorcha—5. See, 'King Gyanendra reinstates House of Representatives', *The Kathmandu Post*, 25 April 2006.

[27] Maoists, responding to a demand by the newly appointed Prime Minister Girija Prasad Koirala, announced a unilateral three-month truce on 27 April 2006.

[28] In 'summit level talks' on 16 June 2006, both the SPA and the Maoist leaders agreed to an eight-point agenda, which includes: framing an interim statute, an interim government, declaring the date for an election to a constituent assembly, and dissolving the revived House of Representatives and the Maoists' People's Governments.

[29] 'Comprehensive Peace Accord signed, armed insurgency declared officially over', *Nepal News*, 21 November 2006.

perpetrated by the newly-emerged armed groups and ethnicity-based organizations, particularly in the southern part of Nepal or the Terai region, has been a major hindrance to the political and peace processes. The government has managed to reach agreements with some groups in the Terai in recent months, but there are numerous issues yet to be addressed.

After long deliberations and discussions, the interim constitution was promulgated by the HoR on 15 January 2007. It was the sixth constitution to have been promulgated by Nepal in the last six decades. Following the promulgation of the interim constitution, the House of Representatives also announced its dissolution.[32] The 330-member interim legislature,[33] convened on the same day, endorsed the interim statute unanimously. With its promulgation, the Monarchy remains a suspended institution until its fate is decided by the constituent assembly. The Seven Party Alliance and the Communist Party of Nepal (Maoist) have accomplished another historic task by forming the interim government on 1 April 2007.[34] Its formation was delayed by the failure of the political parties to reach an agreement on major issues and ministerial portfolios. But the democratic forces have finally inaugurated a new era in Nepal's political history by including the Maoists into the cabinet. Following the signing of a Common Minimum Programme (CMP) by the leaders of the eight-party (SPA + Maoists) alliance, the interim government was formed with the swearing-in of a 22-member cabinet under the leadership of the Nepali Congress President, G.P. Koirala. The Maoists have secured five ministerial portfolios;[35] their participation

---

[32] 'HoR promulgates interim constitution, dissolves itself', *Nepal News*, 15 January 2007.

[33] The legislature has 83 Maoist lawmakers along with 208 lawmakers from the outgoing House and 38 other lawmakers nominated by the various political parties. The list of its 73 MPs from CPN–M (10 others are nominated) includes 22 from the Janajati (indigenous community), 21 Madhesi (Terai community), 28 women, 17 representing martyrs' families and 11 from the Dalit community.

[34] 'PM administers oath to ministers and state ministers; 22 member cabinet unveiled', *Nepal News*, 1 April 2007.

[35] As per the 31 March 2007 agreement between the SPA and the Maoists over the distribution of portfolios, the Nepali Congress, CPN (UML) and Maoists secured five cabinet berths each; NC-Democratic got three berths whereas People's Front (PF), United Leftist Front (ULF) and Nepal Sadbhavana Party–Anandidevi (NSP-A) got one berth each. Altogether there are 16 cabinet-rank ministers and five state ministers.

in this government marked yet another departure from all previous governments.[36]

In February 2007, on the occasion of the 11th anniversary of the People's War, Maoist Chairman Prachanda pronounced his party's approach and position on several major national issues ranging from political governance to ideological perspectives and economic development.[37] His remarks on this occasion explicitly emphasized the change in Maoist policy in the changing political situation. In his first public address after decades of living underground as a fugitive, Prachanda strongly emphasized the CPN-M's commitment to establishing a federal republican structure, adopting a mixed economic policy, and revolutionizing the pattern of land ownership. He also castigated entrenched corruption at the political and public levels and emphasized the need to nip abusive and corrupt practices in the bud. Expressing his strong condemnation of tendencies to derail elections to the constituent assembly, Prachanda warned against anti-democratic designs in the country. A careful reading of the views expressed by the Maoist leader makes it clear that the party that swore by violence and fought for forceful seizure of the state has made several changes in its approach and political perspectives. His explicit remarks on the appropriateness of a mixed economy for the country would definitely provide a greater space for the private sector to operate. Obviously, his remarks indicate that the political realities and constraints leave very limited choices for the political actors, no matter how radicalized, strong and committed they are in upholding ideological positions. This would definitely, in course of time, lead the political actors to compromise and force them to display foresight, innovation and vision.

In April 2007, the Maoists demanded that parliament declare Nepal a republic and began campaigning among the communist parties

---

[36] The Maoists secured five ministerial berths and named its important leaders for each ministry. These are: Krishna Bahadur Mahara, party spokesperson and team leader in the cabinet for the Ministry of Information and Communication; Dev Gurung for the Ministry of Local Development; Hisila Yami for the Ministry of Works and Physical Planning; Matrika Yadav for the Ministry of Forest and Soil Conservation; and Khadga Bahadur Biswokarma for the Ministry of Women, Children and Social Welfare. 'New cabinet to be unveiled in the parliament today', *Nepal News*, 31 March 2007. In recent developments, Matrika Yadav resigned from the cabinet on 2 August 2007. J. Hemnath, 'Senior Maoist leader quits Nepal cabinet', *The Telegraph*, 3 August 2007.

[37] 'Maoists want democratic republic with mixed economy, radical land reform: Prachanda', *Nepal News*, 13 February 2007.

to push forward their demand.[38] The Maoists have held out this new demand mainly to recover from the damage that they suffered recently, particularly in the Terai, and to allay their fears that the Nepali Congress leadership favours the continuation of Monarchy. Despite the constituent assembly elections being scheduled for 20 June, the Maoists wanted the interim parliament to proclaim Nepal as a republic before the elections to justify their decade-long armed struggle and coerce the other political parties to endorse their agenda. On the other hand, the Nepali Congress and NC-Democratic (Nepal Congress-Democratic) have started reviewing their policies and have initiated talks to reunite the two parties. The rising disunity among the parties in the government has nurtured mistrust and disrupted the peace process and poll preparations for the elections.

While political confusion continues, the Election Commission (EC) said that it was technically impossible to conduct free and fair constituent assembly polls on 20 June, as decided by the ruling eight-party coalition.[39] The Chief Election Commissioner (CEC), Bhoj Raj Pokharel, said, 'Besides election-related technical aspects, peace and security situation of the country hasn't yet become stable,' and added, 'It may create further complications if we go to elections without addressing all the other political issues related to the electoral system.' Finally, after two months of discussion over these issues, the government decided to hold the constituent assembly elections on 22 November.[40] The EC expressed dissatisfaction over the security situation and strongly suggested that the government improve the security situation in order to hold free and fair polls.

As Nepal was moving ahead in the peace process, the debate on the Monarchy once again came centrestage in June. On 13 June, the interim parliament passed the second amendment to the five-month-old interim constitution, empowering parliament to abolish the institution of Monarchy (240-year-old Shah Dynasty) by a two-thirds majority if King Gyanendra interfered in the elections in November. The King has been stripped of most of his powers, but the Maoists want to abolish the Monarchy so that he cannot play his last card to

---

[38] 'Maoists want House to proclaim republic', *The Kathmandu Post*, 15 April 2007; 'Republic basis for Left unity: Prachanda', *The Himalayan Times*, 24 April 2007.

[39] Ghanashyam Ojha, 'June 20 poll not possible: CEC', *The Kathmandu Post*, 14 April 2007.

[40] 'Govt sets Nov 22 poll date', *Nepal News*, 24 June 2007. This date was also postponed in September 2007.

disrupt the polls. This argument has some truth as a large section of the Nepalese media suspect that the former royal ministers had a role in inflaming the Terai and making the region the vortex of Nepalese politics at this very critical juncture. Proof of their involvement is growing and this makes the King a suspect. While the Maoists are pressing parliament to announce Nepal as a 'republic' before the constituent assembly elections, the majority of lawmakers and the political parties have remained firm on deciding this issue only at the first meeting of the constituent assembly. In the present political context, the recent amendment has helped to check the fear of the palace backing criminal elements to stall the elections. However, as predicted earlier, the Maoists used this provision to advance their agenda of declaring Nepal a republic before the elections.

In August, the Maoists' fifth plenum meeting and their pre-poll demands dramatically changed the political situation in Nepal. The Communist Party of Nepal (Maoist) held their fifth plenum between 3 and 8 August in Kathmandu, which was attended by nearly 2,000 leaders and senior party workers, including central and zonal leaders, and the chiefs of the party's various wings. The plenum unanimously accepted the political and organizational report of Chairman Prachanda with some amendments. The report also raised two preconditions for the elections—an immediate announcement of the formation of a republic by parliament, and adoption of proportional representation as the electoral system. The Central Committee meeting, held to implement the decisions of the fifth plenum, decided to restructure the CPN-M. Accordingly, the party dissolved the six military-styled regional commands and replaced them with five political bureaus and 12 autonomous republic departments, and another department to look after international affairs. It also formed separate committees for eight ethnic-based 'states' under a federal structure for the country.

The present pre-poll demands of the Maoists constitute a breach of the interim constitution and the political agreements reached during the April Movement. The Maoists have reiterated publicly in their 12-point agreement with the SPA that they will accept a multi-party system, the rule of law and the verdict of the constituent assembly on Monarchy. It is therefore not appropriate for them to press for the republic through the interim parliament and change the electoral system at this juncture; it is their moral obligation to stand by that promise. Maoist sources, however, claim that the party will form a republican front and launch a people's movement if there is no consensus on their demands.

It has been observed that the Maoists are becoming paranoid over their growing unpopularity and the rise of dissenting voices within the party. The involvement of the Maoist-affiliated Young Communist League (YCL) in various violent activities reported across the country has been condemned by all sections of society. While the Maoists' initiatives to restructure the party exemplify their intention to transform it from a rebel group to a political organization, the activities of the YCL undermine this political transformation and the ongoing peace process. In recent times, groups of Maoists have revolted in Nuwakot and Nawalparasi, apart from a revolt by their Tharu leader. The Maoists have declared their protest programmes in order to mollify internal differences. However, their pre-poll demands have halted the preparations for the elections, as none of the parties is sure about the political direction of the country. Further, no political party in the eight-party alliance is ready to face the elections.

As regards external actors, the initial apprehension over the Maoists has been waning, mainly because of their commitment to the management of arms and armies and their renunciation of brutal violence. The Maoists have raised more demands, i.e. wages for the PLA cadres, facilities in the camps during the registration of arms, but they have placed a 'majority' of their weapons and cadres in the cantonments, which has been appreciated by the UN authorities. The problem of child soldiers was also amicably resolved at the high-level talks with the initiation of the UN Mission in Nepal by Ian Martin. The US authorities in Nepal have been very active and are believed to have emerged as an influential factor in Nepal's political situation. But, the dispute between the US and the Maoists reached its lowest ebb in May 2007. The country report from the US State Department maintained that the Maoists were a terrorist organization; it said, 'Despite the ceasefire, Maoists' rebels continued to conduct abductions, extortion, and violence. In the Kathmandu Valley, Maoists took advantage of their dramatically increased presence and the government's reluctance to upset the peace process to expand their use of extortion and efforts to undermine trade unions and student groups affiliated with the political parties.'[41]

During his tenure, the then US Ambassador James Moriarty held a series of meetings on the peace process in the country. This upset the Maoists who suspected the involvement of the US in their internal

[41] 'United States' Nepal Report on Terrorism', Nepal Monitor, 1 May 2007. http://www.nepalmonitor.com/2007/05/united-states-nepal.htm.

affairs and encouraged the other political parties to act against them. The Maoists have become impatient because of the continuous opposition of the US to their inclusion in the interim government, and the activities of their YCL cadres, which resulted in their pelting stones at the vehicle carrying US Ambassador Moriarty in Jhapa district on 25 May. Despite strong pressure to hold the constituent assembly elections, India continued its financial and logistical support for developmental activities in Nepal. On the recent third deferral of the elections, India's Ministry of External Affairs sources said, 'The repeated postponement of elections erodes credibility and affects the process of democratic transformation and legitimisation in Nepal'; it expressed the hope for the peaceful resolution of all grievances through a free and fair election process. China, Japan, the countries of Europe and international human rights organizations also pledged support for a successful free and fair election and the return of peace in Nepal.

Terai Problem: Major Impediment in the Peace Process

While the CPN-M has officially abandoned its armed struggle in Nepal, there are many new groups using violence to achieve their cause. Among these groups, some are demanding electoral and political representation in the newly emerging political arena, while others have dangerous designs to sabotage the ongoing peace process and thwart the forthcoming elections. Many groups fighting for ethnic and regional representation have agreed to resolve their problems through talks. However, some actors continue to actively organize strikes and perpetrate violence, particularly in the Terai region, to push the country once again into political instability. Although the movement in this region was started with a genuine demand for proportional representation of the Madhesis in the constituent assembly, it was subsequently diluted because of the violence perpetrated by the unemployed youth, royalists, criminals and Hindu fundamentalists operating along the open border.

The Terai region occupies 17 per cent of Nepal's land area and houses within it 48 per cent of its 26 million people. The inhabitants known as Madhesis, are multi-lingual, multi-religious and multi-ethnic. This region is rich in natural resources and with its abundant manpower contributes a major part to the nation's economy through trade and agricultural production. Although Madhesi contributions to the country are significant, their demands for equality and political representation have been ignored by the central administration. After three decades of peaceful political movement and frustration, the Madhesis were lured into the Maoist fold, assured that their political rights along with other marginalized communities would be met. Thereafter, the Maoists have actively operated across the Terai region, using it for their insurgent activities and arms smuggling.

After the Jana Andolan II (People's Movement II or April Movement), Terai issues started making headlines in January 2007, predominantly due to the unprecedented violence perpetrated by groups operating in this region. In recent months, over a dozen groups (many of them minor) became active, raising ambiguous demands. With the Maoist's People's War having successfully concluded, almost all the groups in the Terai strongly believe in and advocate violence as a tool against the state to press their demands. Although many of the Madhesi demands are genuine and legitimate and need to be granted, the brutality prevailing in their movement affects their significance.

The demands of the Madhesi community were only taken seriously by the Nepal government in the aftermath of their protest movements which resulted in heavy casualties and destruction to property. In general, when ethnic and linguistic federalism are denied, it has led to violent conflicts, separatist movements, and formation of new states across the world. At the same time, many violent conflicts were settled and separatist movements died down when the demands for autonomy were properly addressed. It is also important to understand that any demand for ethnic/linguistic autonomy, if granted in the early phase of such movements, can help neutralize separatism. In a conflict situation, a settlement will be harder to achieve once the movement has gained momentum; at that stage coercive attempts to suppress the movement will only add fuel to the fire.

In Nepal, the government's initiatives to suppress the movement at the initial stages resulted in a worsening of the situation and dramatically increased Madhesi participation in the movement. Rejecting the government's offer for talks, the agitating groups continued their *bandhs* (strikes) across the region. However, the government has recently managed to bring the largest Madhesi group, viz. the Madhesi People's Rights Forum (MPRF), to the table for peace talks. In three rounds of talks, many key issues, including the federal system, self-determination and proportional representation, were discussed. However, in the last round of talks on 28 July, the government rejected the MPRF's additional demand to dissolve the interim parliament by granting legislative powers to the government. This demand was not made in the early days of their movement and the group warned of another stir in the Terai if it was not met. By making this difficult demand, the Madhesi group has complicated the process of reaching a settlement. However, the government and the MPRF finally clinched a 22-point deal on 30 August.[42] According to this agreement, the constituent assembly will decide the nature, boundaries and rights of autonomous states under a federal structure on the basis of suggestions from the State Restructuring Commission. Significantly, the MPRF has for the time being relinquished its demand for a fully proportional electoral system to help conduct the polls on the stipulated date.

Apart from the MPRF, two other prominent armed groups of the same name, the Terai Janatantrik Mukti Morcha (TJMM), one led by Jai Krishna Goit and the other led by Jwala Singh, have also been demanding a separate state for Madhesis in the Terai region. Although these groups are known only in the eastern Terai region of Nepal, their presence in these commercially important and densely populated districts is significant. The government is likely to have a difficult time in dealing with these armed groups, especially when it has rejected the Goit faction's demand for UN mediation in the talks, which is a blatant attempt at gaining international attention.

In the larger participatory democratic political system, these newly-emerged armed groups cannot be considered as legitimate political forces because they make use of or threaten to use violence against civilians and unarmed persons. Despite all the problems within the government, its sincere offer of talks had provided an opportunity to translate the Terai problem into peaceful politics. The rejection of this offer will cost the Terai groups dearly as the government is left with no option but to pursue brutal measures to hold the elections in accordance with the popular will. This will certainly cause more bloodshed in the already bleeding country. While the election is a crucial part of the peace process, the continuation of violence in the Terai will have severe repercussions for the conduct of successful elections. While the Terai movements are gaining momentum in Nepal, their trajectories will depend on the response of the state.

---

[42] Kosh Raj Koirala, 'Govt, MPRF strike 22-point deal', *The Kathmandu Post*, 31 August 2007.

The government should immediately ensure safety and security in this region. Mainstream political parties also need to further clarify their policy on the structure of the state and on a framework for social inclusion within a fixed period of time.

CONFLICT MANAGEMENT

Maoist-Political Party Ties: Countering Absolute Monarchy

Despite a four-month long Maoist unilateral ceasefire in 2005 after the King's takeover, the country has witnessed widespread violence and human rights violations. The King rejected providing any political space for the democratic parties, and refused to have peace talks with the Maoists. In this chaotic situation, the political parties and the Maoists forged an alliance and formally agreed to end royal rule in their second MoU reached on 19 March 2006.[43] A four-day general strike from 6 April was jointly announced. On their part, the Maoists lifted their 20-day economic and transport blockade on 20 March in all district headquarters, including Kathmandu, which had been imposed from 14 March. They also decided to withdraw the indefinite strike which was scheduled to begin in April.

The royal government's reaction to the agreement was harsh, branding it as 'unnatural, impractical, inhumane and antinational'. It is unfortunate that the government took no initiative either to reconcile with the political parties or to resolve the Maoist insurgency. Instead, it sought to strengthen the royal government by inviting the parties to join in the ministry under the King. The government's policies did not impress the international community and it was severely condemned. During his two-day visit (1–2 March 2006) to India, President George W. Bush urged the Maoists to abandon violence and said that the King should reach out to the political parties.[44] Following that, the US Principal Deputy Assistant Secretary of State for South Asian Affairs, Donald Camp, visited Nepal for two days (8–9 March) and concluded

---

[43] 'Parties, Maoists make public second MoU', *Nepal News*, 19 March 2006. The first MoU was reached in November 2005, which declared a 12-point programme for a joint movement.

[44] Surendra Phuyal, 'Bush tells Maoists to abandon violence, King to reach out to parties', *The Kathmandu Post*, 3 March 2006.

that there was no possibility of an early breakthrough in the current political deadlock. Significantly, he mentioned that the Maoists may have gained greater legitimacy from their recent alliance with the political parties.[45] The uncompromising attitude of the two parties made the security situation in Nepal more difficult, emboldened the Maoists, and widened the division between the country's legitimate political forces.

Declaration of Ceasefire and Peace Agreement

On 16 June 2006, the Maoist leader Prachanda signed an 8-point agreement with the SPA during summit-level talks and made his first public appearance after 10 years. Further, on 28 July 2006, the Maoists announced an extension of its truce for another three months to facilitate a smooth political transition.[46] Finally, Nepal bypassed major hurdles in the peace process and signed a significant Comprehensive Peace Accord between the Maoists and the government on 21 November 2006, and achieved consensus on a tripartite (Maoist, Government and UN) Arms Management Agreement.[47] The peace accord under 10 sub-headings included among others provisions on human rights, civil and political rights, arms and army management, and, socio-economic transformation, which promised to chart a new destiny for a peaceful and democratic Nepal. Some key aspects of the peace accord include ending the armed struggle and declaration of a permanent ceasefire; stopping further recruitment by the state and the Maoists; and abiding by the values of multi-party democracy. The signing of a peace accord has salvaged the country, which was ravaged by a bloody war and was teetering on the brink of becoming a failed state. It has provided hope for a new dawn of peace, progress and prosperity which was improbable until recently. As an outcome of these agreements, the top leaders on both sides finalized and signed the draft of an interim constitution on 17 December 2006, in which the King was not given even the status of a ceremonial monarch. All

---

[45] 'No possibility of early breakthrough in Nepal's political deadlock: Donald Camp', *Nepal News*, 9 March 2006.

[46] The Maoists declared three-month-long ceasefire on 27 April 2006, immediately after the King reinstated the House of Representatives.

[47] The full text of the Comprehensive Peace Agreement held between Government of Nepal and Communist Party of Nepal (Maoist), Relief Web, 22 November 2006, is available at http://www.reliefweb.int/rw/RWB.NSF/db900SID/VBOL-6VSHK8?OpenDocument

functions were to be discharged by the Head of State, i.e. the Prime Minster. Furthermore, it has made elections to the constituency assembly a certainty, and put to rest the suspicions of the Maoists that the SPA would not hold the elections.

Management of Arms and Armies

After several rounds of high-level talks and the efforts of the UN Mission to Nepal, Maoist Chairman Prachanda and Prime Minister G. P. Koirala signed separate letters with similar content requesting UN assistance in creating an atmosphere conducive to free and fair elections, delineating the entire peace process. In particular, they sought the UN's role in five areas:[48]

1. Continue its human rights monitoring through the UN's human rights office in Nepal (OHCHR);
2. assist the monitoring of the Code of Conduct during the ceasefire;
3. assist management of arms and armed personnel on both sides by deploying qualified civilian personnel to monitor and verify the confinement of Maoist combatants and their weapons within designated cantonment areas;
4. monitor the Nepal army to ensure that it remains in its barracks and its weapons are not used for or against any side;
5. provide election observers for the election to the constituent assembly in consultation with the parties.

Although both parties have submitted their consensus letters to the Mission, the issue of decommissioning of Maoist arms persisted as a bone of contention in the peace process. While the government was urging the Maoists to surrender their weapons, the rebels viewed it as suicidal to do so before the elections. The government considered this a primary objective, but the Maoists have attempted to use the issue as a bargaining tool to settle political issues like declaration of republic, the issues over interim constitution and parliament, and modalities for elections to the constituent assembly.

Following the peace accord, the government and the Maoists signed a deal on management of arms and army personell after

---

[48] 'Army, armed rebels to be confined in separate barracks', *The Kathmandu Post*, 10 August 2006.

hectic week-long deliberations on 28 November. It was sent to the UN Secretary General's Personal Representative to Nepal, Ian Martin, for final approval, who assured immediate UN assistance. According to the agreement the Maoists were allowed to keep 30 arms for the security of each of the seven main camps and 15 arms for 21 satellite camps. The weapons' storage depot would have storage containers with a single lock provided by the UN. The agreement has also ended the controversy over the categorization of the Maoist military, deciding to name the PLA structures simply as 'main camp' and 'satellite camp'. The two sides have also agreed to form a nine-member Joint Monitoring Coordination Committee (JMCC) comprising three members each from the Maoists, the government and the UN.

Further, none of the parties shall engage in movement or redeployment of forces resulting in tactical or strategic advantage. The parties shall promote awareness of this agreement, and adherence to its provisions among their commanders, members and affiliated groups. There are four phases in the agreement:

1. Reporting and verification; 2. redeployment and concentration of forces; 3. Maoist army cantonment, NA barracking (maintaining control and keeping the army inside their camps) and arms control; 4. full compliance with the agreement. Both sides have agreed that the Maoist army combatants and arms shall be confined within designated cantonment camps, and the government will provide food supplies and make other necessary arrangements. Regarding the verification of the combatants, those recruited prior to the signing of the ceasefire code of conduct (26 May 2006), and those who have reached 18 years of age by then, would be kept in the camps.

On 15 January 2007, a 35-member UN advance monitoring team had begun the arms registration process in Nepal. It was completed on 19 February and the UN team confirmed that 30,852 Maoist combatants and their 3,428 weapons had been registered in seven main cantonments and 21 satellite camps. After three rounds of talks with the rebels, the Mission has finally started its second phase of verification of the PLA cadres on 19 June from the first PLA division located at Chulachuli in Ilam district. The Maoists have demanded the immediate implementation of all prior agreements, including a salary of Rs 3,000 for each combatant, facilities at the cantonment sites[49] and an enquiry over the killing of their cadres by the MJF and TJMM.

---

[49] According to the source, the government has provided Rs 1.378 billion for cantonment management alone.

The deadlock over the crucial stage of implementation of the Agreement on Monitoring of the Management of Arms and Armies came to an end after Maoist Chairman Prachanda's meeting with the UNMIN's head Ian martin on 17 June. The UNMIN had also confiscated the Nepal army's arms in proportion to the registered Maoist arms.

Managing Disturbances in Terai

Although the government has acceded to the major demands of the Madhesis at this juncture, the increasing divergence among the Terai groups is a major hindrance to any immediate solution. Three major actors—the MPRF, the Jwala Singh, and the Jai Krishna Goits factions of the Janatantrik Terai Mukti Morcha (JTMM)—and some fringe groups like Madhesi Mukti Tigers have been using the Terai card to promote separate agendas over the Madhesi issues, and the government has to deal with them separately. While Jwala Singh's JTMM accepted the government's offer for dialogue, the Goit's JTMM rejected any negotiation and the MPRF has recently reached a 22-point deal. Terai violence once again looms large and if not handled in time with skill and foresight, the movement could well become another insurgency in the making, forcing the country back to square one. The government particularly has to ensure that no incidents like Gaur[50] will occur again in the country. Recently, some of the armed groups—Madhesi Mukti Tigers, Janatantrik Terai Mukti Morcha–Jwala Singh and Samyukta Tarai Janatantrik Mukti Morcha—have begun talks for unification in order to instigate their armed revolt.[51] Further, these groups have been extensively involved in extortions, abductions, killings, etc. At a time when Nepal has been undergoing a historical process of restructuring its political system, the violence in the Terai region has been a major setback to its progress.

CONCLUSIONS

It is well known that Nepal is at a historical crossroads. On a positive note, the completion of the registration of Maoist weapons and

---

[50] On 21 March 2006, at least 29 people were brutally killed and over 40 injured when Maoists and the MPRF activists clashed with each other in the Rice Mills area in Gaur, the district headquarters of Rautahat.

[51] 'Tarai parties hold unity talks', *The Himalyan Times*, 9 October 2007.

combatants has opened the door for the Maoist political forces to join the government. On the other hand, little progress in electoral preparation, the ongoing unrest in the Terai and other parts of the country, and the continued prevalence of widespread insecurity, are troubling signs indicating that Nepal is far from building a self-sustainable peace process. Therefore, the successful and efficient management of the transition and consolidation of democracy remains the basic task in Nepali politics.

Given the political fluidity and growing unrest, the elections will not be possible in 2007. The political process and electoral preparation are currently moving, far too slowly for the elections to be held within this year. Moreover, although the political leaders acknowledge the difficulties in holding the elections, they have failed to overcome these hindrances. Significantly, the major issue is not only the anticipated delay in holding these elections, but also whether Nepal can hold free and fair elections so that marginalized, under-represented and underprivileged groups are included in the constitution-making process.

At present it is clear that the voters are less prepared for the polls as a majority of the population, especially in rural areas, does not even know what constituency assembly polls mean. While the people remain uneducated about the polls and its purpose, the results of the elections may not yield positive results. It is important to understand that the election is based on the involvement of the maximum number of people in the electoral process, representing all segments of society, so as to take ownership of the constitution framed by the constituent assembly which is constituted from their representatives. If a substantial number of people remain outside the electoral process, the very purpose of the assembly would be defeated.

As predicted earlier, discontent, grievances and frustration are bound to be a part of the transitional period. Nepal's major political parties have not yet been successful in their attempt to formulate a mechanism for maintaining the balance between stability and change. At the same time, the Maoists have failed to convince Nepali society that their love for weapons is a thing of the past, and are yet to be transformed into a competitive political party in the democratic system. So far, the Maoists' walking out of the government has not really affected its administrative functioning capacity. However, assembly elections without the participation of the Maoists would be undoubtedly meaningless, and they retain the capacity to make the country ungovernable if they oppose the ongoing process. At this juncture, it is imperative to understand that the complexities are growing, and violent conflict is not yet over, but has taken new forms and dimensions which will further complicate an already difficult transition to democracy and stability.

The political parties need to demonstrate greater caution and flexibility during the political process, which can be considered complete only after the promulgation of the new constitution, written by the elected constituent assembly. While the government's acid test lies in holding the crucial constituent assembly polls by overcoming all odds, it has the added responsibility to bring about normalcy in the country by providing relief to the people through the successful implementation of short- and long-term development policies.

The need of the hour is for all the political forces, civil society and the international community to create a congenial environment for the polls, which is the only means to settle the contentions that have arisen from different constituencies and interests. Obviously, the main hurdle in holding the elections seems to be the Terai issue, and a collective approach is the only way out. The government has been reaching conducive agreements with smaller agitating groups; the Terai issue could be solved in the same way. Nepal is going through one of the most dramatic periods of its social development and political maturing. It is very important for the Maoists and other political parties to display sincerity and reassess their accountability to preserve and utilize their resources more effectively.

Finally, the present chaotic situation is definitely not what the general public had anticipated, following the success of the April 2006 uprising. The people had great expectations from their political leaders but their hopes are gradually dwindling in the current political chaos and deteriorating security situation plaguing the country. As major tasks lie ahead, political leaders must reconcile their differences within and among the parties, initiate organized collective action, and make quick and meaningful decisions to move the country ahead.

10

Sri Lanka: Thumbs Up to Violence; Thumbs Down to Peace

N. Manoharan

A BRIEF HISTORY

Armed conflict in Sri Lanka is one of the most protracted to figure prominently in the conflict map of the world. Despite heavy costs, both in terms of people and material, the two principal antagonists—the government of Sri Lanka (GOSL) and the Liberation Tigers of Tamil Eelam (LTTE)—are not interested in a peaceful settlement of the issue. Meanwhile, violence reached a new high in 2007.

The history of armed conflict in Sri Lanka is a typical case of a secessionist movement emerging out of mismanaged autonomy demands. It started with the articulation of language rights by Tamils after the imposition of the Sinhala Only Act in 1956. Later, when Colombo started pursuing its colonization programmes by settling rural Sinhala people in the eastern provinces, the struggle by Tamils turned into a demand for autonomy of their 'homeland'. With the passage of the 1972 Republican Constitution that consolidated the domination of Sinhala–Buddhism in Sri Lanka, the Tamil political struggle entered its self-determination phase with the Tamil United Liberation Front (TULF) passing its Vaddukoddai Resolution[1] in 1976.

This was fuelled by the introduction of the 'Standardization Policy' by the Bandaranaike regime in 1972 that gave preference to Sinhalese students as against Tamil students entering professional courses. The lack of opportunities not only frustrated the ambitious educated Tamil youth but also challenged the privileged position of existing

---

[1] Giving the rationale for its secessionist demand, the Vaddukoddai Resolution stated: 'This convention resolves that restoration and reconstitution of the Free, Sovereign, Secular, Socialist State of TAMIL EELAM, based on the right of self-determination inherent to every nation, has become inevitable in order to safeguard the very existence of the Tamil Nation in this Country.'

social groups.[2] This does not mean that social exclusion paved the way for militancy, but it created an atmosphere conducive to the outbreak of organized and collective violence. 'Confronted with political vacuum and caught up in a revolutionary situation created by the concrete conditions of intolerable national oppression, the Tamil youth sought desperately to create a revolutionary political organization to advance the task of national liberation.'[3] They organized themselves into groups and started attacking symbols of state power, assassinating pro-government personnel, robbing banks, and ambushing security personnel in the northeast. At the height of the insurgency in the mid-1980s there were five major and nearly 30 splinter militant groups. Prominent among them were the Tamil Eelam Liberation Organization (TELO), the People's Liberation Organization of Tamil Eelam (PLOTE), the Liberation Tigers of Tamil Eelam (LTTE), the Eelam Revolutionary Organization of Students (EROS) and the Eelam People's Revolutionary Liberation Front (EPRLF). Belief in militancy and sympathy for militants rose uncritically among the Tamil people, especially after the ethnic riots of 1983.[4]

Successive Sinhala-dominated governments have failed to provide manoeuvring space for the Tamil moderate leadership to handle the crisis. Colombo's intermittent gestures for talks were meant to buy time to deal with the militants. Sinhalese society was made to believe that only a military victory over the Tamils would secure peace. The central message, readily accepted by the ethnically mobilized masses, was that this ethnic war had historical antecedents and was just and imperative. It is this combination of state power, religion, mythology, and popular ethnic prejudice that laid the ideological and popular foundations for militarization of the state in the 1980s.

On their part, the Tamil militants justified their violence on various counts. The LTTE, for instance, uses the metaphor of the hydra, which if cut, regenerates itself ten-fold. To counter such beliefs, the government's primary tactic was the so-called 'Guatemalan game plan' of terrorizing the ethnic population until the 'sea' in which the LTTE

---

[2] Sirimal Abeyratne, 'Economic Roots of Political Conflict: The Case of Sri Lanka', paper presented at the Economic Division, Australian National University, Canberra, October 2001.

[3] Anton Balasingham, *Liberation Tigers and Tamil Eelam Freedom Struggle*, Madras: Political Committee of LTTE, 1983, pp. 23–25.

[4] Jonathan Spencer, 'Popular Perceptions of the Violence: A Provincial View', in James Manor, ed., *Sri Lanka in Change and Crisis* London: Croom Helm, 1984, pp. 191–92.

'fish' swam would be poisoned.[5] The moderate Tamil leadership, who condoned violence by Tamil youth in the initial stages as being 'acts of heroism', was also responsible for the rise of militancy.[6]

The Tamil militants drew parallels between Bangladesh and the Eelam, with India as a common factor.[7] Inspired by Bangladeshi leader Mujibur Rehman, they believed that the Sinhala-dominant state would yield to armed violence. A Bangladesh-type operation for the creation of a separate Tamil Eelam was considered.[8] These beliefs intensified after the July 1983 anti-Tamil riots when thousands of refugees fled to India—reminiscent of the events of 1971 in erstwhile East Pakistan when the East Bengalis took refuge in West Bengal following the March 1971 crackdown by Pakistani forces.[9]

The Tamil militants also drew parallels with the Palestinian struggle, convinced that 'violence was the panacea of all ills that was afflicting the Tamil society'.[10] Their belief was strengthened when the United Nations General Assembly recognized the Palestinians' 'right to self-determination'.[11] For about a decade from the mid-1970s, Tamil militant groups were trained by Palestine liberation groups in various training centres in the Middle East. The use of suicide terrorist tactics, networking with the Tamil diaspora for funds, propaganda and other services, its arms transfers, and its methods of motivating its cadres are some of the influences that the Palestinian terrorist organizations had on the LTTE.[12]

---

[5] Margaret Trawick, 'Reasons for Violence: A Preliminary Ethnographic Account of the LTTE', in Siri Gamage and I. B. Watson, eds., *Conflict and Community in Contemporary Sri Lanka—'Pearl of the East' or the 'Island of Tears'*, New Delhi: Sage Publications, 1999, p. 140.

[6] Quoted in T. Sabaratnam, *The Murder of a Moderate: Political Biography of Appapillai Amirthalingam*, Dehiwela: Nivetha Publishers, 1996, pp. 233–34.

[7] TULF leader Amirthalingam firmly believed that India would certainly intervene in Sri Lanka to 'liberate' Tamils on the lines of Bangladesh. See A. J. Wilson, *Sri Lankan Tamil Nationalism: Its Origins and Development in the Nineteenth and Twentieth Centuries*, Vancouver: University of British Colombia, 2000.

[8] T. Sabaratnam, see note 6 above, p. 201.

[9] M. R. Narayan Swamy, *Tigers of Lanka: From Boys to Guerrillas*, New Delhi: Konark Publishers Pvt. Ltd., 1994, pp. 27–28.

[10] Interview with PLOTE leader Mr. D. Siddharthan, October 2001 and July 2005.

[11] UN General Assembly Resolution No. 3236 (XXIX), 22 November 1974.

[12] B. Raman, 'The LTTE: The Metamorphosis Appears, as of now, to be more Opportunistic than Genuine', http://www.tamilcanadian.com/pageview.php?ID=706&SID=123.

With the massive ingress of Sri Lankan Tamil refugees into Tamil Nadu after the 1983 riots, India could not remain unmoved by these events.[13] New Delhi, in view of its national security interests in the region, offered its good offices to resolve the conflict through negotiations. At the same time, Indian intelligence agencies provided military training and arms to prominent Tamil militant organizations,[14] which enabled them to take on the Sri Lankan armed forces with more confidence in 'Eelam War–I';[15] this, in turn, provided the justification for the Sri Lankan armed forces heighten terror in the north to restore 'law and order'. Tamil militants also began indiscriminate executions of 'traitors', extortion, robberies, and assassinations in the Tamil-dominated areas. The failure of various peace missions finally prompted India to enter into a bilateral accord with Sri Lanka 'to establish peace and normalcy' in the Island.[16]

Thereafter, India sent its troops (Indian Peace Keeping Force—IPKF) to the Island. However, unable to fully implement the agreement, the IPKF got embroiled in the armed conflict, fighting the same Tamil guerrillas whom the Indian establishment had earlier trained. The IPKF's operations, especially against the LTTE, became one of the reasons for the exacerbation of violence in Tamil areas. In a surprising

---

[13] Prime Minister Mrs. Indira Gandhi, while rejecting a Bangladesh-type intervention in Sri Lanka on behalf of the Tamils, said in the Indian Parliament that 'India stands for the independence, unity and integrity of Sri Lanka.... However, because of the historical, cultural and other such close ties between the peoples of the two countries, especially between the Tamil community of Sri Lanka and us, India cannot remain unaffected by the events there.' See A. J. Wilson, *The Break-up of Sri Lanka: The Sinhalese-Tamil Conflict*, London: Christopher Hurst, 1988, p. 203.

[14] Rajesh Kadian, *India's Sri Lanka Fiasco: Peacekeepers at War,* New Delhi: Vision Books, 1990, p. 105.

[15] This continued for four years (1983–87) till the IPKF landed in Sri Lanka in July 1987.

[16] The Indo–Sri Lankan Accord was signed by Indian Prime Minister Rajiv Gandhi and Sri Lankan President J. R. Jeyewardena on 29 July 1987 at Colombo. Para 2 of the Agreement enabled immediate cessation of hostilities, merger of northeast of Sri Lanka, holding of provincial council elections, surrender of arms by Tamil militants, confining Sri Lankan security forces to barracks in Tamil areas, general amnesty to Tamil militants, and cooperation between both neighbours in preventing militant activities. Para 6 of the 'Annexure to the Agreement' provided for an Indian Peace Keeping Force to 'guarantee and enforce the cessation of hostilities, if so required'. For a detailed discussion on the provisions of the Accord see S. D. Muni, *Pangs of Proximity: India and Sri Lanka's Ethnic Crisis,* New Delhi: Sage Publications, 1993; V. Suryanarayan, ed., *Sri Lankan Crisis and India's Response,* New Delhi: Patriot Publishers, 1991; N. Seevaratnam, ed., *The Tamil National Question and the Indo-Sri Lanka Accord,* Delhi: Konark Publishers, 1989.

move, the Sri Lankan state turned against India and secretly helped the LTTE against the IPKF.[17] It was much later that Colombo realized this was a mistake. Within a short interval after the IPKF's departure, 'Eelam War–II' broke out between the LTTE and the Sri Lankan security forces in June 1990.

The People's Alliance government that came to office in 1994 headed by Chandrika Kumaratunga looked promising at the start. She initiated serious talks with the LTTE during 1994–95, based on a comprehensive devolution proposal. The talks, however, broke down resulting in 'Eelam War–III'. Chandrika became convinced of the righteousness of the 'war-for-peace' programme after the security forces achieved some spectacular victories in 1995 and early 1996. Jaffna was wrested from the LTTE in December 1995. But the security forces started facing reverses after July 1996 with the launch of the LTTE's 'Oyatha Aligal' ('Unceasing Waves') in three phases.[18] The major blow to Colombo came with the fall of Elephant Pass in April 2000. In the same campaign the LTTE tried to recapture Jaffna, but in vain. Thereafter, a stalemate continued on the military front.

On 22 February 2002, a ceasefire agreement was reached between the Sri Lankan government and the LTTE with the help of Norwegian mediation. However, it became irrelevant in March 2004 when the LTTE split after its eastern commander Vinayagamoorthi Muralitharan fell out with the Wanni leadership, and with the assumption of Sri Lanka's presidency by Mahinda Rajapakse in November 2005. As of end-2007, there was a state of 'undeclared war' in the Island with government forces wresting control of the eastern parts of Sri Lanka from the LTTE, and gradually moving north.

PRINCIPAL ACTORS

The internal actors in the Sri Lankan armed conflict include the Sri Lankan government, the LTTE and paramilitary groups, and the external actors constitute India, Norway, the United States, Japan and the European Union.

---

[17] Ranasinghe Premadasa, who was Prime Minister and took out an anti-accord procession when it was signed, carried on his opposition when he became President in 1988 and asked the IPKF to vacate the Island.

[18] In the first phase (from July 1996) the Tigers wrested Mullaitivu; during the second phase (from September 1998) they overran Kilinochchi; and in the third phase (from November 1999) the entire Wanni was captured.

Internal Actors

Sri Lankan Government

The Government here includes the political executive and the security forces. According to the 1978 constitution, the president is head of state, head of government, and commander-in-chief of the armed forces. The security forces of Sri Lanka include the army, navy, air force, police and paramilitary forces. The Ministry of Internal Security was created in March 1984 to handle rising Tamil militancy. A Joint Operations Command (JOC) was created in 1985 to coordinate the anti-insurgency operations of the security forces. The Sri Lankan army was initially created to assist the police in maintaining law and order. However, the JVP uprising in 1971 and later Tamil militancy underlined the need for professional armed forces. From 1983, modernization of weaponry took place rapidly. The tactical concept of the army was tailor-made to fight an insurgency but it has developed the capability to fight a conventional war as the LTTE has grown into a formidable force.[19] The birth of the Sea Tigers as an LTTE wing has drawn the navy into counter-insurgency operations. The Sri Lankan air force (SLAF) has also been extensively used for bombing missions as a part of the counter-insurgency operations and has become important with the commencement of aerial strikes by the LTTE air wing.

The Sri Lankan police was established by the British in 1833 to take over the law and order responsibilities in the coastal areas from the Gamsabhawa.[20] After independence the police department was transferred from the Ministry of Internal Affairs to the Ministry of Defence. The Police Special Task Force (STF) was formed in 1983, and specially trained to handle insurgent activities in the northeast.[21] It guards police

---

[19] See Sri Lanka Army Online <http://202.51.141.138/Organisations4.htm>

[20] It was composed of principal and experienced men of each village and presided over by a minor royal official known as the 'Vidane' This system of law enforcement dates back to approximately 150 BC, and went through little, if any, change until the collapse of Monarchy in 1815. However, it was only in 1832 that a committee appointed by the governor was instructed to form a police force. It was decided by this committee that this new police force was to be funded by a tax to be paid by the public. Constituted of one Superintendent, one Chief Constable, five constables, ten sergeants and 150 peons, the first police force of Sri Lanka formed in 1833 was responsible for maintaining the law and order in the capital city of Colombo.

[21] See Sri Lanka Police Online <http://www.police.lk/index.html>

stations and devises ways and means to counter terrorism. The training of the STF is entirely military to repulse the enemy, hold back the crumbling frontier and penetrate deep into Tamil territory held by the rebels.[22] An important element of their strategy was arming Sinhala frontier villages, planting new Sinhala settlements along border lands, and training them to fight.

With recruitment and promotions becoming politicized and increasingly based on ethnic grounds, and as a result of the use of armed forces to assist the police during civil disturbances, the problems in the security forces were further aggravated in the mid-1950s.[23] In the pre-1956 period, though Sinhala Buddhists constituted two-thirds of the population, they formed just two-fifths of the officers; Christians, both Tamil and Sinhalese, accounting for only a tenth of the population provided three-fifths of the officers. However, matters took a U-turn with the language policy of 1956. Politicization started in the 1970s with the appointment of influential persons and those who toed the government line into the security forces.

The rise of Tamil militancy in the northeast transformed the security forces into a more professional but biased force due to its ethnic composition. More Sinhalese personnel were sent to Tamil-dominated areas as the government believed Tamil security personnel to be either unreliable or inefficient.[24] The Tamil minority saw the security forces as 'oppressive', having the sole aim of fulfilling the state's majoritarian agenda. A common practice for security forces facing unexpected violence from the militants was targeting the ethnic community to which they belonged as a kind of surrogate punishment.[25]

---

[22] S. P. Dharmadasa Silva, 'Law Enforcement and Human Rights Training: Experiences of Sri Lanka', Paper presented at the Commonwealth Workshop on Human Rights Training for Senior Law Enforcement Officers, 27 November–1 December 1995, Nicosia, Cyprus.

[23] K. M. de Silva, *Sri Lanka: Political-Military Relations*, Working Paper Series No. 3, Conflict Research Unit, Netherlands Institute of International Relations 'Clingendael', November 2001.

[24] Ibid.

[25] Daya Somasundaram, *Scarred Minds: The Psychological Impact of War on Sri Lankan Tamils*, New Delhi: Sage Publications, 1990, p. 14.

LTTE

The origins of the LTTE[26] founded by Vellupillai Prabhakaran on 5 March 1976 go back to youth organizations like Pulip Padai ('Army of Tigers'), Tamil Liberation Organization, Tamil Students League, Tamil Youth League, and finally, Tamil New Tigers. The main aim of the LTTE is to establish a separate Tamil nation, *Eelam*, by armed struggle. The 'cult of martyrdom' and the ideology of vengeance in the LTTE are based on appeals to a heroic Tamil past. The LTTE differs from other classical guerrilla organizations which *do not* promote the cult of a leader. For the Tigers, Prabhakaran is supreme. The Central Committee is the highest decision-making body with Prabhakaran as its Chairman. It has both a political and a military wing. Area commanders are responsible for tactical decision-making. They are men with many years of fighting experience.

At the macro level the Tigers' strategy has four key components:

1. using times of peace to prepare for war, in line with the Maoist doctrine of retreat and recuperate;
2. attaining total control over the Tamil struggle to gain legitimacy as the sole representative of the Sri Lankan Tamils;
3. subordinating the political struggle to the military one; and
4. combining guerrilla and conventional warfare tactics in battle.

In addition, the LTTE makes use of suicide bombers; it is one of the few militant organizations to adopt it as an article of faith. A separate unit, the 'Black Tigers', is for just this purpose.[27]

---

[26] For a comprehensive understanding of the LTTE see Dagmar Hellmann-Rajanayagam, *The Tamil Tigers: Armed Struggle for Identity*, Stuttgart: F. Steiner, 1994; Edgar O'Balance, *The Cyanide War: Tamil Insurrection in Sri Lanka, 1973–88*, London: Brassey's, 1989; Adele Balsingham, *The Will to Freedom: An Inside View of Tamil Resistance*, Mitcham: Fairmax Publishing Ltd., 2001; M. R. Narayan Swamy, *Tigers of Lanka: From Boys to Guerrillas*, Delhi: Konark Publishers, 1994; M. R. Narayan Swamy, *Inside an Elusive Mind—Prabhakaran: The First Profile of the World's Most Ruthless Leader*, New Delhi: Konark Publishers, 2003; Anita Pratap, *Island of Blood: Frontline Reports from Sri Lanka, Afghanistan and Other South Asian Flashpoints*, Delhi: Penguin Books, 2001. Some of the LTTE's publications like *Viduthalaipuligal* ('Liberation Tigers') provide an insight into its thinking and functions.

[27] Statistically, the LTTE has so far conducted over 250 suicide attacks killing hundreds in the process; as of July 2007, 322 Black Tigers have been killed in action. Of these 81 were on land and 241 at sea; 232 men and 90 women.

The Tigers' network extends from Canada and the United States all the way to Australia, in largely as a consequence of Tamil refugees who fled from the ethnic conflict in Sri Lanka. Recent crackdowns on the Tigers by the United States, Canada, the European Union, India, Australia and South Africa have diminished their support base. However, the LTTE's supply-lines are alive as a result of its links with Southeast Asian countries like Thailand, Myanmar and Cambodia. India outlawed the LTTE after it assassinated former Prime Minister Rajiv Gandhi, yet a tenuous support is visible in Tamil Nadu.

Paramilitary Groups

Paramilitary units consist of Home Guards drawn from local communities to provide security for Muslim and Sinhalese communities in the northeast. Paramilitary groups also consist of non-LTTE Tamil militant groups like the EPRLF, PLOTE, EPDP (Eelam People's Democratic Party), and the breakaway Karuna group (TMVP). Sri Lankan security forces rely on these groups as hit squads. Besides, there are some Muslim armed groups operating in the east. The ceasefire agreement (CFA) of 2002 obliged the government to absorb these groups into its armed forces, but the government chose to maintain the status quo.

External Actors

Norway

Norway is one of Sri Lanka's major donor countries. Development works, in addition to its image as a peacemaker, are the two main reasons for the choice of Norway as a facilitator in the Island's ethnic conflict. Oslo was chosen because it was acceptable to both the conflicting parties, as also to India and the US.[28] Norway's involvement in the conflict resolution process commenced in 1997, though Chandrika Kumaratunga made a formal request to Oslo in February 2000.[29] It took two more years for Oslo to start work on the ground when the Sri Lankan government and the LTTE signed the CFA on

---

[28] For detailed information of the Norwegian role in Sri Lanka see the official website of Norway in Sri Lanka <http://www.norway.lk/peace/>

[29] 'Norway as peace broker between Colombo and Tamil Tigers', http://www.priu.gov.lk/news, 4 January 2000.

22 February 2002, which had been monitored by the Sri Lanka Monitoring Mission (SLMM) under the guidance of Norway. Unfortunately, while the Sinhalese hardliners view it as pro-LTTE,[30] the Tigers are also dissatisfied that Oslo had not exerted enough pressure on Colombo.

SLMM

The SLMM was constituted to oversee adherence to the CFA. It initially consisted of members from the five Nordic countries: Norway, Sweden, Finland, Denmark, and Iceland.[31] The entire Island was its Area of Operation (AOO). The SLMM had its headquarters in Colombo, six district offices (DOs), and a liaison office in Killinochchi. In addition, the SLMM had established points of contact (POCs) in various locations in the northeast to make themselves more accessible, as also explore the possibility of establishing contact with the local population. The district officers of the SLMM operated mobile units and extensively patrolled the SLMM's Area of Responsibility (AOR).[32] The SLMM, however, started facing constraints in its operations since the beginning of 2006 when its Batticaloa office was attacked. Following an attack by the LTTE on a Sri Lankan naval convoy manned by the monitors on 11 May 2006, the SLMM announced a 'temporary suspension' of naval monitoring in the northern and eastern waters of Sri Lanka. With the banning of the LTTE by the European Union on 8 June 2006, the Tigers questioned the impartiality of the monitors belonging to the EU countries (Sweden, Finland, Denmark). The LTTE issued the SLMM an ultimatum to withdraw them. That left monitors from two countries—Norway and Iceland—to shoulder the responsibilities of the Monitoring Mission after September 2006, thereby weakening the Mission at a critical period. With the abrogation of the CFA by the GOSL with effect from 16 January 2008, the SLMM ceased to exist from that very day.

India

India's role in Sri Lanka is determined by its geostrategic interests, internal political factors and, as a responsible regional power, its hope to find a permanent settlement to the ethnic conflict; one that would

---

[30] 'Major party wants Norway out of Sri Lanka peace talks', *Aftenposten* (Oslo), 5 May 2004.

[31] With the banning of the LTTE, the Tigers expressed their inability to accept EU members (Sweden, Finland and Denmark) in the SLMM and had given time till September 2006 to restructure the Mission.

[32] For further details see http://www.slmm.lk/

meet the sentiments and rights of the aggrieved Tamil community but without affecting the unity of Sri Lanka. In the early 1980s, New Delhi used its diplomatic skills to help the two contending parties to arrive at a mutually acceptable solution. Partly due to the Tamil Nadu factor, India went to the extent of providing military training to the Tamil militant groups in the 1980s to shore up their bargaining power vis-à-vis the Sri Lankan government. In August 1985 New Delhi hosted talks between the Sri Lankan government and the leading militant groups in Thimpu to work out a solution, but in vain.[33] It had to get directly involved in the conflict through the Indo–Sri Lankan Accord of July 1987. Though the Accord was hastily signed, it had provisions that sought to be fair to all parties to the conflict. But it also faced difficulties from the start because of opposition from within the Sri Lankan government and, most importantly, the LTTE. The Accord committed India to send a peacekeeping force, the IPKF, which did not make much difference to the overall situation and ultimately had to leave the Island unceremoniously in March 1990. In May 1991, the former Indian Prime Minister, Rajiv Gandhi, was assassinated by an LTTE suicide bomber. The Indian position had now became 'twice bitten, ever shy'. From that time on, there has been a consensus in India for an informal 'hands-off policy' on the ethnic issue. However, India did not sever its military and economic cooperation with Sri Lanka. India also provides humanitarian assistance to the war-affected areas from time to time. Government-to-government relations are good, especially in the economic sphere. There is talk of a Defence Agreement between the two countries, but it is on hold due to opposition from Tamil Nadu. Norway periodically consulted and updated India on the issue of conflict settlement in Sri Lanka.

Other Actors

Other important actors include the United States, Japan and the European Union.

The US has never been a direct actor in the Sri Lankan ethnic issue. Traditionally, Washington has been providing monetary support, arms

---

[33] During the talks the Tamil militant groups demanded recognition of: the Tamils of Ceylon as a nation; the existence of an identified homeland for the Tamils in Ceylon; the right of self-determination of the Tamil nation; the right to citizenship and the fundamental rights of all Tamils in Ceylon. All these demands were rejected by the government delegation.

and training to Sri Lankan armed forces.[34] In March 2007, it signed the Acquisition and Cross-Servicing Agreement (ACSA) with Colombo to 'allow the US and Sri Lanka to transfer and exchange logistics supplies, support, and re-fuelling services during peacekeeping missions, humanitarian operations and joint exercises.'[35] The US did not support separation in Sri Lanka, but also wanted the rights of all the communities to be respected. In this regard, it encouraged efforts by other countries, be it India or Norway, to help settle the ethnic issue through political means. It also committed substantial financial and human resources, in concert with the EU, Japan and Norway, to facilitate the peace process. Washington wants the political establishment in Sri Lanka to act in consensus, leaving aside their partisan stand on the ethnic issue. It designated the LTTE as a 'Foreign Terrorist Organization' in 1997 despite heavy lobbying, but maintained that it 'will certainly consider removing the LTTE from the list of Foreign Terrorist Organizations, as well as any other terrorism related designations… if the LTTE is committed to a political solution and to peace.'[36]

Japan's role in Sri Lanka is often described as 'a new phase of Japanese diplomacy'—a major shift from the role of a traditional donor.[37] Tokyo strongly backed the Norwegian facilitation and went on to host a round of peace talks in March 2003. Rehabilitation and reconstruction of the war-ravaged northeast has been Japan's concern. Yasushi Akashi, former Under Secretary for Humanitarian Affairs in the United Nations, was appointed as special envoy by the Japanese government to oversee and advise on this issue. Japan's earlier policy of declining to extend reconstruction aid to Sri Lanka until the warring parties reached a final political settlement to the conflict did not succeed. Its present policy is 'to help consolidate the peace process and help rehabilitation and reconstruction work even before a final settlement'.[38] The LTTE has accepted the fact that Japan's involvement has benefited the peace process.

[34] Washington saw Sri Lanka as a military base during the Cold War to strike the then Soviet Union's 'soft underbelly'. There were serious proposals to set up a Voice of America signalling base on the island in addition to refuelling and recreational facilities for US troops in Trincomalee harbour.

[35] 'US, Sri Lanka sign logistics pact', *The Hindu*, 6 March 2007.

[36] Richard Armitage said this during his inaugural address at the Washington Donor's Conference on 17 April 2003.

[37] Refer to Policy Speech by Minister for Foreign Affairs Yoriko Kawaguchi to the 156th Session of the Diet, 31 January 2003. See for the Full text of the speech http://www.mofa.go.jp/announce/fm/kawaguchi/speech030131.html

[38] Statement of Tetsuro Yano, Senior Vice-Minister of Ministry of Foreign Affairs of Japan, on the occasion of his visit to Jaffna, 3 August 2003.

European countries are playing a major role in the ethnic issue. They have traditionally been sympathetic to the demands of the minority Tamils. A sympathy wave after the 1983 ethnic riots in Colombo, the consequent refugee exodus across the world, and the Tamil diaspora lobby were the main factors sustaining Europe's traditional outlook till the mid-1990s. Even immigration rules were relaxed, apart from providing refugee status to Sri Lankan Tamils. But this sympathy waned when Tamil militant groups started exploiting the space provided to them in Europe. The European countries ran out of patience when the LTTE began assassinating heads of states and governments in Sri Lanka and moderates within its own community, besides indiscriminate destruction of life and property through suicide bombings. Intense lobbying by the Sri Lankan Foreign Ministry also worked. Severe restrictions were placed on fundraising and movements of the militants and their supporters. Britain banned the LTTE, and the EU identified it as a group violating its 'Guidelines on Children and Armed Conflict'.[39] In May 2006, the EU went further to blacklist the LTTE as a terrorist organization. The ban came after several warnings, which the LTTE chose to ignore.[40]

CONFLICT IN 2007

Hostilities gradually increased to reach new proportions during 2006–07 as both antagonists indulged in violence, disregarding the ceasefire agreement that they had signed five years before. The confrontation, which began as a 'proxy war', turned into 'undeclared war' and finally to 'open confrontation'. The resulting humanitarian crisis was immense.

'Proxy War'

The CFA started falling apart when 'proxy war' came to be used by both the Sri Lankan government and the LTTE, both of whom found it the best way to perpetuate violence in order to fudge the CFA and deceive the international community. The most worrying characteristic

---

[39] For the full text of the 29-point Guidelines see http://ue.eu.int/uedocs/cmsUpload/GuidelinesChildren.pdf

[40] For the full text of the Declaration see http://www.eu2006.gv.at/en/News/CFSP_Statements/May/3105LTTE.html?month=3&day=1

of the violence is attacks through ambush. The government effectively used paramilitary groups to attack the LTTE. While in the east the security forces effectively made use of the Karuna group, the EPDP helped the government to check the LTTE's influence in the north. The LTTE, on its part, used its 'invisible hands' of 'Upsurging People's Force' to inflict violence on the security forces and their support groups in the northeast. The LTTE claimed that the 'people' were attacking in retaliation against harassment by the security forces. Even the SLMM was not spared when its Batticaloa district office faced a bomb attack in January 2006. The casualties were close to 100 per month during this phase. Efforts by facilitator Norway to roll back this phase of violence through talks failed.

'Undeclared War'

The upsurge of violence transformed into an 'undeclared war' after the assassination attempt on Sri Lanka's Army Commander, Sarath Fonseka, by an LTTE suicide bomber on 26 April 2006.[41] During this phase, attacks continued using claymore mines, grenades and shootouts. Both parties seemed to be more interested in attacking each other's troop movements. The presence of numerous actors on the scene increased the complexity of the situation that had gone beyond the control of the SLMM. The damage on both sides and the collateral damage were quite high, with an average of six casualties a day. The border districts of Trincomalee, Batticaloa, Vavuniya and Mannar were the worst affected. Skirmishes, especially at the forward defence lines (FDLs), became the order of the day. The hostilities also extended to the sea when the LTTE sea wing attacked the Sri Lankan navy vessels off Vadamarachi on 11 May 2006, resulting in over 60 casualties. One of the Dvora Fast Attack Crafts, escorting the *Pearl Cruise* with over 700 sailors and two SLMM sea monitors on board, was sunk. In the south the LTTE continued its claymore mine attacks and assassination attempts on high-profile targets using its suicide bombers. On 26 June, Deputy Chief of the Sri Lanka Army Staff, Maj. Gen. Parami Kulathunga, was assassinated. The worst incident was a claymore mine attack, allegedly by the LTTE, on a passenger bus

---

[41] The Army Commander, who survived the attempt, but recovered only after prolonged medical treatment abroad, vowed to wipe out the LTTE on assuming office in July 2006.

at Kebithigollewa on 15 June, which killed 64 civilians.[42] All these incidents snowballed into 'open confrontation' as each party looked for a spark to ignite a crisis, which came through Mavilaru.

'Open Confrontation'

The root of the Mavilaru crisis goes back three decades when the government constructed the Mavilaru reservoir to benefit government-sponsored Sinhalese settlements in Trincomalee district. During the Eelam War–III in 1997, the government forces lost this area to the LTTE. When the CFA was signed in 2002, the Mavilaru reservoir fell within the LTTE controlled areas. The recent phase of the crisis started when the people in the 'uncleared' areas, without waiting for negotiations, closed the sluice gates of the anicut stopping water supply to some 30,000 acres of ripe paddy fields and to about 60,000 people.[43] The motives of the Tigers behind this blockade were indefensible. What aggravated the crisis and led to the present war situation was the government's belief in settling the issue by military force. When negotiations mediated by the Monitoring Mission and some Buddhist monks were about to commence on 26 July, the army launched 'Operation Watershed' to address an 'urgent humanitarian need'.[44] The LTTE immediately withdrew from the negotiations and launched 'defensive actions' to 'neutralize the Sri Lankan military's attacks on civilian targets'. The ensuing hostilities clearly signalled the beginning of the end of the 53-month-old CFA. There was no turning back after that.

The Sri Lankan army, ably assisted by its air force and the Karuna group, started advancing its forward defence line (FDL) in the east. The air force also conducted precision air strikes deep inside LTTE controlled areas. While the Sri Lankan forces used aerial bombings and multi-barrel rocket launchers, the LTTE employed its artillery. The FDLs at Omanthai (in Vavuniya district) and Muhamalai (in Jaffna district) have shifted several times. The LTTE meanwhile continued its targeted assassinations: killing Upul Seneviratne, Director (Training) of the Special Task Force (STF), in Digana on 7 August 2006, and Katheeswaran Loganathan, Deputy Secretary-General of the

---

[42] *Daily Mirror* (Colombo), 16 June 2006.
[43] *The Morning Leader* (Colombo), 2 August 2006.
[44] *Daily Mirror* (Colombo), 27 July 2006.

Secretariat for Coordinating the Peace Process (SCOPP), in Colombo on 12 August 2006. The Tigers also attacked the Pakistan High Commissioner's convoy in Colombo on 14 August 2006. The Sri Lankan air force's bombing of the Sencholai children's home in an LTTE controlled area on the same day, killing 51 children, was tragic. The government, however, justified this by saying they acted on precise 'intelligence' information that identified the children's home as an 'LTTE training centre with firing ranges and fortifications'.[45] Fearing LTTE retaliation, the government ordered the closure of all schools in the Island until 28 August 2006.

In the ensuing months, the LTTE began to face reverses in the east, losing one base after another in Amparai, Batticaloa and Trincomalee. Sampur was the first territory to be transferred from the LTTE to government control by military means on 27 August 2006.[46] Vakari fell in January 2007. This was the last major bastion of the LTTE in the east. With this military advantage on the ground, President Mahinda Rajapakse called upon the LTTE leadership to lay down its arms and come for negotiations. The President was determined to 'tame them' in case the Tigers failed to respond to the peace offer.[47] The government went on a recruitment drive to shore-up its military manpower. In February 2007 alone 2,700 people were recruited, in addition to the return of 2,500 deserters.[48] Brushing aside the government's call for peace the LTTE did the unexpected: it launched its first ever air strike on Kattunayake air base.

In the early hours of 26 March 2007, two light aircraft of the *vaanpuligal* (Air Tigers) flew all the way from Wanni and returned safely after inflicting considerable damage on the air force fleet in Kattunayake.[49] In less than a month, the LTTE launched a second attack at 0120 hours on the Palaly airfield of the SLAF on 24 April 2007. Once again two light aircraft were involved, but this time they took the sea route to evade detection by the armed forces at the FDLs.[50] The damage on the government side, however, was limited

---

[45] Dushy Ranetunge, 'Prabhakaran's "orphanage": ready to supply cannon fodder', *Daily News* (Colombo), 16 August 2006.

[46] See SLMM statement dated 26 September 2006 (Ref. SLMM/HOM/8624).

[47] BBC, 3 August 2006.

[48] *Daily News* (Colombo), 3 February 2007.

[49] The two light aircraft used by the LTTE were Czech-made Zlin Z-143, allegedly smuggled from Indonesia by the Sea Tigers and later assembled locally by the LTTE.

[50] D. B. S. Jeyaraj, 'The Vaanpuligal takes off', *Himal South Asian*, June 2007.

due to timely activation of its air defence systems by the SLAF. Yet, the fact that the Tiger craft could return to base safely is a cause for concern for the Sri Lankan forces. A third attack was launched on 29 April 2007. It targeted the petroleum storage tanks in Kolonuwa and Muturajewela near Colombo, creating more panic than destruction.[51] A combined air and ground attack was launched by the LTTE on 22 October 2007 at Anuradhapura air base causing damage worth $40 million.

The primary objective of the Air Tigers was to counter the SLAF, which was instrumental for the Tigers' reverses in the east. According to the LTTE, 'The attack is not only pre-emptive but also to safeguard our people from indiscriminate bombing by the SLAF'.[52] Secondly, the Tigers wanted to avenge the enormous destruction caused to the LTTE infrastructure and people by the SLAF's aerial bombings. Thirdly, Tiger chief, Velupillai Prabhaharan, had been under tremendous pressure to do 'something spectacular' and boost the dwindling morale of his cadres. At this juncture, there was nothing more daring than to use its *vaanodis* (aircraft). Fourth, the LTTE also wished to prove to the Tamil community that its strength had not waned due to reverses in the east. It wanted to demonstrate its 'statist' capabilities. In its statement after the attack, the LTTE said, 'Our military infrastructure operates in the very same way as any other conventional military infrastructure of a state'.[53] At the same time, by attacking only the air base and not the adjacent civil airport, the Tigers wanted to send a signal to the international community that they were not a 'terrorist' organization, but well organized 'freedom fighters'.

Downplaying damages caused by the first air attack, the government tried to project the air power of the LTTE as a 'threat to the region' so as to further isolate the LTTE internationally.[54] Colombo was, however, disappointed by the muted reaction of the international community. While India situated the air attack within the context of the general

---

[51] Iqbal Athas, 'Govt. takes off for sky war', *Sunday Times*, 6 May 2007.

[52] Statement by LTTE military spokesperson Rasaiah Ilanthirayan, www.tamilnet.com, 26 March 2007.

[53] Statement to the media by the LTTE political wing chief, S. P. Tamilselvan, on 29 March 2007 in Kilinochchi. Quoted in *Tamilnet*, 30 March 2007.

[54] The Minister for Highways Jeyaraj Fernandopulle said, 'This is a threatening situation, not only to Sri Lanka, but also to the entire region. India should be on alert about the situation since there are possibilities the LTTE may help other terror organisations too.' Quoted in *Daily News*, 27 March 2007.

escalation of violence in Sri Lanka,[55] the United States observed that Sri Lanka 'now has an important opportunity to achieve peace'.[56] The LTTE, air capability is a serious development in the region.

The LTTE's air attacks further exacerbated the violence. Aided by aerial bombardments, the government forces are determined to continue their 'encirclement' of the Tiger territory and 'strangulate' the LTTE. The SLAF could strike a key Sea Tiger base at Puthukudiyiruppu and the LTTE intelligence unit in Kilinochchi. The government forces also took full control of the Mahaoya–Chenkalady A-5 highway in April 2007 after fourteen years. With the capture of the Toppigala (Kudumimalai in Tamil) jungles in July 2007, the government announced the recovery of the entire eastern region from Tiger control.[57] The Sri Lankan military had to face stiff resistance from the LTTE, apart from extensive land mine and booby traps. The government maintained that its next plan is to move north and capture the LTTE controlled districts of Killinochi and Mullaithivu. The government's forces were, as of end-2007, extending the FDL in Mannar district by capturing the coastal areas of Silavatturai and Arippu.[58] The major concern, however, was to consolidate the captured areas. The Tigers, although accepting the loss, called it a 'strategic' move to make the government forces 'walk into a trap'.[59]

Effects and Side-effects

The impact of intense hostilities was felt in two main arenas: human rights abuses and economic downslide.

Human Rights: This was the most worrying effect of the ongoing confrontation for which both antagonists are responsible. The significant dimensions of rights abuses are worth highlighting:

---

[55] During his briefing to the media at the 14th SAARC summit the Indian Foreign Secretary said, 'To pick on individual incidents of violence, I do not think helps to solve the root cause of the problem. The cause of the problem is the conflict which has escalated terribly in the last few weeks and that does cause us great concern.' For the full text of the briefing see http://meaindia.nic.in/pbhome.htm

[56] Interview with Robert O. Blake, US Ambassador to Sri Lanka, *Daily News*, 2 April 2007.

[57] Iqbal Athas, 'Toppigala: a victory, but bitter battle ahead', *Sunday Times*, 15 July 2007.

[58] 'Army moves into Silavatturai', *The Sunday Times*, 9 September 2007.

[59] Interview with S. P. Tamilselvan, Head of the political division of the LTTE, *Tamilnet*, 25 June 2007.

Child Soldiering: The Special Advisor to the UN Representative on Children and Armed Conflict, Allan Rock, visited Sri Lanka in November 2006 to ascertain the ground situation in the conflict zones, especially compliance with the Action Plan for Children Affected by War by the government and the LTTE.[60] During his 10-day mission, Rock found that the LTTE was yet to comply with the Action Plan to release all child soldiers before 1 January 2007. According to UNICEF figures, there were nearly 1,598 pending cases for the release of children by the LTTE. Instead, the LTTE continued to recruit children and failed to show any signs of implementing their undertaking to UNICEF. The most startling finding of the Special Advisor was the complicity of some elements of the Sri Lankan security forces with the breakaway LTTE faction led by Karuna involved in child conscription, especially in the eastern parts of the Island. Backed by 'eyewitness and anecdotal evidence', Rock asserted that 'Sri Lankan security forces rounded up children to be recruited by Karuna group'.[61] Complicity was also evident in the failure of the security forces to prosecute or investigate those responsible for the conscription of children. Pleas from parents to spare their children were generally ignored. Allan Rock maintained that the real figure could be three times higher than official claims, and there was 'evidence that this trend is accelerating'. The Sri Lankan army, 'while dissociating itself from these allegations vehemently', denied having 'any involvement whatsoever with the LTTE breakaway group'.[62] The Karuna group also denied the allegations, claiming that it merely 'offered protection to children fleeing the LTTE'.[63]

Shortage of Essential Commodities: In the second week of August 2006, Jaffna came under prolonged curfew for the first time since 2001. In the same month, the government also ordered the closure of A-9 highway, the only continuous land route connecting Jaffna peninsula with the mainland. The LTTE wanted the highway open, but the

---

[60] The Action Plan, the only signed human rights agreement between the LTTE and GOSL, emerged out of the peace process in 2003. The Plan was intended to benefit 30,000 to 50,000 children affected by the conflict in the north and east through a broad range of programmes. A key provision of the Plan was the LTTE's agreement to end child recruitment and to release children from the LTTE's forces. The Action Plan comprised ten main components including *inter alia* monitoring, documenting, vocational training and education of children affected by war.

[61] For the full text of the Report see *Asian Tribune*, 10 February 2007.

[62] *Daily News* (Colombo), 15 November 2006.

[63] BBC, 13 November 2006.

government was unwilling due to 'security risks to the civilians using the road and extortions by the LTTE from the commuters'.[64] The real reason behind the closure was to deny the LTTE income through informal toll taxes on goods and vehicles travelling the road. The government denied that there was any blockade and insisted that the 'sea delivery route was cheaper, more efficient and safer'. However, as against the government's claims, there was a severe shortage of goods and those commodities available in the open market were unaffordable by the common man in Jaffna peninsula. By November 2006 the prices of essential commodities in Jaffna peninsula were over 10 times that in the rest of the Island. Conditions in the LTTE controlled areas were much worse. In Jaffna, the government had been providing commodities to nearly 600,000 people through cooperative stores and military-run shops. The government also made a one-time shipment of goods from India.[65] All these measures, however, could not tackle the huge shortage.

Internal Displacement: Due to the recent escalation of violence, nearly 300,000 persons have been internally displaced, especially in the northeast region. Many of them were sequentially displaced.[66] This apart, the number of refugees who fled to India due to the recent violence touched 19,000. As the military advanced into the LTTE areas in the east, many civilians resident there fled to the government controlled areas. The highest number of displacements was reported from the districts of Batticaloa, Trincomalee, Mannar and Jaffna. While the LTTE was least bothered about those displaced, the government was busy politicizing the issue rather than paying attention to their welfare. A solution to overcrowding was found in haphazard resettlement of the displaced in the newly 'cleared areas'. In fact, despite their refusal to move to their respective villages, fearing renewed violence, many civilians were forced to resettle.

---

[64] For a detailed explanation of the government see 'Alternate Route to Jaffna via Pooneryn—Humanitarian Support to Jaffna Peninsula', Secretariat for Coordination of Peace Process Report, 10 November 2006.

[65] Interview with Douglas Devananda, Minister for Social Services, 1 December 2006, New Delhi.

[66] For detailed information see 'Sri Lanka's Humanitarian Crisis or Crisis of Majority?' *UTHR (J) Information Bulletin*, no. 45, 27 March 2007. See also South Asians for Human Rights, *Report on the Fact Finding Mission to the North & East of Sri Lanka to Assess the State of the Displaced Persons*, August 2007.

Instead of addressing these problems, the government kept extending its Island-wide emergency every month and increasing tight security measures all over the country, much to the discomfiture of the minority Tamils. Three significant measures are worth mentioning: introduction of 'pass system' to the northeast, setting up of a 'high security zone' in Sampur, and eviction of Tamils staying in lodgings in Colombo. For the first time since 2002, a vehicle 'pass system' was reintroduced in the districts of Mannar, Vavuniya, Trincolmalee, Batticaloa and Amparai, making it more difficult for ordinary people to travel to the rest of the Island. Although the government justified the setting up of new 'high security zones' in Sampur and Muttur in June 2007 to 'foster development', the real intention was to consolidate the territories captured from the LTTE. As a result, 4,200 families were displaced.[67] On 7 June 2007, citing security reasons, the Sri Lankan police ordered all Tamils from the northeast, staying temporarily in Colombo, to 'go back to their homes'. The police justified the crackdown as 'part of continuing efforts to stop the LTTE infiltrating the city', as its investigations 'confirmed that some of the brutal killings by Tigers in Colombo were hatched from these lodgings'.[68] The evictions continued till the Supreme Court issued a stay order on 8 June on a Fundamental Rights petition.[69] In the course of a day the police evicted 376 persons and transported them forcefully to Vavuniya. Most of them were in the capital to get their passports or national identification card, or to find jobs or try and go abroad. The decision invited international criticism at a time when Sri Lanka was being watched for its negative record on human rights. It is true that the Tigers had heavily infiltrated into Colombo using the ceasefire as cover. However, eviction as a means to counter this infiltration was not the best measure and clearly indicated the lethargic intelligence network of the government. After all, they could easily have ascertained the reason for each person visiting Colombo. Moreover, stringent registration of visitors at lodgings would discourage those who had no ulterior motive for being there. Such action in the future will further alienate the minorities.

---

[67] 'Sampur HSZ or FTZ?' BBC, 30 June 2007.
[68] 'Police evict Tamils from Colombo', BBC, 7 June 2007.
[69] 'Sri Lanka Supreme Court restraints eviction of Tamils from Colombo', *The Hindu*, 9 June 2007.

Economic Downslide: Although the Sri Lankan economy grew by nearly 7 per cent during 2006–07, the economic repercussions of the recent escalation of violence have been enormous. The economy is affected in two principal ways: significant parts of the country have been closed off for gainful economic activity; and valuable resources have been diverted towards war.

The tourism industry was the first victim. Due to negative travel advisories issued by many countries discouraging travel to Sri Lanka, the flow of tourists dropped substantially. After the air attack by the LTTE in March 2007 and the consequent increase in air fares, Sri Lanka ceased to be one of the cheapest tourist destinations. Closure of the only international airport for night flights for several months made Colombo even more unpopular among the tourists. The violence also shook investor confidence in the Sri Lankan economy. For instance, the Colombo Stock Exchange plunged on the day of the Air Tiger attack due to panic selling, leading to capital losses of about SLR12 billion. This was reflected in equity prices, which trade at a current price/earnings ratio of 10:6 as compared to 18:1 in the Indian market.[70] The Colombo Stock Exchange index around 20 per cent since its all-time high in mid-February 2007. Significantly, foreigners were net sellers. The Sri Lankan rupee also hit a new low of 113.78 to the US dollar in October. However, it was not as bad as it was in the aftermath of the first attack in July 2001.[71]

Public finances were weak. Successive large budget deficits left the government with a public debt of over 90 per cent of the GDP and interest payments absorb over half of tax revenue. The interim solution of printing more currency led to spiralling inflation of around 15 per cent on all commodities.[72] Citing human rights concerns, some donors reduced their aid to the Island. This was a severe blow to the government, forcing it to issue international bonds to raise additional foreign revenues of $500 million. Increased external borrowing not only put pressure on the balance of payments, but also generated an external liquidity crisis for the government.

---

[70] Jo Johnson, 'Threats of civil war hits Sri Lankan economy', *Financial Times*, 31 August 2006.

[71] Post-July 2001, the Sri Lankan economy witnessed negative growth for some time before picking up. This negative growth had forced the government to abandon its 'war for peace' programme and agree to talks with the LTTE.

[72] 'Sri Lanka politicians oppose taxes, while promoting inflation and money printing', *Lanka Business Online*, 5 September 2007.

According to recent estimates, each Sri Lankan owes external funders about SLR 140,000.[73] With a firm belief in the 'war for peace' programme, the Rajapaksa government has unhesitatingly been spending on defence. The government allocated 139.56 billion rupees (about $1.29 billion) in 2007 as against 108.67 billion rupees ($1 billion) in 2006. Increased defence expenditure is necessitated by new recruitment of soldiers, large purchases of military hardware, and overall strengthening of security systems. Sri Lanka has also turned to Pakistan, China and Ukraine for military hardware.[74] An indication of the enormous cost of war can be seen from the cost of each 250-kilogramme bomb used by the air force to attack the LTTE, which is $ 2,000 (more than SLR 200,000).[75]

CONFLICT MANAGEMENT

During 2006–07 conflict management/resolution in the Island tilted towards increasing the intensity of hostilities. Mahinda Rajapakse's victory as Executive President, with the help of the 'unitarist' JVP and JHU (Jathika Hela Urumayia), raised serious doubts about the revival of the peace process. On its part, the LTTE was not hopeful of peace talks and kept provoking the security forces. Efforts at two levels—internal and external—towards conflict management/resolution should be seen against this backdrop.

Internal Efforts

'War for peace' was the clear agenda of Mahinda Rajapaksa on his assumption of office as Executive President in November 2005. The idea was to weaken the LTTE and force them to the negotiating table. Simultaneously, the plan was to convene an All Party Conference (APC) to evolve a 'southern consensus'.[76] Accordingly, the President

---

[73] 'People further burdened with additional taxes: JVP', *Daily Mirror*, 8 September 2007.

[74] 'This is the MIG deal', *Sunday Observer* (Colombo), 19 August 2007.

[75] 'Year of crisis for Rajapaksa', *The Sunday Times* (Colombo), 7 January 2007.

[76] Popularly known as 'Mahinda Chintanaya' (Mahinda's Thinking), the document outlined that if elected to power his initiative would be 'an undivided country, a national consensus and an honourable peace'. For the full text of the document see http://www.president.gov.lk/pdfs/MahindaChinthanaEnglish.pdf

convened an APC in January 2006. The first in the series of consultations with the political parties (represented by 15 parties), the meeting unanimously decided that steps should be taken to resume 'immediate talks' between the government and the LTTE.[77] The President appointed an All Party Representative Committee (APRC) at the sixth session of the APC in May 2006 to meet regularly for deliberations on the constitutional reform process. The APRC consisted of experts, academics and legal luminaries, and was headed by Professor Tissa Vitharana. The APRC held its first meeting on 20 July 2006. Comprising one nominee from each political party represented in the APC, the APRC was tasked to formulate a constitutional framework with the help of an Experts Panel and submit it to the APC. The Panel submitted a 37-page report to the APRC on 6 December 2006. The group recommended that subjects like defence, national security, foreign affairs, immigration/citizenship, communication, national transportation, international commerce/trade, maritime zones, shipping and navigation be reserved for the centre. It recommended an Autonomous Zone Council to address the concerns of Tamils of Indian origin. Ironically, of the 17 members of the group, only 11 endorsed the report, while the other six submitted three separate dissenting reports.[78] One of the main constituents of the government, the JVP, pulled out of the APRC, citing disagreements with the majority report.

The APRC, however, continued with its exercise to achieve a final report with the help of the Expert Panel report. The main challenge before the committee was on evolving a consensus on the 'nature of the state' and the 'unit of devolution'. Parties like the SLFP, JHU and MEP are opposed to a federal arrangement. The SLFP's own proposals, presented to the APRC in May 2007, suggested retaining the 'unitary' character of a Sinhala–Buddhist state and proposed the scrapping of the current provincial council system in favour of devolution on a far more limited scale at the district level.[79] Parties like the UNP, LSSP, CP, CWC, UPF, SLMC and NUA in their proposals to the APRC took the position that the unit of devolution should be the province and

---

[77] 'Resume peace talks—All Party Session', Press Release by Government of Sri Lanka, 20 January 2006.

[78] The four members who submitted the minority report were H. L. de Silva, Gomin Dayasiri, Prof G. H. Peiris and Manohara de Silva. K. H. J. Wijayadasa and M. D. D. Peiris submitted two other dissenting reports separately.

[79] For the full text of the proposals and its critique from a Tamil perspective see *Tamilnet*, 5 May 2007.

the nature of the state should be 'united' as opposed to 'unitary'. The lack of consensus continued to haunt this body and it was not able to meet its several extended deadlines to submit a final report. The failure was mainly due to the SLFP's delayed submission of its own proposals. Frustrated, the main opposition UNP withdrew from the APRC, and the committee was adjourned *sine die*.[80] The President then asked Prime Minister Rathnasiri Wickramanayaka to iron out the differences between the political parties on controversial matters like the nature of the state and the quantum of devolution. It is, however, not clear how the Prime Minister, known for his hardline stance, will forge a 'southern consensus' on a package that is acceptable to the Tamil community.

Concurrently the President initiated exclusive discussions with the UNP in September 2006 to facilitate a political consensus in the south. Based on intense discussions, the two parties signed an MoU on 23 October 2006. It spelled out ways and means by which the two parties would cooperate and formed five sub-committees, including one on conflict in the north and east. The UNP agreed to support the government in parliament and to participate in the APC (so far the UNP had refused to be part of the conference). A high-level committee headed by the President and the leader of the opposition (including an equal number of representatives of the two parties) was formed to oversee the implementation of the MoU.[81] The two parties also decided to re-activate the stalled Constitutional Council. By signing the MoU, President Rajapakse indirectly sidelined the JVP and JHU on whose support he won his Presidentship in 2005. It was considered a historic agreement as the absence of a bipartisan approach on the ethnic issue between the two parties had been a major obstacle to finding a permanent solution to the ethnic crisis.[82] As expected, the MoU was shortlived. When 19 UNP members of parliament crossed over to the government, the UNP leadership withdrew from the MoU, citing 'horse-trading' as the reason. The MoU lasted just 97 days.[83] With this, an opportunity for bipartisanship was once again lost. The President, more concerned with gaining a majority for his government,

---

[80] T. S. Tissanayagam, 'APRC demonstrates the south's inability to meet Tamil aspirations', *The Sunday Times* (Colombo), 26 August 2007.

[81] For the full text of the MoU, see http://www.priu.gov.lk

[82] A similar agreement brokered by British MP Liam Fox in April 1997 failed to materialize. This Agreement was less ambitious compared to the 2006 MoU.

[83] 'SLFP–UNP MoU torn to shreds', *Daily Mirror*, 28 January 2007.

offered ministerial berths to all the UNP dissenters, thus taking the cabinet strength to 108, an all-time high since independence.[84]

External Efforts

The international community has been taking numerous steps to bring both the LTTE and the Sri Lankan government to the negotiating table. During 2006–07, the external efforts towards conflict management were initially more concerned with effective implementation of the CFA and, later, the safety of the ceasefire monitors.

Eric Solhiem's persistence and persuasion paid some dividends in bringing the LTTE to the negotiating table, but only to discuss the 'smooth implementation' of the (CFA), and not a final settlement of the ethnic issue. After sharp disagreements, both sides came midway to agree on Geneva being the venue for talks on 22–23 February 2006.[85] The agreement for talks was significant in two ways: to bring the two parties together after a long gap, and for its potential to lay the foundation for future talks on 'core' issues. Compared to the LTTE, preparations on the part of the government for the talks appeared serious. A group of nearly 25 members known as the Steering Committee on Peace Building (SCPB) headed by Foreign Minister Mangala Samaraweera was formed to help the negotiating team.[86] With a long-term agenda, the SCPB included six Cabinet Ministers, a Deputy Minister, leaders of the ruling coalition and like-minded parties, six Permanent Secretaries, officials of the Peace Secretariat, and other civil and military personnel. The government also organized a two-day workshop and a four-day training programme for its team involving various experts. However, the government team was inexperienced, with none of its members having participated in any of the earlier negotiations with the LTTE.

---

[84] 'Cabinet strength grows to 108', *The Hindu*, 2 February 2007.

[85] While the LTTE insisted on Oslo or any other European venue, the GOSL was adamant that the delegations meet in Sri Lanka or any other Asian country. Oslo was not agreeable to GOSL as Norway was seen as biased by some of the constituents of the government. Since there was a travel ban on the LTTE by the EU, none of the EU countries was feasible. The LTTE cited security reasons against meeting in Sri Lanka.

[86] The LTTE team comprised its political Ideologues Anton Balasingham and Adele Balasingham, Political Head S. P. Tamilchelvan, 'Col' Jeyam, Police Chief B. Nadesan, and Batticaloa District Political Head Ilanthirayan (Marshall). Headed by Health Minister Nimal Siripala de Silva, the other members of the government team were Trade Minister Jayeraj Fernandopulle, and Industries Minister Rohitha Bogollagama; Minister of Housing Ferial Ashraff represented the Muslims.

Despite acrimonious initial remarks[87] by both delegations, the final outcome of the Geneva talks was moderately positive. While the LTTE 'committed to taking all necessary measures to ensure that there will be no acts of violence against the security forces and police', the government of Sri Lanka assured that 'all necessary measures would be taken in accordance with the Ceasefire Agreement to ensure that no armed group or person other than Government security forces will carry arms or conduct armed operations.' Both parties 'reconfirmed their commitment to fully cooperate with and respect the rulings of the Sri Lanka Monitoring Mission'. The most satisfying aspect of the meeting was the decision to meet again at the same venue from 19 to 21 April 2006.[88]

However, the parties did not meet in April. The principal reason was their failure to abide by the commitments made during the first round. While the LTTE continued its covert attacks on the government forces, the government did not make any serious efforts to persuade the Tamil paramilitary groups allied to the army to give up their arms.[89] Meanwhile, Jon Hanssen-Bauer took over as the new Norwegian Special Envoy replacing Eric Solheim. While the government was ready for the next round, the LTTE cited trivial reasons to stay away from the talks. The efforts by Eric Solhiem and Yasushi Akashi did not bring about any breakthrough. The SLMM started losing its authority and, relevance since then. The safety of the monitors was itself in doubt. Partly irked by the LTTE's obduracy and partly by pressure from

---

[87] In its initial remarks the government team termed the CFA as 'contrary to our Constitution and law' and 'prejudicial to the sovereignty and the territorial integrity of the Republic of Sri Lanka.... LTTE had taken undue and unfair advantage of the ceasefire to strengthen its military capability.... [which] underscore the inherent weaknesses in the existing ceasefire agreement as well as the lacuna in setting out norms for its effective implementation.' On its part, the LTTE said the CFA was the 'most constructive achievement' of the Norwegian peace process and 'the foundation upon which the process has to be built'. It identified five Tamil groups working in alliance with the government forces as 'posing a grave threat to peace and stability in Tamil areas and endangering the Ceasefire Agreement'. For the full text of the initial remarks of the government team see Sri Lankan Peace Secretariat media release dated 22 February 2006. For the full text of the initial remarks of the LTTE team see http://www.tamilnation.org

[88] For the full text of the joint statement issued at the end of the talks see http://www.slmm.lk/

[89] In fact Karuna stated: 'Without mincing our words we wish to tell [Prabhakaran] quite categorically that we have our resolve and moral right to hold onto our arms'. See 'Karuna refuses to give up arms', *Daily Mirror*, 27 February 2006.

the United States, the EU imposed a ban on the Tigers on 29 May 2006; with this, the last bastion of the LTTE diaspora support was stormed.[90]

Facilitator Norway, in fact, had gone to the extent of inviting both parties to Oslo to discuss the safety and security of the monitors on 8–9 June 2006. The LTTE team went to Oslo, but refused to meet the delegations of the Sri Lankan government and the SLMM. The Tigers maintained that the government had sent a 'low level' delegation and therefore only the head of its Peace Secretariat Pulithevan could meet his counter-part Palitha Kohana. Further, the LTTE did not want to 'shake hands' with the EU members in the SLMM delegation after the EU ban. As a result, the very objective of the meeting failed. This had forced Norway to 'go back to the basics' by asking the government and the LTTE to respond to five questions:[91]

1. Will the parties stand committed to the ceasefire agreement?
2. Do the parties want the continued existence and operation of the SLMM as a mission coordinated, facilitated and led by the Norwegian government with diplomatic immunity to ensure its impartial operation?
3. Are the parties able to provide full security guarantees for all monitors, employees and physical assets of the SLMM in all situations, in accordance with CFA Article 3.9?
4. Will the parties accept amendments to the CFA's Article 3.5 to enable the continued functioning of the SLMM at its current operational level with the necessary security guarantees?
5. In the event that amendments to Article 3.5 are made, will the parties provide full security guarantees for current SLMM personnel and assets during a six-month transition phase until another solution has been identified, decided and fully implemented?

---

[90] It is not that the EU imposed a sudden and outright ban. In a 19-point resolution issued on 18 May 2006, the EU called on the LTTE to 'resume peace negotiations with the Government of Sri Lanka without delay, to be prepared to decommission its weapons and to set the stage for a final political settlement of the conflict'. The Resolution spelled out active consideration of the formal listing of the LTTE as a terrorist organization. Earlier, another warning was given in September 2005 by imposing a travel ban on the LTTE. There was, therefore, adequate time for the LTTE to pacify the EU. In addition, the EU made it clear that the ban was not final and it was willing to remove the LTTE from the listing if the group 'mends its violent course and return to peace talks'. For the full text of the Declaration see http://www.eu2006.gv.at/en/News/CFSP_Statements/May/3105LTTE.html?month=5&day=1

[91] For details of these five questions and their responses see Norwegian press release dated 22 June 2006 available at http://www.norway.lk/press/

In their responses, while reiterating their commitment to the CFA, the LTTE and the government of Sri Lanka differed on amendments to Article 3.5 which reads 'the SLMM shall be composed of representatives from Nordic countries'. The Tigers argued that after the EU ban, the monitoring of the SLMM members from the EU countries—Sweden, Finland and Denmark—would be 'skewed'. They wanted a reconfiguration of the SLMM by September 2006. For the government, however, any change in the SLMM was 'unacceptable'. Despite various efforts, the LTTE was adamant that only non-EU members constitute SLMM. Accordingly, Finland, Sweden and Denmark left the Mission in September and the burden of monitoring shifted to Norway and Iceland.[92] Swedish SLMM chief Ulf Henricson was replaced by Norwegian Lars Johan Sølvberg. At a crucial time when the services of more monitors were required the SLMM witnessed its downsizing.

Amidst continuing violence both antagonists met in Geneva on over 28–29 October 2006 after nearly eight months. The government set a seven-point agenda that included 'democracy, multi-party system, pluralism, human rights, child recruitment, development of the northeast, and devolution'. The LTTE, however, insisted on addressing 'the urgent humanitarian crisis caused by Sri Lankan state terrorism in the Tamil homeland' and 'the implementation of the Ceasefire Agreement' before taking up the 'core issues'. Not surprisingly, the two-day talks ended in 'zero' results. Once again, there was a stalemate. However, facilitator Norway stated that it would continue to engage in shuttle diplomacy to persuade the two sides to return to talks.

CONCLUSIONS

During 2006–07, Sri Lanka gradually, but firmly, slipped into a 'war mode'. Both antagonists held on to their respective 'maximalist' positions. The government believed that its 'war for peace' approach was pragmatic and commanded popular support. Military victories in the east boosted its beliefs, and the government is confident of 'taming the Tigers' sooner or later. On its part, the LTTE has been preparing for a 'final war'. Losing the east is interpreted not as a defeat, but only

---

[92] The overall strength of the SLMM with monitors from five countries was 60. With the departure of Finland, Sweden and Denmark the strength came down to 20, one-third its original strength.

as 'trapping the government forces'. Now the focus of the war has shifted towards Tiger controlled territory. The ultimate victims of this war are innocent civilians who are being constantly displaced and starved, and suffer all kinds of abuses. Both parties were unable to give guarantees to the Monitoring Mission, and several rounds of talks to bring the SLMM back on track had failed. Overall, the attempts towards conflict management or resolution had been haphazard and insincere. The APC and APRC exercise by the government now looks like an eyewash. More emphasis is laid on a military solution than its earlier stated stand of simultaneously evolving a political package.

The following points should be kept in mind while working towards peace in the Island:

- A 'step-by-step' approach is pragmatic. Cessation of hostilities is the first step for any kind of peace process. It should be followed by some sort of interim arrangement to ameliorate the conditions of war-affected people in the northeast. In the third stage talks should follow in order to find a final settlement. A new peace process should commence at the earliest. If the government ignores the ethnic issue, it might pave the way for strengthening subaltern nationalist groups like the JVP and the JHU by exploiting the economic alienation of the masses.
- It is vital to have some principles in the form of a framework agreement to guide future peace processes. The framework should clearly lay out the plan of action, the participants, facilitators/mediators, and the rules of the game. This agreement should be guaranteed by the international community. There should be a cost if the parties violate this framework.
- The process should be inclusive; otherwise it may not be sustainable. All Sinhalese parties and, at the same time non-LTTE parties and Muslims, should be part and parcel of the process. One of the main drawbacks of the earlier peace process was that it failed to address the Muslim factor, which continues to be a 'weak link' in the entire peace chain. The two main Sinhalese parties—UNP and SLFP—should give up their confrontational politics in the interests of the country. Bipartisanship on the ethnic issue is a must for the settlement. The international community must strive to do something in this regard. Track 2 and 3 levels should be included to widen the base of the process and increase the stakeholders.

- Any peace process will not be credible as long as human rights abuses and humanitarian crises continue. These issues require immediate and serious attention. It will be difficult for the government to win over the Tamil population as long as the security forces are the major cause for human rights abuses. The international community has a major role to play here.
- Neither the LTTE nor the Sri Lankan state is democratic enough to resolve the ethnic crisis. The inherent undemocratic nature of the state institutions—both on paper and in practice— makes it unwilling to accept reforms. So is the case with the LTTE. There is, therefore, an urgent need for democratization.
- Because of its control of territory by the LTTE for nearly a decade, a de facto confederation is already in place. It will be difficult for the LTTE to climb down from this position. This reality should be accepted by the south, while striving for a 'united' Sri Lanka and not being insistent on a 'unitary' Sri Lanka.
- Some kind of interim arrangement in the war-affected northeast is necessary to address the immediate needs of the affected people. At the same time, this should not become an excuse for a permanent stalemate. The mechanism agreed upon by the two sides to address the post-tsunami situation could be extended to other needs as well. This can be a good basis for the compromise.

Notes on Contributors

Bibhu Prasad Routray is a Research Fellow with the Institute for Conflict Management, New Delhi. He received his doctoral degree from the School of International Studies, Jawaharlal Nehru University, New Delhi, for his thesis on 'Articulation of Dissent in an Authoritarian Regime: Case Study of Indonesia under the New Order (1947–85)'. He was also Director of the Institute for Conflict Management's Database and Documentation Centre on Conflict and Development (DADC) at Guwahati, Assam between August 2001 and February 2005. His recent publications include *Tibetan Refugees in India: Religious Identity and the Forces of Modernity* (*Refugee Survey Quarterly*: UNHCR, July 2007) and *Failure of Peace Processes* (*Armed Conflicts and Peace Processes in South Asia*: Sanskriti, 2006). His current projects include Systematizing Response to Urban Terrorism in India.

D. Suba Chandran is Assistant Director at the Institute of Peace and Conflict Studies (IPCS), New Delhi. His primary area of research includes Pakistan's internal security, in particular Balochistan, FATA and Northern Areas. He also works on Kashmir, terrorism, particularly Suicide Terrorism. Some of his recent publications include: 'Sectarian Violence in Northern Areas', in P. Stobdan and Suba Chandran (eds), *The Last Colony: Muzaffarabad-Gilgit-Baltistan* (New Delhi: India Research Press, 2008) pp. 55–86; 'Pakistan: Tribal Troubles in Balochistan and Waziristan', in D. Suba Chandran (ed.), *Armed Conflicts and Peace Processes in South Asia 2006*, pp. 159–79; 'India and Armed Nonstate Actors in the Kashmir Conflict', in W. P. S. Sidhu et al. (ed.), *Kashmir: New Voices, New Approaches* (Boulder: Lynne Rienner, 2006) pp. 80–107; 'Intra-State Armed Conflicts in South Asia: Impact on Regional Security' in Dev Raj Dahal and Nishchal Nath Pandey (eds), *Comprehensive Security in South Asia* (New Delhi: Manohar Publishers, 2006) pp. 159–75.

Devyani Srivastava is a Research Officer for the Institute of Peace and Conflict Studies (IPCS). She holds a Master's degree in International Relations from the University of Warwick, UK. Her publications include 'A season of suicide terrorism in Pakistan', 'The Swat offensive' and 'Web of violence in Jharkhand'. She is currently engaged in a research project that looks at studying the role of civilians in counter insurgency measures of both the government and the non-government sectors in India. As such, the project examines the factors that are instrumental in sustaining various insurgencies being waged in India.

Kanchan Lakshman is a Research Fellow with the Institute for Conflict Management, New Delhi, and Assistant Editor for the Institute's quarterly journal *Faultlines: Writings on Conflict and Resolution*. The primary focus of his research is terrorism and political violence in Jammu and Kashmir and in Pakistan. He received a doctoral degree from the Jawaharlal Nehru University, New Delhi, for his thesis on 'The United Nations Secretary-General: Diplomacy in Conflict Resolution in the Post-Cold War Era'.

Kavita Suri is an accredited journalist and is presently working for *The Statesman* as its Special Correspondent based in Jammu and Kashmir. She covers the entire state, travels to the Line of Control, I nternational border and other conflict areas in all the three regions of Jammu, Kashmir and Ladakh of the troubled State. She possesses a Ph. D. in Education from the University of Jammu and worked on 'Occupational Stress, Role Conflict and Attitude of women teachers, administrators and professionals towards their profession' for her doctoral thesis. She is also a recipient of the prestigious British Chevening fellowship 2005–06 and WISCOMP peace fellow. She has made many documentaries for Doordarshan's satellite Kashmir Channel and Jammu and Srinagar DDKs.

Mallika Joseph is an Assistant Director at Institute of Peace and Conflict Studies and works on various issues relating to South Asian security. She specializes on security sector reforms, human security, left extremism, small arms, landmines and small arms and improvised explosive devices. In 2007 and in 2006, she was part of the DFID high level technical team that offered consultancy for broad-based security sector engagement in Guyana. Her area of consultation was police reforms, community policing and police public relations. She has co-authored three books—*Small Arms and the Security Debate in South Asia, Anti-Personnel Landmines: A South Asian Regional Survey* and *Lethal Fields: Landmines and Improvised Explosive Devices in South Asia*—and was a regular contributor to the *Landmine Monitor* for the country sections on South Asian countries. She has also co-edited four books—*Reintroducing Human Security in South Asia, Consolidating Peace in Jammu and Kashmir, Terrorism and* *its repercussions on International Politics* and *Missing Boundaries: Refugees, Migrants, Stateless and Internally Displaced Persons in South Asia*. She has a Ph. D. in International Relations from Jawaharlal Nehru University, New Delhi.

N. Manoharan is currently Senior Research Fellow at the Institute of Peace and Conflict Studies, New Delhi. He has been South Asia Visiting Fellow at the East-West Center, Washington (2005) and recipient of the Mahbub-ul Haq Award (2006) given by the RCSS, Colombo. His areas of interest include Sri Lanka, human rights, ethnic violence, multiculturalism, and terrorism. His recent publications include *Ethnic Violence and Human Rights in Sri Lanka* (New Delhi: Samskriti, 2007); *Counterterrorism Legislation in Sri Lanka: Evaluating Efficacy* (Washington, D. C.: East-West Center, 2006).

P. G. Rajamohan, till recently, was a Research Fellow at the Institute of Peace and Conflict Studies (IPCS). Currently, he is working on border issues and terrorism in South Asia in general at the Institute and specializes on Nepal's Maoist insurgency and political situation. His recent publications include: (Co-author) 'Soft, Porous or Rigid? Towards Stable borders in South Asia', *South Asian Survey*, vol. 14 (1): 117–28. January–June 2007; 'Connecting India: A Road Map for New Roads', *IPCS Issue Brief*, no. 58, January 2008; 'Nepal: Continuing Violence', *Armed Conflicts and Peace Processes in South Asia 2006* (Samskriti, 2007), pp. 102–17; 'State Restructuring and Accommodating Madhesi Aspirations', *World Focus*, July 2007; 'Tamil Nadu: The Rise of Islamist Fundamentalism', *Faultlines*—Writings on Conflict & Resolution (vol. 16).

P. R. Chari is a former member of the Indian Administrative Service (1960 batch/Madhya Pradesh cadre). He served in several senior positions in the Central and State Governments, and sought voluntary retirement in 1992 after 32 years in the government. During the course of his official career he served two spells (1971–75 and 1985–88) in the Ministry of Defence. His last position there was Additional Secretary. He was Director of the Institute for Defence Studies and Analyses (IDSA), New Delhi (1975–80), International Fellow, Centre for International Affairs, Harvard University (1983–84), Visiting Fellow, University of Illinois, Urbana-Champaign (1998), and currently is Research Professor at the Institute of Peace and Conflict Studies (IPCS). He has worked extensively on nuclear disarmament, non-proliferation and Indian defence issues. He has published over 1050 op-ed articles in newspapers/websites and over 110 monographs and major papers in learned journals/chapters in books abroad and in India.

Shanthie Mariet D'Souza is Associate Fellow at the Institute for Defence Studies and Analyses (IDSA), New Delhi and is currently working on the project 'US Counter terrorism Objectives in South Asia'. She has expertise in US policy towards Afghanistan, Terrorism, Indo-US relations, and Indo-Afghan Relations. She was awarded the doctoral degree from the School of International Studies, Jawaharlal Nehru University, New Delhi on the topic 'United States and the Emergence and Decline of the Taliban'. She has conducted field studies in the United States, Canada, Pakistan, Afghanistan, Jammu and Kashmir and India's North East. She has presented papers at international and national conferences on Afghanistan and has a number of publications to her credit.

Smruti S. Pattanaik is a Research Fellow at the Institute for Defence Studies and Analyses, New Delhi. She holds a Ph. D. degree in South Asian Studies from the School of International Studies, Jawaharlal Nehru University, New Delhi. Her area of specialization is identity politics, security and foreign policy issues pertaining to India's neighbourhood. Her research project under the Kodikara fellowship sponsored by the Regional Centre for Strategic Studies, Colombo is published as a book titled as 'Elite perceptions in Foreign Policy: Role of Print Media in Influencing Indo-Pak Relations, 1989–99'. She received the Asia Fellowship in 2003 and also its follow-up grant in 2006 and was a visiting Asia Fellow at the Department of International Relations, Dhaka University from February–December 2004 and May–September 2007. During this period, she worked on 'State formation in South Asia: Role of Identity and Nationalism in the Making of Bangladesh'. She has published many research articles and chapters in various journals and books both nationally and internationally.

Index

Abdullah, Farooq 92, 98, 111
Abdullah, Omar 92, 98, 111
Abdullah, Sheikh 92
Achik Matgrik Liberation Army (AMLA) 158
Achik National Volunteers Council (ANVC) 158–9
Afghan National Army (ANA); COIN force 23–4, 25
Afghanistan 12–14, 44; Ahle Hadith and anti-Shia jihad 48; al Qaeda, local support 34–6; anti-Pakistan feeling 89; anti-US feelings 89; Arab–Afghan population 90; armed conflicts in 11–15, 79; armed groups international networks of 36; Civilian casualties 35; civilians killing 80; Conflict within 85; Constabulary Force (CF) 46; DDR 44; Deobandi–Shia 50; Disarmament of Illegal Armed Groups (DIAG) 44–5; displaced 34; Islamist militancy 49; Jamaat-e-Ulema Islam, the JUI 36; Jirga recommendations by 38n; Joint Co-ordinating and Monitoring Board (JCMB) 30; Karzai Government 33–34, 46; Pak Peace Jirga 38–9; Quick Reaction Force (QRF) 46; 'regional conflict formation' 44; Suicide attacks in 31–2; Sunni–Shia violence 47–9; Violence 30–3
Afghanistan Independent Human Rights Commission (AIHRC) 35
Agency Coordinating Body for Afghan Relief (ACBAR) 33
Ahmed, Khaled on sectarian violence 48–9
Ahmed, Samina 57
Akashi, Yasushi 249, 264
al Ghalib, Asadullah 195; chief of AHAB, 198
al Qaeda 7, 9, 12–13, 21, 23–4, 74; and Taliban 7, see also Taliban; Talibanization
Alhe Hadith Andolan Bangladesh (AHAB) 195

Ali, Hazrat 64
All Bodo Students' Union (ABSU) 156
All Jammu and Kashmir Muslim Conference 92
All Parties Hurriyat Conference (APHC) 115
All Tripura People's Liberation Organization (ATPLO) 157
All Tripura Tiger Force (ATTF) 158
All Tripura Tribal Force 158
al-Masri, Abu Khabab 73
Alvi, Fazal Hussain 63
al-Zawahiri, Ayman 73
American–Soviet negotiations 11
Amo, Charlton Lien 185
Andhra Pradesh Civil Liberties Committee (APCLC) 127
Ansaar-ul-Islam 55–6
anti-Hindu riots 14
anti-Muslim riots 14
Anti-Terrorism Act (ATA) 66
armed conflicts 1–4; features of 5–10
armed force, use of 3
armed groups 121–4
Asom Gana Parishad (AGP) 155
Assam 166–9, 178–80; Black Widow faction of the DHD 160; ceasefire with the NDFB 180; counter-insurgency operations 178; ISI and the Bangladeshi DGFI 167; Islamist militancy 160; KLNLF 160; outfits 181; People's Committee for Peace Initiatives in Assam PCIPIA) 179
Association for the Protection of Democratic Rights 127
Awami League (AL) 190–2
Azad, Ghulam Nabi 110
Aziz, Shaukat assassination plots on 64

Babri Masjid's demolition (1992) 14
Baig, Muzaffar Hussain 110–1
Balochistan attack by storming PPL's installations 73; FATA 74–5
Balochistan Liberation Army (BLA) 59, 73

Banglabhai in Dhaka 16
Bangladesh 18, 189; Al Haramain foundation 197; Alh e Hadith movement 194–5; anti-Soviet jihad in Afghanistan 195; Armed Groups: 194; armed revolution (kital) in 195; arrest of JMB and JMJB leaders 198; arrest of Mufti Hanan 198; Arresting militants 207; 17 August, bomb blasts 203–4; banned HuJi 204; BNP government 191–2, 196–7, 206; Christina Rocca's visit 198; Civil Society Actors 195–6; conflict in 206–8; conviction of Aminul Haque 201; empowering women 208–9; execution of JMB and JMJB leaders 208; External Actors 196–8; funds for *madarssa*s and maktabs 197; funds for militants from zakat 200; Government Actors 191; ICS (Islamic Chatra Shibir, student organization of JI) 200; Insaf Dal—a faction of Alhe Hadith (AHAB) 202; IOJ [Islamic Oikyo Jote]) 190; Islamic parties 191–3; Jamaat Islami 190, 199; link between Jamaat, JMB and JMJB, 208; mlitant Islam in 189, 201–2; NGOs 196–8; politics of religion in Bangladesh 209; radical groups 209–10; Rapid Action Battalion 203; sentencing JMB activists 207; Talibans and al Qaeda in 189; trends in the Conflict 204–6; US training the Bangladesh police 198; Wahabi Islam 198; Zadid al Qaeda and bomb blasts 204; zakat 196
Bangladesh National Party (BNP) 189–96, 206–7
Bari, M. A. 195
Begum, Haseena 106
Bhaban, Hawa 191
Bhambri, C. P. on 'the politics of violence' 150–1
Bharatiya Janata Party (BJP) 98
Bhutan 5, 18
Billo, Haji Hanif 56
bin Laden, Osama 21, 89
Blair, Tony 67
Bodo Liberation Tigers (BLT) 156
Bodoland Territorial Council (BTC) 156
Bombay blasts in 1993 14

Brar, T. P. S. 112
Brasstacks Exercise (1987) 5
Bru Liberation Front of Mizoram (BLFM) 159
Bru National Liberation Front (BNLF) 161, 185

China and the erstwhile Soviet Union 4
Chittagong hill tracts 12
Choudhury, Anwar 198
Choudhury, Badal 173
Chure Bhawar Ekata Samaj (CBES) 219
Communal violence 2, 14
Communist League (YCL) 217, 227–8
Communist Party of India (Maoist) 123–6
Communist Party of Nepal-Maoist (CPN-M) 15, 130–1, 213–14, 217, 223, 226; abandoned armed struggle 228
Coordinating Committee of Maoist Parties Organizations of South Asia (CCOMPOSA) 128

Dadullah, Mullah death of 35
Dal, Allar 201–2
Danish aid and development organization (DACAAR) 32
Dar, Abdul Majid 99
Dima Halim Daogah (DHD) 156
Directorate General of Forces Intelligence (DGFI) of Bangladesh 155
Dutt, D. N. 159

ethno-political conflicts 3

Fair, Christine 59–60
Farooq, Mirwaiz 113, 117
Farooqi, Maulana Zia-ur-Rehman 54
Faryad, Abdullah 64
Federally Administered Tribal Area (FATA) history of 7, 12, 73–5

Gandhi, Indira 16
Global War on Terrorism (GWOT) 26
Gogoi, Tarun 168, 178–9
Gujarat (2002) 14
Gurkha Interim Task Force (ITF) 221–2
Gyanendra, King 225; changed three governments 215; Emergency of 214; repressive regime of 220

Hanan, Mufi 205
Haq, JUI-Samiul 68
Haqqani, Siraj 84
Haque, Aminul 202
Harkat-ul-Jihad-al-Islami (HuJI) 24, 194, 209
Harkat-ul-Mujahideen 24, 65–6
Hezb-i-Islami 17
Hindu–Muslim communal riots 3
Hizb-i-Islami 22
Hmar People's Convention-Democracy (HPC-D) 165
human rights, violation of 18
Hynniewtrep Achik Liberation Council (HALC) 158
Hynniewtrep National Liberation Council (HNLC) 158, 186

Iffat, Idris on sectarianism 50–1
Ikhwanis (former militants) in Kashmir 16
Ilyas, Mufti 64
India 18; –Pakistan 'composite dialogue' 10; and Bangladesh 8, 19; and Pak border 13; and Sri Lankan relations 7
India–Pakistan conflicts 96–7
Indus Waters Treaty (1960) 10–11
insurgency 21–2, *see also* Karbi insurgency; Nagaland, insurgency in; Mizoram, insurgency in
Inter-Services Intelligence (ISI) of Pakistan 155
Inter-Services Public Relations (ISPR) 77
intra-state conflicts 8
Iranian arms 28
Isak-Muivah faction (NSCN-IM) and the Khaplang faction (NSCN-K) 154
Isar-ul-Qasimi, Maulana 49
Islamic Chatra Shibir (ICS) 190
Islamic extremists 9
Israeli–Palestinian negotiations 11

Jaffna peninsula 12
Jagrata Muslim Janata Bangladesh (JMJB) 190–2
Jaish-e-Muhammad (JeM) 24, 66
Jamaat-ul-Furqan 24
Jamatul Mujaheedin Bangladesh, The (JMB) 189; women cadres of 189
Jammu and Kashmir (J and K) 96, 98 Afghan mujahideen 95; Agnishekhar 111; armed conflict decline in 101–3; Bus Services 114–15; ceasefire along the LoC 102; civilians killed 102; conflict in 92; Cross-border infiltration 104; declining recruitment 103–4; demilitarization 116–17; Dukhtaran-e-Millat led by Asiya Andrabi 107; Fidayeen attacks 104–5; Foreign militants 104; high-tech terror 105–6; Hizbul Mujahideen 95, 99, 108–9; human rights violations 110; Ikhwans 100; Indian National Congress 93; infiltration 104; Internal ceasefire 111–12; jihadi groups 97; Jihadis: Lashkar-e-Toiba and Jaish-e-Muhammad 99–100; migrant groups 111; Militants 99; NC formed the government 95; NC, People's Democratic Party (PDP) 98; Non-State Actors (NSAs) 98–100; Over-ground Conflict (OGWs) 107; Police lead 116; policy for Kashmiri Pandit migrants 109; Round Table Conference on J&K 101; Special Operations Group (SOG) 98; Treaty of Amritsar 93; UN Security Council adopted a resolution 94; war in Kargil 95; Women as perpetrators 106–7; women's wing as Khwateen Markaz 107; Working Groups and Round Table Conferences 109–11, 115

Jammu & Kashmir Liberation Front (JKLF) 95
Jammu & Kashmir National Conference (NC) 92
Jana Andolan II (People's Movement II or April Movement) 229
Janatantrik Terai Mukti Morcha (JTMM) 218, 235
Jhangvi, Maulana Haq Nawaz 49, 54
jihadis in Pakistan 10
Jinnah, Mohammad Ali 93

Kamruzzaman 199
Kamtapur Liberation Organization (KLO) 159
Kangleipak Communist Party (KCP) 156–7
Karbi insurgency 156

Karbi Longri North Cachar Hills Liberation Front (KLNLF) 156
Kargil War 4–5, 104
Karuna in eastern Sri Lanka 16, *see also* Liberation Tigers of Tamil Eelam
Karzai, Hamid 12, 14, 23, 40, *see also* Afghanistan
Kashmir, Panun 111
Khajuria, Ashok 111
Khaleeq, Maulana Abdul 199, 201, 204
Khan, Riaz Mohammad 112
Khan, Amanullah 95
Khel, Yargul 84
Khun Hynniewtrep National Awakening Movement (KHNAM) 184
Kochekkan, E. J. Major General 170
Koirala, Girija Prasad 221, 223
Kuki Liberation Army (KLA) 171
Kumaratunga, Chandrika 242

Ladakh Union Territory Front (LUTF) 111
Lapang, D. D. 184
Lashkar 108–9
Lashkar-e-Islam 81
Lashkar-e-Jhangvi (LeJ) 48, 50–4, 65; Sipah-e-Sahaba Pakistan (SSP) 50; Muhammad Ajmal alias Akram Lahori 51; Mufti Eid Mohammed 53; militant Deobandi groups 52; murder of American 53; Daniel Pearl 53; Abdullah Faryad 53; Fayyaz Dada 53; Zahoor alias Choota Waqar 53; Usman Chotu 53; Arshad Satti 53; Mohammad Ali alias Mama 53
Lashkar-e-Toiba 37, 66
Lashkar-i-Islam 55–6, 62
leftist extremists 9
Liberation Achik Elite Force (LAEF) 164, 176
Liberation Front (EPRLF) 239
Liberation Tigers of Tamil Eelam (LTTE) 9, 239–40, 245–6; assassinations 7, 250–68; air strike on Kattunayake air base 253; 'Black Tigers' 245; as 'Foreign Terrorist Organization' in 1997 249; it's 'Oyatha Aligal' 242; and paramilitary groups 242; Sea Tigers as an LTTE wing 243; vaanpuligal (Air Tigers) 253–4

Line of Control (LOC) 10; fencing of 111–12; in Kashmir 13, 17; as Line of Peace 112–13; *see also* Jammu and Kashmir
Lyngdoh, R. G. 184

Madhesi Mukti Tigers (MMT) 218–9
Madhesi People's Rights Forum (MPRF) 218, 229–30
Maldives 5
Malik, Yasin 97
Manik Sarkar 186
Manipur 161–2, 180–1; insurgent groups 161; KYKL and its Yawol Lanmi 161; Meira Paibis 180; Naga-Kuki clashes in 171; 'Operation Khengjoi' 170; PREPAK and its army wing Red Army 161; security situation in 169–71; Unified Command Structure 181; violence by the Naga group1 173
Mansoor, Saifullah 35
Maoist Communist Centre (MCC) 124–5; in Bihar 120
Maoist Communist Centre of India [MCC-I]) 124
Maoist, insurgency 9, 128, 212–15; political party ties 231–2; and the Seven Party Alliance 219; demands 224–5; People's War 15, 211–12, 215, 222
Marwein, Bobby 176
Mazumdar, Charu 119
Meghalaya 184, 175–7; ANVC cadres 164–5, 176; Assam-based UPDS 184; Cheristerfield Thangkiew 176; HNLC 184; neutralization of the HNLC 176; NSCN-K 164; NVC 184; ULFA in 177
Mehsud, Abdullah 72
Mehsud, Abid 65
Mehsud, Baitullah 72
Menon, Shiv Shankar 112
Militancy in Meghalaya 158
militants 74–5
Mir, Javid 95
Mizo National Front (MNF) 157
Mizoram 165, 178, 185, BLFM cadres surrendering 185; BLFM militants 178; BNLF and BLFM 165; HPC-D to the negotiating 185, insurgency in 158–9
MMA Muttanida Majlis-e-Amal 67, 89
Mohammad, Maulana Faqir 64–5

Mohammad, Nek 72, 87
Mostafa, Nadim 202
Muhammad, Noor 54
Mukherjee, Pranab 113
Musharraf, Pervez President 53–4, 68; assassination plots on 72; 'enlightened moderation' 70; 'war against terror' 65–6
Muslim United Liberation Tigers of Assam (MULTA) 156
Muttahida Quami Movement (MQM) 56

Naga insurgency 153–9; Black Widow group 156; Bodo Accord 156; Kuki tribals 157; Naga-inhabited' areas of Assam 182; 'Nagalim' logjam 187
Naga National Council (NNC) 154
narcotics traffickers 36–7
Narcotics trafficking combating 40–1
National Democratic Front of Bodoland (NDFB) 156
National Human Rights Commission 127
National Liberation Front of Tripura (NLFT) 157–8
National Socialist Council of Nagaland Kaplang-K 164, 174–5, 182–3
National Socialist Council of Nagaland (NSCN) 154
National Socialist Council of Nagaland-IM and 157, 163–5, 174–5, 182–3, 187; clashes with NSCN-K 171
NATO 22, 30; mission of 26–7
naxalite 9; against Sethusamudram Ship Canal Project 151; Andhra Pradesh 134–5; attacks against civilians 142; attacks on Security Forces 140–1; ban on the main naxal group (the PWG) 144; in Bihar 136–7; Central Bureau of Investigation (CBI) 128; in Chhattisgarh 135–6; Chief Ministers' Conference on Internal Security 143; Civil Society organizations 127–8; civilian armed counter-naxal group 126–7; Committee of Concerned Citizens (CCC) 127; conflict 132–40; conflict management 142–8; counter-naxal strategy 122; CPI (Maoist) 124–5; CPI (Maoist) Unity Congress 149; deploying the Sashastra Seema Bal (SSB) 145; Estates Acquisition Act 119; external actors 128–9; Forum for Fact-finding Documentation and Advocacy 127; government actors 122–3; history 119–21; use of Improvised Explosives 141–2; in Jharkhand 137; Joint Coordination Committee (JCC) 147; in Karnataka 139; kisan sabhas (peasant unions) 119; Land Reforms Act in 1955 119; Left Wing Extremism 149; Sahni on 151; in Madhya Pradesh 139; in Maharashtra 138; Mahendra Karma against the 126; Manmohan Singh on 121; MCC-I and PWG merge of 125–6, 129; militancy 15; movement 129–30; Naxalbari as peasant uprising 119; Orissa 136; the Party Unity (PU) 124; profile of violence 140; Strategies and tactics 131–7; in Tamil Nadu 139; United Struggle Committee against Fake Encounters 127; Village Defence Committees (VDCs) 147; in West Bengal 132–4

Nazir, Maulvi 84
NC-Democratic (Nepal Congress-Democratic) 225
Nehru, Jawaharlal 93
Nepal 18; April Movement in 2006 211; armed groups in 235; arms and armies 233–5; Ceasefire and Peace Agreement 232–3; child soldiers 227; Chinese Cultural Revolution 212; Common Minimum Programme (CMP) 223, 226; government's policies and international community 231–2; history 211–12; Joint Monitoring Coordination Committee (JMCC) 234; multi-party system 216; Peru's Left-wing extremist guerrilla movement 213; Sendero Luminoso (Shining Path, founded in 1980) 213; Seven Party Alliance (SPA) 214–16, 220, 223, 226; Terai groups 217–19; Terai problem 228–31, 235; UN's role in 233; US Ambassador James Moriarty on the peace process 227–8
Nepali Congress 225
NLFT 187
North West Frontier Province (NWFP) 58, 71

northeast India 3; conflict in 166–78
Northern Alliance 14, 88
Norwegian mediation in Sri Lanka 242, 246–7; Lars Johan Solvberg 266; Jon Hanssen-Bauer 264; Eric Solheim 1, 264; Ulf Henricson 266

OEF–ISAF (International Security Assistance Force) 26–7
Om, Hari 111
Omar, Mullah 21
'Operation Bluestar' and 'Operation Silence' 16
opium trade 37–8; *see also* narcotics traffickers
Orakzai, Ali Muhammad Jan 59

Pakistan-occupied Kashmir (PoK) 194–5
Pakistan 18, 28; Abdullah Mehsud group 59; against India 4; agreements—Shakai and Sararogha 91; Ansaa-ul Islam 81; Bus services 10; civilians death 70; de-weaponization drive 91; FATA reforms 85, 90; FCR Reforms Committee 89; Fencing and Mining the Durand 87–8; Hisba Act (in NWFP) 67; history 71–3; Hizb-ul-Mujahideen 66; Inter Services Intelligence (ISI) 20, 88; International Crisis Group (ICG) 68; jihadi seminaries 57; John D. Negroponte on 67–8; Khilafat system 54; Khilafat-i-Rashida 65; Khudamul Islam 65; Khyber Agency in FATA 55; kidnappings 78, 82–4; Lal Masjid bombing 16, 77–79, 87; *madrassa* reforms 68–70; military response 86; missile attack in North Waziristan 77; Multan Anti-Terrorism Court 63–4; peace agreements 87; Provincial Reconstruction Teams (PRTs) 41–3; Pukhtoon militants 64; sectarian violence in 57, 60–1; sectarianism in the NWFP 58; Sharia court 78; Special Investigation Group (SIG) 58; spreading anarchy 79–83; suicide terrorism in 78, 85; Takhim-e-Solh or 'Strengthening Peace' 40; taking hostages 82–3; Wafaq-ul-Madaris 68

Palestinians' right to self-determination 240

Panag, General 102
Pashtuns 7
Pati, Shivraj 110
peace processes 4, 9–10, 223, 267
Pearl, Daniel abduction and murder of 53, 60, 64
People's Liberation Army (PLA) 156, 222
People's Liberation Guerrilla Army (PLGA) 125
People's Liberation Organization of Tamil Eelam (PLOTE) 239
People's Revolutionary Party of Kangleipak (PREPAK) 156
People's Union for Civil Liberties (PUCL) 127–8
People's Union for Democratic Rights (PUDR) 127
People's United Liberation Front (PULF) 157
People's War Group (PWG) 120, 124–5, *see also* Maoist, insurgency; naxalite
Phizo, A. Z. 155
Pokharel, Bhoj Raj 225
Prabhakaran, Vellupillai 245, 264
Prachanda 224, 226
Prevention of Terrorism Act [POTA] 144
Provincial Reconstruction Teams (PRTs) 27
Proxy war 4–5

Qasmi, Maulana Eesar-ul-Haq 54
Quami *madrassa* 189, 207–9

Rahman, Abdur and Sajjad 200
Rahman, Mostafizur 203
Rahman, Moulana Sayeedur alias Abu Zafar 202
Rahman, Saidur 199–200, 203
Rahman, Sheikh Abdur 190
Rahman, Sheikh Abdur 194–5, 204
Rahman, Tareque 192, 207
Rahman, Tariq 191
Rajapakse, Mahinda 242, 255, 262, 264
Ramesh, Jairam 113
Rao, Varavara 151
Rashtriya Swayam Sevak Sangh (RSS) 9
Rehman, Maulvi Inayatur 64–5
Rehman, Mujibur 240
Rehman, Sheikh as JMB chief 199–204
Rio, Neiphiu 183
Rizvi, Hasan-Askari 67

Rohingya Student Organization (RSO) 195
Rouf, Maulana Abdur 202
Royal Bhutan Army (RBA) 155
Royal Nepalese Army (RNA) 216
Rumsfeld, Secretary of Defense 21

SAARC 2, 18–19
Saeed, Mohammad Hafiz 99
Saifullah, Pir 81
Saifullah, Rao 54
Saifur Rahman 190
Salafi, Maulana Abul M. 204
Salwa Judum 126–7; in Chattisgarh 17
Samaraweera, Mangala 263
Sanyal, Kanu 119
Sarbaharas 192
Sayeed, Mufti Mohammad 110
sectarian and ethno-political violence 7
Shah, Najaf Ali 62
Shah, Syed Ali 62
Shahabuddin 64
Shahjahan, A. S. M. 201
Shahjalal shrine bomb blasts 198
Shakir, Mufti Munir 81
Shia–Sunni violence in Pakistan 3
Shillong Accord 154
Shrestha, Pushpa Lal 212
shura committee 194
Shura, Majlis 203
Singh, Harshdev 111
Singh, Maharaja Gulab 93
Singh, Maharaja Hari 92–4
Singh, Manmohan 101, 113
Singh, Nirmal 111
Singh, Okram Ibobi 170
Sinhala Buddhists 244
Sinhala–Tamil ethnic conflict in Sri Lanka or Pashtun–Uzbek clashes 3
Sipah-e-Mohammed Pakistan 55
Sipah-e-Sahaba Pakistan (SSP) 53–4
Soz, Saifuddin 111
Sri Lanka 5, 14, 18; Acquisition and Cross-Servicing Agreement (ACSA) 249; agenda of Mahinda Rajapaksa 260–1; All Party Conference (APC) 260–1, 267; All Party Representative Committee (APRC) 261–3, 267; and India 247–8; bombing of the Sencholai children's 253; Ceasefire Agreement 266; Child soldiering 256; conflict management/resolution 260–6; economic downslide 259–60; Eelam People's Revolutionary 239; Eelam Revolutionary Organization of Students (EROS) 239; Eelam War 241–2, 252; European Union 248–50, 265–6; government of Sri Lanka (GOSL) 238, 243–5, 266; Guatemalan game plan 239; history 238–42; Human Rights 255–68; Indian Peace Keeping Force (IPKF) 241–2; Internal displacement 257–8; Japan 248–9; Joint Operations Command (JOC) 243; Open confrontation 252–5; Paramilitary groups 246–8; People's Alliance government 242; Police Special Task Force (STF) 243–4; proxy war 250–1; shortage of essential commodities 257–8; Sinhala Only Act in 1956 238; SLMM 247, 251, 266; Steering Committee on Peace Building (SCPB) 263; Tamils in 10; and United States 248–9; upsurge of violence 251
Sri Lanka Monitoring Mission (SLMM) 11, 264
Sri Lankan air force (SLAF) 243
SULFA (Surrendered ULFA) in Assam 16
Sunni and Shi'a extremists 9
Sunni Tehreek (ST) 56–7

Taliban 12–13, 17, 29–33, 37, 48, 59; –al Qaeda in 24–5, 29, 44, 72, 74–5; captured Kabul 20; regime 20–1; insurgency 22n, 24; kidnappings in 32–3; killings 35–6; -led insurgency 44; Pervez Musharraf on 40; reconciliation 39–40; training at jihad camps 36; and US 21
Talibanization 79, 82–3
Tamil Eelam Liberation Organization (TELO) 239
Tamil United Liberation Front (TULF) its Vaddukoddai Resolution, 1976 238
Tanweer, Shahzad 67
Taqi, Hafiz Muhammad 56
Tarigami, Mohd Yusuf 111
Tariq, Maulana Azam 54
Tehreek-e-Jaferia Pakistan (TJP) 55
Tehreek Nifaz Fiqahe-Jafria (TNFJ) 55
Tehreek Nifaz-e- Shariat-e-Mohammadi (TNSM) 64–5

Terai Cobra 218
Terai Janatantrik Mukti Morcha (TJMM), one led by Jai Krishna Goit 230
Terrorism Convention, The 15
Tripura 172–3; ATTF, and NLFT 173, 181–2; Bodoland Territorial Council (BTC) 168; counter-insurgency policy 172; KLNLF and Black Widow 168–9; militant outfits in 162–3; Phalendra Reang abduction 173; Ranjit Debbarma-led ATTF 162
Tripura National Volunteers (TNV) by B. K. Hrangkhawal 157
Tripura, Manyakumar 173
Turabi, Allama Hasan 63

UCDP definitions 6
Ullah, Kaleen 54
UN Office on Drugs and Crime (UNODC) 36
United Committee of Manipur (UCM) 181
United Liberation Front of Asom (ULFA) 154–6, 186–7; backed People's Consultative Group (PCG) 179; military wing 159–60
United National Liberation Front (UNLF) 156
United Nations Assistance Mission in Afghanistan (UNAMA) 32

United People's Democratic Solidarity (UPDS) 156
United States 25; Central Intelligence Agency (CIA) 20; 11 September 2001 (9/11) attack 21; led forces in Nek Mohammad killing of 75; coalition forces in Afghanistan 33, 39, 77, 88; Operation Enduring Freedom (OEF) 21; Operation Anaconda 72
unmanned aerial vehicles (UAVs) 9
Uppsala Conflict Data Program (UCDP), The 2–3
Ussuri clashes 4
Uzbek, and Pashtun communities, divide between 14; militants 76, 84

Vishwa Hindu Parishad 9

Waheed, Abdul 54
Warlords 25
Waziristan Agency 12
weapons of mass destruction (WMDs) 9

Yuldashev, Tahir 76; and al Qaeda divide 84

Zada, Zahid Husain alias 64
Zia, Khaleda and Sheikh Hasina arrest of 16
Zia-ul-Haq, General 48–9